Henry C. Lucas, Jr.

Henry C. Lucas, Jr. is currently Professor of Information Systems at the Graduate School of Business Administration, New York University. He received his B.S. from Yale University and his M.S. and Ph.D. from the Sloan School of Management, Massachusetts Institute of Technology. His research interests include implementation, systems analysis, expert systems, and the management of information processing. He has published articles in computer and management journals including *Management Science, Decision Science, Communications of the ACM, MIS Quarterly, JMIS,* and *The Computer Journal.*

Professor Lucas is the author of *Introduction to Computers and Information Systems,* Macmillan, 1986, and *Coping with Computers: A Manager's Guide to Controlling Information Processing,* The Free Press, 1982. He also has written four monographs, *Toward Creative Systems Design,* 1974, *Why Information Systems Fail,* 1975, and *Implementation: The Key to Successful Information Systems,* 1981, all published by Columbia University Press, and *The Implementation of Computer-Based Models,* National Association of Accountants, 1976.

MACMILLAN SERIES IN INFORMATION SYSTEMS

Henry C. Lucas, Jr., Editor

Lucas: *INTRODUCTION TO COMPUTERS AND INFORMATION SYSTEMS*

Lucas: *MANAGING INFORMATION SERVICES*

Turban: *DECISION SUPPORT AND EXPERT SYSTEMS*

Laudon/Laudon: *MANAGEMENT INFORMATION SYSTEMS*

Managing Information Services

Managing Information Services

HENRY C. LUCAS, JR.
New York University
Graduate School of Business

Macmillan Publishing Company
New York

Collier Macmillan Publishers
London

PRINTED IN THE UNITED STATES OF AMERICA

Macmillan Publishing Company
866 Third Avenue, New York, New York 10022

Collier Macmillan Canada, Inc.

Library of Congress Cataloging in Publication Data

Lucas, Henry C.
Managing information services / Henry C. Lucas.
p. cm. — (The Macmillan series in information systems)
Includes index.
ISBN 0-02-372231-2
1. Information services—Management. I. Title. II. Series.
Z674.4.L8 1989
020'.68—dc19 87-29801
CIP

Printing: 1 2 3 4 5 6 7 8 Year: 9 0 1 2 3 4 5 6 7 8

To Scott and Jonathan

Preface

This book is intended for a course in managing information services. The primary audience is students majoring in information systems; the book is also relevant for MBAs who expect to be involved in making decisions about information processing. The book assumes some prior computer background on the part of the reader, either from courses or from work experience. In particular, the student should have some familiarity with systems analysis and design, computer hardware and software, and a procedural programming language.

The objective of the book is to explain the issues in managing information services and to recommend management actions to the reader. Some background in the field is necessary in order to understand the management of systems analysis and design, programming, and microcomputing, to name only a few of the topics covered in the book. Since the book assumes familiarity with the major building blocks of the information systems field, it does not explain fundamental concepts. For example, Chapter 5 presents trends in the technology and their implication for management. The chapter does not try to offer a tutorial on the underlying technology.

The first chapter presents a framework that has been used to organize the text; this framework emphasizes the process of management and the specific areas with which management has to be concerned. For example, the book stresses the development of a plan for information services and discusses the planning process in detail. Given a plan, management in information services has to be concerned about end-user support, computer capacity, and areas like office automation, communications, and factory automation. A hypothetical case study appears throughout the book to illustrate the concepts presented in each chapter.

There are several key themes in the book. First, it is expected that information processing will continue to be distributed to end users. The power of 32-bit microcomputers equals that of the mainframes of a few years ago. Given the price/performance ratio of these computers, individuals can easily be furnished with very powerful personal workstations. As a result, information processing will expand until almost every information worker in a firm will have a workstation.

The expansion of computer power means that divisional and departmental managers will have to concentrate on the management of information processing, something they could leave to a centralized information services group in the past. This broad diffusion of computing throughout the organization raises new challenges for managers in information services. In particular, information services is giving up power and control to users; instead of directing, IS managers now must manage through influence and consultation.

A major theme of the book is the changing role of the computer professional. From the systems analyst and programmer to the CIO, personnel in the systems area are becoming consultants and advisors. By and large, we view this trend as healthy, since the experience of having the IS staff in total control has been less than successful.

The diffusion of computing and the new role of IS management create a number of problems for both senior management and IS personnel. Distributed and decentralized processing still needs to be coordinated to avoid costly duplication and wasted effort. However, coordination must be accomplished with good taste and sensitivity to those who are being coordinated. Otherwise, coordination becomes a form of stifling bureaucratic control that can be counterproductive.

Probably the most important objective of this book is to prepare the student to manage information services in both today's and tomorrow's environment. We have developed an incredibly powerful technology. Changes in this technology and management's vision of how it can be employed in the organization create tremendous opportunities for information services employees. To be successful in the future, senior management of the firm and managers within information services must meet the challenges of managing information processing technology. This book is intended to contribute to their efforts.

H.C.L.

Contents

PART **I**

Information Services and the Organization

1

PART II

The Information Services Environment

PART III

Managing Information Services

12

13

14

Managing Operations 265

15

Control and Audit of Information Services 281

16

Capacity Planning 302

19

Managing Office Automation 358

20

Managing Communications 376

PART V

Management Issues

21

Evaluation and Management Control 399

PART I

Information Services and the Organization

1

Introduction

What is the information resource? What are the challenges of managing it? Organizations have long processed information; now they are beginning to realize that information is a resource to be managed. It has been easy to ignore information itself and focus on business functions like manufacturing, finance, and marketing. In today's increasingly complex technological environment, success depends on the firm's ability to manage information and take advantage of the opportunities presented by the technology.

Why Process Information?

Computers have become pervasive in business, stimulating users and managers to focus on information as an entity in itself. As an example, consider a manufacturing company. Information about orders is needed for the firm to know what to produce and ship to its customers. Manufacturing management requires information on what goods are in production and inventory in order to control operations. Financial officials in the firm need information on cash flow, including anticipated income and expenses, in order to finance operations.

In addition to these operational uses of information, the management of many firms is interested in how it can use information resources to compete more effectively. One way to use information is to help reduce costs in order to follow a strategy of being the low-cost producer in the industry. How does information help to achieve this goal? Information can be used to run a plant or deliver a service efficiently. Production control, materials requirements planning, and just-in-time inventory approaches all require information to function; this information is usually processed on some type of computer.

Another way to use information to gain an edge on the competition is to develop a special product that fits into a niche in the market. Merrill Lynch used information and modern processing technology to create a new product, the Cash Management Account (CMA). This account "sweeps" the cash in a customer's brokerage account into a money market fund so that the customer earns the maximum return on his or her funds. The CMA allowed Merrill Lynch to expand the number of customers it serves and to increase the size of its money market funds, from which Merrill derives considerable management fees. It is interesting to note that in this example, the technology became a part of the product itself.

Our manufacturing company in the earlier example could also use information to reach customers more effectively. For example, the firm might place terminals in customer locations; the customers could use the terminals to enter orders directly, saving time and effort. A strategy such as this ties customers more closely to the manufacturer and makes it easier for them to place orders.

Firms process information for a variety of reasons. Historically they have used it to operate and control the business. Information has always played a role in supporting decisions as well, such as the decision by a financial officer on how much money to borrow or invest in order to ensure an adequate cash flow. More recently, information has been seen as a strategic resource, something that allows the firm to obtain a competitive advantage.

Managing Information Processing

In the early days of commerce, information was managed as a part of doing business. Information was not identified as a resource, nor was some functional area of the firm designated to manage it. Accountants took care of all information needed for accounting; they collected the data and processed them as needed. Manufacturing management provided information to accounting because it was needed and collected its own data to control manufacturing. The skills needed to process information before the advent of electronic computers were available within most departments.

The development of electronic computers fundamentally changed our ability to process information. Computers introduced a new set of dependencies into the organization. No longer could a single department afford the skills to process its own information. In the 1950s and 1960s, it was far too expensive to have a mainframe computer and programmers available at the departmental level. Instead, departments had to rely on a central group, often called the *electronic data processing* (*EDP*) department, to create systems and operate them. The department now depended on EDP to process its information.

This situation continued until the development of minicomputers, devices that were often sold to departments. Since these machines are simpler than centralized mainframe computers, departments were able to operate the computer themselves. However, it was still necessary to have some kind of specialist work on programming and run the computer.

Today we are confronted and, in some instances, overwhelmed by personal computers. These microcomputers make it possible for many individuals in the firm to process their own information. A typical user works with an electronic spreadsheet package to help make decisions, a word processor to prepare documents, a file management system to keep track of data, and/or a presentation graphics system for preparing documents for presentations.

The Goal of the Book

The goal of this book is to prepare the reader to assume a management position in information services from which he or she can help to improve the effectiveness of information processing in the organization. The book stresses the emerging role of the chief information officer (CIO); in addition, it discusses significant management positions in an information services organization.

Management Challenge

Why, if users are using their own computers, are we still concerned with the management of the information processing resource? Can we not rely on users to manage their own use of computers and information? The computer revolution and the rapid proliferation of mini- and microcomputers has brought the organization a variety of options. Consider the computer alternatives available now:

- Supercomputers
- Mainframes
- Mini supercomputers
- Super minicomputers
- Minicomputers
- Supermicrocomputers
- Microcomputers

The preceding list is just for hardware; what about software?

- Custom-developed systems
- Fourth-generation languages
- Packages

Next, consider where processing is to be done:

- In a central location
- Decentralized, at various locations
- Distributed, with communications among processing sites

Lastly, there is the question of where this system is managed:

- Centrally
- By users and managers at remote sites
- By some combination of central and local managers

Overview of the Book

The purpose of this chapter is to describe the tasks associated with the management of information services in an organization. The rest of the chapter presents a framework for management and then describes various managerial positions in information processing. This first chapter also provides an overview of technological trends that are important to management. Trends in the technology have a dramatic impact on the type of information processing possible in an organization. Finally, we introduce CMI, a hypothetical firm that will be used to illustrate some of the concepts discussed in the text.

Part I (Chapters 1–6) of the book deals with the organization and how it affects the management of information services. This section discusses the role of various managers in information services and the internal and external structure of the information services department. Chapter 5 goes into more detail on new technology and computer applications. The technology is changing the way organizations compete and the way individual users interact with computers. This section concludes with a chapter on planning for information systems (IS), one of the most important activities in information services management.

Part II (Chapters 7–11) is concerned with the information services environment. Topics such as leadership and the management of IS personnel are covered. Systems development is a major activity in information processing; this section of the book contains five chapters devoted to systems analysis and design, implementation, and alternatives to traditional design practices.

Part III, Chapters 12–17, on managing information services addresses the management of operations and the support of end users. This section concludes with chapters on the control and audit of information systems, capacity planning, and the acquisition of hardware, software, and services.

Part IV, Chapters 18–20, deals with the management of three areas that are becoming increasingly associated with traditional information systems in the firm: factory and office automation, and communications. Forecasts suggest that in the future organizations will increasingly include responsibility for all aspects of technology under the position of CIO.

The final section of the book deals with the evaluation and control of information services. In many organizations, senior management is uneasy with information services. Part of this uneasiness comes from management's problems in evaluating and controlling information processing. The last chapter is intended for managers who are not directly involved in the management of information processing; it contains advice and suggestions on how these managers can work more effectively with IS managers and obtain the maximum return from their investment in the technology.

A Management Framework

The task of managing the information resource has become more complicated, rather than less so, as a result of advances in technology. Now we find individuals who are not computer professionals making significant decisions about information processing and technology. Management is needed to coordinate, support, and control information processing. New technologies also offer the firm tremendous strategic opportunities, as described previously; to take advantage of these opportunities will require the ability to manage information processing successfully.

Figure 1-1 presents a framework to guide managers in the information services department (ISD) in their efforts to manage the information resource. Much of this book is organized around discussions of the activities in Figure 1-1.

As the figure shows, top management and the CIO must determine the role of information processing in the organization. Is its role to support operations, decision making, or strategy? Or is it some combination of these functions? The CIO and senior management are responsible for developing a vision for information processing in the firm.

From a knowledge of the firm's priorities and new technology, management and the ISD staff develop a 3- to 5-year plan for information processing. The plan identifies applications areas to receive attention and discusses the structure of information processing in the firm. First, there is the structure of information processing within the organization: What is the pattern of processing? Where are the computers located? How are they connected? What discretion does local management have with respect to information processing?

The CIO also has to be concerned with the internal organization of the ISD. Of paramount importance is the management and leadership of information services in the firm. Under these headings, we are concerned with IS personnel, the management of systems development, end user support, operations, and the management of related technologies like office automation, factory automation, and communications.

Within systems development, IS management must look at alternatives for developing applications, project management, and the ultimate success-

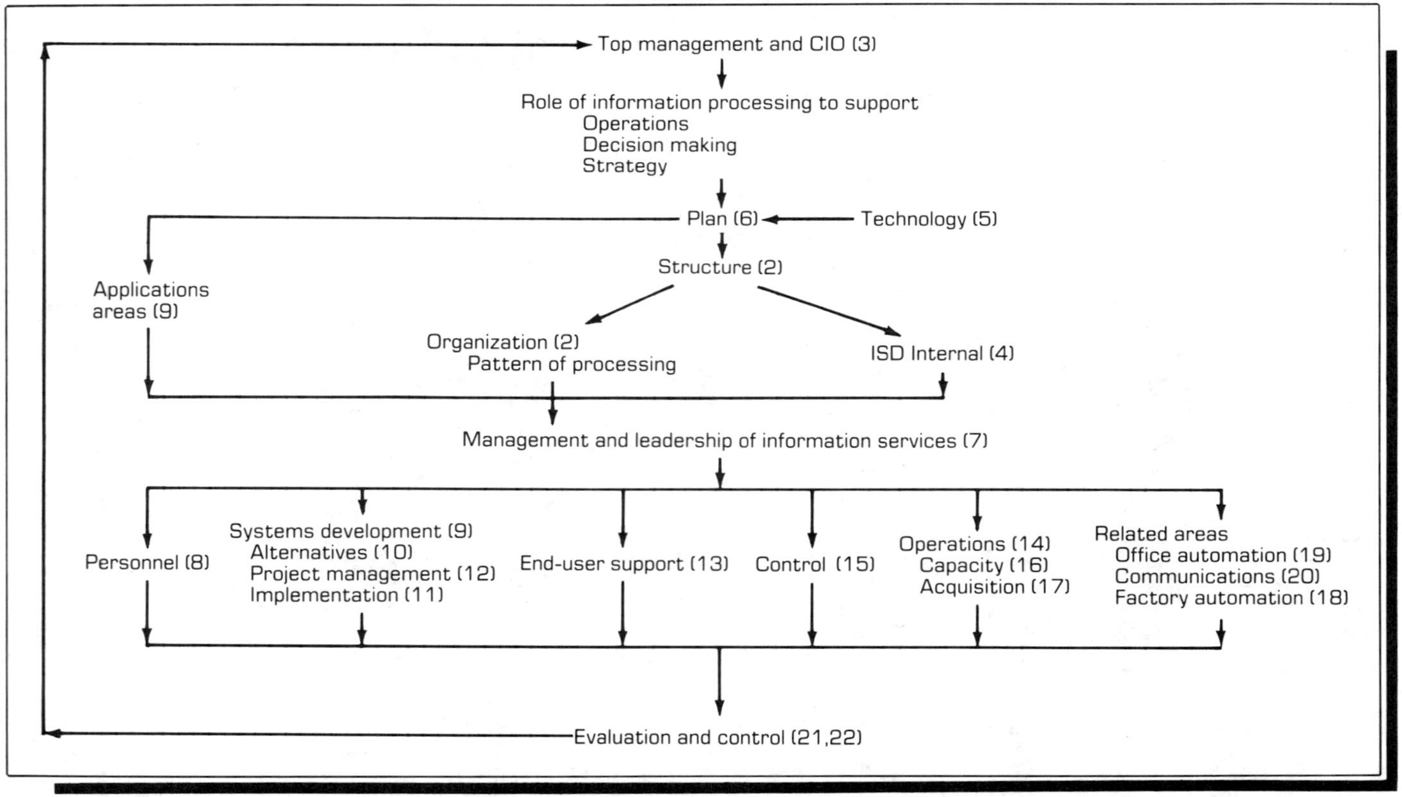

FIGURE 1-1 Management of the information resource: A framework. Numbers in parentheses refer to chapters in the book in which the topic is discussed further.

ful implementation of individual systems. Operational concerns include capacity planning and the acquisition of hardware and software. Each of these topics will be discussed in much greater detail in subsequent chapters, as indicated in Figure 1-1.

Management Positions

What are the different management positions within information services? See Table 1-1.

Chief Information Officer

The position of CIO is emerging in many leading corporations. It is estimated that about half of the Fortune 500 companies now have a senior-level manager who occupies the CIO position. The CIO is the highest-level manager in the organization who has full-time responsibility for information processing. What distinguishes this person from the traditional manager of information services? The CIO position has emerged as information processing has become more important to organizations. Typically, one finds a CIO today in

TABLE 1-1 Management Positions in Information Systems

Position	Description
Chief information officer	Oversees technology; bridge between users, managers, and the technical staff
IS manager	Responsible for daily operation of the ISD, including systems analysis and design, user services, operations, etc.
Department manager	Manages a local ISD; may report to IS manager or to user management
Systems manager	Responsible for all systems analysis and design projects
Programming manager	Manages and consults for the programming staff
Manager of operations	Responsible for all systems that are in production; schedules computer use and plans for new capacity
Manager of end-user computing	Supports various users who work with special languages and microcomputers
Database administrator	Responsible for defining and maintaining applications, using database management systems
Manager of quality control	Some firms have formal quality groups that verify changes made in existing applications, and review and accept new systems
Project manager	Leads a team developing a new computer application
Manager of systems programming	Responsible for the technical support of the computer and systems software

financial services organizations like brokerage firms; these organizations depend on information and information products to remain competitive and serve their customers.

Whether or not an individual is called a CIO, the concept of a senior officer of the firm managing information services on a full-time basis is important. This IS manager should report to a high-level manager in the firm, preferably the chief operating officer. In many organizations, the highest-level IS officer is responsible for traditional information processing on computers and for communications and office automation. A manager of information services who reports to someone four or five levels below the chief operating officer does not fit the model described here. In the future, we expect to see more senior level managers with full-time responsibility for information services and continued growth in the number of CIOs.

The CIO should oversee all of the firm's technology, including computer systems, office automation, and telecommunications. This individual should concentrate on long-range issues like planning and strategy; the day-to-day operation of information systems should be handled by the IS manager.

IS Manager

Before the development of the CIO position, the IS manager was the highest-level manager with full-time responsibility for information processing. The IS manager is concerned with the daily operations of information services, ranging from computer operations to systems analysis and design to planning. Because many IS managers have a technical background, they have had difficulty communicating with senior managers. In addition, the routine demands of the ISD are great, tending to drive out planning and strategic considerations.

The creation of a CIO position reflects management's growing realization of the importance of information and the need for someone to supplement the traditional ISD manager. Of course, in firms without CIOs, the ISD manager will have to undertake the activities that would normally be handled by the CIO.

Department Manager

Within a large organization, there may actually be several ISDs, for example, one at each of three manufacturing locations. A department manager is concerned with many of the same issues as the CIO, only on a more local scale. The department manager is likely to have to coordinate and control actions with the corporate ISD manager or the CIO.

Systems Manager

Many ISDs have managers of systems, who are responsible for the overall management of a firm's portfolio of development projects. This person must be concerned with the resources allocated to projects, the management of individual projects, staff assignments, and all other aspects of systems development.

Programming Manager

There may also be a manager of programming in a firm. This person is responsible for programmers; he or she is a manager and consultant for the programming staff. A good manager in this position will constantly strive to find improved programming techniques and ways to increase the productivity of the programming staff.

Manager of Operations

The two positions just described deal with the development of new applications. Once an application is finished, it is placed in production and becomes the responsibility of the operations department. The manager of operations must ensure that computer jobs are run on time and correctly. For on-line systems, he or she must be concerned with the availability of the computer and with response time. A constant problem for the operations staff is the need to do maintenance on systems, to enhance or repair systems that are currently in production. Often programmers who work with systems software (systems programmers) report to the operations manager.

Manager of End-User Computing

With the proliferation of microcomputers, there is a relatively new management position in the ISD, the manager of end-user computing. In some firms, a comparable job title is *manager of microcomputing* or *manager of the information center.* This person, regardless of the title, is the individual responsible for supporting various users in their computing activities.

Other Managers

In addition to the managerial responsibilities just described, there are other duties that must be performed in an ISD. In smaller installations, these tasks may be the part-time responsibility of an individual. Included in this category are a database administrator, manager of quality control, project manager, manager of R&D, manager of systems programming, and manager of maintenance programming.

The database administrator (DBA) is responsible for defining the relationships that constitute various databases in the organization. He or she also must be concerned with the integrity of the data stored in the database. This individual works closely with programmers and systems analysts to define data structures and to code the data definition language to set up a database for a new application.

The manager of quality control is concerned with new applications and maintenance. He or she must accept a new application and agree that it is ready for production. In a similar manner, when an existing system is modified, the quality control area tests the system with the new changes before agreeing that it can be placed in production.

Many times systems development is accomplished by a project team consisting of users, systems analysts, and programmers. One individual has to manage the team and is designated as the team leader or project manager. This position is temporary and lasts as long as the project.

Many mainframes and minicomputers require systems programming support. Systems programmers work with operating system software and systems software like telecommunications monitors. These programmers make modifications to the software, install new packages, and update existing systems. Maintenance programming is very similar, except that the term generally applies to applications developed within the organization.

Challenges of IS Management

The preceding discussion suggests that the task of managing the information processing resource has become more complex over time. How have we reached this point? How has the management of information processing progressed from its early days in the 1950s?

Stage Models

One famous approach to describing information systems management is the *stage hypothesis* suggested by Nolan (1979). Nolan stated that an organization goes through a series of identifiable stages in managing information services. At first, he proposed four stages, which later were expanded to six.

During *initiation* the computer is introduced and users are encouraged to make use of the system. Because users have little knowledge of computing, there is not a large demand for services. There are simple applications, often of an accounting nature. Most processing is centralized because users are not familiar with the technology.

In *contagion* users become enthusiastic about computers and request many applications. The computer group tries to expand in order to provide service; expenditures on staff and equipment rise dramatically during this stage. Typically, there is little planning and control during this period of rapid growth.

Control is soon sought by management when it becomes alarmed at the budget increases required to maintain momentum in information processing. The growth rate of information services budgets is reduced or even stopped; management wants to know what return they are receiving for their investment in information processing. The ISD may place emphasis on control and management, for example, by introducing a chargeout system to allocate expenses to user departments.

During the *integration* stage, the ISD takes advantage of new technology like database management systems (DBMSs). The department becomes more professional and takes a wider view of the organization, trying to integrate different applications.

Integration leads to *data administration,* in which the ISD provides database management support for different applications. There is much more of an emphasis on sharing data in the organization.

Finally, the firm achieves *maturity* in information processing, though few organizations have reached this level. At this point, the computer is integrated into management processes. The applications are in harmony with information flows in the organization; users and the ISD have joint responsibility for information processing.

The Nolan model, while cited often, has proven quite controversial. Many managers feel that it provides significant insights into the adoption of computerized information processing in organizations. Researchers, on the other hand, have failed to find much empirical support for it. The model is a purely descriptive one that provides little help in understanding why different events happen. A student of IS management should be familiar with the Nolan model because it is so frequently cited.

Gibson and Nolan (1974) described different management strategies that are appropriate at different stages. The difficulty with their proposals is that few firms ever fit exactly the profile for a given stage. What actions should they take? Similar issues are undoubtedly faced by different organizations as they adopt computing, but the stage hypothesis is not adequate to explain the complex phenomenon of information processing in the organization. For our purposes, the model in Figure 1-1 will be used to explore the complex issues of managing the information resource.

Technological Evolution

One can identify various stages of technological advancement by the computer industry. These changes in technology have driven a number of management decisions about information processing (see Table 1-2).

The First Generation

In the early days of computing in the 1950s, a typical organization acquired a single computer. These computers were all mainframes, and management generally began an EDP department or turned an existing tabulating card operation into such a department. All applications were centralized; a group of analysts and programmers developed batch processing systems, usually in assembly language.

The Second Generation

When the second generation of hardware appeared, with transistors replacing vacuum tubes, the number of computers installed was expanded.

TABLE 1-2 Evolution of Technology and Management

Generation (Years)	Hardware	Software	Management Response
1 (1950s)	Centralized mainframe	Assembly language	Centralized EDP department, usually under accounting
2 (1958–1964)	Mainframes	Movement to COBOL and operating systems	Mainframe at different locations (e.g., in a factory)
3 (1964–1970)	Mainframes Beginning of minis	Operating system required, COBOL standard, first database management systems	Centralized computers in large data centers for economies of scale
4 (1970–present)	Micros Minis Mainframes	Fourth-generation languages, packages, user-friendly microcomputer software	Distributed processing, user reactions against mainframes and computer professionals

A large firm might place several second-generation computers in different locations, each with its own EDP department developing new applications. Many firms began to use COBOL extensively in developing new applications, and operating systems came into widespread use.

The Third Generation

When integrated circuits replaced discrete components, the third generation was born. Software became much more of an issue because of the need to convert existing programs. There were far more programs to change in going from the second to the third generation than from the first generation to the second. (Remember that the machine languages of most computers at this time were incompatible with each other, even among computers from the same vendor!) Increasing use of COBOL and the first use of DBMSs characterized the third generation.

Because the third generation featured computers whose power increased with their price, there were economies of scale. Grosch's law was thought to prevail: the power of a computer increased as the square of its price. A computer that was twice as costly as another was four times as powerful.

Such economics suggested that companies should centralize computing; the dispersed computers of the second generation should be gathered into computer centers. Because computers now routinely supported remote data transmission and even on-line systems, there was no need to have local computers. The organization would gain by having a few large, central computers.

The Fourth Generation

Unfortunately, it has proven very difficult to provide good, responsive service from large, centralized information processing centers. When minicomputers came along during the 1960s, users were eager to take advantage of this new technology. A department or plant could justify the use of a minicomputer and operate it without requiring assistance from a large, central ISD. The same logic has led to the explosion in the use of microcomputers. Users are largely motivated by negative reactions to the services provided by computer professionals.

The fourth generation has witnessed the rise of fourth-generation languages (4GLs), which are often offered to end users. Through support centers, users learn how to write programs in a 4GL and how to solve some of their own information processing problems. ISDs may also adopt these languages, at least for some tasks, as a replacement for or supplement to COBOL.

Distributed processing was a major theme of the fourth generation. Instead of the third-generation economies of scale argument, the minicomputer vendors and communications firms suggested that computing would be more responsive if the firm bought many smaller computers and connected them using communications networks. Grosch's law was repealed by the economies of chip fabrication, which led to the development of minis and, later, of micros.

Microcomputer vendors today are fanning resentment of unresponsive central ISDs. However, seeking an opportunity to offer total solutions, the vendors suggest that the next step is to tie everything together in a network so that the user can access the mainframe's databases easily from the micro.

This history has been brief, but hopefully it has demonstrated that technology, rather than management considerations, has often seemed to drive decisions about information processing. The technology is a given; it may allow the organization to follow a certain path or it may limit the firm in some way. The important point to remember is that *the firm should manage the technology instead of reacting to it.* In subsequent chapters, we shall see how to actively manage the information processing resource. We shall pay particular attention to the planning process, in which the organization determines what technology is most appropriate for it, given the technology that is available and foreseeable in the next 3 years or so.

The Current Status of IS Management

In most organizations we have visited, the ISD is not very popular; this impression is supported by trade press reports about these departments. What are the problems and complaints?

1. The ISD can never create systems on time and in budget.
2. The applications developed do not meet our needs.
3. It is impossible to get a system changed or to obtain a new report.
4. Systems are highly inflexible.
5. The computer is never up.
6. Response time is very slow.
7. We were told that it would be 2 years before the ISD could start work on our system.
8. There are many errors in the database.
9. Our reports are always late.

10. Costs for information processing keep going up, while the service gets worse.

We could continue this list, but these 10 items are representative of many user complaints. Managers have even more serious objections:

1. I don't feel we are getting a good return for the money we invest in information services.
2. I think information processing is out of control.
3. I get more complaints about information systems than about any other area of the company.
4. We just can't get good management in the information processing area.
5. I don't like the manager of ISD; there is no way he could become a vice president or CIO.

It appears that being a manager of information processing today is one of the most challenging and frustrating positions available. What is the reason? Are all managers in this field incompetent? We suspect that there are a number of problems that contribute to a difficult management situation in information processing. These problems include the following.

Technology

Most managers and users who have nontechnical backgrounds do not understand technology, either its capabilities or its limitations. Many users seem to fear the technology, since it does seem foreign.

Invisible Procedures

A user or manager can observe materials entering a factory and watch machines transform the materials into a finished product. Even if the individual does not fully understand the process, a great deal of it is visible. The procedures executed by computers are just the opposite; there is no way to see what is happening.

Complexity

There is no question that computer technology is complex and is becoming more so. We use technology in general to hide complexity from the user, but in turn create more complexity within our systems. A good example is the automatic transmission in an automobile; this device has simplified the user's interface with the automobile at a cost of much greater complexity in the transmission. As we make computer technology more convenient to use, for example, through on-line systems, we increase the complexity of systems in order to reduce complexity for users. These complex systems are often hard to maintain and prone to failure.

Apathy

The chief operating officer of a firm probably knows less about information processing than about any other area of the business. This executive probably knows a great deal about finance, marketing, production, and so

TABLE 1-3 The Challenges of IS Management

Supporting the organization's strategy
Meeting the demand for computer power and smooth operations
Dealing with aging information systems
Reducing the backlog of applications
Supporting end users
Managing IS personnel to reduce turnover and enhance skills
Developing a vision of the role and contribution of technology to the organization
Defining an overall hardware and software architecture, including micros, minis, mainframes, and communications
Coordinating processing decisions across the organization

on, but knows little about information processing. In addition, many managers seem to feel that information processing is so uninteresting that they should know little about it. This negative attitude is very difficult to overcome and creates constant problems in information processing.

Computer Professionals

Just as managers can be criticized for apathy and disinterest, a number of problems come from computer professionals who fail to understand management and its objectives. For most firms, the goal of the organization is not to create bigger and better information systems.

Too many computer professionals are mired in the technology; they are unable to function as managers to control information processing. This problem, combined with the apathy of management, makes it difficult, if not impossible, to establish a well-managed ISD.

Current Challenges

From a managerial perspective, what are the most important challenges for information processing management during the next 5 years? See Table 1-3.

Supporting Strategy

Most information services managers believe that their primary role is to provide a service to the organization. For the past 20 years, this goal has probably been enough. Today, however, organizations are interested in using the technology strategically. In the future, the ISD will still have to provide a service, but at the same time it will have to think much more about how to support the strategy of the firm.

Operations

There is no way to avoid concern over computer operations. The more applications developed, the more demands placed on systems hardware and software. On-line systems require reliable service and good response. Planning for hardware capacity and operations is a critical concern today.

Aging Systems

A number of ISD managers have complained about the aging systems they must maintain and enhance. The investment in some of these systems is so massive that even if they are 10 years old or more, the firm cannot afford to replace them. Various jury-rigged solutions are used to get around this problem. For example, one firm may use a specially programmed microcomputer to create a new user interface for one of its older systems. The micro and its programs create a new interface that replaces the standard interface provided by a previously dumb terminal.

The Application Backlog

Many organizations report a huge, visible backlog of applications. There are so many demands for new applications and so few staff resources that it is not unusual to wait for 2 years before a new application can be started; combined with the length of time needed to develop the application, this delay means that the user may wait for 4 years or more for a system. Not only is there evidence of a known backlog, it has been observed that there are as many applications waiting to be suggested as there are on line.

End-User Support

The problems previously discussed may make the reaction of users to mini- and microcomputers seem more understandable. Realizing that they cannot afford to wait for the computer professional, users are "doing it themselves." While this approach leads to a number of problems that we will discuss later, it does relieve the ISD of some of the development demands on it. At the same time, it places new demands for support on computer professionals.

Managing IS Personnel

The IS industry has always been characterized by high turnover; rates of 20 per cent a year are not uncommon. Since the productivity of applications development is directly related to people and to the firm's investment in them, managing IS personnel is an important challenge.

Lack of Vision

One serious challenge is to overcome the lack of vision that characterizes the management of both the firm and the ISD. Both groups need to discuss the strategy of the firm and the status of the technology. What is their joint vision of the future? How does information technology fit in? A vision is crucial to planning and controlling information processing.

Lack of Architecture

Organizations are acquiring hardware and software at a rapid pace; the lack of an overall architecture for computing in the organization makes it hard to decide if requests make sense. A vision of the firm leads to the development of an overall architecture for hardware and software; the architecture, in turn, helps guide the acquisition of hardware, software, and services. An architecture may establish a set of standards for hardware and software in the firm.

Coordination of Processing

Given today's trends toward decentralized and distributed processing, one of the most serious challenges facing management is how to coordinate information processing without stifling initiative. In later chapters, we shall discuss methods of coordination that are designed to balance the needs of the firm with the creativity of individual users.

Technological Trends

Technology has changed rapidly and dramatically. Previously we criticized organizations for being too heavily influenced by vendors and their latest technology. Given the pace of technological development, however, it is hard not to be unduly influenced. Technology is an enabling factor; it allows the organization to develop systems and products that would be impossible without it. Our task is to understand the coming technology and use it to advantage. The challenge is to manage the technology rather than letting it manage us. See Table 1-4 for a summary of important trends in technological development.

TABLE 1-4 Technological Trends and Their Implications

Trend	Implications
Less expensive processors	Processing will be widely available for many tasks at an acceptable cost
Workstations	Information and knowledge workers will use workstations as a routine part of their activities
Communications networks	Firms will connect diverse types of computing equipment to facilitate access to data and communications
Electronic connections	Increase communications speed and reduce the use of paper
4GLs	There will be more end-user computing, demands for support, and custom development of systems using 4GLs
Systems development	Productivity will be improved due to packages, programmer/analyst workstations
Input/output advances	Simpler ways will be developed to communicate with computers, which will encourage more extensive use of computer systems
Optical storage	Massive, easily distributed databases will become feasible
DBMSs	Extensive use will make development more productive and data easier for users to access
Artificial intelligence	Expert systems offer new opportunities
Office automation	This provides a new way to communicate and improve productivity
Varied patterns of processing	There will be more end-user computing and local control over information processing; greater distribution of processing

Less Expensive, More Powerful Processors

The trend toward less expensive, more powerful processors should continue. Beyond 32-bit chips for microcomputers, further improvements in cost and performance will come from refinements in the chips and from lower production costs. Several vendors have introduced computers that employ reduced instruction sets; only the most frequently used instructions are "wired into" the chip. Reduced instruction set computers (RISC) may offer a speed advantage, since they contain a smaller number of instructions that can execute more quickly than those of conventional processors.

Another way of obtaining more processing power is to use novel computer architectures. A number of experiments are now underway to determine the advantages of alternatives to the conventional von Neumann architecture, with data and programs flowing to and from a central processing unit. The most promising ideas at the present time are for computers that use many processors working in parallel to solve problems. The drawback to this approach is the problem of coordinating the processors and breaking the problem into parts that can be worked on in parallel.

As hardware prices are reduced, applications that were once only marginal become feasible. A lower-priced computer makes it possible to undertake a task that would have been too expensive with more expensive machines. No one could have afforded to provide each worker with a mainframe computer of the 1960s, yet today's desktop microcomputer has that much power or more.

New architectures and less expensive fabrication of custom logic make it feasible to dedicate computers to particular tasks. There have always been some specialized computers—for example, communications controllers. However, now it is possible to envision computers dedicated to special tasks such as scientific computations, graphics processing, and imaging.

Workstations

The workstation described previously will become an increasingly common sight in offices. It will be built around a 32-bit microprocessor; it will feature a high-resolution color graphics display, a large hard disk with 40 to 100 million bytes of storage, a draft printer, and a modem for communicating with other computers. There will also be specialized peripheral devices, depending on the way the workstation is being used—for example, optical disk readers for access to large amounts of data (see the section "Optical Storage" below).

Because it appears that workstations can dramatically improve managerial productivity and the quality of work, organizations in the 1990s will create an environment in which there is likely to be more than one workstation per professional employee. Key executives will have workstations at home as well as at the office.

Communications Networks

The proliferation of microcomputer-based workstations, the increasing trend to connect organizations with suppliers and customers, and the growing popularity of electronic communications all provide impetus for a growth in communications networks.

At the present time, with the deregulation of AT&T, it is difficult to foresee the environment for networking. It is likely that there will be a variety of services available for wide area networks, connecting locations separated by a few miles or thousands of miles. The common carriers will offer switched services for digital transmission, and packet networks like Telenet will continue to be popular.

Some firms will want to control their own communications and bypass phone companies. Private networks to accomplish these purposes, such as the one created by Citibank, are very expensive and are likely to be developed only by the largest firms.

The use of local area networks (LANs), which tie together computers and other devices on one or two floors of a building, should expand rapidly. It is likely that two or three standard networks will emerge, each of which will support most vendors' products. The use of LANs is now constrained by the high cost of connecting each computer to the network and by confusion over standards for the networks. Costs should drop, making it economical to connect computers to local networks, and two or three approaches like Ethernet and the IBM token passing scheme should become standard.

Electronic Connections

There are often several purposes for connecting firms electronically. One objective is to reduce the amount of paper that has to be processed. Millions of purchase orders, invoices, and similar documents are now being transferred electronically directly between firms. Commercial time-sharing vendors are marketing networks to connect different companies. Firms like General Motors and Sears have invested in their own networks to make electronic document interchange possible.

In addition to reducing costs by eliminating paper processing, a firm can create stronger links with its customers, tying them more closely to the firm. An electronic connection also makes it possible to provide additional services—for example, to let the customer inquire about inventory balances before placing an order.

Fourth-Generation Languages

A 4GL is a language that functions at a much higher level than COBOL or FORTRAN. These languages feature statements like "SELECT EMPLOYEE

WHERE SALARY GT 30000 AND YEARS GT 10." This statement retrieves the names of all employees who have a salary of over $30,000 per year and have worked more than 10 years for the firm. In COBOL, it would take many statements to accomplish this processing task, especially for printing a report with the results.

A 4GL makes it possible to reduce programming time, since the level of detail of a language like COBOL is not required. These languages have become popular with users who write their own programs rather than wait for a computer professional to become available. They have made end-user computing possible. As long as the information desired exists on the computer and is not spread across too many different files, a user can retrieve and manipulate the required data relatively easily with one of these languages.

We also expect to see firms using 4GLs for their production programming in place of COBOL. One experiment has shown that there is great potential for increasing programmer productivity with these languages, but that there may be a cost in execution time. Since programming and systems development creates such a bottleneck, firms will make the decision to purchase more powerful hardware, if required, to obtain greater programmer productivity through the use of 4GLs.

Systems Development

In the past 5 years, packaged software has become a significant force in information processing. The costs and time required for systems development, plus the frequent inability to produce a good system, have made custom-developed applications much less appealing today.

The quality of applications packages has increased as new generations of software have been released. Many packages have been around for over 10 years and have experienced constant improvements during this period. Also, the mass market for microcomputer software has forced vendors to develop software packages that are appealing and easy to use. Packages will continue to grow in popularity: the first question will be "Can we find a package for a new application?" rather than "How much will a custom system cost and how long will it take?"

Workstations will be developed to assist analysts and programmers when it is necessary to develop a custom system. The jobs of the programmer and systems analyst will continue to merge. The final objective will be to have automatic programming packages so that the systems analyst can generate programs after entering a description of the system's requirements into a workstation. Such systems should reduce the need for programmers and change their role to one of developing software for packages and specialized uses. The work of the programmer will be leveraged; instead of developing a custom system, he or she will develop systems capable of producing custom applications.

Input/Output

Providing input and producing output continue to be a bottleneck for computer systems. An increase in systems that link organizations together will reduce the amount of duplicate data entry, for example, by sending orders electronically so that the recipient does not have to key the order. However, computer input will continue to require a significant amount of human effort.

For factory applications, there will be extensive use of bar codes that allow the movement of parts and materials to be tracked with little or no keying of input. For office work, there will be increased use of electronic transmission of documents rather than paper copies. A copy on paper will be printed for review or for making notes, but most documents will be exchanged electronically. When it is necessary to work from a paper copy, optical character recognition (OCR) readers will handle input.

Many systems will feature natural language or restricted natural language inquiry. The user will not have to remember command syntax to ask a question of a database. Other interfaces will allow the user to make an inquiry by giving an example. The objective is to make it easier for a user to interact with data.

Voice recognition technology has the potential to reduce the number of key strokes required to enter data. Current voice systems are very limited in what they can recognize. However, there are promising developments that may produce a breakthrough in understanding speech. It is likely that in the 1990s a significant number of nontypists will communicate with computers using brief spoken commands. It is also likely that these individuals will be able to dictate short letters and memoranda into a machine that will convert the words to written text. However, for individuals accustomed to working with a keyboard, the keying of commands will probably be faster and more natural than the available speech recognition systems.

Optical Storage

Optical disks offer the potential for vast amounts of storage at a relatively low cost. One of today's optical disks can store 200 million bytes of data, or enough characters for about 1000 books. It is now possible to buy a database on the 10,000 publicly traded firms in the United States that contains historical financial statements, excerpts from Securities and Exchange Commission documents, the text of security analysts' reports, and abstracts of magazine articles about the firms. The database comes with an optical disk reader that is used with a microcomputer. The low cost of mass producing data for distribution on optical disks suggests that much information that could be sent over communications lines will be distributed in physical form via a disk.

Today's optical disks are read-only; at most, one can write data once. Optical disks that can be erased are now in the laboratory and should soon be available. This technology will probably eliminate or drastically reduce the use of magnetic tapes and will eventually replace magnetic disks, though probably not until after the year 2000. Optical disks offer a firm many exciting possibilities for the storage and distribution of vast amounts of data.

Database Management Systems

DBMSs have been available for over 15 years, at least for mainframe computers. There still are many organizations that have not adopted this technology; however, their number is steadily decreasing. For multiuser applications on mainframes and minicomputers, the 1990s should bring a database environment to most organizations. This environment will be characterized by a DBMS (probably relational), a highly integrated data dictionary, and a query language or 4GL for programming.

On the microcomputer scene, personal filing and storage systems will become the third most popular use of a personal computer after spreadsheets and word processing. Current DBMS software on micros is beginning to approach the ease of use of spreadsheets; by 1990 this kind of program will be common on managerial workstations.

Artificial Intelligence

Artificial intelligence is being applied to business applications primarily in the form of expert systems. These systems capture the rules used by human experts and place them in a knowledge base. Expert systems are in use for configuring DEC VAX computers, and two firms offer expert systems for providing financial advice, one of which contains 6000 rules. More expert systems will be developed to give the firm an edge on its competition, though many firms today regard expert systems as research projects having more risks than conventional applications.

Office Automation

Office automation is an amalgamation of a number of tools, including electronic mail, word processing, and personal services like electronic calendars. Office automation and communications will be integrated under information services and will report to the CIO. Electronic mail will become more prevalent and will be used to entice managers to try hands-on use of computers. Voice mail systems will also be used, since they do not require a terminal and are an advantage where travel is involved. Office automation will be a feature of vast computer networks connecting many of a firm's processors.

Pattern of Processing

Several of the trends just discussed suggest an evolving pattern of processing in the organization. First, the economics of hardware versus labor to produce software favor continued substitution of hardware for systems development and programming time. Organizations will be forced to adopt analyst/programmer workstations and 4GLs if they are to complete even a fraction of the applications demanded by users.

This high demand for and low supply of systems development resources will lead to a dramatic increase in the amount of computing done by end users working with micros and 4GLs. As users undertake more computing and become accustomed to functioning with a workstation, office automation and traditional forms of information processing will merge. The workstation will perform local processing, make inquiries of a mainframe computer's database, and handle office automation tasks. Capabilities such as these require networks of computers that are able to communicate with each other.

At first, we will see more distributed processing as users continue to acquire micros and departmental minis. However, as the burden of supporting equipment continues to rise, there will be a trend toward asking a centralized information processing group to take more responsibility for operations, support, and service. Users will find that they do not want to run their own computer centers.

As software and hardware become easier to use and networking increases, the actual location of data and processing power should become less important. Certainly there will be distributed processing in the microcomputer-based workstation. However, for access to data and programs and for specialized computing demands, the user should not be concerned with whether the computer is next door or thousands of miles away. Of course, this system will work only if a professional computer staff is successfully able to operate a complex of computers and communications networks.

Summary and Implications

The trends we have described have a number of implications for management and the organization. First, information processing involving computers and communications networks will become even more integral to the functioning of the firm. The firms that succeed in the coming years will be those able to manage information processing technology and use it to gain a competitive advantage.

Management can also expect to spend an increasing amount of money on information processing. Traditional operational systems will continue to expand in scope and will handle larger numbers of transactions. At first, a few banks had automated tellers connected to their central computers; now banks are joining in regional and nationwide networks of automated tellers to increase the level of service they provide to customers. Costs and the banks' dependence on the technology will also increase.

There is no one right amount of money to spend on information technology. Firms will cost justify some systems and will undertake other applications because management feels that the firm may gain a competitive advantage by doing so. Firms will move toward the use of steering committees for making decisions on new proposals for the use of the technology in order to obtain widespread input and judgment. Cost savings will be used less to justify these investments in technology. Instead, managers will evaluate objectively and subjectively how much a new application will contribute to the goals of the firm.

Finally, managers and others will be more involved in information processing technology than ever before. Managers will use the technology for personal support, look for ways to use it to gain a competitive edge, and spend a considerable amount of time managing information processing itself.

Technology and Management Challenges

Table 1-5 shows the contributions the previously discussed technological trends make to meeting the management challenges presented earlier in the chapter. Advances in networks and greater connectivity among firms provide more support for the use of technology as a part of corporate strategy. Strategic applications frequently involve links to customers or suppliers; networks make these links easier to develop. Artificial intelligence and expert systems may also help a firm gain a competitive edge.

Many aspects of the coming technology should help meet the challenges of operating a modern computer system. Less expensive processors, workstations, and communications, along with advances in systems development techniques, should help to replace aging systems entirely or conceal them with new interfaces. This same type of technology may help to ease the applications backlog. However, it is unlikely that any coming technology can create the enormous improvements needed in our ability to do systems analysis and design.

Workstations and less expensive processors, combined with greater connectivity, will provide support for end-user computing. The technology, however, will have little impact on the challenge of managing IS personnel. Networks and communications, along with office automation and various options for the pattern of processing, are important to the firm in developing its vision for information services. Workstations, networks, communications, and office automation, combined with the available patterns for processing, influence the firm in choosing an architecture; these technological variables also determine the amount and type of coordination needed for information processing.

Chapter 5 discusses some of the trends in technology in more detail in order to better predict the impact of technology on the management of information services. The challenges of managing this function introduced in this chapter will be covered in more depth in succeeding chapters.

TABLE 1-5 Interaction of Technological Trends and Management Challenges

Management Challenges	Technological Trends: Cheaper Processors	Work-stations	Net-works	Electronic Connec-tions	4GLs	Systems Develop.	I/O Advan.	Optical Storage	Database Manage-ment	Artificial Intelli-gence	Office Auto-mation	Pattern of Processing
Support for strategy	2	2	1	1	2	2	2	2	2	1	2	2
Operations	2	2	1	1	1	1	1	1	1	2	1	1
Aging systems	1	1	1	1	2	1	3	3	2	2	3	3
Applications backlog	3	1	1	1	1	1	3	2	1	2	3	2
End-user support	1	1	1	1	1	2	2	2	2	2	1	2
Managing IS personnel	3	2	2	2	1	3	3	3	2	2	1	1
Vision	2	2	1	1	2	2	2	3	3	2	1	1
Architecture	2	1	1	1	2	2	2	3	2	2	1	1
Coordination	2	1	1	1	2	2	3	3	2	3	1	1

1 = Major contribution of trend to meeting challenge
2 = Some contribution
3 = Little contribution

TABLE 1-6 CMI, Inc

CMI	Charleston	Fremont	Omaha	Chicago
Business	Headquarters	Printed circuit boards	Electromechanical switches	Metal parts fabrication
Computer	IBM 4300	DEC VAX 8700	IBM System 36	Hewlett-Packard Spectrum
Applications	Finance, accounting	Order tracking, production control, billing, shipping	Order processing, production, shipping	Production control, shipping
ISD	Manager 3 consultants 1 planner/R&D 1 DBA 1 mgr. of micros 2 analysts 3 programmers 3 operators 2 data entry clerks	Manager Manager, operations 2 analysts 3 programmers 3 operators 1 data entry clerk	Manager Manager, operations 2 analysts 4 programmers 4 operators 2 data entry clerks	Manager Manager, systems and programming Manager, operations 1 DBA 3 analysts 4 programmers 5 operators

Technology, organizations, and the business environment are constantly changing. Much of the study of information services focuses on the management of change. As long as managers and users remain creative and vendors develop new technologies, the management of change will be a major component of the management of information services.

CMI: A Hypothetical Example

A hypothetical company, CMI, will provide an example to illustrate the topics discussed throughout the book. In this chapter, we present the background of the firm by way of introduction. CMI resulted from a merger of the Carson Corporation and Midcontinent Industries in 1988. The firm has its headquarters in Charleston, South Carolina, and three major divisions located in Fremont, California; Omaha, Nebraska; and Chicago, Illinois. Table 1-6 describes information processing at CMI.

The firm is in three basic businesses. In Fremont, CMI operates a plant that makes printed circuit boards for the electronics industry. This product has to be constructed to high tolerances and shipped to electronics firms. Customers use the board to mount various circuit components and computer chips to make a product such as a computer modem.

In Omaha, CMI manufactures electrical switches and relay equipment; these products are used primarily by the building industry for homes and offices. The switches are similar to the kind used for the lights in a home. However, the firm also makes a number of heavier-duty switches for electrical equipment, such as the switches and relays found inside an air conditioner. This branch of the firm is currently investigating automotive electronics to see if it can make products for this market.

In Chicago, the company operates a precision metal parts manufacturing company. This subsidiary uses highly complex machining centers to turn out custom metal components. Its customers include the aerospace industry, computer vendors, and the U.S. government.

As a result of its merger, CMI has a number of dissimilar computers at different locations. In Charleston there is a medium-sized IBM 4300 mainframe computer that handles corporate accounting and finance. Fremont has a VAX 8700 computer for order tracking, production control, billing, and shipping. Certain engineering calculations are done on the VAX. In Omaha there is an IBM System 36, which is used for order processing, accounting, and shipping. Chicago has a Hewlett-Packard computer that runs a software package for production control and shipping. Finally, each location has a number of personal computers, and the engineering department at Chicago has a Prime computer.

There are also a variety of staff members in the ISD. The CIO is at Charleston, and he manages a group of three corporate consultants, one planner, and a manager of microsupport. There are also a DBA, two systems analysts, and three programmers. Finance and accounting also jointly hired a manager of user department computing to support their micros.

Chicago has a manager of information services and a manager of systems and programming. There are a DBA, three analysts, and four programmers. The ISD in the plant employs a manager of operations and five operators, along with three data entry clerks.

In Fremont there are a manager of IS, two analysts, and three programmers. Here there are three operators and one data entry clerk reporting to a manager of operations. Finally, in Omaha there are a manager of IS, two analysts, and four programmers. The manager of operations has four operators and two data entry clerks reporting to him.

Summary

In this chapter we have introduced the environment surrounding the information resources of an organization. The purpose of this book is to prepare the reader to manage and control information processing effectively. A large number of actors are involved in information processing, ranging from senior management to users and computer professionals.

It is important to remember that information services provides more than just a service to the modern organization. Today we have to think in terms of its contribution to the purpose and objectives of the firm. Can information technology advance the organization's strategy?

To contribute to corporate strategy, the information services function has to be well managed; its staff must meet the challenges described in this chapter. We must change the negative perceptions of information services and convince members of the organization that information processing can make a significant contribution to them and to the firm. Only if the information processing function is well managed and controlled will the organization receive the full benefits of a powerful technology.

Recommended Readings

Cash, J., F. W. McFarlan, and J. L. McKenney, *Corporate Information Systems Management*, 2nd ed. Homewood, Ill.: Richard D. Irwin, 1988. (A text oriented toward the senior manager who must deal with the information services function.)

Gibson, C., and R. L. Nolan, "Managing the Four Stages of EDP Growth," *Harvard Business Review*, vol. 52, no. 1 (January–February 1974), pp. 76–88. (Describes the management implications of the original four-stage theory.)

Lucas, H. C., Jr., *Coping with Computers: A Manager's Guide to Controlling Information Processing*. New York: Free Press, 1982. (A discussion of a framework for managers to use in controlling the information processing resource.)

Nolan, R. L., "Managing the Crises in Data Processing," *Harvard Business Review*, vol. 57, no. 2 (March–April 1979), pp. 115–126. (The expanded stage theory; this descriptive model is widely cited, though it has its limitations.)

Discussion Problem

1.1 Kolton Industries is a manufacturer of high-quality optical devices such as lenses for binoculars, submarine periscopes, and similar applications. The design of lenses is a very complex engineering task, and the firm first invested in computers to help engineers. Scientific calculations determined what computer to buy. A lens analysis package was available for a particular brand of computer, so the firm chose it.

Later, as an afterthought, the company considered using the computer for routine business applications. Because of the historical origins of computing, the manager of the ISD was an engineer. He gave first priority to lens design problems and very low priority to business applications. As an engineer, he was used to approximations. Engineers do not expect 100% accuracy; they wanted enough accuracy for their designs to work. The manager of the ISD applied this same idea to business processing. "I don't understand why accountants get so upset about a few pennies out of hundreds of millions of dollars," he was heard to say.

Management at Kolton became concerned over deteriorating relationships between users and the computer group and asked for consulting assistance. What would you recommend to the firm? How can they reduce information processing problems?

1.2 The manager of a medium-sized garment firm, Fashion Designs, was very concerned about his computing operations. "I am spending millions on accounting and computers. How much should an organization of this size spend for these services? I don't know, but I do know that we spend too much."

His vice president for operations was very concerned with the president's statements. She said, "How do you answer a question like that? What is the right amount to spend on advertising, on a new design for our products? We have to account for our business; we have to process orders on computers because we couldn't afford to hire enough people to do the job manually. But how do I answer the president's question without looking silly?" What can you suggest to the vice president of operations?

Questions

1. How does a modern corporation use information?
2. What is unique about the Merrill Lynch CMA?
3. Why were the first computers centralized?
4. List some of the types of computers available today.
5. Why is it a good idea to have a plan for information processing in the firm?
6. Describe two management positions in information services.
7. What is the difference between the jobs of the CIO and the manager of the ISD? What are the similarities?
8. What trends have led to the creation of a position of manager of microcomputing?
9. What are the problems with the Nolan stage model of the development of IS in a firm?
10. Why did some experts suggest that computers should be located in central places during the third generation?
11. Why has the IS field tended to be so heavily influenced by the technology? What is the alternative?
12. What are the major complaints about ISDs today?
13. What are some of the reasons that firms have difficulty coping with information processing?
14. Why is the coordination of processing in a large company important?
15. What are the benefits of cheaper processors for users and the firm?
16. What is a workstation for a manager? How does it help the manager?
17. What is a 4GL? Why might an organization want to use one?
18. What is the promise of optical storage technology?
19. What is an expert system?
20. Define office automation.
21. What is a pattern of processing? What pattern do you expect to see in many organizations in the next 5 years?
22. What are the implications of the pattern of processing for users and management?
23. Why does a firm like CMI have so many different brands of computers?
24. What do you think the highest-priority problem is for the CIO at CMI?
25. What problems will CMI encounter if it tries to move to one brand of computers across the firm?

2

Organizational Structure

A fundamental problem for management is to determine the structure of the organization. Managers are constantly changing reporting relationships, the definition of a business unit, and even the lines of business in which the firm engages. Usually there is some reason for making a change in the organization—for example, to improve managerial control or to increase the profitability of a unit.

Information services have been organized in a number of different ways throughout the relatively short history of this function. They have moved from centralization to decentralization and back to centralized processing with the third generation of equipment. Now they are in a period of more distributed and decentralized processing. In the last chapter, we observed that much of the structure of information processing had been dictated by technology rather than management considerations. In this chapter, we shall review several important considerations in choosing an organizational structure and apply them to the information services function.

Management Theories

There are many books and articles on how to organize; we shall discuss a number of variables and see how they can help in determining the structure for an information processing unit. Table 2-1 summarizes the key concepts discussed in this chapter. The discussion is applicable to the overall structure of information processing for the organization and for determining the internal structure of the ISD, a topic discussed in Chapter 4.

Variables

Management theory is concerned with two important variables that influence how an organization is structured. The notion of uncertainty is extremely important in understanding organizational design (March and Simon, 1958). Uncertainty is a lack of knowledge about a condition or event. As an example, many firms regard future sales as highly uncertain.

There is inherent uncertainty in the environment, and organizations create uncertainty through their operations. Uncertainty from sales comes from unpredictable product demand from the environment. Uncertainty about the ability to produce a product according to the shipping schedule requested by the customer arises from the way the production process is organized; this uncertainty is created by the operations of the firm.

It is interesting to note that the ISD copes with a great deal of uncertainty. Does the analyst understand the needs of the user? Will programs be completed on schedule and perform adequately? Will the on-line system

TABLE 2-1 Management Terms

Terms	Classification*	Definition
Uncertainty	Variable	Lack of knowledge about events or states of the world
Coordination	Variable/Action	Acting together for the benefit of the organization
Rules and programs	Strategy	Procedures for work
Hierarchical referral	Strategy	Appeal to management
Targeting and goal setting	Strategy	Establishing performance standards to reduce communications needs
Slack resources	Strategy	Extra margins to act as a buffer
Self-contained tasks	Strategy	Work group has all of the resources it needs for its assignment
Vertical information systems	Strategy	Systems that pass information upward in the organization
Lateral relations	Action/Strategy	Liaisons to coordinate across organizational boundaries
Integration	Action/Strategy	Pulling together units with diverse tasks
Interdependence	Condition/Strategy	Work groups that depend on each other to accomplish their goals
Power	Behavior/Condition	The ability to influence the behavior of others

* Variable = an entity that takes on different values
Action = action taken by management
Strategy = organization design strategy
Condition = a result of some action or strategy
Behavior = individuals' actions

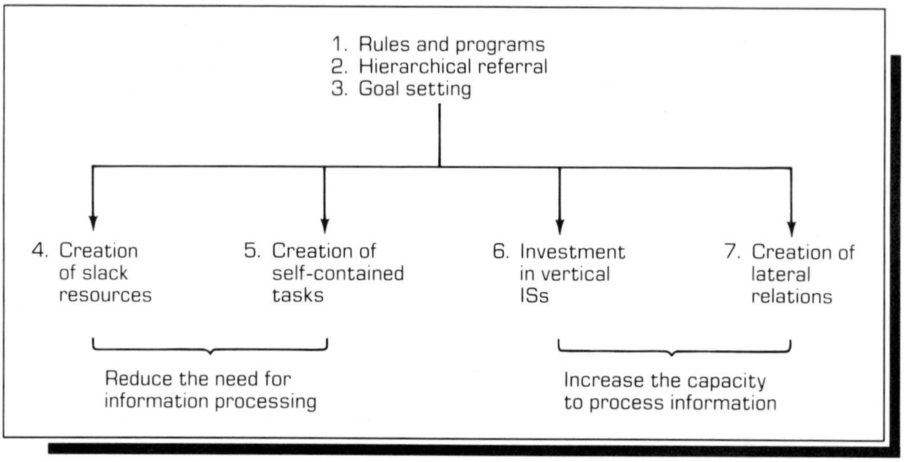

FIGURE 2-1 The Galbraith model, showing some strategies that can be used in organizational design. (From Galbraith, 1973)

have adequate response time and availability? When will the software fail next?

A second important organizational variable is coordination. As tasks become more specialized the ISD has to be concerned with coordination (March and Simon, 1958). For a simple, small computer installation, one or two individuals may be sufficient to operate and program the system. As the installation grows, more specialized roles develop such as systems analyst, applications programmer, maintenance programmer, and systems programmer. Soon it is necessary to add managers of systems and operations to coordinate the activities of the various specialists.

Information Processing

Galbraith (1973) offers an information processing view of the organization. He argues that firms are organized around the need to process information, a view that fits nicely with our interest in information services. It is important for the organization to coordinate its activities, and information is what allows coordination.

Figure 2-1 shows some of the strategies that can be used in organizational design. First, a firm may use rules and programs to operate and coordinate tasks. For example, a payroll clerk may be given a series of rules about who is eligible for a certain benefit and how the benefit is to be calculated. Such a rule might be that an employee has to have worked for the firm for 5 years to be eligible for 3 weeks of vacation. Since the rule is well known, the payroll clerk can easily determine the amount of vacation for each employee. There is no need to involve other individuals or process additional information.

Other examples of using rules and programs occur in factories. The set procedures of the automobile assembly line represent a series of rules; the worker is taught what to do as each car passes his or her station. Many rules and procedures are encoded in computer programs; the hope of the designer is that most routine cases will be processed automatically, with only a few rejected for further attention.

Often, however, it proves impossible to define rules and procedures that cover every situation. There will always be exceptions and special circumstances; to handle these situations, the organization refers the issue to someone higher in the management hierarchy. Exceptional conditions, great uncertainty, and nonroutine problems are referred upward to managers. Many managers complain that they spend a great deal of time "fighting fires," yet according to Galbraith, fire fighting is one of their most important functions.

The hierarchy of managers supplements the rules and procedures; it becomes involved when rules and programs cannot handle the situation. Hierarchical referral has been used for centuries, but this approach to information processing is limited by the capacity of the managerial hierarchy.

As the amount of uncertainty surrounding a task increases, the managerial hierarchy may become overloaded. One approach to reducing information processing is to set targets or goals for subtasks. In information processing, we might break a large systems development project into smaller modules and describe the design goals for each module. The team members working on each module are responsible for meeting its design goals.

In addition, if we provide information on how all modules will be linked, the designers' end products should all fit together. Since all of the individuals working on the project are interdependent, there must be some overall coordination and determination of the rules and procedures.

In a manufacturing environment, management might decentralize responsibility to workers by setting targets. For example, a plant might be given goals regarding the number of units to produce, quality standards, and profitability. If all goals are met, central management does not have to worry about the details of plant performance. Some conglomerates are run exactly this way: autonomous divisions submit plans for approval. Once approved, the division has to report back only if it deviates from the plan.

Sometimes even the three strategies for processing information just described are not enough. As the uncertainty surrounding tasks increases, the number of exceptions and unusual conditions may become so great that rules, the managerial hierarchy, and goal setting are inadequate to coordinate the actions of the firm.

Galbraith suggests four design strategies to cope with these high levels of uncertainty. The first two reduce the need for processing information; they are the creation of slack resources and the creation of self-contained tasks.

Slack resources provide a buffer against uncertainty or too difficult a goal. As an example, U.S. firms have frequently used large work-in-process inventories as a form of slack. Having a large work-in-process inventory means that one part of a factory is less dependent on the performance of the operations that precede its function. The cost of slack resources can be considerable; in the factory, a great deal of material and labor value is added to goods in a state of partial completion. In addition, extensive effort may be required to keep track of in-process work and orders. Finally, production control and scheduling costs may be very high.

There are many examples of the use of slack resources. A physician uses the time of patients as a slack resource. One generally always waits for a doctor; by scheduling several patients at the same time, the doctor has a pool of slack resources on which to draw and is never idle. In the computer field, slack hardware resources are often provided to meet peak processing needs. An on-line system has a great deal of slack during the evening but may run at close to capacity during the day.

The firm can also create self-contained tasks to reduce information processing and management coordination. Each group of workers has all of the resources it needs to complete a task. Instead of working as a specialist on one function, the worker becomes a part of a group whose work is self-contained.

In the computer field, maintenance programming is typically organized by function. There are a series of maintenance programmers, each of whom works on one or more requests, with little coordination among them. In designing new applications, the tendency is to put together self-contained design teams. Exceptions and problems are reported to management, but in theory the design team has all of the resources it needs to complete the assigned task.

Galbraith suggests two design strategies that can be used to increase the organization's capacity to process information: an investment in vertical information systems and the creation of lateral relations.

Readers should be very familiar with the role of vertical information systems; these systems report information to various levels of management. The information serves to reduce uncertainty directly and to notify management of where it may need to take action. Vertical systems that serve this purpose include budgeting, project management, and financial statements.

Lateral relationships serve a coordinating role in the organization. A lateral relationship might involve a systems analyst assigned to a user department but reporting to information services. The purpose of this individual is to relay concerns and information directly between the two departments, dispensing with formal channels of communication.

Engineers in a manufacturing environment often form an integrating or lateral relationship. Industrial engineers are concerned with how processes work and with the link between production control, manufacturing, and quality control.

Galbraith's model can be applied to the organization as a whole or to individual functional areas in the firm. For example, in developing information systems, an ISD may have a rule about using a data dictionary to coordinate different programmers working on a project. However, the dictionary may prove to be insufficient, so project managers resort to setting goals for the performance of individual programmers' modules—goals like maximum program size and execution time. User liaison persons who work for the ISD in user departments are an example of lateral relationships for improving coordination.

Integration

As organizations become more specialized, the need arises to integrate their activities. Lawrence and Lorsch (1967) have used the term *differentiated* to describe the tendency for organizational subunits to become quite different

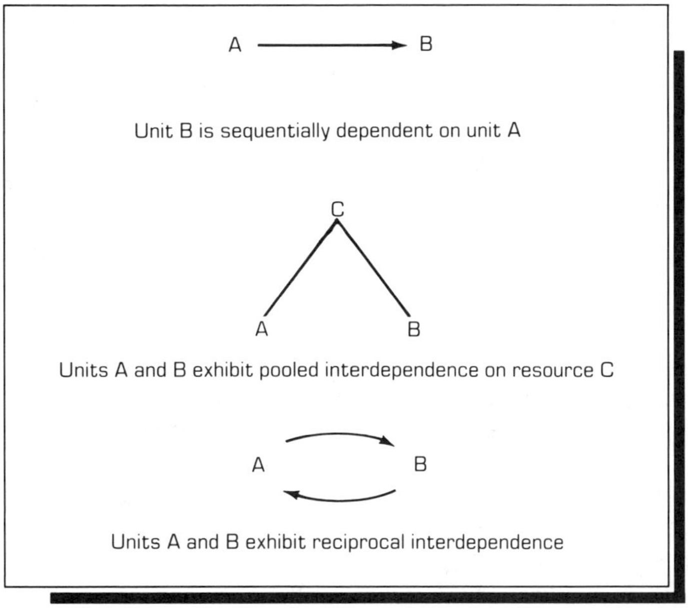

FIGURE 2-2 Organizational dependencies.

from each other. In a study of a small number of firms, they found that success was associated with highly differentiated firms that also provided integrative mechanisms.

As an example, a chemicals firm might have a special group of engineers whose responsibility was to integrate the work of diverse plants producing different products. Such integrators might look for economies of scale or opportunities to use common equipment or suppliers. This notion of integration influenced Galbraith's previous strategy for design, the creation of lateral relationships. Integration is also a form of coordination, something that will be very important to us when we consider alternative ways of organizing information processing.

Interdependence

Workflows influence the creation of uncertainty and the need for coordination. Different units in a firm exhibit different types of interdependence. Thompson (1967) has identified three classes of interdependence: sequential, pooled, and reciprocal. See Figure 2-2.

Sequential interdependence is the easiest to coordinate; an assembly line is based on this form. Each station on the line is dependent only on the preceding stations.

In pooled interdependence, two subunits depend on a common pool of resources. In the CMI case introduced in Chapter 1, each operation must draw on the total capital for investment available to the entire firm; for capital budgeting purposes, Fremont, Omaha, and Chicago exhibit pooled interdependence.

Reciprocal interdependence exists when two subunits depend on each other to accomplish some task; it is the hardest type of interdependence to coordinate. In information processing, systems analysts and users are reciprocally interdependent. The analyst depends on the user to provide the data and requirements for a new system; the user depends on the technical skills of the analyst to design an application.

Power

The preceding discussion of organizational design may be considered lacking in one area: the politics of the firm. Variables like dependence, coordination, and uncertainty imply a certain rationality on the part of the members of the organization. A sociologist or political scientist would argue that much of what happens in an organization is related to departmental loyalties, the reward structure, and power.

One theory of power (Hickson et al., 1971) suggests that there are four conditions that cause a department to become powerful in a firm. The first of these is high coping with uncertainty. As we would expect from our earlier discussion of uncertainty, a department that copes with a great deal of uncertainty ought to be powerful, since uncertainty reduction is a constant goal of the organization. A department for which it would be hard to substitute is also likely to be powerful; if we cannot do without a department, we do not have much control over it.

Departments that are connected closely to other departments in terms of workflow are also likely to be powerful, depending on the nature of the connections. Power from workflow will be greater if the impact of a stoppage is immediate. If the legal department stopped working for a week, the immediacy of the impact would usually be small. If the manufacturing plant stopped working for a week, the impact would be immediate and severe.

The last condition leading to high power is interdependence; a department on which many other departments depend will be powerful.

In a study of the power of information services, we found some rather surprising results (Lucas, 1984). Based on the conditions hypothesized to lead to high power just described, we expected the ISD to rank as a powerful unit in the organization. The results suggested, however, that the ISD has relatively low power.

Information services does cope with uncertainty for other departments. For example, the information provided by vertical information systems is used to reduce uncertainty. In addition, information processing actually creates uncertainty that only the ISD is capable of resolving. When a new application is installed, the users become dependent on the ISD. There is more uncertainty on the part of users about whether they will be able to accomplish their tasks, as now they must have cooperation and good performance from information services.

The connection of the ISD to other departments is strong in most firms. As companies install more and more applications, there are few departments whose workflow is not influenced in some way by information services. The immediacy of the impact from a work stoppage in the ISD depends on the nature of these applications. For example, the breakdown of on-line systems for making airline reservations would have an immediate negative impact on the airline.

In a firm that has a 15- or 20-year history of using computers, we would expect to find high levels of interdependence between the ISD and other departments. A large number of applications will have been developed, and many of these are likely to be crucial to users. As a result, they will depend on information services. The ISD, in turn, depends on users to provide input, use the systems, and provide input for the design of new applications.

Our study included manufacturing plant managers in five departments: accounting, engineering, marketing, production, and information services. We asked a number of questions related to the four variables thought to be associated with high power. To our surprise, information services was ranked lowest of the five departments on power and influence.

There are several possible explanations. The organizations in the study were all manufacturing companies; many of the plants featured rather mundane batch processing systems. Under these conditions, it is possible that information processing did not have a significant impact on the plant itself.

Another explanation is that the power of information services exists, but that it is concealed from users. An individual user generally sees one or two applications in his or her department; few users are aware of the total number of applications that have been developed in the firm. In fact, there are many managers of information services who do not think about all of the applications they operate because their focus is usually on an immediate problem with one or two systems and users.

A factor that is likely to contribute to these findings is centrality. For these manufacturing plants, and possibly for other organizations as well, information services may not be seen as central to the mission of the firm. In the study, production, marketing, and engineering were rated as influential and powerful; these functions are central to the operation of a manufacturing plant.

It appears to us that information services is central, but it may not be perceived as such in many organizations. Managers in information services may have to devote some effort to marketing information processing and convincing managers and users that it deserves their support and interest. A number of IS organizations are now instituting marketing programs to help users understand the IS function and its services.

Organizing for Information Services

In this section we shall apply the preceding discussion about organizational design to the structure of information services in the entire firm. Refer to Table 2-1, which summarizes the key concepts of organizational design presented in the last section. In Chapter 4 we consider the internal organization of information services.

Motivation

Figure 2-3 shows the factors influencing the structure of information services. The actors involved in this process include senior management, the CIO, and probably users and user management. In Chapter 1 we observed that one trend today is toward more distributed and decentralized processing. Why is this so?

Figure 2-3 begins at the top with a variable reflecting the power of information services. This power is increased (though possibly this is not recognized by users) by the dependence of other departments on information services. Dependence, as discussed previously, tends to be reciprocal, which is the hardest form to coordinate. The lack of centrality of the ISD, on the other hand, tends to reduce the perceived power of this department.

Whatever power the ISD is viewed as possessing, perceptions of poor service and backlogs of requests exert strong pressure for user control over information processing. User control may take many forms—for example, distributed or decentralized processing.

In decentralized processing, equipment is placed and managed at remote sites. There is no communication among computers, and there may be little coordination.

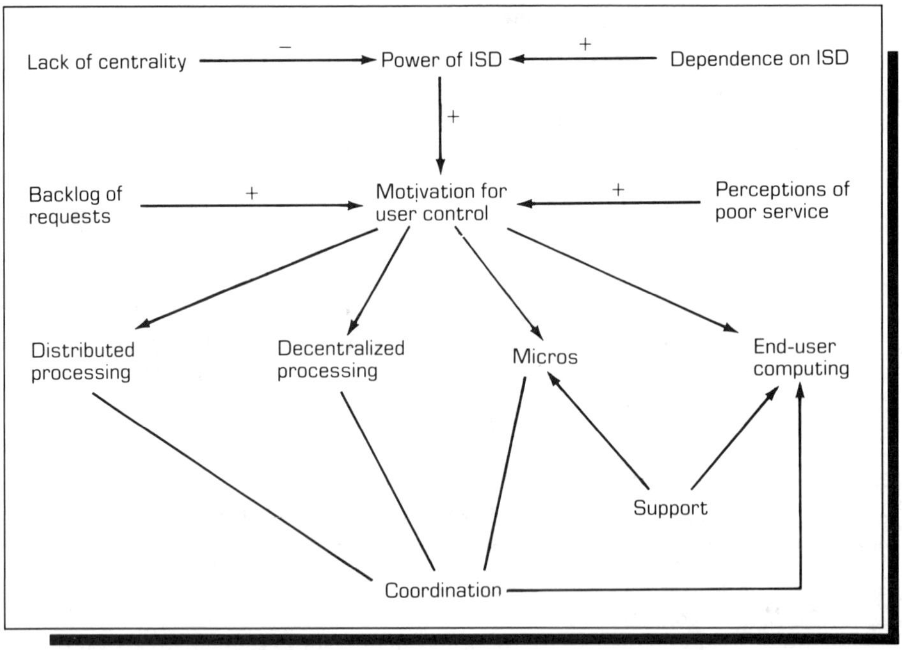

FIGURE 2-3 Factors influencing ISD structure.

Distributed processing features remotely located equipment, but the various computers are connected for some portion of the day in a network. Distributed processing therefore requires a great deal of coordination.

Another reaction to the unresponsiveness of the information services staff and the clumsiness of the tools available for professional programmers is the movement toward microcomputers. The software for micros has tended to be several orders of magnitude more friendly than the software developed by computer professionals for computer applications in the firm. Micros are "mine" and are under the control of the user.

Another phenomenon that is associated with user control is *end-user computing*. This term is associated with 4GLs, which, as noted in Chapter 1, are higher in level than COBOL or FORTRAN. Users can work with these languages to produce simple reports or even complete systems. Since the languages are often accessing data stored on large computers, the ISD staff must support end-user computing.

All of these forms of end-user control require coordination to prevent the information processing environment in the firm from degenerating into complete chaos. In this case, users are allowed and encouraged to become more independent, to become capable of handling some of their own computing needs. As we have seen, one of the costs of specialization or differentiation is the need to coordinate, to integrate the activities of diverse individuals in order to be sure that the firm maintains control over information processing in the aggregate.

Prototypical Configurations

In later chapters we shall discuss how the firm can organize to support end-user computing and how to deal with micros. This section presents some of the alternatives for structuring mainframes, minicomputers, and microcomputers to form a pattern of processing for the firm.

There are three components to the structure of information processing: the location of information, equipment, and the management of processing. Note that the structure of information services is frequently described according to the location of computers. As we shall see, the location of computers is not nearly as important as the managerial control over them.

Table 2-2 arrays the three preceding factors and categorizes them as centralized or decentralized. (*Distribution* refers primarily to a method of connecting computers; it is not really a type of management or a location for information.) This combination of factors, with the two polar extremes of centralization and decentralization, yields eight possible configurations. Of these, two are rather unlikely and will not be discussed (3 and 7).

The first prototype (I) is very common and was the one favored during the third generation; everything is highly centralized. (See Figure 2-4.) Even given the prices of today's computers, this alternative probably has the lowest total cost for information processing. Its major drawback is that users feel that centralized computing is unresponsive. If management chooses this

TABLE 2-2 Organizational Design for Information Services

Real System Type	**I**	**II**		**III**
Potential System Type	**1**	**2**	**3**	**4**
Information	Central.	Decent.	Central.	Decent.
Equipment	Central.	Central.	Central.	Central.
Management of ISD	Central.	Central.	Decent.	Decent.
Comment:	Very common, e.g., batch systems	Common,,e.g., on-line systems	Rare	Unusual, e.g., on-line systems local computer dept.
Real System Type	**IV**	**V**	**7**	**VI**
Potential System Type	**5**	**6**		**8**
Information	Central.	Decent.	Central.	Decent.
Equipment	Decent.	Decent.	Decent.	Decent.
Management of ISD	Central.	Central.	Decent.	Decent.
Comment:	Common, e.g., data collection from remote sites	Computer staff, management coordinate decentralized operations	Rare	No coordination, complete local autonomy

Processing patterns can be characterized by the structure of information, equipment, and the management of information sources. This table illustrates the possible processing patterns when each variable is centralized or decentralized.

alternative, it should take special steps to try to make systems more responsive. For example, the company could encourage end-user computing and provide information centers throughout the firm to consult with users. Users would be encouraged to access the centralized computers from their own locations.

The second configuration, (II) shown in Figure 2-5, includes decentralized information with centralized computers and management. This prototype suffers from the same problem as the first: unresponsiveness. However, given the decentralized information, one is likely to find many on-line systems, so that data can be entered remotely. These systems, if run well, can appear highly responsive to users; consider, as an example, the highly successful airline reservations systems. Because there must be coordination among users working in different geographic locations, the nature of the application dictates central coordination through an on-line system.

The third prototype (III) is more unusual; it includes centralized equipment with decentralized information and management of information services. See Figure 2-6. With communications facilities, this configuration is one way to reduce equipment costs. Large centralized computers are accessed remotely. Local management retains control over information processing and sets development priorities. If the equipment and communications links work well, this alternative can provide responsiveness to users at a reasonable cost.

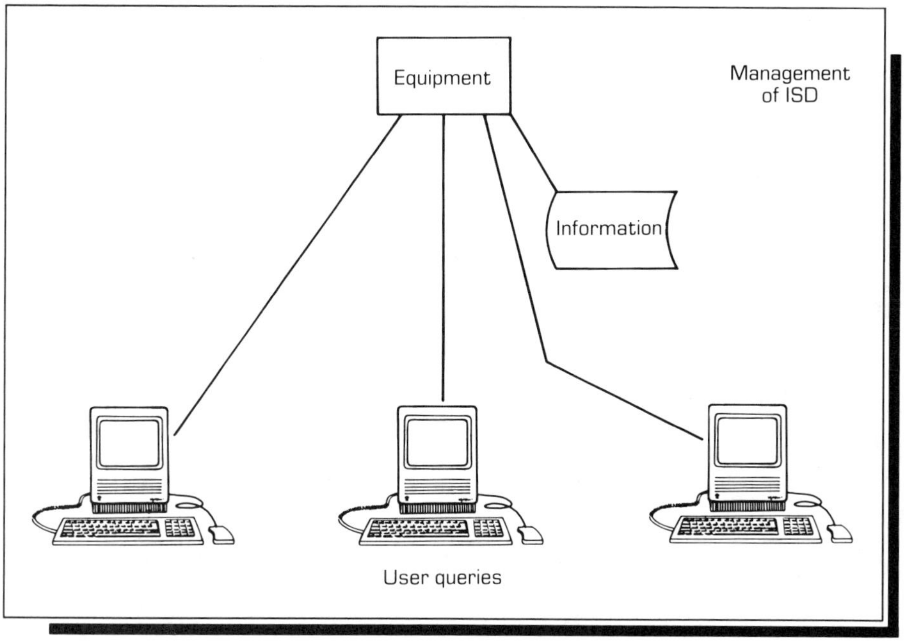

FIGURE 2-4 Configuration I: Centralized.

The fourth example in Table 2-2 (IV) features decentralized equipment with centralized management and information. In Figure 2-7 we might find local computers, say at manufacturing plants, sending data to a common database at a central location. In order to provide coordination, there is centralized management of information services, though it is likely that some autonomy is granted to the locations with their own computers.

Note, however, that local autonomy is not necessarily required. Distributed processing is not necessarily associated with user control. A grocery store scanning system would fit this model. Decentralized information is transmitted from a store computer to headquarters each day. The headquarters store downloads prices to the stores in the morning and processes reorder information at night. The local store has no development capability and no management influence on the system.

The fifth alternative, V, has decentralized equipment and information, but management in this case is centralized. See Figure 2-8. This structure is typical of an organization that has many different divisions but retains a strong corporate staff. The central staff does not actually control the day-to-day operations of each local computer, but instead is a kind of supreme consulting group with the responsibility of reviewing local decisions.

The last alternative, VI, is for complete decentralization; this model shown in Figure 2-9, is probably not suitable to most organizations. There are too many opportunities to suboptimize for the entire organization when there is no central coordination of processing. If a firm wants to have complete decentralization, it will probably soon end up paying rather high costs to integrate processing.

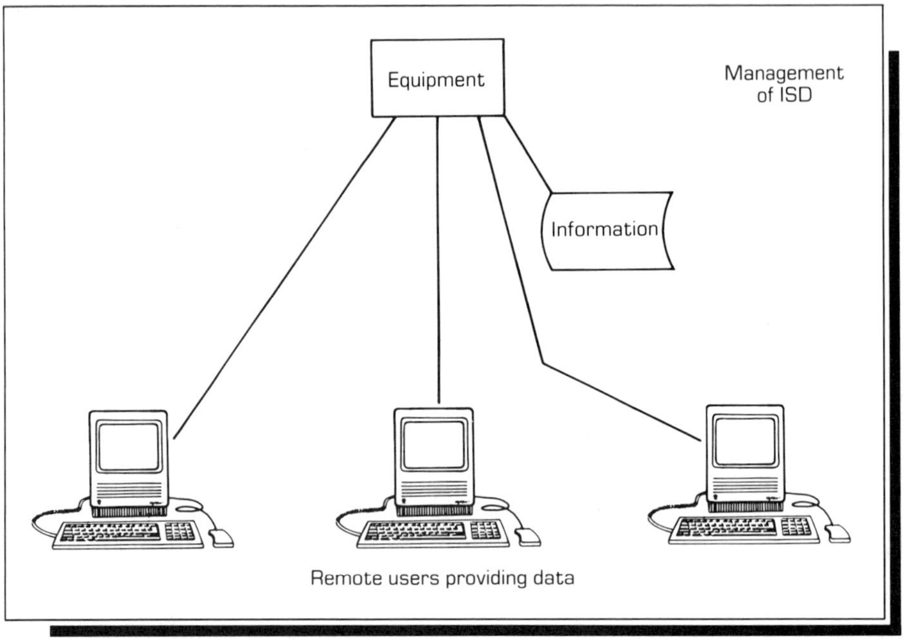

FIGURE 2-5 Configuration II: Decentralized information, centralized equipment and management.

Choosing a Structure

What is the best alternative? As with any question of organizational design, there is probably no one best solution for a company. The first step in choosing a structure is to determine what the firm wants to accomplish. Is the objective cost minimization? If so, one might recommend centralization. If the objective is to become more responsive to users, some form of decentralized or distributed processing is a good candidate. Prepare a table like Table 2-2 and weigh different possible structures against the firm's evaluation criteria. One might even try to give each structure a score on critical evaluation criteria, such as a rating from 1 to 7 on how well that structure accomplishes a given goal.

Even with a firm objective in mind, it is also necessary to consider the implications of technological trends and user demands. First, many experts feel that the current situation, with a separate mainframe, centralized computer operations coexisting with departmental and plant minicomputers, and hundreds of unconnected microcomputers, cannot last. There is a great deal of emphasis today on tying together various computers using networks.

If most devices will eventually be connected, why does one have to be concerned about an organizational structure for information services? The answer to this question is that some group in the organization has to take responsibility for providing information services and for managing all of the networks in the organization. Even with a responsive network, there are many management tasks in providing service and ensuring that there is a high degree of connectivity among the computers purchased for the firm.

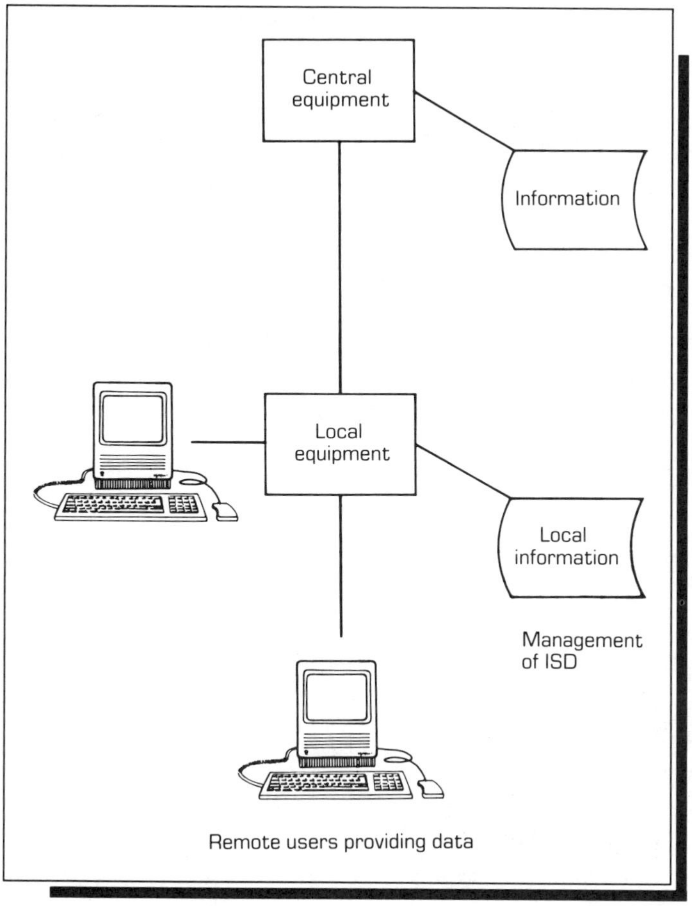

FIGURE 2-6 Configuration III: Decentralized management of ISD and decentralized information with centralized equipment.

While users will develop some of their own applications, the vast majority of large computing systems will be designed by computer professionals, especially transactions processing systems that are fundamental to the firm. Even though telephone service is widespread and reliable, there are central organizations (telephone companies) to develop and maintain the network and the services it offers. Highly connected computers throughout an organization will place even more demands on the traditional ISD.

Given these assumptions, then, alternative V in Table 2-2 is a good model for a starting place. This model is responsive to users in that equipment and information can be decentralized. There is still centralized management control, but in today's environment, significant amounts of that control are likely to be decentralized to local users and managers. Central management becomes a coordination and research and development (R&D) function.

It is unusual to be asked to design a complete information services structure for an organization from the beginning. In a more likely situation, one is asked to change an existing organizational structure to accomplish some goal. It is

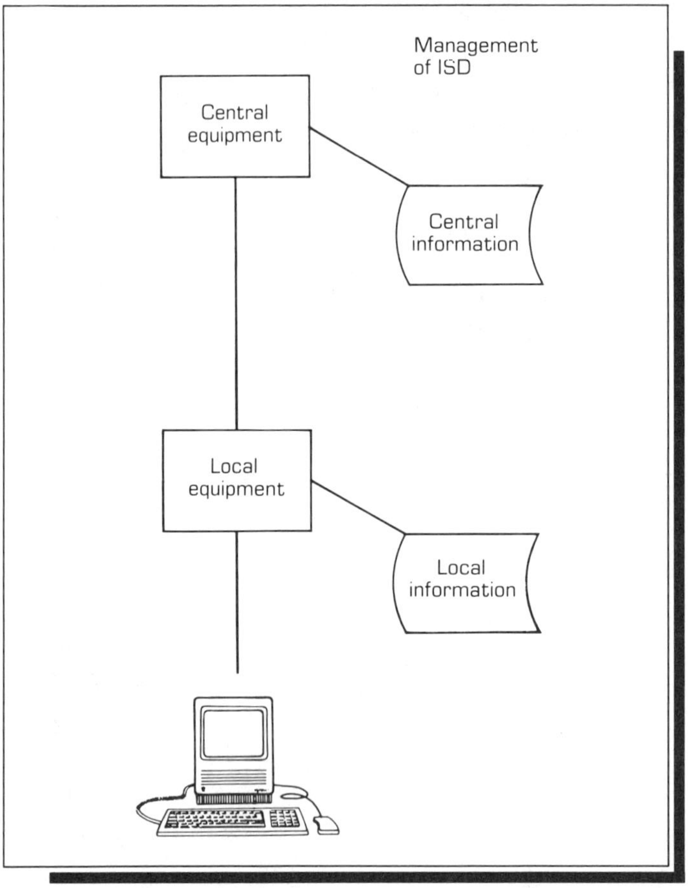

FIGURE 2-7 Configuration IV: Centralized management information, with equipment largely decentralized.

important to have a reason or goal for changing the organization and to evaluate the results of the change. Given today's situation, the goal is probably to become more responsive to users. Under these conditions, one would recommend distributing more responsibility for management decisions to local managers while still retaining some central coordination and control.

This advice, however, is not always easy to implement. One firm decided to develop a systems staff under each of three division managers. Previously, the bulk of the processing needs for the three divisions were met by one centralized computer and the systems staff. Moving the staff to the divisions was fairly easy, but the existing applications on the mainframe were not segregated by division. To install equipment at the divisions and convert the applications was forecast to take over a year and to cost several hundred thousand dollars. In addition, because the staff was being split up, there was a need for more operations personnel, managers, and probably programmers and analysts than currently existed at the central site. Management decided to proceed, but then had to cancel its plans when business conditions turned against the industry and sales dropped.

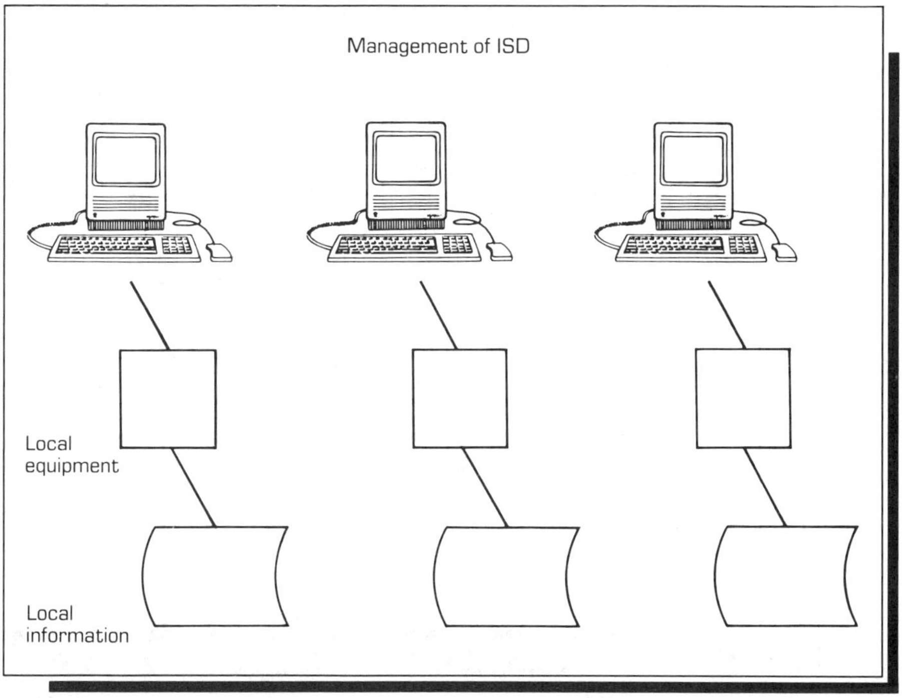

FIGURE 2-8 Configuration V: Centralized management with decentralized equipment and information.

Coordination

One variable is extremely important in choosing an organizational structure for information services: coordination. If there is a tendency toward more decentralization of the responsibility for decision making on information processing, coordination becomes a key variable if not the key variable in planning.

What are some of the things that can go wrong in the absence of coordination?

1. Subunits of the firm can purchase highly incompatible computers, making it difficult to communicate among them at some later date, to share data, share programs and systems, or to take advantage of shared expertise about the systems.

2. Subunits of a firm can purchase software in ignorance of each other's needs. The results will be failure to take advantage of quantity discounts and suboptimization from the inability to share expertise.

3. Subunits of a firm may undertake the development of applications that are common to several units. As an example, if three nearly identical manufacturing plants all decide to write a new payroll system and remain ignorant of each others' efforts, the firm will probably pay two to three times more than is necessary for the resulting applications.

Given some of these problems that result from a lack of coordination, why not coordinate? The problem is one of motivation and the ability to

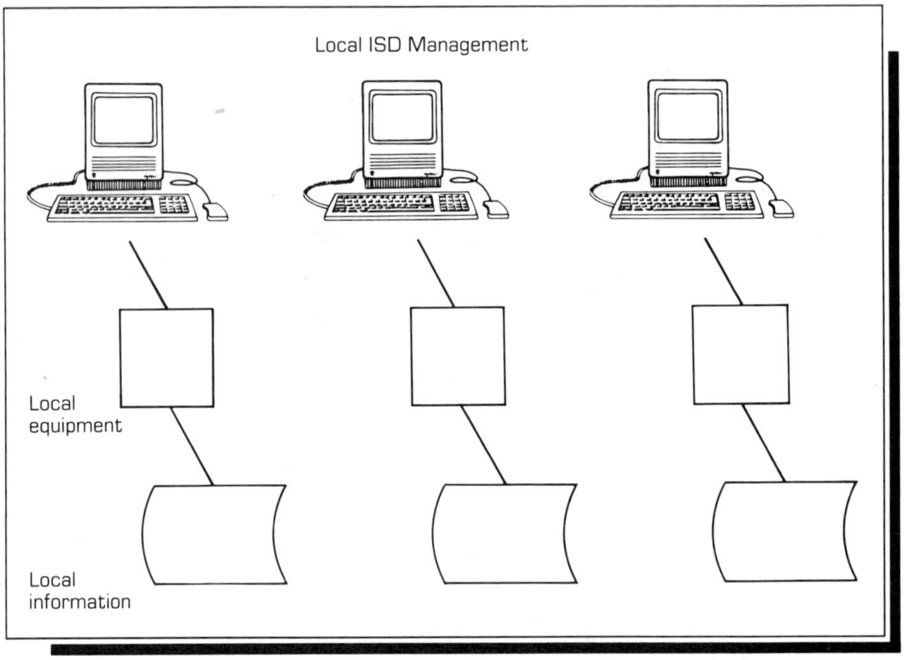

FIGURE 2-9 Configuration VI: Decentralization.

coordinate with good taste. The tradeoff might look something like the following:

Coordination ← versus → Responsiveness

Users have sought more influence over processing decisions because centralized staff groups have proven unresponsive; the user wants to get away from the bureaucracy. Most forms of coordination, however, require a local manager and user to follow some procedures and to wait for approval. As a result, there is a direct contradiction between coordination and remaining responsive.

If a firm wants to coordinate processing, which it should, it will have to make a strong effort to maintain responsiveness in the process.

Some possible coordination mechanisms help illustrate how to keep control and remain responsive. Assume, for this discussion, that there is a central coordinating group of consultants at a headquarters location.

1. The central staff develops, as part of a 3- to 5-year information processing plan, a list of vendors and equipment that may be purchased without approval. One mainframe and several minicomputer vendors are likely to be on the list. The list might also contain the names and models of two to four microcomputers which the firm is prepared to support.

2. Deviations from the list must be justified and approved by the central staff; it will not take more than 2 weeks for this review, or the local manager may proceed.

3. The central staff will visit each remote computing location at least twice a year. At least every 6 months, there will be a meeting of all information processing staff members of the firm at a different location.

4. Local computer groups are required to notify the central staff of any systems development efforts or applications packages purchased that are anticipated to cost more than $20,000. The central staff will maintain a database of applications that are under development and will publish an applications newsletter every quarter describing each application in case other locations can take advantage of it.

5. The central staff will conduct R&D on new software, hardware, and development approaches. The results will be published and disseminated throughout the organization.

6. The central staff will be responsible for ensuring that local computer sites have appropriate steering and maintenance committees in place and functioning. (A steering committee provides guidance for the IS group, while a maintenance committee sets priorities for maintenance and changes in applications.)

7. The central staff will be responsible for developing an overall plan for information processing for the firm, and will define hardware and software architecture for the organization.

8. The central staff will provide consulting assistance to locations that request it.

9. The central staff will negotiate purchase agreements and publicize their existence.

10. The central staff will set standards for systems development, documentation, quality assurance, backup, controls, and so on.

This list should provide an idea of the type of coordination that is needed for a firm with a number of different computer installations and local management autonomy in managing them. The challenge for the central staff is to make coordination work by remaining responsive to users.

Information Processing Committees

We mentioned two committees in the previous discussion. For many years, different committees have been recommended to help coordinate decisions about information processing.

The first committee is an executive steering committee. This committee consists of the top managers of the firm; its purpose is to review a corporate plan for information processing and to set priorities on development efforts. It must also decide how much to budget for information processing for the year. These committees have worked successfully when information services has provided them with relevant information to make decisions and has been able to carry out the decisions made.

As an example, in one firm where many applications had been requested, a group of senior managers quickly agreed that a sales application had highest priority. This application involved putting terminals in the offices of major customers so that they could order directly from the company's computer without having to call the sales department. The sales staff estimated that, if successful, the application would save the firm $1 million a year in order processing costs. Other managers said that their applications could wait because this one was obviously so important to the firm.

A corporate steering committee can and should be supplemented by similar committees at whatever level managers can make decisions about what applications to undertake. The choice of applications is too important to be left up to the computer staff; computer professionals are rarely in a position to know the priorities of management with respect to applications.

Another important committee is one for determining maintenance priorities. Maintenance is a critical issue in many firms. Just as there are insufficient resources to develop all requested applications, there are usually too few resources to handle all maintenance requests. Should information services determine what maintenance is done? A better solution is to have a committee of users who review requests for changes and enhancements in existing systems and assign priorities.

For this committee to work, information services must provide good information. For example, a monthly report should go to the committee describing how many hours were spent on maintenance, the number of requests completed, the number remaining, and the hours required for the remaining changes. The committee can then see how much progress is being made and adjust priorities accordingly. It can also lobby for more resources for maintenance.

The last committee typically found in information processing is a temporary one: a project design team. Most organizations today design applications with the participation of users, managers, and systems analysts. This design team may be headed by a user; the analyst then acts as a consultant and provides staff support to the committee.

One way to view the computer professional is as a tour guide advising the travelers on the committee. The analyst describes the path and presents alternatives and their tradeoffs; the committee decides which ones to include in the system.

A number of organizations have tried using different types of committees for information processing and have disbanded them. The major problems in these companies appear to be a lack of purpose and poor staff support. The computer staff must prepare carefully for meetings and provide issues for decisions that are relevant for the specific committee. Discussion items for a design team are very different from those for the executive steering committee. Committees offer a tremendous opportunity for users and managers to develop a greater understanding of the technology. They also provide an opportunity to market information services.

IS Structure in User Areas

In addition to an overall structure for information processing in a firm, we must consider how to organize information processing in a division or even a local department.

The case for a division is fairly easy; the division will mirror the type of structure found in the organization. In some firms, divisions are as large as small companies; the division needs to consider the same issues previously discussed. What structure balances costs against responsiveness? What coordination mechanisms are needed?

As divisions become smaller, say to the point of a plant having a single computer facility, the issues remain. Even if there is a single computer, it is likely that there will be requests for departmental mini- or microcomputers. Local management needs a plan and a mechanism to manage information processing.

While the local manager is interested in autonomy, he or she will also want to take advantage of common applications, purchase discounts, and so on. As a result, local managers should find it in their best interest to cooperate with the coordination effort of the headquarters staff group.

As we move to the level of the individual department, the structure of information processing becomes less of an issue. A department manager may have one or two employees who operate a computer part-time. If the department is involved in developing applications, the department manager may have analysts or programmers on the staff. It is more likely, however, that some sort of central pool will provide staff support to single departments.

When local management generally supports end-user computing, there will be a need for a consulting group such as the one found in an information center (see Chapter 13). The consultants teach users how to work with software and help users access files in local and remote computers.

Most local managers today are confronted with a management problem created by microcomputers. The issues here, however, are familiar as well. Micros need to be coordinated, whether by local management or a central staff group. Incompatibilities become obvious when two individuals in adjoining offices cannot share programs and data and are unable to communicate with other computers. Policies on what brands of computer to purchase and consulting support for micros are some of the organizational solutions we shall consider later.

The Structure at CMI

Figure 2-10 shows the structure of information services at CMI. The model most closely fits Type V in Table 2-2. Tom White is the CIO; he reports to the chief operating officer. Tom has responsibility for information processing for the corporation. The four information services managers at headquarters, Fremont, Omaha, and Chicago report to the managers of the respective divisions. Mary Watson, who handles headquarters processing, reports to the financial vice president, Bob

Carlson, since most of the headquarters processing deals with accounting and finance.

Each of the division ISD managers has a dotted line responsibility to Tom White. Tom describes his role as "coordinating what a diverse group of user divisions wants to do. We have to be sure that no one goes completely haywire. We maintain a staff of three consultants who visit the divisions, hold reviews and project walkthroughs, and respond to division requests for equipment."

White continues: "We have three vendors who are approved since we inherited the equipment: IBM, DEC, and Hewlett Packard, if someone wants to buy a mainframe or a mini. We will also consider Prime, since an engineering department has one. On micros, we will take IBM compatible or HP; I have a volume purchase agreement with Zenith for personal computer compatibles that is working quite nicely now.

"If anyone wants something else, like a Sun or Apollo workstation for an engineer, their manager has to approve it, along with my staff. We try to get back in 2 weeks for a request and are pretty reasonable. Stand-alone machines used for a special purpose like engineering, especially with a knowledgeable user, aren't a real problem.

"The toughest thing we have to do is be a liaison with senior management of the firm and, at the same time, with division and lower-level managers. The divisions are pretty independent; they don't like us interfering in their affairs. On the other hand, I have to represent the best interests of CMI, so sometimes we are pretty unpopular.

"We have steering committees at the corporate level and in each division. I use them a lot in developing a plan and setting priorities. My real problem is that dotted line responsibility. I don't really have any control over whether the computer staff in Fremont fouls up or not, yet I am making a commitment to senior management that we will get a certain system done by a certain date for a given cost. This CIO job literally involves being the man in the middle!"

White goes on to explain that the divisions are free to decide on new applications areas and have to notify him only about something that will cost more than $25,000. He and his staff make regular visits to the divisions and try to keep abreast of all applications under development. Since there are only three divisions and headquarters, it is easy to look for opportunities to share applications or packages.

"My other problem," White continues, "is that we only advise the divisions. It took a long time hammering on Omaha to get an agreement to set up an end-user support group. Management in Omaha didn't see any need for it, yet I knew the users were screaming and criticizing the local ISD staff. It wasn't their fault; they had no support from management to get into end-user computing. I guess we have to give the local guys the final authority, but we seem to always get caught in the middle."

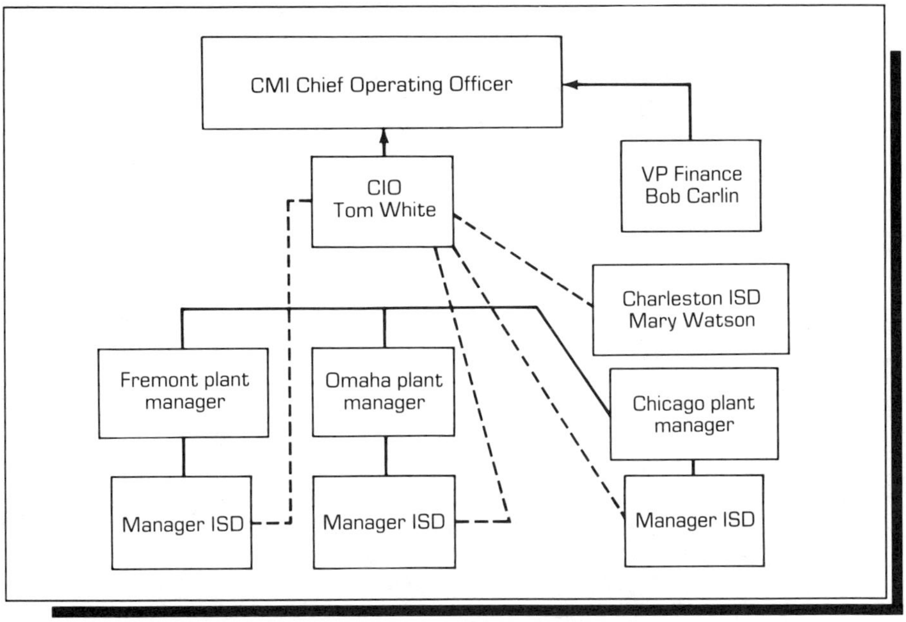

FIGURE 2-10 The structure of processing at CMI.

Recommended Readings

Galbraith, J., *Designing Complex Organizations.* Reading, Mass.: Addison-Wesley, 1973. (An excellent book with an information processing view of organizations.)

Hickson, D. J., C. R. Hinings, C. A. Lee, R. E. Schneck, and J. M. Pennings, "A Strategic Contingencies Theory of Intraorganizational Power," *Administrative Science Quarterly,* vol. 16, no. 2 (June 1971), pp. 216–229. (A somewhat technical article on the power theory discussed in this chapter.)

Lawrence, P., and J. Lorsch, *Organization and Environment.* Boston: Division of Research, Graduate School of Business Administration, Harvard University, 1967. (The study of differentiation and integration cited in the text.)

Lucas, H. C., Jr., "Organization Power and the Information Services Department," *Communications of the ACM,* vol. 27, no. 1 (January 1984), pp. 58–65. (The power study described in the chapter in which ISD ranked lower than other departments on power and influence.)

March, J., and H. Simon, *Organizations.* New York: Wiley, 1958. (A classic book of organization theory.)

Thompson, J., *Organizations in Action.* New York: McGraw-Hill, 1967. (An enjoyable book about how organizations are structured and how they function.)

Discussion Problems

2.1 The chairman of a major insurance company was convinced that most of the problems with information systems at the company came from a badly structured organization. Information came into the firm from countries all over the world; some of it was correct, but much was inaccurate. The firm maintained several regional processing centers, the largest of which was at its headquarters in the United States.

The chairman hired a consultant and presented him with several different organization charts for immediate comment. There seemed to be little difference among the charts, and the chairman could not state his reasons for preferring one over the other. The consultant tried to figure out how to help the insurance company and its chairman. What do you recommend?

2.2 The ABZ Corporation was experiencing great difficulty with maintenance. There was an increasing backlog of user requests for changes to systems. Some of the changes were minor and would require only a few hours of effort. Others were estimated to take several days. Requests requiring more than 4 person-weeks of labor were considered new development projects and had to be submitted as if a new application was being requested.

The manager of information services at ABZ was not sure of what to do about the maintenance problem. He assigned about 25% of his resources to maintenance, saying, "If I put any more people on maintenance, we won't be able to design any new systems." One user felt that this would be a good idea; he suggested a moratorium on the development of new applications until all existing maintenance requests were satisfied. At the rate new requests arrived, it was likely that if the user's proposal were accepted, there would never be any new development.

Think about the organizational design issues discussed in this chapter and develop a proposal for ABZ to consider. The proposal should explain what organizational considerations led to your recommendations.

Questions

1. What is uncertainty? Why is it important in the design of organizations?
2. Can you use the variable of uncertainty to explain price fixing on the part of senior managers?
3. How does the ISD cope with uncertainty?
4. How do rules and programs contribute to the management of a firm?
5. What is the role of the organizational hierarchy in Galbraith's model of organizational design?
6. What are targeting and goal setting? How do these strategies help coordinate projects?
7. What is an example of slack resources in an organization? In an ISD?
8. How do self-contained tasks contribute help to reduce the need to process information?
9. What is the role of lateral relationships in the firm?
10. Explain the concept of organizational integration.
11. Describe the three types of interdependence. Which is the easiest to coordinate? The most difficult?
12. What is organizational power? How does it differ from the power exhibited by countries?
13. What are the four conditions that Hickson et al. (1971) believe cause a unit to have high power in the firm?
14. Describe how the ISD fits the Hickson power model.
15. Why do managers appear to find information services of little importance in the firm?
16. Is information processing central to the mission of the firm? If so, in what kinds of firms?

17. Why is it important to consider the location of the ISD staff and management, as well as the equipment, when describing the structure of information processing in an organization?
18. What are the advantages and disadvantages of a totally centralized ISD in which a central group controls equipment, the systems staff, and the management of information services?
19. What are the advantages and disadvantages of complete ISD decentralization?
20. Why is coordination important in information processing?
21. Can there be too much coordination of the ISD? What is the likely effect?
22. What is the role of an executive steering committee for information services?
23. What factors should a division manager consider in structuring the ISD in his or her division?
24. Why does Tom White at CMI want to be notified if a new application is being planned that costs more than $25,000?
25. What is the disadvantage of requiring users to notify the CIO of their plans for information services?

3

The CIO and Other IS Managers

The CIO

In the early days of computing, the person in charge of managing the systems effort was the manager of data processing. When emphasis shifted to management information systems (MIS), the data processing manager was elevated in title to "manager of MIS." Unfortunately, in many firms the MIS manager is viewed by other managers largely as a technician. The new role of the CIO is to be a liaison with other managers; he or she must bridge the gap between senior managers, users, and the more technical management of the ISD. The CIO's job is important and exciting, but is also complex and frustrating at the same time.

Since the position of CIO is relatively new, the tasks associated with it are not entirely clear. At American Airlines, where computers play a central role, the CIO manages about 4000 employees and has an annual budget of $400 million. This manager is also responsible for selling American's Sabre reservations system to other airlines. Sabre contributed 6% of American's revenues in 1985 and 28% of its profits.

For American, the CIO is responsible for marketing a technological product. At other firms, the CIO attempts to define how the company can use the technology strategically. In most instances, the day-to-day operations of the computer center are delegated to someone else. The CIO at CMI does not have a data center reporting directly to him. However, it is likely that the typical CIO will have responsibility for selecting and installing all of the firm's technology, including equipment and staff for computer processing, office automation, and telecommunications.

One major characteristic of all CIO positions is access to and membership in top management. The CIO is a combination of superconsultant and coach, explaining the technology to nontechnical managers and others. The CIO has to relate the needs of the business to technology and show how computers contribute to the mission of the firm.

Why does information processing deserve to be led by a senior, highly paid manager? The expenditures for information processing by many organizations are sizable. One large Los Angeles bank has an annual budget of $300 million for information systems. Other firms have larger budgets, particularly if one includes local computers, office automation, factory automation, and telecommunications.

Beyond expenditures, however, we see a number of firms for which information processing is a part of strategy. American automobile manufacturers have stated that the only way they can be competitive with foreign firms is to become low-cost producers; the route to efficiencies in production is through automation and computerized factories.

Financial services firms use technology to offer new products and deliver services to customers. Airlines use their computer systems strategically to encourage travelers to take their flights; the reservations systems also generate revenue, since competing carriers pay a charge if one of their flights is booked. When TWA changed ownership, the new chairman sold a half interest in TWA's computer-based reservations system to Northwest Airlines for a reported $140 million.

Reporting Levels

One important question is at what level the CIO should be located in the firm and to whom he or she should report. Because information processing is so important to a number of firms, more and more CIOs are found at very high levels of management. It is important for the CIO to have access to senior management and to learn about the plans and strategy of the firm. One cannot suggest how to use technology strategically if the firm's strategy is a secret! Most CIOs are at the level of vice president or senior vice president in the firm.

A more difficult problem is to whom the CIO should report. In many organizations, it would be best for this individual to report to the chief operating officer of the firm, usually the president. The president should know the plans of the firm and be in a position to help the CIO allocate scarce resources to different areas of the firm requesting systems.

Historically, the manager of information services has reported to the

TABLE 3-1 The Mintzberg Roles

Role	Activities
Interpersonal	
Figurehead	Symbolic duties
Leader	Set directions, motivate staff
Liaison	Coordinate with others
Informational	
Monitor	Follow the environment
Disseminator	Communicate within the organization
Spokesperson	Communicate outside the organization
Decision making	
Entrepreneur	Look for opportunities
Disturbance handler	"Fire fighting"
Resource allocator	Provide resources
Negotiator	Resolve conflicts

financial vice president because many early applications were financial. However, reporting to a functional area like finance, accounting, or even manufacturing presents a number of problems for the CIO. In this situation, it is natural for the majority of applications to be developed in the area of reporting; there will be more finance applications in firms where the CIO reports to a vice president of finance. Unfortunately, when manufacturing or marketing want applications and have to wait, they feel that finance is favored.

To summarize, it is best for the CIO to (1) report to the highest level possible in the firm and (2) report to a neutral manager who does not represent a functional area of the business.

Managerial Roles

Each of us plays a number of roles in life, including student, family member, employee, and colleague. Mintzberg (1973) conducted a study of the role played by the most senior managers in a series of firms. See Table 3-1. Mintzberg spent a week with each manager, making detailed notes of each activity and interaction observed. After finishing his observations, Mintzberg sorted and collated the various behaviors and grouped the managers' activities into roles.

These roles represent the different ways in which the managers functioned during the week. There are three categories of roles: interpersonal, informational, and decision making.

Interpersonal Roles

In the interpersonal role category, the manager acts as a figurehead. In this role, the CIO might sign a letter of appreciation for an employee or might represent the firm at a professional meeting or conference.

In an extremely important interpersonal role, the manager acts as a leader. Many books have been written about leadership and how one exhibits this characteristic. Managers seem to feel that they have less influence on subordinates and the organization than they actually do. We have talked with managers who are discouraged about their inability to influence subordinates; subsequent discussions with subordinates indicate that they observe their managers closely and try to respond to their cues.

Mintzberg has described this aspect of leadership well: ". . . leadership permeates all activities; its importance would be underestimated if it were judged in terms of the proportion of a manager's activities that are strictly related to leadership. Each time a manager encourages or criticizes a subordinate he is acting in his capacity as leader . . . in virtually everything he does, the manager's actions are screened by subordinates searching for leadership clues . . . the key purpose of the leader role is to effect an integration between individual needs and organizational goals . . . it is in the leader role that managerial power most clearly manifests itself. Formal authority vests the manager with great potential power; leadership activity determines how much of it will be realized. . . . Thus, through the leader role the manager welds diverse elements into a cooperative enterprise" (pp. 61–62).

The manager also serves as a liaison with other managers and functions in the firm. The liaison role is a horizontal one in most cases. For the CIO, liaison roles are crucial, since information processing is a resource for almost all parts of the organization. Liaison work is important because information systems span many departmental boundaries; various constituencies have to be included in the development, operation, and management of information systems.

Informational Role

The manager must monitor the environment to understand what is taking place both inside and outside of the organization. The manager is looking for changing conditions and new opportunities; there may be threats from competitors or things to be learned from them.

In the rapidly changing environment of information technology, monitoring is very important. The ISD is responsible for bringing new technology to the organization; the staff must remain aware of trends and new technology, and decide whether or not an innovation makes sense for the firm. Many organizations have failed to keep up with the technology and have suffered as a result.

The manager, because of his or her access to information, plays a role as disseminator of information. For the CIO, one important function is to learn what the strategy and goals of the organization are in order to disseminate this information within the ISD. Knowledge of strategy and current managerial interests will help in deciding how to undertake new applications and will assist project managers in allocating resources within information services.

The manager is also a spokesperson. The CIO carries information from senior management back to middle managers and others in the ISD. The CIO represents the interests and concerns of the information processing staff in talking with senior management. Here the CIO is a linking pin, coordinating the concerns of managers above and below the CIO's level.

Decision-Making Role

We expect a manager to be involved in a number of decision-oriented roles. The first decisional role is that of an entrepreneur. This role is well suited to the CIO; the technology offers many opportunities for innovation. Financial services firms, for example, offer new products based on computer systems. The information processing staff may find a new way to use the technology to gain an edge on the competition, for example, by developing a new product based on computer technology. The entrepreneurial manager is always looking for opportunities; he or she also seeks entrepreneurial ideas from others and then gives the originators assistance and encouragement.

The manager frequently acts as a disturbance handler. When problems cannot be resolved at lower levels in the organization, they are usually brought to the attention of the senior manager. While the entrepreneurial role is an active one for the manager who seeks out opportunities, disturbances are thrust upon the manager by others in the firm.

Within information processing, the predominant mode of operation seems to be disturbance handling, at least for operating managers. One major criticism of information services is its orientation to disturbances as opposed to planning. Such an orientation, however, is forced upon information services by the state of the technology. Computers go down, programs fail, and operator errors require reruns. The operational uncertainties for information services create a number of problems that have to be resolved. Applications development is hardly any better; projects tend to be over budget and behind schedule. Thus, it is quite natural for managers within information services to be heavily involved in disturbance handling.

Managers also have to allocate resources. Within information services, there are a number of serious allocation decisions that affect the relationship between this area and users:

1. What resources for applications development are allocated to what users?
2. What resources should be allocated to the support of end users?
3. Should resources be allocated to an information center?
4. What resources should be allocated to maintenance versus new application development?

The CIO has to be concerned about what organizational resources in general are allocated to information processing. Also, how many of these resources should be the responsibility of the information services area? With more and more processing distributed to end-user areas, the CIO influences a smaller percentage of the resources allocated by the organization to information processing.

The last decisional role involves the manager as a negotiator. There are many times when issues are resolved by negotiation. Many of the resource allocation problems previously described require negotiation. Some authors have suggested that systems development is really a process of negotiation; different users have different views of what a system should do. In addition, the information services analyst may feel that design should follow a certain direction. All of these potentially conflicting views have to be resolved; the project leader may turn out to spend most of his or her time negotiating solutions to design problems.

Time Allocation

Ives and Olson followed Mintzberg's methodology in a 1981 study of IS managers. (There were few CIOs in 1981.) In terms of time distribution, they found that the IS managers spent their days as follows:

Activity	Percentage of Time
Desk work	19
Phone calls	9
Incomplete calls	1
Scheduled meetings	48
Unscheduled meetings	20
Tours	2

These data, though for only a small sample, suggest that an IS manager spends a great deal of time in meetings. It is also interesting to see with whom the manager interacts:

Person	Percentage of Time
Superiors	7
Immediate subordinates	38
Lower-level subordinates	23
Users	8
Corporate services (e.g., personnel)	8
Vendors	9
Others	7

These data were published in 1981; if the study were repeated today, we would expect to find much more of the CIO's time spent with superiors, particularly in firms that are using the technology as a part of their strategy. The other change in time distribution would involve more time spent with users. End-user computing means that more and more individuals are working with computers in their own locations; the CIO is probably spending more time with these users and with their divisional management.

Demands on the CIO

The preceding description of the job of the CIO portrays a challenging and exciting position in the organization. What are the drawbacks? What are the

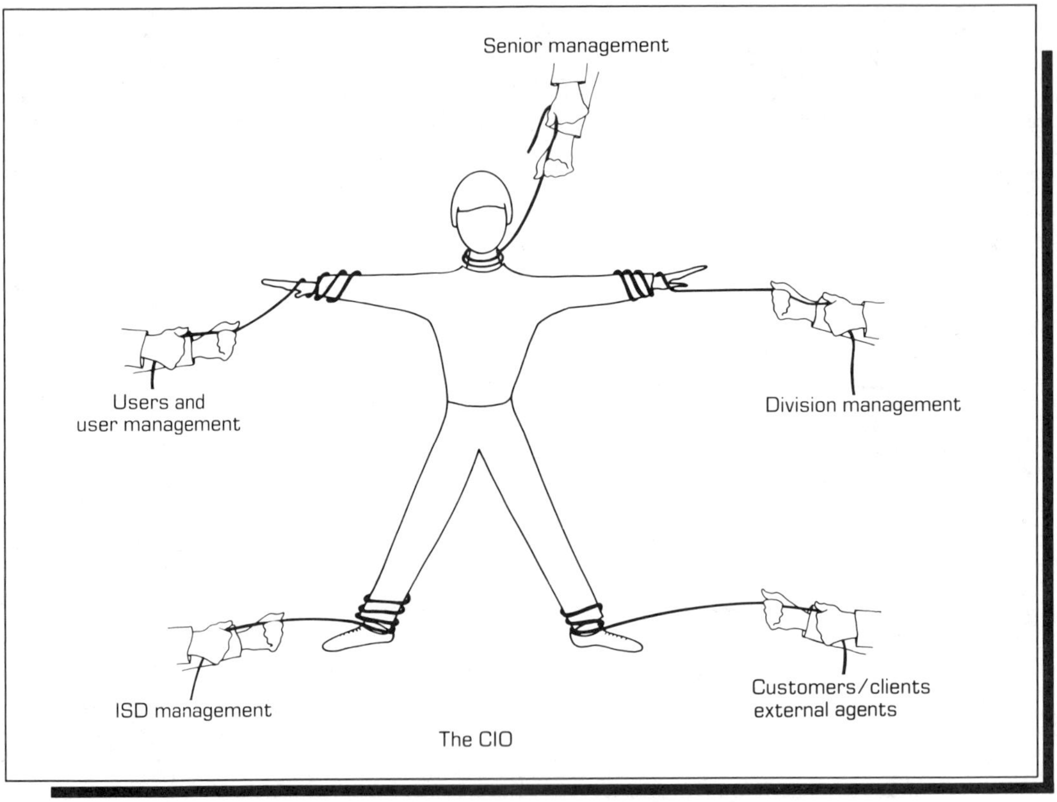

FIGURE 3-1 Demands on the CIO.

frustrations and conflicts of the CIO's position? Figure 3-1 shows some of the constituencies with whom the CIO must interact; individuals in these different categories make a variety of demands on the CIO, often conflicting demands.

The first group that places demands on the CIO is senior management. Senior managers often are concerned with costs: Why does it cost so much to operate our computer area? What should a firm spend on information processing? Why are there so many complaints about information services? Is information processing under control in the organization?

The CIO is often confronted with a management that does not understand the capabilities or problems of modern information processing technology. Most senior managers today understand a great deal about finance, accounting, manufacturing, and marketing; their knowledge of technology is much more limited. Some managers view information processing as only a service; it should take care of itself. If the CIO has constructive ideas on how to use the technology actively in the firm, a passive management will prove very frustrating.

With the spread of distributed processing and end-user computing, the CIO finds computers and users in various places in the organization. One group asking for help will be division management; in large firms, the division may be a company in its own right. Division managers will have some of the same concerns and demands as senior management, but they will focus on their division rather than on the corporation as a whole.

Users and user management have always placed demands on information services. These individuals are the final customers of the services offered by the CIO. Relationships with users are rarely smooth. The user is placed in a position of dependence on information services whenever a new system is developed. Users may develop their own applications on a microcomputer, but a multiuser system will usually involve some assistance from a professional systems analyst working for the ISD.

As previously described, there are many opportunities for conflict in the development of systems. The professional analyst may be in the position of negotiator; since negotiation often results in compromises, so that no one gets exactly what was wanted, users may blame information services for their disappointments.

Professionals in information processing also have rather a dismal record of design. We shall discuss some approaches to systems development to improve communications and performance in Chapters 9 and 10. Historically, information services has tended to deliver systems late and over budget; in addition, these applications often have not met the expectations of users.

Once a system has been designed and installed, the ISD is responsible for operating it on a routine basis. Users depend on the system for part of their work; the ISD depends on users to provide input and make use of output. The integrity of the database is also the responsibility of the user. When the system fails for some reason, software or hardware, users are very frustrated. Sometimes users even blame the ISD when they themselves have failed to update the database.

The CIO must manage the personnel in information services; these individuals also make demands. There are many different factors that motivate information processing professionals; these individuals seek support and resources that the CIO is thought able to provide. There is a large difference between the development part of information services and operations; the CIO has to respond to both groups. Systems development is a creative, long-term task that is usually carried out by a group. Operations, on the other hand, is more like running a factory; there are deadlines, equipment maintenance considerations, and products that must be delivered to users.

Finally, the CIO deals with customers, clients, and external agents like vendors of hardware, software, and services. As organizations come to depend more on information systems, they will connect their computers with those of other firms. The CIO must now be concerned with the demands and challenges of individuals outside of the organization. Some of these individuals become new types of users—users external to the organization who are probably very important to the business.

Success Factors

One popular approach to strategic planning is to ask managers what factors are most important to the success of their organization or function. Martin surveyed 15 managers of ISDs in 1982 to determine their perceptions of the factors critical to the success of IS. He developed the following list:

- Systems development
- Operations
- Human resource development
- Management control of information processing
- Relationship with the rest of the organization
- Support of the organization's objectives
- Management of change

Based on the previous discussion, these factors are probably not too surprising. The managers surveyed reported concerns over project selection, project management, and the ability to respond to user needs in a timely fashion. The other major task within information services is the operation of systems. An on-line system that is always down, late reports, and continual errors destroy the credibility of information services.

A manager must also be concerned with human resources—the development of the information services staff. There are severe shortages of qualified systems analysts and programmer shortages in some areas. Managers have to upgrade the capabilities of their staff members for the benefit of the staff and the organization.

The overall control of information processing is of concern to senior management and the CIO; we shall discuss control further in Chapter 15. The managers in Martin's survey were concerned about planning, budgets, and adherence to standards and procedures in the company.

We have described some of the demands placed on IS by users; the managers expressed the need to develop good relations with users. Five of the managers also stressed good relationships with top management.

If information services is to contribute to the firm, it must support the firm's objectives and plans. Managers feel that IS must be responsive to user priorities. To succeed in this effort, IS personnel must learn the objectives of the firm and the priorities of users. Martin suggests that concern over the firm is particularly crucial when high-level decisions are made about the allocation of resources to activities like systems development.

Forty percent of the managers mentioned the management of change; their focus was on long-range technological planning to take advantage of new developments. In addition to this expressed concern, we must point out that every activity undertaken in development and planning for IS implies some type of organizational change. The CIO is in the business of creating change in the organization.

The New Role of the CIO

In the previous chapters, we have discussed some of the major changes in the computing environment; chief among these are end-user computing and distributed processing. This chapter describes a fairly traditional role and set of concerns for the CIO.

The proliferation of personal computers, minicomputers, and distributed processing centers under the control of local management has occurred for two main reasons. The first is technological; the cost of processing power has dropped dramatically, so that an end user can now buy a microcomputer for the price of a good electronic typewriter. The second factor responsible for these dramatic changes is the perception that the information services area is incompetent.

It has proven very difficult to satisfy users and senior management with the traditional form of information services: a central computer facility staffed by professional systems analysts and programmers. Users feel that it takes too long to develop applications; that they must wait for several years for other systems to be completed; and that the system, when completed, is over budget, behind schedule, and does not meet specifications. Less expensive hardware has given the user a chance to take control of information processing.

In later chapters we shall talk about some of the problems that these trends toward more user control create for the ISD, the organization, and users themselves. However, the important result of these changes for the CIO is a major alteration in his or her role in the firm. It has been estimated that 10 years ago the CIO controlled 85 to 95 per cent of the total expenditures in the firm for information processing. Today that figure is more likely to be 60 per cent and is dropping fast.

In the last chapter we saw a typical organizational structure with significant amounts of processing at CMI under the control of division management; the ISD managers at the plants had only a dotted line relationship to the CIO. As we move to individual users working with micros and minis, the control of the CIO almost vanishes.

However, it is important for management to realize that one does not have to control in order to influence. The role of the CIO, then, is changing from direct control over information processing to providing advice to the organization about information systems.

In this new role, the CIO and others in information services act as consultants and advisors. They seek to influence the firm's policies toward information processing and provide guidance on how to organize and coordinate information services with the entire firm. The behavior of an advisor is very different from that of a commander. The advisor does not issue orders; he or she suggests a course of action and presents the pros and cons of the suggestion. Senior managers may disagree, and the advisor will have to compromise.

As part of this role, the CIO and other staff members educate users and other managers about information processing. Since these managers and end users are devoting considerable resources to information processing, education should be a positive benefit for the firm.

Some managers may resist the loss of power and control that is occurring. However, the trend is clear and trying to retain power will only hasten its loss. On the positive side, managers have not been able to provide the kind of service that organizations and users demand when given control. As advisors, their time and effort are leveraged since those they advise will manage and develop systems. It should be far more satisfying to advise an organization successfully than to control an information processing effort that is widely perceived to be a failure.

The CIO at CMI

In the last chapter we saw Tom White, the CIO at CMI. Tom has a bachelor's degree in economics and an MBA from a leading university. His first position was that of a systems engineer for a computer vendor. "I learned how computers worked, especially the software in the days of the mainframe," he remarked.

"After 3 years I decided to go back for an MBA. Fortunately, I could major in information systems. The MBA program presented a lot of new ideas, especially about the management of information services. From where I sat with a vendor, it was hard for me to understand why IS had so many problems in our client organizations. Now I see some of the complexities of trying to manage in this environment."

Tom went on, "The users really don't understand technology. One of my mistakes was to think that users were as interested and enthusiastic about computers as I was as a new systems engineer. A lot of users are afraid of computers, though less so today with so many micros around. During my MBA studies, I began to see some of the conflicting demands on people who work in information services. The job involves a lot more than being a technical expert.

"At CMI, most of my work is with management and users. I have to influence the divisions to follow the policies that make sense for the corporation. Only the division managers don't always see things that way. The division IS staff members don't report directly to me; it is a dotted line relationship, which means that I have some influence, but no control. In a way, this kind of organizational structure makes it easier for me. It is very clear that I represent senior management; what I am recommending is best for the company, not best for headquarters or the finance department."

Tom concluded, "When I finished my MBA, I worked as a consultant for a big firm for 5 years and then became the manager of a medium-sized information services department. From there I came to CMI because it looked like a great opportunity. I think I understand the technology—not the bits and bytes, but I can deal with technical issues. Most of this job involves being a management consultant on information services. What's my business? Number 1 is change and number 2 is control. We develop information processing systems to change (improve) what we do around here. In order to prevent total chaos, I have to help control and coordinate information processing activities undertaken by a diverse group of people."

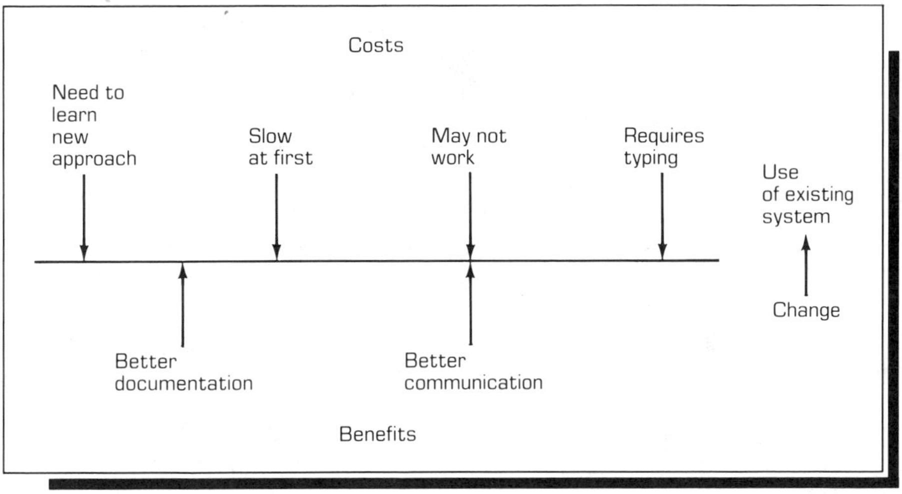

FIGURE 3-2 The force field.

The Management of Change

One theme in this chapter, echoed by Tom White, is that information systems are developed to make changes. The changes may be made to increase efficiency, improve ties with customers, offer a new product or service, or accomplish some similar objective. However, all of this effort implies change.

In Chapter 11 we will talk about change in the context of implementing systems. However, management with information services is involved in myriad changes. In some cases, IS will be responsible; in others, it will act as a consultant. Change is most common when a new system is installed, but there are many other kinds of changes associated with information processing.

Suppose the manager of systems and programming wants the systems analysis staff to use a new design tool. This manager must work on a program to encourage the analysts to change their behavior by incorporating the new tool. There is much to a project such as this one. There is a technical component that involves selecting and testing the new design tool. There is a component that we shall call *project management,* a topic we address in greater detail in Chapter 12. Finally, there is a need for the analysts to change their behavior.

For most change efforts, the hardest component to manage is behavioral change. A psychologist named Lewin suggested a framework for human change in the 1940s, and his approach is still very useful today. Figure 3-2 describes the Lewin force field.

Lewin asks us to visualize three stages in a change process: unfreezing, moving, and refreezing. During unfreezing, individuals become ready to change; they are motivated to consider an alternative. During moving, the individuals learn a new behavior; they actually change what they have been doing. During refreezing, the new behavior becomes permanent.

One way to visualize the change process is with the force field shown in Figure 3-2. We can see a line that represents current behavior. The objective of the change effort is to move the line in a certain direction—say, upward in the figure—and then maintain behavior at this new equilibrium. Note that there are forces that act to keep the line in its present position. Some forces act to inhibit change, others to encourage it. The arrows pushing down on the line represent inhibiting forces or the costs of change. The lines pushing up represent encouraging forces or the benefits of change.

In our example, the benefits of the new design tool are better documentation and improved communications among members of the design team and with users. The inhibiting factors are the need for the analyst to learn a new approach, the fact that the tool will be slower at first, fears that the new technique will not work, and the fact that the analyst will have to spend a lot of time typing at a terminal to use the system.

To make a change, it is necessary to reduce the inhibiting forces or increase the encouraging ones. In the example in Figure 3-2, the manager of systems and programming might consider providing some evidence that the new tool is effective. One approach would be to visit a firm that is successfully using the tool and find out about their experiences. Perhaps the tool does not require too much typing and is easier to learn than was believed. If the organization has found total development time reduced, it would change the picture in the figure.

In thinking about managing change that involves any type of alteration in behavior, the force field can be a useful diagnostic tool for the manager. What is necessary to change the current equilibrium? How do those involved perceive the costs and benefits of the proposed change? What can be done to decrease the inhibiting forces and increase the encouraging forces?

We are in the business of change; change management, then, is an important determinant of the success of information services. From the programmer to the CIO, change is to be expected.

Other IS Managers

This chapter has concentrated on the CIO, though there are many other managers in information services. In this section, we will discuss the roles of some of these individuals. In a given company, the titles and duties may differ, but the positions described here are fairly typical.

Manager of the ISD

The role of the ISD manager depends largely on whether or not the firm has a CIO. If there is a CIO, the manager of the ISD is responsible for the day-to-day management of information services. The CIO links information services to senior management. A strong manager in the ISD means that the CIO can devote his or her efforts to communications, liaison, planning, and strategy.

If there is no CIO, the manager of ISD is the highest-level manager concerned full-time with information processing. In this role, the ISD manager must handle both day-to-day operations and liaison with senior management and users. Without a CIO, the manager of the ISD has to depend heavily on other managers in the department or on a deputy to manage the department.

The creation of the CIO role provides evidence that the manager of ISD in most firms has been unsuccessful in fulfilling the liaison role with senior management. The daily fire-fighting involved in running the ISD and the technical problems in this department prevent the manager from performing planning and consulting activities. Since the manager of the ISD often has a technical background, it is very difficult for him or her to be perceived as a senior manager by top management.

We expect to see more and more firms moving to the CIO form of management for information services. Under this scheme, there will be a highly capable manager of the ISD who is concerned with the active management of information processing. This individual may have a career path that includes becoming a CIO, but he or she will have to demonstrate management, planning, and liaison skills to secure such a position.

Manager of Systems and Programming

The manager of systems and programming is concerned with the overall management of systems development. Typically an organization has a group of analysts and programmers; they are assigned to different projects by the manager of systems and programming. This type of organization is called *matrix management;* the programmers and analysts form the columns of a matrix, and the individual projects are the rows. Each individual, then, has two potential leaders: the manager of systems and programming and a project leader for the project on which the individual is working.

The manager of systems and programming is responsible for bringing new technology to the development process. Until recently, the development of IS has been a very labor-intensive process. Now there are some new tools and techniques that can facilitate systems analysis and design. However, there are many competing tools for this purpose, and the degree of improvement with each is not clear.

Figure 3-3 shows some of the conflicts faced by the manager of systems and programming. Typically this individual reports to a manager of information services. This immediate superior wants systems that are developed to be responsive and completed on time and within budget. However, this same superior may, from time to time, preempt programmers for a special project or change development priorities, making it difficult to complete projects already underway.

The manager of systems and programming also has to contend with division management, who want to be sure that the division's investment in

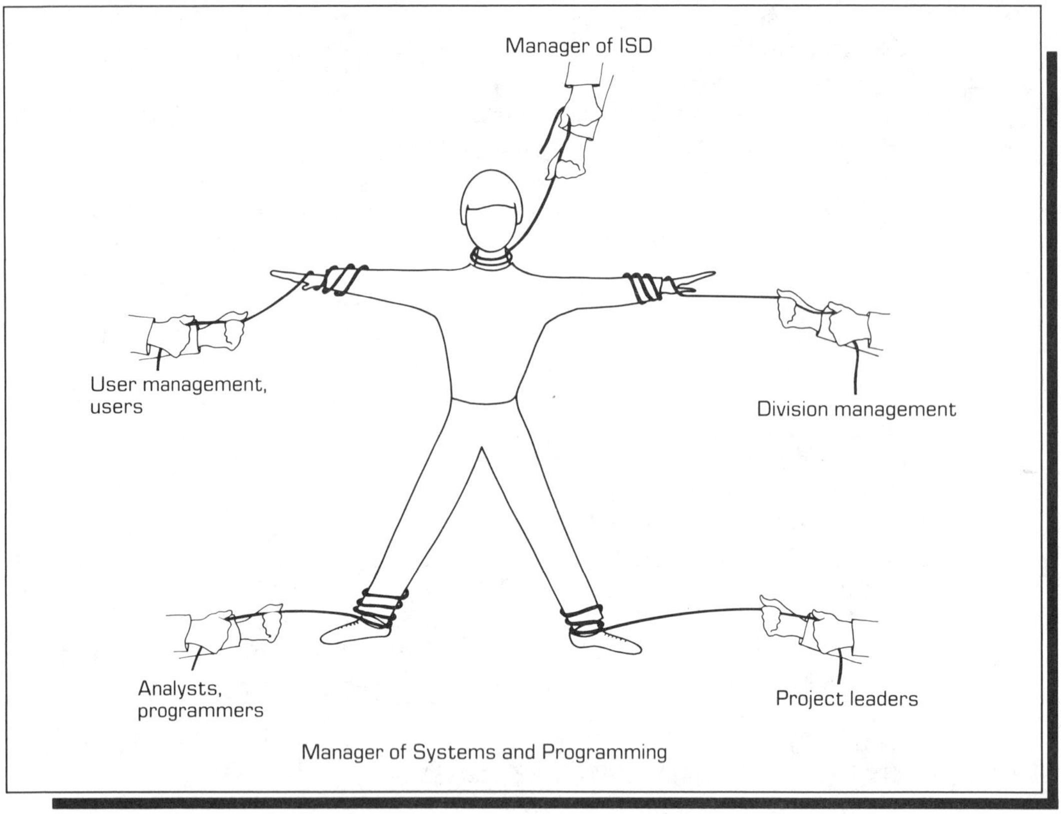

FIGURE 3-3 Demands on the manager of systems and programming.

systems pays a return. These individuals are impatient for results and often are interested in systems that can be shown to save costs.

The manager of systems and programming also has to respond to his or her immediate subordinates, the analysts and programmers. These individuals are professionals; they tend to be independent and are often dedicated to their profession rather than their employer. Conflict arises when the analysts and programmers are criticized by users or when they fall behind schedule on a project.

Finally, the manager of systems and programming must deal with a number of project leaders. In some firms, the project leader may be a user rather than a computer professional. Project leaders demand more resources for their projects; each one wants the "best" analyst and programmer.

The manager of systems and programming has a diverse constituency that makes a number of competing demands. The position combines project management, personnel management, and all-around leadership skills.

Manager of Operations

The manager of operations has the same reporting relationship as the manager of systems and programming. To some extent, this individual en-

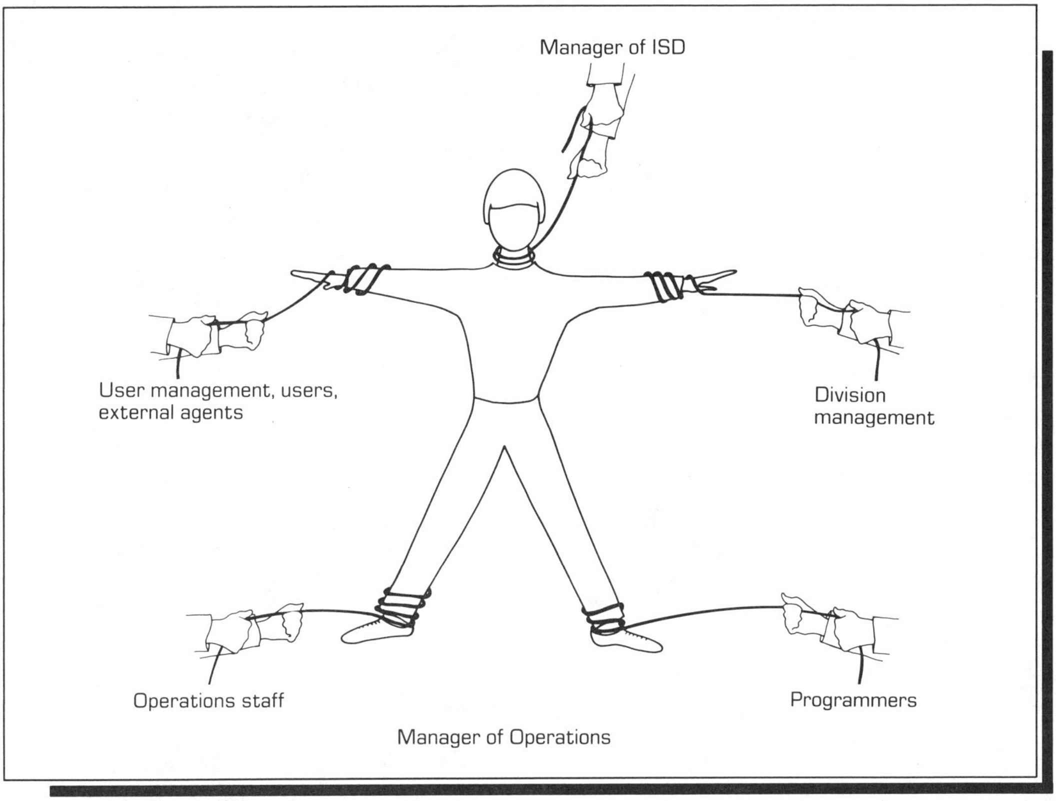

FIGURE 3-4 Demands on the manager of operations.

counters the same cast of characters as well. However, the operations manager is responsible for a very different resource: the computers and processing capabilities of the firm. See Figure 3-4.

Division management is concerned with results; it wants good response times and minimum down time. These managers depend on information processing; they want reliable processing and accurate output.

Users and user management have these same goals. Users are dependent on computer operations; these operations must be reliable and accurate. External agents, like customers or suppliers, connected to the computer also have the same goals.

The manager of operations has to contend with the operations staff. This staff includes computer operators, librarians (for tapes and disks), control clerks, and possibly schedulers. Operations are typically a two- or three-shift-per-day business, so that a large number of individuals may be needed to staff this department. Much of the job is clerical and manual; there are problems attracting qualified employees.

In some firms, operations is also responsible for maintenance and systems programmers. Maintenance programmers do limited enhancements and repair programs when a new bug is discovered. Systems programmers are responsible for the systems software of the computer; they may install new releases, modify code, or correct errors.

The manager of operations is involved with the IS quality control department; this department may report to operations. The acceptance of a new system for production or the modification of an existing system has implications for operations. The job of quality assurance in IS is to be sure that systems operate properly when they are put into production.

Finally, the manager of operations must contend with applications programmers. These individuals are often behind on their schedules and want additional test time. Unfortunately for the programmers, the first objective of this manager is to keep operations running. The firm must maintain normal operations even if a programmer's new project is late.

The manager of operations comes the closest to running a production line of anyone in information services. Systems development is a creative task, and operations is a line management task. There are machines (computers) and a certain amount of work. The machines must be operated to complete the work, and this is the task of the operations manager. As a result, the operations manager must forecast the demand for service and plan for the acquisition of more processing power.

Project Manager

We mentioned project managers earlier; these individuals have overall responsibility for a development project. Historically, project managers have come from the ranks of systems analysts. More often users are put in charge of systems as a way to encourage more user input in the design process.

Figure 3-5 shows some of the pressures on project managers. The manager of systems and programming is the superior to whom the project manager reports. As mentioned before, this manager wants to see the project completed on time, within budget, and in accordance with specifications.

Division management and users and their management share the same goals. However, they may not realize the amount of cooperation required on their part to achieve these goals. Obtaining user input in the design process has proven very difficult, which is why some firms make a user the project manager.

The project manager also becomes the first-line supervisor for analysts and programmers working on the project. Since this individual is likely to be an analyst, he or she may manage a systems analyst on one project and work for that same individual on another one. Analysts and programmers want more resources to help them, more input from users, and often more computer time.

Systems development is where the relationship between users and information services begins. If the project leader is successful, subsequent dealings with users should be much easier. On the other hand, if the project is late, over budget, and does not meet specifications, a group of users has been turned into a group of vocal critics of information services.

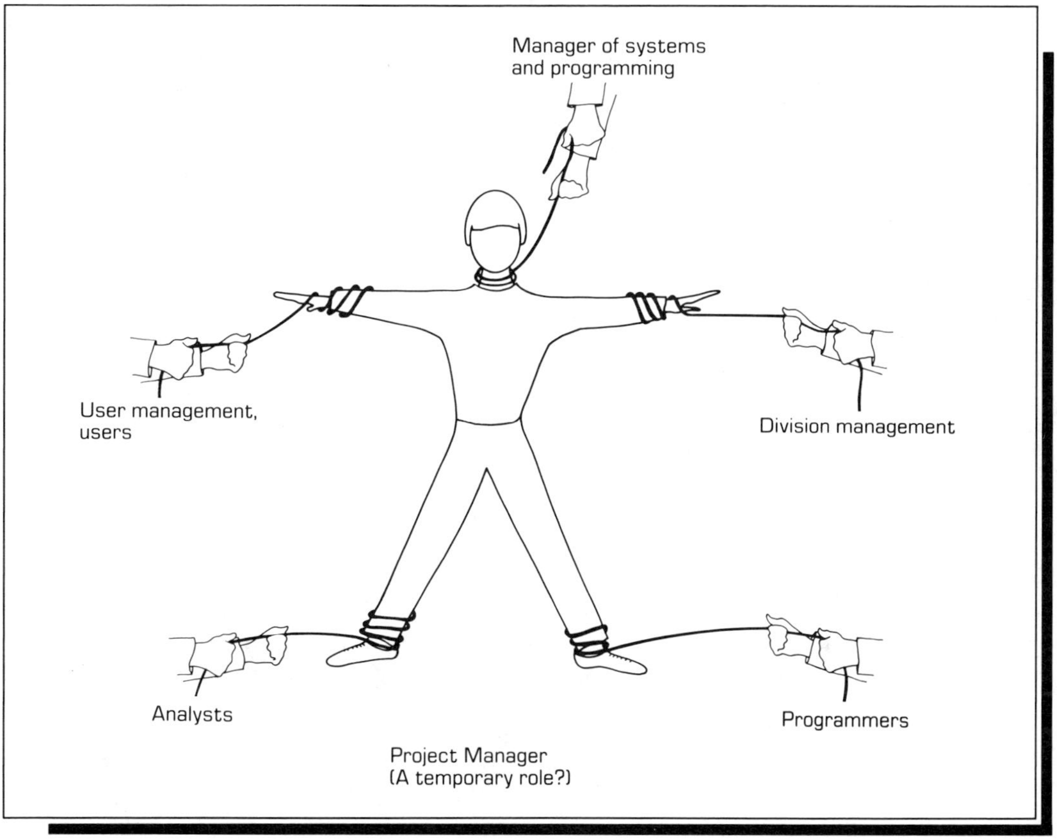

FIGURE 3-5 Demands on the project manager.

End-User Support/Information Center

With the explosion of end-user computing and distributed processing, some firms have established special consultants to aid end users. Sometimes these individuals report to end-user areas, but it is more common for them to be a part of information services. An information center is a physical location staffed by consultants; it usually offers a variety of tools for users who want to access existing data files or develop simple systems.

Managers of these areas, which deal with end users, have to be oriented toward consulting; they cannot be individuals who are used to being in charge. These staff members are advisors and educators; their clients and students are users in the firm. A manager with these assignments must continually look for ways to serve users and for new tools for users to adopt.

R&D Manager

The position of R&D manager does not exist in many information services organizations, but it should. Because the technology is changing so rapidly, the organization needs to devote resources to testing and planning for new technology. An R&D manager keeps abreast of technology and, in particular, tries to assess how it can be used in the firm. What are its implications for the way the firm does business? Does the technology enable the firm to do something better? The R&D manager brings new technology to the firm and experiments with it. He or she evaluates new developments to see how they might help the firm.

Database Administrator

Many organizations use database management systems; this software automates part of the task of systems development. Typically a DBMS provides a model of data such as a hierarchy, network, or relational model; a data dictionary to keep track of data items and structure; access routines; and a query language.

Firms have found that in order to use these systems effectively, they need a DBA. This individual is an expert on the database management system used by the firm. He or she uses a data definition language to describe the structure of the database to the system. This manager is also responsible for the data dictionary, a listing of all variables and their meaning. Finally, the manager is concerned with data integrity and the protection of company records.

The DBA can play an important role in systems development. The needs of various users must be incorporated into a physical database. A DBA can help take the users' logical view of data and create a unified physical view as a part of the database.

Conclusions

There are many different management positions in information processing. The ones described in this chapter are typical, though a large company will have layers of middle management between the positions described here. Their objective, however, is the same. They must effectively lead, control, and manage information processing in the firm.

For all of these managers, the pace of change is rapid. Managers within the ISD are giving up control and power to end users. In the future, managers in information processing will accomplish their goals through influence and competence rather than authority derived from the structure of the organization. Such a change in role is difficult for current ISD staff members, but it should result in more effective information processing.

Recommended Readings

Ives, B., and M. Olson, "Manager or Technician? The Nature of the Information System Manager's Job," *MIS Quarterly*, vol. 5, no. 4 (December 1981), pp.

49–62. (The article discussed in the chapter in which the authors followed information processing managers to observe their activities.)

Martin, E. W., "Critical Success Factors of Chief MIS/DP Executives," *MIS Quarterly*, vol. 5, no. 2 (June 1982), pp. 1–9. (A look at what 25 IS managers feel is crucial to the success of their areas.)

Mintzberg, H., *The Nature of Managerial Work.* New York: Harper & Row, 1973. (An excellent book on how chief executives actually manage; good reading for any manager.)

Discussion Problems

3.1 Carole Jackson is manager of systems for the AgChem Division of United Chemicals. In this role, she functions as the manager of the ISD and reports to the division president. There are senior-level managers in information processing at headquarters, but as yet no CIO.

Carole has a problem with one of her staff members, Harold Gray. Harold has been with the company for 15 years; his background is in operations research. Harold's current position is senior systems analyst.

The problem, as Carole sees it, is that Harold has failed to adapt to modern technology and systems. "He is back in the days of operations research, which is where he started. Clients were in awe of the mathematicians doing OR work. There was no question of who was in charge. Today, we have to be willing to let the user determine the solution and Harold hasn't accepted that approach."

What solutions can you recommend to Carole?

3.2 Jim Dolan, manager of the ISD for Ajax Manufacturing, began his career as an applications programmer. From there he moved into systems programming, where he was responsible for keeping the operating system and computer running for several IBM mainframe computers.

When the previous occupant of his job left, Ajax interviewed several people before choosing Jim for the position. The major drawback was Jim's technical background and lack of a college degree. He had a reputation for dealing abruptly with users. However, in his favor was the fact that Jim was a known quantity and that it was hard to attract people to Ajax's location.

Senior management is now in a quandary. It appears that Ajax should have a CIO at the vice presidential level. However, no one wants to promote Jim. There is widespread fear that if someone is brought in over Jim, he might resign. Jim has a great deal of knowledge about the firm, and his loss would be a major blow.

What would you advise Ajax to do?

Questions

1. What are the primary responsibilities of the CIO?
2. To whom should a CIO report?
3. Why is it likely that the manager of the ISD will not be promoted to CIO?
4. What is the primary function of the manager in playing the interpersonal role?
5. Describe your own view of leadership.
6. Why are a leader's actions important, even when this individual feels that he or she is not really leading?
7. What is the informational role for a manager?

8. To what extent do managers spend most of their time making decisions?
9. Why is there so much disturbance handling in information processing?
10. Should the CIO be expected to spend a lot of time in meetings? Why or why not?
11. What are the key success features for a CIO?
12. Why is the CIO a change agent in the organization?
13. Describe the new role of managers in information services.
14. Why might ISD professionals resist their new relationship with users?
15. Describe the Lewin model of change.
16. How might the force field model apply to the change in ISD personnel from controlling projects to acting as project advisors?
17. What is the difference between the manager of the ISD and the CIO?
18. What are the duties of the manager of systems and programming?
19. What is different about operations when compared with other management tasks in ISD?
20. What are the duties of quality assurance?
21. Should there be an R&D manager in information services? Why or why not?
22. What is the role of the DBA?
23. What trends are responsible for end users taking more control over processing?
24. Is it only large organizations that should consider a CIO position? Explain your reasoning.
25. What has been the contribution (or lack of one) of ISD management to the often negative perceptions users have of information processing?

4

Internal Structure of the ISD

In Chapter 2 we discussed different ways to structure information processing in the organization itself. That discussion stressed the fact that there is no one perfect structure for information processing. Instead, there are many different ways to organize. The firm has to consider its objectives and situation, and then evaluate the pros and cons of different organization structures.

The same considerations apply to choosing an internal structure for information services. We shall describe some functions that are likely to be included in ISDs and one way to organize them. It is important to remember, however, that there will be different structures for different situations. In this chapter, we first discuss the components and tasks of a typical IS area and then recommend an organization structure for the ISD.

Components of the ISD

Table 4-1 shows the major activities of an ISD. Whether an ISD is found at the corporate or division level, management must decide how to organize it. Who will be responsible for systems analysis and design, end-user support, and so on? This section describes some of the activities in information services and how they are typically organized.

Systems Development

The task of systems development involves the design and installation of a computer application. A typical design effort involves the formation of a design team consisting of users and personnel from the ISD. The team meets for an extended period of time, ranging from several months to several years for a large system. The team must determine the functions a system is to perform, how it is to work, the contents and structure of the database, the interface with users, and so on.

Why is systems development important to information services? It is the initial point of contact with a user; the relationship between users and the ISD begins during the system development process. Design is also important because of the product, the system itself. Some employees in the firm will spend much of their day using the system that results from the design process. If it is poorly designed or does not work well, these users will be frustrated. Their jobs will be made less interesting rather than helped by the computer system.

As systems are used, it must be expected that individuals will want changes. It is difficult to design a computer system in the abstract; we have

TABLE 4-1 ISD Components

Components	Task	Objective	Characteristics
Systems development	Design and install applications	Meet user specifications, schedule, budget	Creative, team oriented, high risk
Data administration	Design/maintain databases	Productivity and data integrity	Design, R&D, administration, change control
End-user support	Help users make tools available	End-user competence	Consulting
Information center		Make users aware of tools	Consulting/teaching
Personal computer (PC) store	Demonstrate, teach	Encourage PC use	Consulting/teaching
Consulting	Direct, assist	End-user competence	Consulting/teaching
Operations	Run systems	Meet schedule uptime, response time	Factory-like
R&D	Search for opportunities	Bring new ideas and technology to firm	Research is future oriented
Planning	Develop plan for IS	Plan accepted as road map	Group involvement Boundary spanning
Quality	Assure accuracy and integrity of results	Minimum errors	Uncertain, constant testing

trouble visualizing how the system will actually work. Once completed, there are likely to be many areas for improvements. A system that is well designed will be flexible, that is, designers will be able to make changes easily because of the way the system has been developed. We shall explore ways to design more flexible systems in Chapter 9.

The design process is characterized by creativity and high risk. There is a risk that the project will not be finished on time or within budget. There is also a substantial risk that the system will not meet its original specifications and that even if it does, the original specifications will not necessarily reflect what users want. How can the design team perform so poorly?

There are a number of reasons for problems in design. The first is the fact that there is often inadequate management interest in the design process. A manager may initiate a systems development project and then turn it over to subordinates to complete. Unless the manager provides input, attends review meetings, and otherwise shows an interest in the project, subordinates are likely to assign the project a low priority.

Another problem arises with expectations. It is important for the IS staff to manage user expectations and to ensure that they are realistic. If expectations are too high, users are bound to be disappointed by the results. The traditional ISD does not have a good reputation in most organizations. The ISD provides a service on which users depend; it is easy for problems to occur and hard to excel. The services users demand routinely requires consistent outstanding performance by the ISD staff, particularly given the problems of the technology.

Users and designers have many communications problems. The specifications for a computer system are not easy to read, and computer professionals have a history of not documenting systems development. An architect draws plans for a building, using a set of standards that are understood by other architects and the people working on the construction of the building. In contrast, there is no one standard for representing a systems design, and many systems analysts do minimal documentation. As a result, users have an incomplete or even misleading picture of how a system is supposed to work.

Finally, conditions change during the design process. Personnel move to new positions and new individuals become involved with the system. In addition, business conditions change. One ISD had to stop work on all projects to make modify an existing system that priced goods. The manufactured product contained expensive metals whose prices were fluctuating. As a result, the company decided to price its products on shipment rather than when accepting the order. This change in business philosophy necessitated extensive changes in computer systems, a process that delayed all new applications.

Chapter 9 addresses approaches to mitigating these problems. However, there is no magic solution, no organizational structure that will prevent problems from arising. One helpful technique is to have users on the design team and to put a user in charge of the design project itself. In this approach, the professional systems analyst becomes a guide, explaining what the next issue should be to the design team. The professional designer also prepares information to support design decisions. There are hundreds of ways to build a system; the professional must choose several alternatives that are appropriate and present them to the design team for consideration.

Database Administration

The last chapter discusses the role of the DBA. This individual works in a database administration department, which has two responsibilities. The first task of the database group is to assist in the design of new computer applications. As mentioned earlier, the DBA can help designers take users' logical views of the data and develop a single, unified view that becomes the input for the actual design of a database to support the new application.

A second important task for the database group is to maintain existing databases. Individuals in this group are responsible for the security and integrity of existing data in the firm. They must be concerned about adequate backup and about changes made to systems that require changes in the definition of existing databases.

End-User Support

End-user computing is a relatively new phenomenon; at first, it referred to users who generated their own reports from mainframes or minicomputers. These users would run query languages to inquire against a database. Alternatively a user could work with a 4GL to generate reports. This approach to computing is a partial solution to the maintenance problem.

The typical ISD spends 50 per cent or more of its discretionary resources—systems analysts and programmers—on maintenance. What is maintenance? In some instances, it involves fixing errors that occur in programs. However, surveys have shown that the actual amount of time spent on repair of systems is relatively small, under 10 per cent. Most maintenance consists of enhancements, changes that users want, a special report, or some similar request. (At some point, a request requires so much change in a system that it becomes a new development project.)

One appeal of end-user computing, then, is that users can perform some of their own maintenance. If users want a new report, they can work with a 4GL to produce it. Instead of putting in a maintenance request and waiting for ISD staff to find time for it, they can solve their own problem.

Is there a flaw in this reasoning? If so, it is in the fact that while users do answer some of their own requests, end-user computing can lead to more requests. How? Consider the end user who asks for data that are not in the database. Most ISDs feel responsible for maintaining the integrity of the firm's data; they will not allow an end user to modify corporate databases. Now the end user is back where he or she was before the development of end-user computing: waiting for resources from the ISD to modify existing applications so that the requested data will be available.

The other problem with end-user computing is preparing and motivating end users to participate in it. For this reason, many ISDs have support centers, special places with staff members to assist users. IBM popularized the name *information center* for this kind of support group.

The information center should have a physical location where users can come for assistance. A typical center will be staffed by several consultants who are well versed in the query languages and 4GLs being used in the firm. The consultants will also know something about existing applications so that they can help users access the data in which they are interested.

This matching of user needs to existing systems is one of the most important tasks for the consultants in the information center. The consultants' other major responsibility is to teach end users how to work with the tools available to them. The consultants, therefore, need to be particularly oriented toward users. In this assignment, technical skills are secondary to interpersonal ones.

The term *end-user computing* has been expanded in some organizations to include the use of microcomputers. As a part of supporting users, then, an information center or some other group is often set up to provide assistance in learning how to use a personal computer. In the case of a 4GL or query language, the type of advice is determined by the tools and applications available. For personal computing, users encounter a variety of problems:

1. Do I need a personal computer?
2. If so, what type should I buy?
3. If I buy a personal computer, how should it be configured? How much memory is necessary, what kind of printer, color or monochrome cathode ray tube (CRT), and so on?
4. What software should I buy?
5. What word processors does the firm support?
6. How do I use each specific package?
7. Do I want to connect to other computers? If so, how?

To help solve these problems, some firms have established microcomputer stores and/or consulting groups. The store may display several brands and configurations of microcomputers that the company is willing to support. The user can try different software packages on different computers to aid in selecting a machine. The store may also offer courses and individual instruction to help users become comfortable with micros.

The person in charge of consulting and the personal computer store is sometimes given the title *manager of microcomputers*. This individual consults in the ways previously described and is also available to handle phone calls and help requests from users. This manager and his or her staff also will install micros and upgrade existing machines, for example, by adding more memory or installing a hard disk. The micro staff may also install a series of machines and a LAN in a department.

The area of end-user support is vital. One investment banking firm in New York hired a new manager of information services at the partner level, the highest level in the firm. This person turned around a mediocre department by bringing in 4GLs and generating a large number of systems for the mainframe. Unfortunately, he was replaced, partially because he had allocated only 2 support staff for some 500 microcomputer users.

While end-user computing and micros have expanded the number of users and individuals who are able to do processing, this phenomenon has been a mixed blessing for the ISD. It is true that there are not enough professionals to develop all of the applications and handle all of the maintenance requests from users. However, as many more users try to expedite matters by solving some of their own problems, they create a tremendous demand for support from professionals.

These demands are quite different from those that users have historically placed on information services. End-user support clearly shows the transition facing computer professionals; the role of controlling systems development has clearly shifted, in this area at least, to advising, consulting, and teaching users.

If processing is the responsibility of the divisions, then division management should seriously consider a support center. Informally, a user help network will develop, with users as experts in certain packages. At first, this informal network will probably be sufficient. However, as end-user computing becomes more prevalent in the division, users will need support by a full-time staff of consultants. End-user computing is a healthy trend, but it is not free.

Operations

The mission of the operations group is clear: it must execute existing applications. Management and users will judge operations by whether it meets processing schedules, whether computer systems are up and running, by response time for on-line systems, and by errors in processing. Operations resembles a production line environment as compared with the more research-oriented nature of systems development.

The operations group has two distinctly different types of responsibilities, depending on the mode in which an application operates. For batch processing in which users submit data, files are updated at one point in time, and reports are generated, the operations area is responsible at least for the integrity of the database and the accuracy of reports. Generally the user area takes responsibility for the submission of input data, particularly when inputs are collected on line. There are some systems remaining in which an input section within operations keys input documents in to a system; in this case, the operations area is responsible for data transcription accuracy.

Operations has a slightly different set of responsibilities for systems that operate totally on-line. Here, once in production, the operations group monitors response times and provides file backups. The user is responsible for input and queries, and ISD produces the routine, periodic reports as scheduled.

Today's operations environment is characterized by a large number of hybrid systems; some parts operate in batch mode, while others are on line. One manufacturing company operates a materials requirements planning system. The system "explodes" incoming orders into the components needed to manufacture the products ordered. The programs compare actual orders with forecasts and generate a master production schedule; other programs release work orders to the factory for production. Clerical personnel in the factory key the movement of orders in to CRT terminals during the production process. The generation of a master production schedule and certain updates of production status occur in batch processing runs overnight, while movements are updated on-line for inquiry purposes. There are many similar hybrid systems that combine some aspects of on-line and batch processing.

Operations staff members have to worry about capacity: Is there sufficient computer capacity to handle the expanding workload? Why is this workload always expanding? It is rare to find a computer application that is discontinued; about the best we can hope for is a new version that replaces and updates an existing system. More typically, the systems development group is developing new systems. If the firm invests several years and hundreds of thousands or even millions of dollars in an application, it expects to use it for a long period of time. For mainframes and minicomputers in a business environment, there are few one-shot applications. As a result, the number of jobs and the amount of processing required both tend to increase. If a firm is doing well, it also expects that the volume of information being processed will expand. As a result, operations will need new secondary storage space, and possibly new memory or central processing unit (CPU) capacity.

As the need for more capacity grows, the firm is likely to be faced with the need to acquire new hardware and/or software. Operations, then, must play a role in obtaining this new technology.

Research and Development

R&D within information services is seen as a luxury by many organizations; as a result, the majority of firms probably do not have a separate R&D organization. Does this mean that there is no R&D? Probably not; someone in operations or the systems area looks at new products, services, and trends.

Given the rapid changes in the technology and the pace of new applications, it is important for an organization to keep abreast of what is happening in the information systems field. An R&D group serves this role within the ISD. In addition to surveying what is available and what new ideas are coming from universities and industrial development laboratories, the R&D group can run its own experiments.

As an example, suppose that a department is interested in developing a LAN to tie together its microcomputers. An R&D group within information services could investigate different vendors' products and acquire one or two for evaluation. This group would set up the network, possibly in a laboratory setting, and determine if it meets the needs of the department. While this seems like a lot of attention to the needs of one department, it is an investment in the future. The R&D group would expect other departments to be interested in this technology; having gained experience and selected one LAN, they are ready to assist the rest of the firm.

Planning

Given the scarcity of information systems plans, one could argue that the existence of a plan should be worth at least a grade of B+. We have been continually surprised by (1) the number of firms that have no plan beyond a current year's budget for the ISD and (2) the poor quality of the plans that do exist. Chapter 6 is devoted to a discussion of planning itself; in this chapter, we discuss organization structures for planning.

For a plan to be successful, it must be accepted and used to operate the business. Information services, then, cannot develop a plan in a vacuum, since it is dependent on senior management and users to determine the direction for the development of information systems. ISD planning needs a structure that facilitates input from outside the department.

One possibility is to have a separate planning subunit in the department, even if it consists of only one individual. The planning subunit is responsible for developing a 3- to 5-year plan for information processing in the firm and for a detailed 1-year operational plan and budget. The planning group must provide liaison with others in the firm to obtain their inputs and commitment to the plan.

In a small organization, it may be possible to have a part-time planner; in larger firms, where potentially hundreds of individuals should be involved in planning, the information services planning department may have 5 or 10 individuals. At the division level, a planner will have to coordinate with corporate planning and with plans developed by other divisions.

Quality Control

The duties associated with quality control are often assumed by an individual as a part of his or her normal tasks. However, given its importance, it is a good idea to make quality control a separate area. What does quality control mean with respect to information systems?

The first task of a quality control group is to accept new applications. The development group must meet the appropriate standards of quality control for testing and documentation before a system is placed in production. Just the presence of this check can do wonders for the quality of the design effort. In firms without a quality control function, the development group often merely declares that a system is ready or that all it has to do is convince the operations group that the system is working.

A formal quality control acceptance procedure for a new system will help the organization install systems that are easier to modify and that execute with a minimum of errors. Quality control has the final say in when an application is ready to be classified as in production status.

Quality control has another important role to play. Before modifications are allowed to go into actual use, this group has to agree that the changes made in the modified system actually work. Quality control will run the new system in a test mode to check a standard series of transactions that have been run through the production version. This group has to be satisfied that the changes (1) accomplish their objectives and (2) create no unanticipated errors in other parts of the system.

Summary

Table 4-1 summarizes the functional components of a typical ISD. While these different tasks may not be labeled as in the table, the ISD must accomplish them in some way. In the next section, we talk about how an ISD might organize to perform these tasks.

Organizational Structure

Figure 4-1 shows a typical organization chart for an ISD. There is an overall manager of the department; reporting to him or her are three major subunits: systems and programming, operations, and end-user services. The last group is new and may not yet be found in all organizations.

Despite the fact that the units are likely to be small, it is a good idea to have the planning and R&D functions report directly to the manager of the ISD. The activities of both of these groups are very important to the future of the ISD; they need the ongoing encouragement and support of the manager.

Within systems and programming, one finds the matrix management

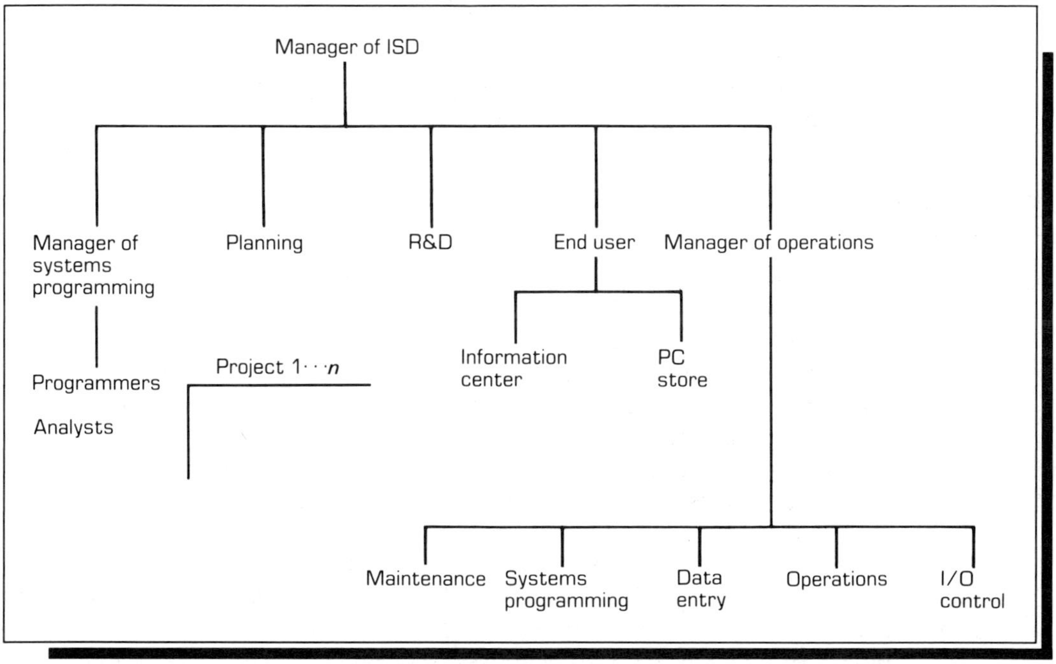

FIGURE 4-1 A typical structure for ISD.

described in Chapter 3. Programmers and analysts report to the manager of systems and programming. However, project leaders and this manager assign analysts and programmers to work on different projects. In this matrix the staff has two reporting relationships: the manager of systems and programming and one or more project leaders.

In a large firm, there may be managers who report to the manager of systems and programming and who, in turn, supervise various programmers and analysts. In some organizations, particularly large ones, systems and programming is organized by functional area. For example, a bank might have one group of programmers and analysts that specialize in systems for the trust department, another for retail banking, a third for commercial banking, and so on. Within each of these functional areas, programmers and analysts are still assigned in matrix fashion.

Operations is often organized into the operation of systems, data entry, and input/output control. With more and more distributed processing and an effort to eliminate batch input, data entry should be a vanishing subunit within the ISD. I/O control will probably exist until users are able to trigger the production of reports and verify their accuracy. For the immediate future, most operations groups will have to check the output from the computer.

Operations also frequently contains the systems and maintenance programming staffs. Remember that systems programmers tend the programs that direct the computer system, while systems designers develop applications software. Systems programs are closely associated with the day-to-day operation of the computer, and systems programmers are most often found in the operations group. Since maintenance programmers' most critical duties are the repair of production applications that fail, at least some maintenance programmers are assigned to the operations area.

As mentioned previously, end-user computing is likely to be organized into an information center, personal computer store, or both. Another option is to have an umbrella group called, for example, *end-user consulting.*

Rationale

Why is the structure in Figure 4-1 or some close approximation found in so many organizations? There are a number of rationales for structuring an organization. Earlier we discussed sequential, pooled, and reciprocal interdependencies. Often organizations group together activities exhibiting reciprocal or joint dependence, since these are the hardest to coordinate.

Another practice in designing organizations is to put in close physical proximity individuals who have to communicate with each other frequently. Since individuals in the same department are often interdependent and therefore must communicate to accomplish their assigned tasks, these two variables usually are associated with each other.

In the ISD, the individuals within operations need to communicate a great deal. Data entry prepares data for the individuals who operate computers; input/output control checks the output. Systems programmers keep the computers' systems programs running, and maintenance programmers are on call when there is a problem in a production system. By grouping systems programming and maintenance programming together, the organization designer tries to make communications as efficient as possible.

Another technique often used in the design of organizations is to group individuals together according to the types of tasks and the management required. Since systems design differs markedly from operations, the development group is separate from operations. Also, aside from requiring computer time, there are very few interdependencies between developers and operations staff, at least on a daily basis. Of course, the kinds of systems developed have an impact on future computer needs, but this kind of dependence can be handled through the planning process.

Following the same logic, end-user computing represents a third type of management activity within the ISD. The end user group, as mentioned earlier, has to be concerned with teaching, consulting, and advising users. As such, the group has contact with both the design groups and operations. End-user consultants may need to call on the design group for help in modifying an existing application to make data more accessible to end users. Consultants also depend on operations to execute the 4GLs and query languages that end users need for their own computing. If micros are connected to the mainframe or minis run by operations, end-user consultants have to work with the operations group to resolve problems.

In general, then, the organizational structure presented in Figure 4-1 tends to group tasks together in order to keep interdependent individuals in the same subunit and to put individuals in the same unit who need to communicate often. This structure also tends to group individuals together based on the kind of tasks and management needed. Systems development is research oriented and is done in a group; operations faces day-to-day deadlines and pressures. End-user computing advises but does not control any type of computing in the firm.

The Manager of the ISD

The discussion in this chapter should suggest why the task of managing information services is so complex. The manager of the ISD in Figure 4-1 has a variety of individuals reporting to him or her. These individuals are responsible for many different kinds of tasks, ranging from the "think tank" of R&D to the "factory" of operations. While the managers of individual groups can specialize in the needs of their subunits, the manager of the ISD has to adopt the perspective of each subunit in managing the department.

In this respect, the manager is like the coach of a ball team. Each player responds to a different style of management because he or she faces a different set of problems and has a unique personality. The wide receiver has to worry about speed and the defensive backs; the quarterback about the execution of the play. The tasks in the ISD represent different types of problems; the ISD manager has to respond to the creative, project-oriented nature of systems development and the factory-like environment of operations.

Committees

Companies form committees as a way to supplement the normal structure of the organization; a committee is like a task force, which was discussed as one organizational coordination mechanism in Chapter 2. What committees are usually associated with the ISD? (See Table 4-2.)

We have discussed three types of committees: executive steering committees, steering committees, and maintenance committees. An executive steering committee consists of the senior officers of a firm who meet to set the direction for information services. This committee should include the CIO and the head planner for information services. The executive committee probably meets only two to four times a year. It discusses trends in processing and how the technology can be used to accomplish corporate objectives. This committee may choose areas for applications development.

A steering committee is also helpful within divisions or at different physical locations to make detailed resource allocation decisions and to choose among competing alternatives for the design of a new system. Such a group might exist at a factory; the corporate executive steering committee has indicated that technology for reducing manufacturing costs is a key priority. The local committee will decide how to accomplish this reduction; for example, it may decide that it needs a quality control system, while a neighboring plant chooses materials requirements planning. Given the choice of a strategy, the factory steering committee evaluates different alternatives for improving quality control with a computer system, alternatives like a packaged system, a custom-designed system, and so on.

A final committee is for maintenance; users decide what requests for maintenance and enhancements will receive priority. This committee should consist of users who work with systems on a daily basis and who represent their departments, along with the most senior IS employee involved in maintenance. A user should definitely chair this committee.

Local Variations

The prototypical structure for an ISD discussed in this chapter will be found, with many variations, in different organizations. The functions to be performed will be the same, however. One firm may contract out all systems

TABLE 4-2 IS Committee Structure

Committee	Duties
Executive steering committee	Senior officers set direction, develop and approve IS plan, set priorities
Steering committee (divisional)	Plan for divisions, choose applications alternatives
Maintenance committee	Users decide what priorities to place on maintenance requests

development to consultants; another may choose to have its processing done by a time-sharing service bureau so that it does not have to manage operations.

Within one organization, we may find differences. One local division may draw on a headquarters design group for systems development. Another might join a neighboring plant in setting up a single computer facility that both will use. A third plant might decide to process on corporate mainframes rather than have its own mainframe or minicomputer.

The important thing to remember is that there is no one right structure within the ISD, just as there is no one right structure for information processing in the whole organization. The functions described in this chapter have to be performed somewhere and by some group. The important questions are: What is the objective of the organization? What are its management capabilities for information processing? What principles of organization design apply to developing a structure for information services?

The ISD at CMI

Figures 4-2 to 4-5 show the internal structure of the ISD at CMI's four plant locations. Note the relatively flat organizational structures; only Chicago has a manager for systems and programming reporting to the manager of the ISD. These structures reflect the fact that CMI has not yet invested heavily in information processing for its plants. Even headquarters in Charleston, with its small mainframe, does not need a manager of operations.

If CMI invests more in systems, it will probably find that more managers will be needed. In fact, Mary Watson in Charleston has now asked to hire a manager of operations and a systems programmer.

Her argument is that operations are becoming more difficult to control. "I am spending too much of my time worrying about operations; almost everyone with a machine this size has a manager of operations to keep the thing running. We also need a systems programmer; we are running CICS, a teleprocessing monitor, VM, a virtual machine operating system, and a version of DOS, the IBM disk operating system. With a database manager in addition, we are always calling the vendor for expensive systems engineers to fix things. Last year I spent $40,000 on this kind of outside help. For not much more money, I can have a full-time systems programmer."

Mary continued, "The operations area is a pain in the neck; there is always some little problem. I sit down to think about planning, and all of a sudden there is a crisis because some application died or the on-line systems are down. If nothing else, the manager of operations could take care of users with operations problems."

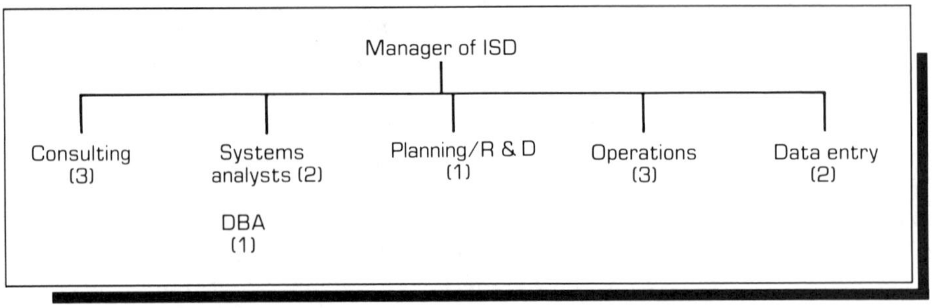

FIGURE 4-2 CMI Charleston ISD.

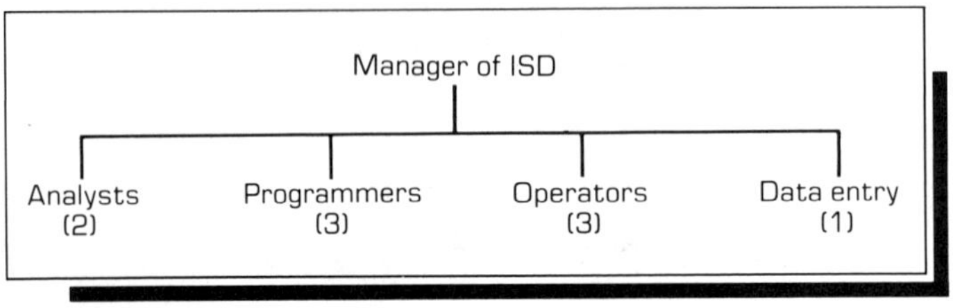

FIGURE 4-3 CMI Fremont ISD.

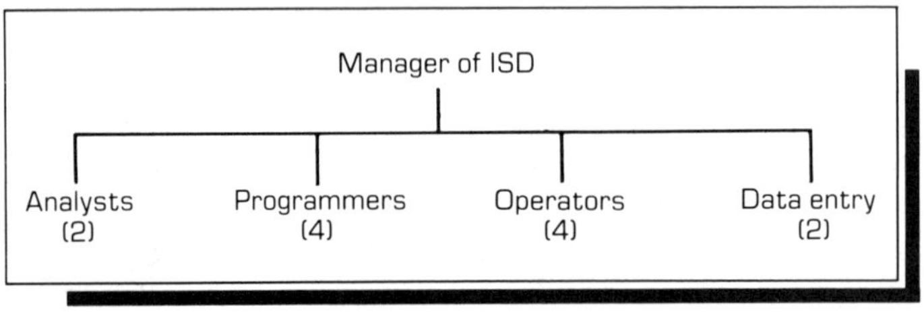

FIGURE 4-4 CMI Omaha ISD.

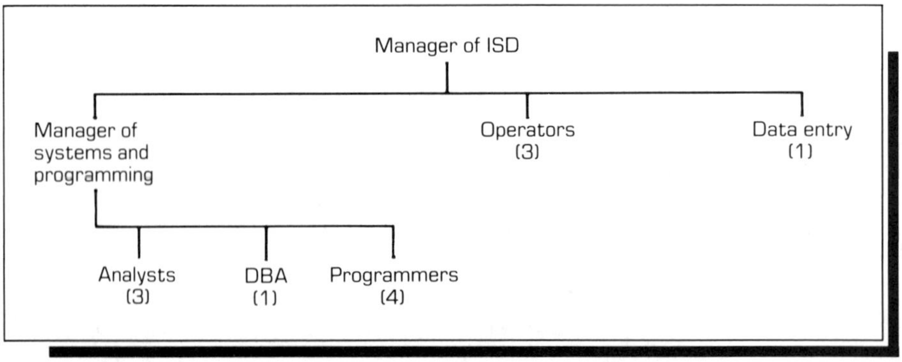

FIGURE 4-5 CMI Chicago ISD.

Mary started to work on a memorandum to her vice president, Bob Carlin, with a copy to Tom White, the CIO for CMI. She outlined her arguments from an organizational standpoint and with the objective of providing better service. As she started to dictate the memo, her phone rang again with the news that an operator error in mounting a tape had forced the data center to abort a lengthy run; the operators wondered if they should work overtime after midnight to rerun the job. . . .

Recommended Readings

Nolan, R., "Managing Information Systems by Committee," *Harvard Business Review,* vol. 60, no. 4 (July–August 1982), pp. 72–79. (An influential paper on how committees have been used to improve the management of information services.)

Zmud, R., "Design Alternatives for Information Systems Activities," *MIS Quarterly,* vol. 8, no. 2 (June 1984), pp. 79–92. (A particularly modern approach to the functions that should be included in an ISD.)

Discussion Problems

4.1 The Morris Manufacturing Company had a long history of stormy relations between the ISD and users. At one point, the firm became so disgusted with computer services that it fired most of its information processing staff and brought in an outside consultant to act as a facilities management contractor.

One of the first acts of the consultant was to form an executive steering committee. There were so many requests for new systems and for changes to existing applications that the consultant's staff did not know where to begin. The first steering committee meeting was an informal one in which several managers caught the manager of the ISD in the hall and took him to a conference room to complain. Reputable sources said later that several reports were thrown either at the manager or at least across the room.

After this episode, the steering committee met monthly to talk about how to set priorities. Generally, the managers lacked knowledge about how systems functioned; they also were very impatient with how long it took for the ISD staff to make changes or develop new systems. Soon the steering committee stopped meeting and there seemed to be little communications among users, managers, and the ISD staff. What do you think went wrong? How could Morris and the consultant revive the steering committee?

4.2. Amalgamated Industries is planning to decentralize information processing to three divisions. The bulk of current processing is done on a large mainframe computer, and the divisions constantly complain about the service they receive. The division managers also feel that there is a great deal of overhead in information services. They are convinced that the divisions can get better processing for less money if they do it themselves.

The manager of corporate processing has reluctantly agreed to go along with the proposal, since he sees no way around it. However, he wonders how the divisions can do processing for less money. "All of our programs are designed to be run in a centralized manner on the IBM 370 architecture. We can't just take one division and give it the code; the programs will have to be changed to run for a single division. Our logic now, right or wrong, is that of one large program with branches in it for each division."

He also feels that the divisions are getting into more than they know: "None of these managers has the slightest idea of how to manage information services. They will try to do it with the minimum staff possible and will soon be having the same problems they have with us. Only these managers won't have professionals to help them solve their problems."

What is your evaluation of the split into divisions? What can Amalgamated do to ease the transition? What do you think has motivated the division managers?

Questions

1. What is included in systems development?
2. Why is systems development such an important activity for the ISD?
3. What are some of the problems with systems analysis and design?
4. What is end-user computing?
5. What is required to support end users?
6. What is an information center? What should it contain?
7. What might the duties be for a manager of microcomputing?
8. What is the role of operations?
9. What are the differences between batch and on-line applications where operations is concerned?
10. Why should an ISD consider having an R&D function?
11. What are the duties of R&D within information services?
12. Why is there a need for a planning function within ISD?
13. What is quality control with respect to information systems?
14. How should a quality control or quality assurance group interface with operations? With systems analysis and design?
15. Describe matrix management.
16. Why is matrix management so popular for systems analysts and programmers?
17. Why might a large firm have systems development groups organized by function? For example, why might a large bank have a systems development group and even a computer center for its trust operation?
18. Why is management information services such a complex task?
19. What is the purpose of an executive steering committee?
20. How do the functions of a local steering committee in a division differ from those of an executive steering committee?
21. How should a maintenance committee function?
22. Why is there no one right structure for information services?
23. What design principles help in deciding what kind of structure to recommend for the ISD?

5

New Technology and Applications

The management of information processing has often been driven by technology. Rather than determining what kind of organization management wants and then choosing appropriate technology, firms have let technological fads and fashions determine how to manage information processing. Figure 5-1 depicts the role of technology in the management of information processing. In the next chapter, we discuss planning in some detail. It is important for management not to assume that one form of processing or technology is necessarily best. It should determine, first, the goals of the organization: what kinds of services should be provided? Then it should choose the most appropriate technology, whether distributed processing, microcomputers, mainframes, or some combination of these options.

The available technology provides choices for processing information. Ten years ago, it was far too expensive to provide individual users with computers; today the investment for a personal computer is not much more than for a sophisticated typewriter. Ten years ago, then, we could not consider providing computers to users; today that is an important and often chosen option. Changes in the technology and its costs have thus created a new opportunity; however, the fact that the opportunity is there does not mean that it is necessarily the solution for every problem.

In this chapter, we explore what some of the new technologies mean for the organization and for managing information services. It is assumed that

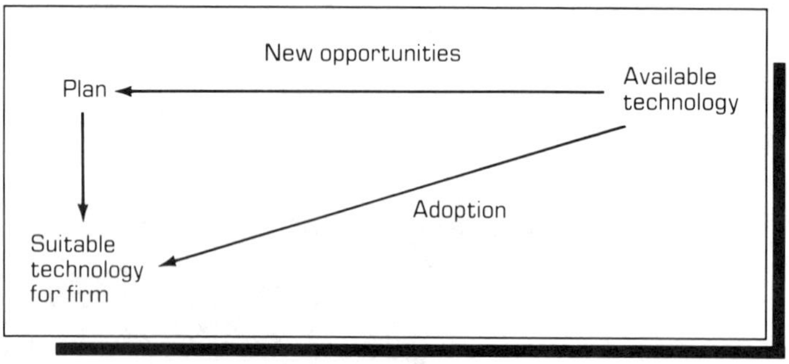

FIGURE 5-1 The role of technology.

the reader is familiar with the details of the technology; for an explanation of computer technology for management, see Lucas (1986). We shall concentrate on the *implications* of the technology for the organization, rather than on details of how the technology functions. See Table 5-1.

Patterns of Processing

Earlier we described distributed processing, the interconnection of computers at different locations. Without planning or management intervention, it appears that the natural trend today is toward distributed processing. While at first users may enjoy the independence created by decentralization through local departmental minis and micros, they soon want to access large databases stored on computers at different locations.

Connecting to different computers, even for only a short time, requires that the firm support distributed processing. Technological developments in the information processing industry today focus on allowing computers to communicate with each other. See Table 5-2.

Networks

When computers are connected for communication purposes, they form a network. The simplest network is the one offered by common carriers like

TABLE 5-1 Technological Trends and Their Implications

Technology	Implications
Networks	Plan for networked environment and consider compatibility today
DBMSs	Plan for DBMSs, especially relational models
4GLs	Adopt for end-user computing and systems professionals
Expert systems	Investigate opportunities
Workstations	Develop and install networked workstations
Applications	Look for competitive and strategic applications

TABLE 5-2 Some Distributed Processing Communications Alternatives

Common carrier dial-up service
Private lines leased by the organization
Value-added networks (VANs), e.g., packet switched data networks offered by common carriers
LANs
Private branch exchanges (PBXs)
Direct micro–mainframe links

the telephone company. As an example, consider the ability to dial a university computer from a remote location such as a dormitory; the regular switched voice network provides the connection.

For a relatively local organization like a university, the cost of dial-up service is reasonable. However, if the individuals who need to connect with a computer are dispersed over a wide region, the organization may want to consider a private network of some kind.

Basically, in a private network, an organization leases lines that are permanently assigned to the firm. The firm creates a network of these lines to carry traffic among its terminals and computer devices. Usually a combination of lines of different speeds is used, depending on the traffic between nodes on the network.

As an example, consider an airline reservation system. The American Airlines system supports some 65,000 terminals, which are connected to 4 large IBM mainframe systems (with a fifth computer on standby for backup purposes). The network for this system consists of a variety of lines and devices to combine traffic from low-speed terminals and send it over higher-speed lines. (High-speed lines cost less to lease than the equivalent capacity from a group of lower-speed lines.) A firm with a major nationwide on-line system can and must have a group of experts on the staff to plan and manage its network.

A smaller firm may imitate what American has done; it can develop a network appropriate to its situation. Alternatively, it can choose a different alternative, a service provided by a common carrier. Recognizing the market for networks, a number of firms offer their customers the opportunity to use an existing network. Usually these nets are packet switched, that is, a packet of data is assembled and sent over the network. One message may consist of several packets. The network routes the packets to their destination and reconstructs the message from the packets.

Firms like Telenet offer packet switched networks. One can also use services provided by AT&T and MCI and avoid the construction of a private network. Whatever the choice, there are a number of options for constructing this type of wide area network.

At the other extreme, consider a single department that may want to share computers or devices on a local network. For example, a group of users may want to share the services of a large, hard disk. The group may invest in one laser printer to serve 8 or 10 users, since it is hard to justify the investment required to provide each user with a laser printer.

The LAN is enjoying rapid growth. Typically it is used to link together a group of personal computers that are reasonably close to each other. Most of the networks require users to purchase a special interface board, and all require that some computer memory be dedicated to the network software when a computer is active on the network. A LAN has much to recommend it; however, organizations find that LANs may require a relatively high cost for each machine on the network. As costs come down, we may expect LANs to become commonplace in organizations. The LANs will also have gateways (connections) to other wider area networks.

The PBX

Fourth-generation private branch exchanges (PBXs) offer competition to the LAN for connecting computers. The first generation of PBXs was like a telephone central office switch installed in a private location. Operators worked with cords to link extensions to outside lines. Second-generation systems during the 1970s introduced software to direct calls automatically, replacing the electromechanical switches of the first generation. In the 1980s, third-generation PBXs routinely carry both voice and data transmissions. These devices also feature call accounting and automatic route selection to connect with the lowest-cost long-distance service.

The fourth generation integrates LANs into the PBX. Third-generation devices transmitted at a rate of 56 to 64 kilobits per second. New cable-based LANs operate at speeds of 5 to 50 megabits per second, and fourth-generation PBXs are trying to achieve speeds closer to those of LANs. These more advanced systems digitize voice signals and combine them on the line with digital data from computers.

A major trend in PBX design is to distribute more of the intelligence to local devices. In the first generation, the central switchboard was crucial. Today there are PBXs that contain no central logic; all intelligence is located at local nodes. More common is a mixed system, containing both central logic and local processing. For example, digital PBXs generally digitize the voice at the telephone instrument, using special chips in the handset. The PBX offers a possible alternative to creating a network in an office. Combinations of a PBX to handle low-frequency data transmission and a LAN to handle large volumes of data are one communications strategy.

Micro–Mainframe Links

Another type of distributed processing occurs when a user connects a personal computer to a mainframe to download data. In most instances the direction is from the mainframe down, as information services personnel are reluctant to let users input data to databases unless IS professionals have designed input edits and controls. Inputs and updates to databases should come through regular transactions so that they are carefully edited and validated.

In this application, users want to turn their micro into something more than a terminal; they want to capture data from the mainframe and put it on a disk or diskette on the micro for further processing. This operation requires users to have software that runs on the personal computer and on the mainframe. Users must also know how to extract the data they want from the mainframe; the software must transfer the data to the personal computer, where it is stored. The software must also format the data so that programs on the personal computer can access it.

Compatibility

A major issue in distributed processing and the creation of networks is compatibility. If all of the devices on a network have the same machine language and use the same code for communications, the creation of a network is much easier. What happens if different computers are incompatible? What happens if some use one type of machine language and communications code, while others use different conventions? Creating a network is not impossible under these conditions, but it becomes more complicated. Some kind of processing must be done to interface the various devices on the network.

A common carrier that offers network services has to provide these interface devices. A private network developer must be concerned about compatibility; he or she will have to find networks that support different types of computers and communications protocols.

Digital Equipment Corporation (DEC) has been making inroads on IBM's customer base because DEC's computers are all based on the same architecture; they can communicate with each other easily and exhibit high connectivity. IBM has recently consolidated its computer lines, but it is still faced with four architectures that its networking products will have to support: the IBM personal computer on the micro end; the System 36 and System 38 architectures in the minicomputer market; and the 4300 supermini and 3090 Sierra series, which follow the old 360/370 architecture. To ameliorate some of the problems of compatibility, IBM has introduced the 9370, a departmental computer with the 370 instruction set. This move will let users run programs for the 370 across a wide range of computers. However, there are still systems software incompatibilities among operating systems that will create barriers to complete compatibility such as that offered by DEC, with its VAX system and VMS operating system.

Future Trends

It is likely that communications among computers will increase, probably for business reasons rather than dramatic cost reductions or breakthroughs in the technology. There has been more competition in the telecommunications industry since the breakup of AT&T; however, historically, computer hardware costs have fallen much faster than communications costs.

We shall continue to see private and common carrier services used for wide area networks. Firms will experiment with LANs, but we may require the next generation of micros, with much larger primary memory and possibly built-in network interfaces, before LANs become commonplace. After all, many users want personal computers to be independent of other machines. A LAN means sharing resources and the user wanted to get away from sharing when he or she acquired a micro!

The common carriers are developing integrated services digital networks (ISDNs) in an attempt to capture a firm's total communications activities. An ISDN supports data communications directly, since the underlying technology is digital. Sampling techniques are used to encode the human voice so that the digital network can also be used for voice communications.

The move toward ISDN-type services suggests that firms are likely to view voice and data communications as integrated rather than completely separate organizationally. Whether communications will become a unique organizational entity or will be subsumed under information services because of the volume of communications among computers remains to be seen.

Many attempts are also being made to define standards among organizations in order to encourage communications. A manufacturing automation protocol (MAP) is being developed for factory communications. The automobile industry is supporting committees working on electronic data interchange. The purpose of this effort is to develop common purchase order and invoice documents so that suppliers and purchasers of goods can communicate electronically rather than on paper.

Other industries have developed standards in order to apply technology more effectively. For example, the grocery industry and food packagers have agreed on the Universal Product Code for store scanner systems for customer checkout. The airline industry has a message switching network that is used by major airlines, and there are a number of standards for processing information electronically in the banking industry.

In the future, we expect to see wider adoption of electronic interchange among organizations, not only in the same but in different industries as well. By transmitting information electronically, organizations will reduce the amount of data entry required and will increase the accuracy and speed of communications.

Opportunities

The tremendous flexibility provided by communications means that the organization can contemplate putting computers anywhere it likes. The technology exists to provide remote access to highly centralized computer facilities. There is also the option of placing smaller computers in a number of locations and sharing data among them. The technology will provide very little help in making this kind of decision; instead the ISD manager and senior management will have to consider the variables and issues discussed in Chapter 2 when deciding what kind of processing best fits the organization.

Existing and coming technology for communications will facilitate a movement toward more intraorganizational systems. One way to obtain a competitive advantage with computers is to connect systems directly to suppliers to reduce costs. For example, Detroit auto manufacturers are establishing links with their suppliers to better coordinate the shipments of parts to factories.

The trend toward intraorganizational processing depends completely on the availability of telecommunications capabilities. As users exhaust the capabilities of their personal computers, they will want to join networks in order to access data from corporate computers. While not necessarily elegant, technology exists today to make this kind of connection possible.

Current telecommunications and future technology are enablers at this point; technology will contribute to organizational plans, not inhibit them.

Challenges for Management

While in theory all of the components are present, configuring, installing, and operating a network are still complicated tasks. One firm simply wanted to place a terminal displaying three different screens in customer locations. The company contracted with one of the packet switched carriers so that it would not have to develop its own network. Despite the relatively small amount of programming required and the fact that only three or four customers were involved at first, the project took over 6 months and, at last report, the system was not operational. ISD staff involved in the project encountered many problems in working with the equipment installed to interface their computers with the network. There were also problems in training customers to use the system.

The point of this story is that firms have to manage the development of networks carefully. One reason to have a plan is to anticipate the kind of networking that will be needed in the future. Then today's decision on equipment can be made with future networking considerations in mind. While it is possible to interface various types of incompatible equipment, the development of networks will be simpler if devices are as compatible as possible. Chapter 20 discusses some of the operational problems of managing communications in the firm.

Database Management Systems

DBMSs do not represent a particularly new technology. Thus, it is surprising that many firms have not yet invested in these systems, which can dramatically improve the quality of applications and their speed of development. There are a number of reasons for using a DBMS.

1. A DBMS creates more independence between data and the programs that access them, facilitating changes. Data independence is so important that it is sometimes called the *database concept;* the greater the separation between data and programs, the better.

2. It reduces the duplication of data. Variables are stored only once, rather than maintained in separate files, when common data are used by more than one application.

3. It provides the DBA with a language to define the logical and physical characteristics of data. This language is often called the *data definition language;* it provides a common way to describe data in the firm.

4. It provides file access routines; the system builds directories and keeps track of pointers so that the programmer does not have to do so.

5. It also provides facilities to help protect the integrity and security of data.

6. Increasingly, it is built around a data dictionary. The dictionary is a repository of information about each data element. The dictionary shows the data structures of which the element is a part. It also defines the element and has a list of modules that use the data. If it is necessary to change the definition of the data, the DBA knows immediately all programs that are affected by the change.

7. It is usually packaged with a query language; this language facilitates ad hoc inquiries of the database. With some training, users should be able to formulate requests with this language so that the programming staff does not have to be involved when the user has a simple query.

A DBMS is a software product; it is not a hardware device that is subject to technological breakthroughs. Today the software technology is gradually moving to relational databases. The relational model appears to be the easiest for users to understand and manipulate. The vast majority of DBMS packages for micros are constructed around the relational model.

The standards set by microcomputer DBMS packages should improve the quality of packages for mainframes and minis. The micro systems have to be easy to use so that a nonprofessional can build a system with them. Mainframe packages today belong to the DBA, systems analysts, and professional programmers. Vendors are rushing to add and integrate data dictionaries with their mainframe DBMS packages and to make their query languages more powerful.

Opportunities

A DBMS is a systems development tool for the professional systems analyst and programmer. There is a steep learning curve and a high cost to the acquisition of this software. An organization with a large mainframe can expect to invest $250,000 to $1 million in purchasing a DBMS and training the staff to use it.

The purpose of this investment is to increase productivity in several ways. First, once implemented, the DBMS makes it possible to define data structures and create the database with far less programming than is required using a normal development language like COBOL. Second, because the investment in programming is less, the DBMS makes it easier to change the system while it is under development. Finally, the DBMS makes it easier to change an application after it is operational; this should reduce the maintenance programming task.

Challenges for Management

The first management challenge is to select a DBMS, whether for a mainframe, mini, or micro. There are a number of competing products, and the organization will have to delineate its needs, study the options, and choose the most appropriate package. It is important to choose a system that will grow with the firm; changing from one system to another is not recommended.

The next challenge involves training and motivating the staff to use the system. The organization will need a DBA to manage the system and its applications. The first application undertaken using the system will probably take longer than predicted until the staff gets used to the system. However, the investment is for subsequent applications, which should proceed more quickly with the system than without it.

This discussion implies that the DBMS is not so integrating that we lose the concept of separate applications. Is there not one large database for the entire organization? Conceptually one could think of all the data in a firm as constituting its database. For most organizations, however, the size and complexity of the results make it impossible to consider creating a single database for the organization. Instead, firms tend to use a DBMS for a number of different applications. Compared to the use of COBOL programs and sequential files, a single application using the DBMS would encompass the functions performed by a number of separate systems in the days before database development. However, if there are no data in common between a system to manage inventory and one to do standard cost accounting, why complicate the development process by trying to force the systems into the same database?

Fourth-Generation Languages

The definition of a fourth-generation language (4GL) is not very clear. During the period when COBOL was becoming the language of choice for developing commercial applications, some vendors began offering programs that they called *report generators.* A user specified the contents of a data file and the format of a report. The report generator then retrieved the data requested and produced a report.

Gradually, the capabilities of the generators expanded. They began to process complex queries with different logical conditions like AND and OR. They usually gave the user the ability to do calculations on the records retrieved, and possibly to do calculations on a record before deciding to include it in the report.

Because the languages were intended to speed the generation of reports, they tended to accomplish a great deal with one statement. The language might include a command like SUMMARIZE BY REGION to produce a control total for sales in a region. To accomplish the same task in a procedural language would require many statements. Vendors began referring to these expanded report generators as *nonprocedural languages;* the user came closer to telling the computer what should be done rather than how to do it.

Is there a language that is totally nonprocedural? For commercial processing, the answer is probably "no." The system has to have some procedures for processing. However, a nonprocedural language reduces dramatically the amount of coding that must be done for a given task. Since the languages are considered higher in level than COBOL and FORTRAN, which are third-generation languages, these more nonprocedural languages have been labeled *fourth-generation languages.*

These languages, along with query languages from a DBMS, made end-user computing possible. Because the languages are sufficiently higher in level than COBOL, they can be taught to users. If users are given some help in defining the file contents, they can generate some of the reports needed without having to wait or take the time of the professional computer programmer.

Opportunities

The 4GLs generally put users in touch with data stored on a mainframe computer. One of these languages, FOCUS, comes with mainframe, mini, and personal computer versions. However, at first it ran only on large mainframe computers. The term *end-user computing* has now been expanded to include all of the work done by users on micros.

End-user computing provides many advantages for the ISD. First, it reduces some of the department's workload; users can now do some of their own computing. In the early days of telephones, projections were done showing that every man, woman, and child in the United States would have to become a telephone operator if the rate of phone calls was maintained. As a result, the phone company brought in new technology: the central office with automatic switching equipment. In effect, the phone company made everyone a telephone operator for local calls. Many years later, the phone system did the same thing for station-to-station long-distance calls.

End-user computing can help accomplish the same thing for information services. There is too much demand and too few human resources to meet every user's request for systems and services. Only by doing some of the processing themselves will users be able to obtain the information they want.

In addition, end-user computing should help users understand more about the technology and its limitations. We have mentioned that most individuals in the firm seem to know far more about all other aspects of the business than they do about information processing. Hands-on experience should help users to understand the technology better.

One New York investment firm brought in a new CIO who immediately stopped development in COBOL. He hired several analysts and brought in ADABASE and NATURAL. ADABASE is a DBMS and NATURAL is a 4GL that works through the DBMS. This CIO's objective was to increase the productivity of systems development dramatically at the cost of using more hardware resources. (It is generally agreed that 4GLs use hardware less efficiently than languages like COBOL.) The plan succeeded in that an exponentially increasing number of systems were completed and put into production.

Challenges for Management

End-user computing is a mixed blessing. A number of ISD managers have been less than enthusiastic about supporting it. Information services must provide consulting assistance and training for users. One manager was reluctant to let users work with a newly acquired 4GL because he was afraid that they would put too much of a demand on his mainframe computer. This manager failed to understand that hardware is available and cheap; users would join him in a request for a more powerful machine if they were satisfied with the results they were getting from a 4GL. Some managers predict that within 5 years they will have more hardware devoted to users who run their own programs than to the conventional production systems now run by the ISD.

Management, then, has two problems. The first is to train and support users working with 4GLs; the second is to prepare the staff for a 4GL. End-user computing must be included in hardware and staff support plans.

Finally, if ISD management wants to use a 4GL for development work, it must determine what projects will be most beneficial and convince the staff to work with the 4GL. In an application for motor vehicle registrations and drivers' licenses in New Jersey, a consulting firm used a 4GL for all programs in the system. Because the 4GL had efficiency problems, the entire system was unable to provide an acceptable on-line response or to finish batch processing in the time available overnight. A 4GL can be a productivity tool in systems development, but it must be used with discretion.

Expert Systems and DSS

There is much current interest in an applied branch of artificial intelligence known as *expert systems (ES).* An ES captures the knowledge of a human expert as a series of rules. These rules and facts about the application domain constitute the knowledge base of the system.

ES languages, or shells, interpret the rules when asked a question. For example, an ES might be used to diagnose problems of engine maintenance. The user inputs the symptoms of the problem and the system consults its rules to suggest the probable problem.

A number of firms report that they are developing ES, but say little about them because they hope that the system will provide an edge on the competition. For example, several commercial systems are offered to financial consultants. These systems contain a series of investments and the complicated rules that determine when the investment is appropriate for a given client.

ES are exciting because they represent a new use of the computer—not just processing data or transactions. With an ES, the computer processes symbols and engages in extensive pattern matching. There are ES shells for mainframes, minis, and micros. Since the language LISP is often used for building a system or a shell, one can also purchase a computer whose machine language is LISP, to be used in developing an ES.

We expect to see continued interest in the use of ES. These applications are particularly attractive when it is helpful to make expertise more widely available in the organization or when there is much routine advice that can free an advisor for more complex tasks. ES technology is also appropriate when key individuals are likely to retire or leave the organization and there is no real replacement.

Decision support systems (DSS) have been around for a long time; the term was first used to try to distinguish between computer systems that primarily process transactions and those that aid decision making. Early DSS applications were for mainframes or minicomputers and generally fell into one of two categories: data analysis or model based.

A system for data analysis provides an extensive database and a series of analytical tools. Users retrieve and process the data of interest to them. As an example, one large manufacturing firm maintains an extensive database of all of its equipment; it tracks customers and the products they have installed. Planners access this database to answer a number of questions. A planner might be investigating a new attachment for a particular piece of equipment. This individual can obtain a list of all customers having the equipment and can forecast market potential for the product.

A model-based DSS includes some kind of model, often an optimizing operations research model. One airline developed a model of where to refuel its planes and saved $6 million in the first year of use. On the basis of relative fuel costs, the model showed where the airline should buy fuel and when a plane should carry extra fuel to avoid refueling at a high-cost airport. Before the use of the DSS, operators calculated a manual fuel plan once a month or less; the DSS can be run in 20 minutes to generate plans when fuel prices change.

The DSS just described were developed by company staff members or consultants. The greatest expansion in the development of DSS applications has come from the microcomputer and its spreadsheet programs. When an individual builds a spreadsheet model, it is often used for decision making and therefore qualifies as a DSS.

Given the dramatic expansion of end-user computing, it is likely that the DSS and ES fields will grow. As users become more familiar with the power of the computer, they will look for more advanced ways to solve problems. The technology behind DSS and ES will provide this power.

Opportunities

Transactions processing systems provide great benefit to a firm; in some cases, the tasks performed would be impossible without a computer. Consider trying to provide thousands of travel agents with the ability to make airline reservations and calculate fares under deregulation. This task would be impossible without elaborate airline reservations systems connected to travel agents' offices.

However, there is also much to be gained by using a computer for more decision-oriented tasks. A single DSS may save the firm millions of dollars each year by allowing it to manage its cash more efficiently. Another DSS might help managers decide whether to merge with another firm. An ES could provide a competitive advantage by dramatically lowering costs or capturing the imagination of the consumer. Will the first automobile company that has a complete ES resident at each dealership for diagnosing and repairing its cars have a major advantage?

Challenges for Management

One of the major problems with DSS and ES technology is the fact that there is no guarantee of results. Particularly with today's ES, one cannot promise that an application will provide benefits to the organization. To some extent, the same is true for DSS, though this technology is more mature and there are systems that clearly benefit the firm.

The design of an ES or DSS requires a great deal of input from the manager or expert involved. The decision process is so central that in most cases the manager cannot delegate DSS design to subordinates. The ISD must also use different design approaches in building these systems; prototyping is particularly appropriate. Despite these problems, DSS and ES offer a way to develop systems that perform well and have high visibility. With the potential of high rewards, however, firms must also accept a greater risk that the projects will not succeed.

Workstations

A workstation is a computer device dedicated to a particular function. The first workstations were developed in the engineering field; an engineer worked with a powerful minis or micros to perform tasks like circuit design. With low-cost micros now available, the idea of the managerial workstation is being developed.

A workstation for a manager would include a spreadsheet program, word processor, database manager, communications and electronic mail capabilities, and some form of presentation graphics. There would also be special programs for the individual's functional area, such as accounting or finance.

In the future, we expect to see personal computers being turned into workstations. To achieve this evolution, the personal computer has to have a hard disk of its own or share one in a network. The hard disk makes it possible to store and quickly use the variety of programs necessary to provide the functions of the workstation. There will also be some kind of overall manager, such as a shell, hiding the operating system from the user. These shells, which are available now, allow the user to load a program into memory and begin executing it with the use of a few keystrokes.

Several leading firms have announced plans to provide, within a few years at least, one terminal or personal computer for every professional employee, including secretaries. Both IBM and Travelers Insurance have ambitious programs to expand computing facilities to their employees. It will not take long for terminals and small personal computers to turn into full-fledged workstations.

Opportunities

As with end-user computing, the proliferation of managerial workstations offers added resources for the ISD. Managers will see that the technology can play a part in their daily lives; computer systems will not be isolated and used only by clerical employees.

Challenges for Management

The risk with workstations, as with end-user computing in general, is that managers will become less and less satisfied with conventional systems. The software and user interface for the mass market confronted by microcomputer software vendors has set new standards. The workstation will provide a much more pleasant environment than the typical application designed by ISD personnel.

All of the optimistic projections for workstations assume that the technology will work. Who will train the users? Who will ensure that the data a user might want to access from the mainframe are available? If there is inadequate support, users may turn out to be as disappointed with managerial workstations as they are with some of the conventional systems in the firm. The challenge for the ISD is to test the technology in advance and to provide support so that users of managerial workstations will become enthusiasts for information systems.

Applications

We have already sketched some applications, such as expert systems and decision support systems. Probably the greatest interest today is in the strategic use of the technology. Can the firm devise applications that will give it a competitive edge?

In 1982 Lucas and Turner suggested that a firm can use technology strategically in three different ways. First, the firm can develop traditional computer applications that result in greater efficiencies, contributing to the overall performance of the business. Second, the firm can use technology as an aid in strategic planning, for example, through a DSS for planners. Finally, the firm at the most sophisticated level can use information processing as part of its strategy.

There are three widely discussed generic strategies that a firm can follow. The first is to become the low-cost producer in the field; here strategy dictates high levels of efficiency. Firms have used computers extensively to cut manufacturing and inventory costs to achieve low-cost production. A company like Tandy (Radio Shack stores) is a low-cost producer.

The next strategy is to differentiate one's product. Companies like BMW and Mercedes Benz have enjoyed huge profits by differentiating their cars from domestic automobiles and charging the buyer a large premium. One can envision using computer support to enhance product differentiation—say, by having totally automated parts inventories, roadside service, and so on.

Finally, a firm can attempt to fill a particular market niche. In the computer industry, Compaq is a good example of this strategy. IBM did not make a transportable personal computer at first; Compaq established itself in that market and developed a good enough product that IBM was unable to market its own model successfully.

A good example of technology in strategy is the Merrill Lynch Cash Management Account (CMA). Originally, investors who bought stocks and bonds through Merrill Lynch did not earn interest on the idle funds in their accounts. An individual in the firm had the idea of sweeping customers' funds into one of Merrill Lynch's liquid assets funds automatically each day. The idea expanded to include a credit card and check-writing privileges. The CMA has been tremendously successful; over 1 million customers now receive this type of service. Merrill Lynch has earned over $50 million by managing the liquid assets funds holding customers' cash. The only lost revenue is the interest that the firm no longer earns on the idle cash.

In this example, the technology became a part of strategy and a part of the product sold by Merrill Lynch. How does a firm decide whether or not it can use the technology strategically? Cash, McFarlan and McKenney (1988) have suggested a framework for the strategic relevance of information technology, as shown in Figure 5-2.

In the strategic cell of the figure are companies for whom information processing is critical to operations. New applications are of crucial importance for competitive success. Examples of firms in this category are those that process information as a basic activity, like banks and insurance companies.

Turnaround companies receive IS support through operations but are not completely dependent on this support to achieve their objectives. Cash, McFarlan and McKenney cite a manufacturing firm in which IS technology

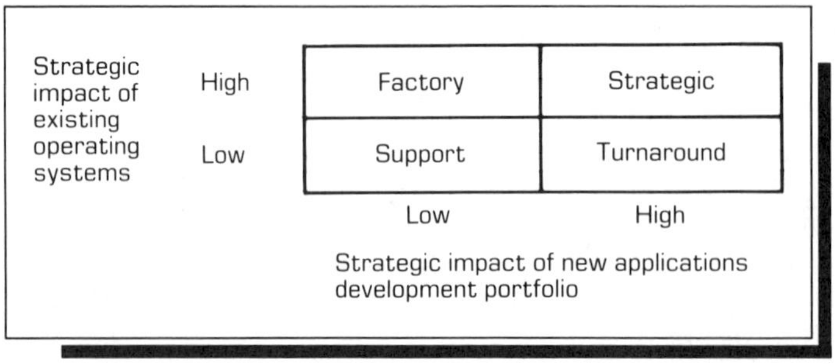

FIGURE 5-2 The Cash-McFarlan-McKenney framework. (From Cash, McFarlan and McKenney, 1988)

was embedded in accounting and factories but was not essential for continued functioning of the firm.

Firms in the factory cell are dependent on cost-effective, reliable systems. Applications in firms in this cell are dominated by maintenance; the systems are not fundamental to the firm's ability to compete.

Support category firms are not dependent operationally on the computer, nor do they use systems that have great strategic impact. In these firms, one usually finds more mundane, clearly cost-justified applications; ISD is lower in the organization and receives less senior management attention.

The framework presented in this figure is a popular one, yet it is unsatisfactory because of what it implies. Looking at Figure 5-2, we could argue that only firms in the strategic cell need to be concerned about information processing. A firm in the support cell needs only to keep on developing its applications.

The framework's view of the world allows senior management who wants to ignore information processing to do so in great comfort. However, this policy is perhaps shortsighted. Not every firm will find a strategic application, but the potential payoff from finding one is so great that we should never stop looking. In addition, as the trends discussed previously are realized, all firms, even those in the support cell of Figure 5-2, will find that information processing technology has a dramatic impact on the organization and the way individuals work. The pervasiveness of workstations and applications demands management attention. No organization can afford to ignore information processing technology if it is to flourish in the next decade.

Opportunities

The opportunities for developing new and exciting applications are limitless. Systems development is a creative activity; so is the task of deciding in what area the firm should develop a system. Strategic applications may occur through bottom-up invention, in which someone below the top levels of the organization is working on a project that will have strategic significance when completed. Another approach to finding strategic applications is through top-down scanning; senior managers are constantly monitoring the environment, looking for opportunities and threats. In today's highly competitive world, the strategic use of technology becomes another opportunity to gain a competitive edge.

Challenges for Management

The greatest management challenge for the strategic use of technology is competence. There are many firms where it would be unwise to undertake a strategic application. In such firms the ISD does not perform well; there are bitter relations between computer professionals and users and management. A strategic application often involves individuals or firms outside of the organization; failure is far more evident than with an internal system. To enjoy the benefits of a strategic application, the firm must be able to manage information processing well. In some instances, it may be necessary to contract out the development of a strategic system if there is too little confidence in the ability of the firm's own ISD.

A Scenario

Based on the predictions in this chapter, we can sketch a scenario for a leading firm in the coming decade. Most individuals in the firm use a computer in their daily work. Professional workers have managerial workstations that provide spreadsheet programs, word processing, database management, and presentation graphics.

The production staff and clerical workers have terminals and microcomputers for data entry. Manufacturing processes are largely monitored and controlled by computers. The firm is connected electronically to suppliers and customers so that the amount of duplicate data entry among organizations is minimized.

Employees communicate with each other using electronic and voice mail systems; they also communicate electronically with relevant individuals outside the organization. For example, customer services sends electronic messages to and receives messages from customers.

The pattern of processing is not too important to users because the quality of service is high. Almost all computers are on a network, and there are gateways to the networks of other firms to facilitate intrafirm communications. Since the network functions well and users have substantial computer power on their desks, the actual location of minis and mainframes is not an issue.

However, the issues of who design systems and where designers are located are still important. Divisional and departmental managers have to decide whether end users are to develop an application and whether it is to run on a micro, mini, or mainframe. Local management must also decide whether to support local professional systems analysts or rely on a central group. The technology will offer many options; management has the difficult task of deciding which options make the most sense for the organization.

An Example

An example will help demonstrate how the technology and management considerations are intertwined in the development of a competitive application. The system in this example was developed by a major money center bank. The application involves customer cash management.

Prior to the development of the system, the treasurer of a firm doing business with the bank had to plan the disposition of cash each day. The treasurer probably has multiple accounts in 5 to 15 or more banks. In the morning, the treasury staff at the firm determines its cash balance in all banks and accounts.

In the early days of computing, treasury staff members had to call banks for this information. The next step was for the banks to post their balances to an on-line system, which could be accessed by customers. With either the phone or the inquiry method, the treasurer had to work with a series of handwritten numbers on various forms representing balances in different accounts. There were many errors, which were aggravated by the time pressures involved. By noon or 1 P.M., the treasurer had to decide whether to move money to various accounts, invest excess funds, and/or borrow short-term funds to cover the firm's cash requirements.

The bank in this example developed a microcomputer system to aid the treasurer in managing cash. The system stores the reporting formats for 80 to 100 different banks; early in the morning, it automatically dials the banks with which a given customer does business and retrieves the firm's balances. The balance information is posted to a spreadsheet that the treasurer can use to plan his or her actions. The micro allows the treasurer to initiate wire transfers and to invest extra cash or borrow automatically.

The system has many functions beyond those described. It serves to bring the customer closer to the bank. Since the bank earns fees from transactions, the microstation generates revenue as customers use it as their primary method for wiring funds. The microstation also draws the customer closer to the bank; it encourages the customer to do more business at the bank, according to bank client representatives.

A number of competitors of the bank tried to develop similar systems; many were unsuccessful. The bank in this case began work on the system using the staff from an internal time-sharing subsidiary. However, this staff wanted to design a system that had the microstation serving as a front end for the time-sharing computer in order to maintain work on the time-sharing system.

As the project developed, the goals of the designers and the time-sharing development team diverged to the point where the developer turned to an independent contractor and bought a new, but very similar, system from an outside vendor. The new system has been a tremendous success for both the bank and its customers. One customer explained that this system was superior to those offered by the competition because the bank took the time to look at the treasurer's function from the treasurer's point of view rather than the bank's.

In this case, development of the microstation did not proceed smoothly. However, the firm was able to manage the project and to deal with crises as they developed. There was leadership, project management, and technological knowledge. Success comes from a combination of factors; the technology, present and future, is only one component. It is important to take advantage of what the technology has to offer, but technology will not substitute for effective management.

Recommended Readings

Cash, J., F. W. McFarlan, and J. McKenney, *Corporate Information Systems Management: The Issues Facing Senior Executives,* 2nd ed. Homewood, Ill.: Richard D. Irwin, 1988. (A useful book stressing top management's view of information systems.)

Lucas, H. C., Jr., *Information Systems Concepts for Management,* 3rd ed. New York, McGraw-Hill, 1986. (A book intended for a person with an MBA who wants an overview of systems, management, and technology.)

Lucas, H. C., Jr., and H. Krcmar, "Developing Strategic Information Systems," (1988), forthcoming. (A case study of the development of competitive application.)

Lucas, H. C., Jr., and J. Turner, "A Corporate Strategy for the Control of Information Processing," *Sloan Management Review,* vol. 23, no. 3 (Spring, 1982), pp. 25–36. (A framework for the use of technology and corporate strategy.)

Discussion Problems

5.1 Many managers resist adopting new technology; they prefer to take a conservative approach and see if the technology works and offers something to their firm. Such caution is highly advisable because often technology is used to solve problems for which it is not the best solution.

However, one can err in the other direction. In an effort to maximize yearly earnings, the Bank of America economized on expenditures for information processing technology. As a result, the bank fell behind its competitors. Branches lacked information on all of the business that customers had with the bank and, as a result, missed marketing opportunities.

The bank had to budget large amounts of money for information technology and undertake many projects at one time in order to modernize its systems. How could management have prevented this problem? How can a firm determine if a new development is a fad or a major advance?

5.2 An electronics equipment manufacturer developed a state-of-the-art order entry system in the 1960s. The system expanded gradually to become the administrative backbone of the company. With thousands of terminals and hundreds of different functions, the system is irreplaceable. On the other hand, much of the technology is old and the system does not present an attractive interface to the user.

A manager responsible for the system described his problems with it: "We need to redo the system, but the investment and disruption would be high. Right now we are thinking of building an interface on a personal computer to try and make the user interaction with the system a little better. I don't know what we will do for the long term."

Do you have any ideas on how a system like this one can be updated?

Questions

1. What is the role of technology in managing information services?
2. What is the motivation for networking?
3. What is the difference between dial-up service and leased lines?
4. Why would a department want a LAN?
5. What is the difference between a PBX and a LAN?
6. What is a micro–mainframe link?
7. Why does a user want compatibility among computers?
8. What is the database concept?
9. What are the advantages of a DBMS?
10. Define a fourth-generation language (4GL).
11. Are 4GLs only for end users?
12. Why is end-user computing both a solution and a problem?
13. What is an expert system (ES)?
14. What is a decision support system (DSS)?
15. What are the similarities between ES and DSS?
16. Why are ES and DSS a problem to implement?
17. What functions might be included in a managerial workstation?
18. What is the major insight provided by the McKenney and McFarlan framework for strategic IS?
19. Why should the firm consider strategic applications? What are the necessary preconditions for undertaking such applications?
20. What were the major technological problems in developing the cash management microcomputer system in the bank described at the end of this chapter?
21. What advantages over the competition did the system in Question 20 provide for the bank?
22. Should management adopt the latest technology? Why or why not?
23. What role does the R&D group within the ISD play in adopting new technology?
24. Is technology responsible for success in information processing?
25. What firms should not consider developing strategic applications, at least at the present time?

6

Planning for Information Processing

Why do organizations plan? Planning is an attempt to deal with the future effect of current decisions. Planning is not forecasting the future. These two statements are important in understanding planning and its objectives. The key objective of planning is to evaluate today's decisions in light of where management wants the firm to be at some point in the future.

Consider a firm that is trying to decide whether it needs a policy to deal with the spread of personal computers in the organization. What is the future effect of having a policy versus having no policy? With no policy, it is likely that users will buy a number of different brands of personal computers and different software packages. Management may feel that individual choice is very important and that there is little need for sharing or communicating electronically among users of different personal computers. Under these conditions, the future impact of a current decision to have no policy on personal computers is acceptable to management.

Another firm might look at the future effect of a policy that restricts users to one brand of computer and one piece of software for each task, for example, the use of one spreadsheet package by everyone in the firm. Some time in the future, this firm will want to establish a computer network and have all of its personal computers connected to it. The future impact of a strict policy that the firm will acquire only one brand of personal computer will facilitate this future objective of having a network of computers.

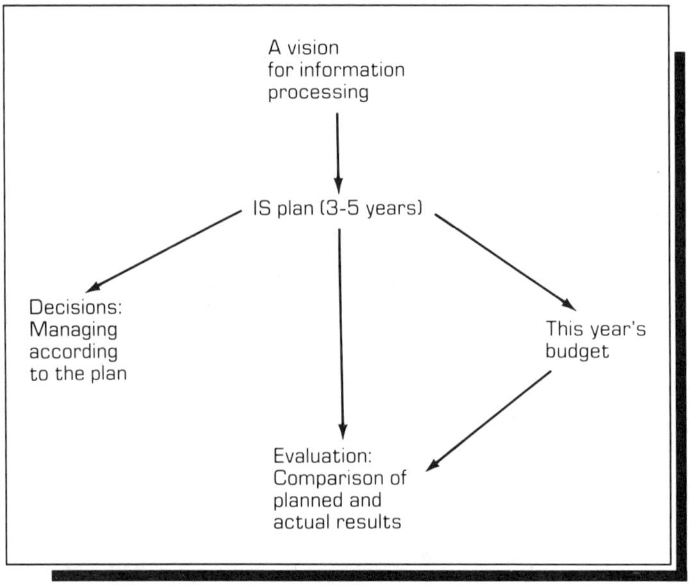

FIGURE 6-1 The role of an IS plan.

In one firm, the ISD resisted the development of a plan; their objective was to gain approval of an annual budget to do what they felt was best for the firm. The management of the ISD did not want to be influenced too much by company management! Hopefully, this kind of attitude is not prevalent today. However, the general status of planning for information services is dismal. Few organizations have plans, and those that exist are often of poor quality.

Why does the IS manager want a plan? See Figure 6-1. A plan is a road map; it provides guidelines for making many decisions about what applications to undertake, what hardware and software environment to develop, staffing requirements, and all aspects of managing information services. The long-range plan is also the basis for developing this year's budget for IS.

What does senior management gain by planning for information processing? A plan can be an excellent tool for evaluating and controlling information processing. When ISD management asks for approval of requests, senior managers can evaluate these items in terms of how well they fit with plans for information services. When senior management evaluates information services and the CIO, the plan is the benchmark against which the evaluation is undertaken.

Senior Management's Perspective

Senior management has great difficulty in coping with the information processing function of the organization. A framework to assist senior manage-

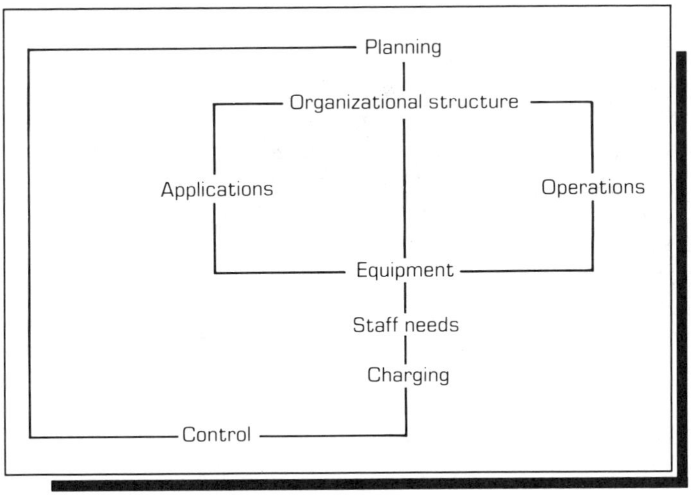

FIGURE 6-2 Management control of information processing. (From Lucas, 1982)

ment is shown in Figure 6-2. The development of a systems plan is a key component of the framework; the plan is the road map showing how information processing will deliver services and contribute to the organization in the future.

One important outcome of planning is agreement on the structure of information processing for the firm. In Chapter 2, we discussed a number of options and variables that influence the organization of information processing. Planning offers a forum for raising issues of organizational structure and deciding what pattern of information processing best fits the firm.

A plan also contains application areas; in some cases, it describes specific applications that are to be undertaken. The development of computer applications places heavy demands on the ISD; new applications constitute the varying part of the load on the department. It is difficult to alter the resources needed for operations, but discretion can be used in undertaking systems. New applications also generate demands for maintenance and enhancements once they have been installed.

Operations refers to the task of keeping existing applications running. The past load is known, and it is fairly easy to estimate the processing demands of applications that will be finished in the near future. With this information, one can plan for the resources required for operations.

New applications and ongoing operations are the source of demand for hardware, software, and ISD staff members. Since few applications are discontinued, management can expect to see constantly expanding demands for hardware and software resources. The plan explains why new resources are needed and suggests when additional capacity should be added. Planning for new staff members is fairly clear for operations; it is more difficult to estimate what resources are needed for new applications, since there is a great deal of uncertainty associated with systems design.

The framework in Figure 6-2 also includes questions of charging and control. Charging is one mechanism for controlling the use of information processing. It has been suggested that a firm wishing to encourage the use of computers charge their expenses to overhead. An organization with fairly inexperienced users might follow this approach. A company that wants to ration usage and has more sophisticated users might want to charge costs back to users or their departments. See Chapter 15.

Overall control of information processing requires more than charging for services. Management must look at various indicators to see if information services is performing at an adequate level. On the operations side, management can request information on user satisfaction, reruns, late reports, response time, and computer availability. For systems development, management consults the plan to determine if projects are on target; it must also find out from users if systems are meeting their objectives.

If the plan states that certain goals to be accomplished each year, management should evaluate performance against the plan. Performance in information processing has many components; the plan is a very useful place to begin in evaluating the contribution of information services to the organization.

The Planning Process

Organizations have a variety of approaches to planning; many firms do not have plans that are promulgated widely in the organization. The plan for one insurance company existed only in the mind of its chairman; he would not commit it to paper for fear that a competitor might see it! Of course, this meant that no one in the firm had a clear picture of the plan, either. At the other extreme is a firm like IBM, where planning is an ongoing and highly formal process; the company is managed according to the plan.

Two IS Planning Methods

Most firms developing an IS plan follow their own approach to planning. Various vendors and consultants have developed planning methodologies, which they sell to clients who need assistance in planning. A review of two of these approaches will help show the key components of a planning methodology.

Business systems planning (BSP) was originally developed by IBM for its internal use, but was later applied to customers. BSP is undertaken by a team of IS personnel and managers in two phases. Phase I consists of developing a broad understanding of the firm and how it is supported by information systems. The team identifies the gross information systems required by the firm and assigns priority to the most important applications.

Phase II focuses on the creation of a long-range plan for the development of the information systems identified in phase I. Included in the study is an assessment and critique of current information systems. The team identifies data elements and places where data and processes are shared by users. The results of phase II are a long-range plan with detailed specifications for systems to be developed during the planning period.

BSP can proceed in the absence of an organizational plan or strategy; it is not tightly coupled to the plans of the firm. The approach has been criticized for requiring extensive detail, since the applications are outlined at a fairly low level. Given dynamic business conditions, it is possible that applications identified and specified for implementation in 4 or 5 years may never be developed.

One of IBM's European subsidiaries has modified the BSP approach to reduce the amount of detail required and has used it successfully with clients. Because BSP is a one-time study, a firm must also develop the internal capacity to update its plans. A mechanism is needed to turn the planning process from a one-time task force into an ongoing activity within the firm.

Another planning technique has recently become popular. Rockart (1979) applied an approach used for many years in strategic planning to planning for information services. He advocates the critical success factors (CSF) approach to information systems development. In this approach, a planner and designer asks chief executives to give the four or five factors that are most critical to the success of the organization.

CSFs are developed during interviews; a group of managers and planners go through several group meetings to eliminate duplicate CFSs and to choose those that are the most critical. Then designers suggest information processing applications that provide information for meeting the firm's CSFs. One consulting company has adopted and extended this approach to develop an overall plan for information processing in a firm.

Both BSP and CSF approaches to planning result in a plan for new applications. However, as we saw in discussing the management framework, a plan has more components than a list of new applications. Applications are important, but the primary purpose is to develop a planning document that provides guidelines for the overall management of information processing. High-priority applications will be a part of this plan, but there will be many other components as well.

The major contribution of any planning methodology is that it encourages planning and suggests what steps to follow to create a plan. An organization is well advised to study different approaches to planning and then to devise its own approach. Key considerations include the following:

1. Who should be involved in the planning process?
2. What information should be included in a plan?
3. How will the plan be used?
4. Who will contribute to the plan and who will review it?
5. How will the plan be approved, and by whom?
6. What is the time horizon for the plan?

A Planning Approach

Planning literature is full of prescriptions. Unfortunately, this literature offers little information about what has proved successful. We have used the approach described in this section with some success, but in too few cases to claim that it will always work well.

Planning is often described as *top-down* or *bottom-up*. As the names suggest, top-down planning involves management; senior managers set the goals and objectives and lower-level employees fill in the details. Bottom-up planning works in the other way; low-level organizational units submit their plans, say for the coming year, and senior management reviews them in coming up with a final plan. Usually the two approaches are mixed. Planning cannot succeed if there is a vacuum at the top; senior management must have goals, and in the final analysis, this is the only group that can resolve conflicts and allocate resources. Senior management, however, cannot have detailed knowledge of what is happening at the operating levels of the organization; it must gather this information from lower-level management.

The objective is to develop an ongoing planning process for information services. The output each year should be a 3- to 5-year plan and a detailed operating plan and budget for the coming year. What is the best way to accomplish these objectives?

The first step is for information services to assign the planning task to one individual. This person should be at a fairly high level, and should optimally have experience in planning. This person, or a consultant if no one is available, will be the facilitator. He or she must apply pressure at the right places in the organization to ensure that a plan is developed.

Senior management must be willing to participate in the planning process. It should also describe the goals of the organization and its plans for the future. Even if these plans are not available in a written statement, they can be developed during group discussions.

Why should senior management devote time to IS planning? Remember that the mission of information services has changed. Nine out of 10 CIOs would probably reply that IS exists to provide a service to the organization. IS, however, can and should do more. The firm can use information technology to accomplish its goals, as a part of strategy and as a way to gain a competitive edge. This creative use of technology depends on management as well as the ISD. The final reason that senior management should be involved in the planning process for IS is that information processing is not well managed in most organizations. The kind of plan we are discussing will aid nontechnical managers in controlling information services.

A Process

Let us assume that the organization is developing an IS plan for the first time. The planner from IS should arrange a meeting that includes the chief operating officer of the firm and senior levels of management. Also included are the planner and the CIO. This senior-level planning group meets to discuss the overall objectives and strategy of the organization. At the first meeting, it may not be appropriate to discuss information technology, depending on how much agreement there is on the firm's objectives and plans. See Table 6-1.

Next, the planning group considers the role of information technology in achieving the firm's objectives. At this point, it is not interested in identifying specific applications; the focus of the meeting is on what opportunities the technology provides. The planner and CIO might discuss other firms using the technology creatively to stimulate the planning group. They might also present the results of a technology forecast: what technology is likely to be available for this firm and for its competitors in the future?

The relationship between planning and technology suggested above is shown in Figure 6-3. Technology plays two important roles in the planning process. First, the planning group asks how technology can affect the firm's competitive position. The ability to ask and answer this question depends on whether this group has a vision of the firm in the future. Given an answer to this future-oriented question of technology and strategy, the group begins a planning process that considers how the technology can support the firm in a variety of ways, from transactions processing to competitive applications.

In subsequent meetings, the planning group identifies key applications areas. Members of the committee may want to meet with subordinates to learn about their needs for information processing and to learn what they are facing from their competitors. It would be very appropriate for each senior manager to convene a planning group in his or her area for this purpose.

Before going into a detailed discussion of each application, the planning committee should ask: "What kind of information processing environment do we want in 3 to 5 years?" The CIO and this planner can help this process by developing several scenarios showing what is possible with the technology. For example, they might sketch a scenario of a manager with a work-

TABLE 6-1 The Planning Process

Meet with the chief operating officer and senior managers to discuss objectives and strategy of the firm.
Meet with this group to discuss the role of information technology in achieving these objectives.
Determine how technology can help support the firm; see Figure 6-2.
Identify key applications areas through discussions with senior and middle management.
Develop scenarios of how users and managers will interact with the planned information systems environment.
Develop an organization structure and pattern of processing for information systems.
Estimate resource requirements for the plan.
Hold a review meeting with all planning groups.
Develop a draft plan and review it.
Develop a consensus on the plan.
Manage according to the plan.
Update the plan regularly.

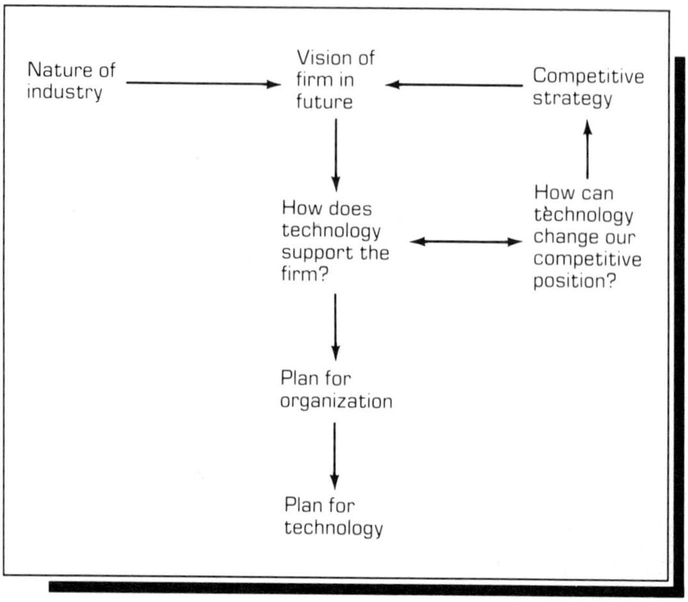

FIGURE 6-3 The relationship between planning and technology.

station and show how this person's activities would differ from his or her routine today. A useful scenario should seem possible and plausible to the reader. In some instances, a planner will want to provide more than one scenario to help planners choose among different alternatives.

Consideration of the information processing environment leads to a discussion of organizational structure. The CIO and the planner should present the factors discussed in Chapter 2 for debate. Does the firm want to be decentralized, distributed, or centralized with respect to processing? Who should have the authority to make decisions about applications, regardless of where hardware is located? Who will develop applications and where? What type of coordination, if any, is desired?

Given the applications areas and a structure for information processing in the organization, the ISD can estimate the processing needed to meet present operating requirements and the needs of new applications. All of these factors combine to yield a forecast of the staff required for systems development and operations.

At this point, the firm is ready to have a larger meeting, a retreat with the lower-level planning groups that have been meeting with the managers on the committee. The results of the meeting can be presented tentatively at this point for user reactions. This meeting allows senior management to test its assumptions about the most appropriate pattern of processing and the kinds of applications that are important to the firm. For example, if the structure for processing is distributed, how do users who will have major responsibilities for information systems in their departments react? Is there agreement that some type of coordination is required?

After the large meeting, the planning group should have gathered data that is both top down and bottom up. The meeting represents the intersection of the top-down approach followed by the planning committee and the bottom-up detail gained from meetings conducted by senior managers in their areas of responsibility. At this point, the planner may be able to develop a draft plan that is acceptable. If more work is needed, the senior planning group can respond, as can the lower-level groups; another meeting of all personnel concerned may be necessary.

The planner, after iterating through a number of cycles of meetings as just suggested, should be developing successively refined versions of a plan. When completed, the plan will be a road map for future information processing activities. The process of task forces, committees, and meetings is suggested for several purposes. First, it provides needed data, both the top-down overview from management and the bottom-up detail from operating personnel. Second, the process helps gain commitment to the final plan; the plan will not be a surprise, and many individuals will have contributed to it. Finally, the process of planning should be an educational one for the individuals involved in it. They will learn about technology and some of the problems of developing applications. They will also see that there are many alternative ways of delivering information processing services.

Ongoing Planning

The preceding scenario assumes that the organization is developing a plan for the first time. Should it develop a 3-year plan every 3 years? One could probably plan in this manner, but after 2 years the pace of change would make the plan obsolete. Instead, each year the plan should be updated, using some of the same processes just described.

Since it takes a long time to develop and install applications, major portions of the plan will not change. However, it is quite possible that certain applications areas will no longer be critical and that new ones will have taken their place. Changes in the technology may also make it feasible to undertake application that were postponed because the technology was not available or was too expensive.

The review of the plan also provides an opportunity for management to evaluate information services and the CIO. What has been accomplished, given the original goals of the plan? Is progress being made toward establishing the kind of processing environment envisioned originally? Are major applications projects on schedule?

An ongoing review and update of the plan should also include information on the competition. In what new ways are competitors using the technology? What is the firm's response? Have new opportunities arisen since the plan was developed? The review process should generate a revised plan that will be a road map for the next 3 to 5 years.

Managing According to the Plan

At the beginning of this chapter, we emphasized that planning was not forecasting; it is an attempt to deal with the future effects of current decisions. Given a request for a new system, the CIO and senior management on a steering committee can use the plan to see how the application fits the current agenda of development projects. Does it have a higher priority than systems to which we are already committed?

Using the plan this way can help senior management respond to suggestions for new applications. In approving development projects, managers are often frustrated because they function in a vacuum. The plan provides a frame of reference and a way to calibrate a suggested application.

The plan serves the same role with respect to requests for hardware. For example, if the firm has adopted a strategy for processing that stresses Hewlett Packard computers for factory floor systems, a good case must be made by a division in Detroit that wants to acquire a Prime computer. If the Prime is a serious contender, the factory proposing it will have to answer a series of questions that are dictated by the plan. For example, assume that the plan envisions a corporate network. Adherents of the Prime will be asked how it will connect with the network and how it will communicate with Hewlett Packard processors already installed in the plant. The plant will also have to show that it can support the Prime, since the central information processing group does not.

The role of the plan in evaluating information services was discussed in the section on "Ongoing Planning." The plan is a commitment from the CIO and information services that, given the resources required, they can deliver what is in the plan for the coming year. The plan, then, forms the basis on which senior management can evaluate the performance of information processing. This evaluation component is extremely important and is missing from planning approaches like BSP and CSF. Applications are an important part of the plan, but it includes much more.

An Insurance Company Plan

In this section, we shall see the outline of a plan developed for a worldwide insurance firm. This company had lagged behind in the development of systems; it had saved money on computing, but was now constrained because its present systems would not let it develop new lines of business easily.

Planning was complicated by the lack of an overall plan for the company. A management group was appointed to oversee the information processing area; one of its first tasks was to undertake a planning process. The chairman (the same one described earlier in the chapter) would not write anything down about his plans for the future. His goals were easy to state but hard to accomplish; a 20% growth in sales and earnings each year.

Executive Summary

The plan began with a short executive summary. The plan itself was expected to be quite lengthy; a summary was necessary to communicate with senior management, who would not take the time to read a long, detailed plan. In fact, the summary is a bit of top-down design in the sense that it gives the reader a sense of where the plan is headed before going into detail. A good executive summary is an important part of a plan.

Goals

While the plan was being developed, the firm was strongly batch processing oriented. There were few master files; the concept of a database or DBMS was foreign. In fact, given the emphasis in the firm on cost reduction, the suggestion of spending several hundred thousand dollars on a DBMS would not have been well received. To create management reports, a program had to summarize a large number of transactions reports.

The goals of the plan were ambitious. Since the company operated worldwide, the management committee felt that it would best be served by moving information processing power closer to the users. Lengthy transmission time and the lack of good telecommunications capabilities in places like Africa hindered processing. Users also had little faith in the information services area. Moving equipment and control of information services closer to end users was felt to be a popular suggestion that would gain support for the plan from others in the firm.

There were a number of goals that were considered primarily as platitudes. The ISD needed to become more responsive to users; the processing environment should move toward more on-line interaction with computers; and the ISD had to develop the ability to make processing changes more easily and quickly than at present.

Assumptions

The basic assumption in the plan was the chairman's stated 20% a year increase in sales and profits. This assumption was used as a basis for projecting increases in business and information processing requirements.

Scenario

The plan contained a scenario of what different users would see when interacting with computers. The scenario served to make abstract statements and goals more concrete; it showed what would actually result from implemention of the plan.

The scenario could be read by a nontechnical audience. It was an extremely important part of the plan, since readers could relate to it and understand the implications of this lengthy document for them. We would recommend using a device like a scenario, both for discussion purposes in developing the plan and in the plan itself.

Applications

Almost all planning techniques include a delineation of high-priority applications. Whether using BSP, CSF, or some other approach, planners have to elicit from members of the organization their most important applications.

In this company, the problem was compounded because the manager of information services wanted to be responsive; he accepted every suggestion that was made. No one in the ISD knew the number of applications promised or the resources required to develop them. In this firm, one purpose of an applications list was simply to determine what had been committed to users and to add up the resources required to meet the commitments.

In addition to what had already been promised, of course, it was important to learn about new applications that might help the firm gain an edge on its competition. In this plan, the applications section was overflowing with ideas.

Operations

In most firms, the demands on operations are fairly predictable. The ISD knows the number of people required to run existing systems and can usually predict what will be needed as new applications are implemented. For the insurance firm, the plan for operations had to include resources to bring existing operations to a minimally acceptable level. The manager of the ISD had spent his first year trying to bring some order out of the chaos of operations. Controls and documentation were inadequate or lacking entirely.

Maintenance and Enhancements

Many individuals in an organization have no need for a new application. They are, however, vitally interested in modifications to existing systems. A plan should indicate what kinds of resources the organization wants to dedicate to maintenance and enhancements for existing systems.

Surveys have suggested that, on the average, a firm may allocate 50% of its programmer/analyst support to maintenance. Some firms put so much effort into maintenance and enhancements that there is virtually no applications development effort for new systems.

Organization Structure

As mentioned earlier, one objective of the plan was to move computing closer to the end user. The plan contained information on where computers would be located. It was also necessary for the management committee to discuss how systems would be developed. Because of cost considerations, the planners favored fairly tight central control of development to promote sharing of applications.

The management group thought it would be a major improvement for users to have reliable computing operations provided by distributed hardware. The users, they felt, should be willing to accept common applications in return for better operating service.

Impact of the Plan

The management committee suggested the need for a section of the report dealing with the impact of the plan. The first issue was the financial impact; how much money would this plan cost? In addition, there was concern over the impact on individuals in the firm. Could users in Third World countries adapt to the use of on-line computer systems for input?

Impact considerations also included the positive benefits from systems. Would a competitive system generate so much business that the normal processing load would grow out of control? Once the firm became more competitive, what would be required to stay that way?

Implementation Risks

An ambitious plan for information processing is not without risks. In this organization, which was lagging so far behind its competitors, the fear was that users and managers would not be able to implement the plan. The plan also could have turned out to be so costly that senior management would reject it.

Given the quality of information services, the firm had trouble attracting ISD personnel. Could they hire qualified individuals to implement the plan? Was the company capable of managing the changes that the plan implied? Could a firm used to making short-range decisions stay with a longer-range plan that involved a significant investment before much return was evident?

Conclusions

We would like to say that this plan met with great success and was implemented enthusiastically by the firm. Unfortunately, the chairman was also an impatient man. After 6 months he decided that enough time had elapsed, and he replaced the CIO. The new CIO wanted to start with a completely new management structure, so the old management committee disbanded.

In this instance, there was not enough high-level support for planning. The chairman did not want to participate in the process, but his support was needed, along with some patience. Can anyone develop a plan under these circumstances? Possibly if the management committee that the chairman appointed had reported more regularly to him, the plan could have been completed. On the other hand, given the personality of the chairman, managers tended to avoid him whenever possible.

CMI's Plan

CMI has developed a broad 3-year plan for information processing, with a 1-year plan in detail. Following is the executive summary of that plan to provide another idea of how a plan might look. The entire plan covers 60 pages, much too long for inclusion here. The summary, however, describes the high points of the plan and demonstrates the directions in which CMI wants to move.

Introduction

The major objective of information processing at CMI is to contribute to the goals of the firm. In particular, the ISD should provide a service and should introduce technology that will help CMI implement its corporate strategy.

For the next 3 years, management and the ISD have identified several critical areas in which information technology can make a contribution to the firm.

1. In manufacturing plants:
   a. Just-in-time (JIT) inventory
   b. Supplier communications
   c. Electronic mail
   d. Factory automation
2. In the office:
   a. Electronic mail
   b. Professional workstations
   c. End-user inquiry
3. Management:
   a. Greater coordination of information processing activities in the firm
   b. Integration of traditional information systems, communications, and factory automation

Senior management envisions moving CMI toward the configuration of an electronic firm. It wishes to replace as much paper processing as possible; computer technology will be crucial in achieving this objective. In particular, the firm must move toward a more networked environment in order to support a variety of workstations and terminals, which will need to access various computer systems.

The plants view the implementation of JIT inventory as a key factor in reducing production costs; major revisions in communications with suppliers and in existing production control systems will be required to implement this concept. They will start with the Omaha operation and use it as a test case during the coming year.

Since both the office and the plants want more intracompany communications, a high priority for the coming year is to conduct research and select an office automation system, particularly one with electronic messaging.

High-Priority Applications

The high-priority applications then become:

1. An order entry system link to customers so that they can place orders with the firm electronically.
2. JIT inventory coordinated with production control in Omaha.
3. Electronic mail.
4. Data center preparation for the future: 4GL selection, DBMS selection, and systems development productivity tool acquisition.

Structure

In general, management is satisfied with the existing pattern of information processing. Local ISD managers are responsible directly to a local manager and have a dotted line relationship with the CIO at headquarters. The firm will move to strengthen this relationship through greater coordination. Quarterly meetings are planned for ISD staff members across the firm and monthly headquarters visits to each location.

Operations and Maintenance

Operations receives satisfactory marks from each location. Detailed needs for each location are contained in the plan.

Maintenance is running at about 33% of discretionary resources. This percentage will be retained, which will allow slightly more total resources for maintenance throughout the firm.

Impact and Implementation

If this plan is successful, we feel that CMI will be better able to compete. The JIT inventory will help CMI become the low-cost producer in several markets. Electronic links to customers and suppliers will also drive down costs and improve the speed with which manufacturing can respond. The costs will move the firm from about 3.5% of gross sales spent on information processing to close to 5% by the end of the third year.

There are implementation risks and obstacles. The JIT philosophy is untested at CMI; it could fail in the pilot test. There is low risk for electronic messaging because the technology is in place in many firms. The major risk here is that individuals inside and outside CMI will not use it; the management committee has agreed to become users, which will help the implementation effort. We also have no control over customers; we shall try to make the order entry operation appealing enough for them to adopt it readily.

Conclusions

Is it ever appropriate not to plan for information processing? It is hard to think of a situation where some effort devoted to planning will not be rewarded. A plan is an attempt to make today's decisions with their future impact in mind. Managers have reported difficulties in making decisions about information processing; a good plan should help reduce this uneasiness.

At the same time, the plan is a benefit to the CIO and the ISD staff. They can use it to evaluate requests and to coordinate information processing. If a user proposes a system that does not fit with the plan, the ISD can work with the user to find an approach that is consistent with it. Over time, fewer past decisions will turn out to be incorrect because no one knew the direction of the organization with respect to information processing.

To learn about what is happening in the firm in order to make an immediate contribution, the new CIO manager of the ISD should develop the kind of 3- to 5-year plan described in this chapter. The plan will then become the guideline for managing information services.

Recommended Readings

Dickson, G. W., and J. C. Wetherbe, *The Management of Information Systems.* New York: McGraw-Hill, 1985. (Contains a comprehensive chapter on planning for systems, including an attempt to synthesize several approaches.)

Henderson, J., J. Rockart, and J. Sifonis, "Management Support Systems in Strategic IS Planning," *JMIS,* vol. 4, no. 1 (Summer 1987), pp. 5–24. (An expansion of CSFs to planning.)

Lucas, H. C., Jr., *Coping with Computers: A Manager's Guide to Controlling Information Processing.* New York: Free Press, 1982. (See especially the chapter on planning.)

Pyburn, P. J., "Linking the MIS Plan with Corporate Strategy: An Exploratory Study," *MIS Quarterly,* vol. 7, no. 2 (June 1983), pp. 1–14. (A study discussing factors that the author feels are associated with planning success.)

Rockart, J., "Chief Executives Define Their Own Data Needs," *Harvard Business Review* (March–April 1979), pp. 81–93. (A description of critical success factors for IS design.)

Discussion Problems

6.1 The president of a garment manufacturing firm asked for help in developing a plan for his company. Basically, he was dissatisfied with information services, but had very little experience with which to compare present operations. "I know that we spend too much and get too little," he said on several occasions. However, because the president had worked in the firm for a decade, he had no benchmarks for comparison.

Despite his dissatisfaction with the firm's information processing at present, the president was quite willing to try again. He hired a consultant and was willing to support the consultant in any way possible. Given this kind of situation, what recommendations would you make to the company president? How should the company proceed to develop a plan? What is the president's role in this process?

6.2 The chairman of General Motors has been quoted frequently in the press as stating that the only way for the firm to compete in the future will be with technology and automation. As a result, GM has purchased EDS, a large consulting firm, and given it responsibility for operating and integrating all of GM's computer facilities. EDS is building a large network and assisting in factory automation. GM has also purchased Hughes Aircraft in order to expand its capabilities with technology.

At the same time, GM has experienced significant difficulties in implementing automation. Several plants that are highly automated seem to have a number of problems and have not yet reached full production. The president of EDS, who was a board member at GM, has publicly criticized the giant manufacturing company for its bureaucracy and its slow response to the market.

How do you plan for information processing in this kind of turbulent environment? Given an organization the size of GM, describe what kind of IS planning you would implement. Would it be top-down or bottom-up? How would you coordinate processing in a firm of this size?

Questions

1. Define planning.
2. How does planning differ from forecasting?
3. Is there a role for forecasting in planning?
4. Why should management encourage planning?
5. How does a plan help determine an organizational structure for information services?
6. Why do planning techniques like BSP and CSF not lead to comprehensive plans?
7. What is the role of new applications in the plan?
8. What is a critical success factor?
9. Define top-down planning and contrast it to bottom-up planning.
10. What is the role of senior management in planning for IS?
11. What is the role of corporate strategy in the development of an IS plan?
12. What does one accomplish during a review meeting on a plan?
13. Should the plan be considered complete? Why update it?
14. What is the role of new technology in the plan?
15. How does the plan serve as an evaluation mechanism for the ISD?
16. What is meant by managing according to the plan?
17. Describe an example of a present decision that will have a future impact on the firm. How does a plan influence this decision?
18. What was the major problem in the insurance company planning example in this chapter?
19. What was the problem with the insurance company chairman in this example?
20. Can you think of conditions in which it is not necessary to plan for information services?
21. Why do you think that so many organizations do not plan for information services? What can be done to encourage them to plan?
22. How does the CIO use the plan on the job?
23. Why might one include a section in the plan on risks? What kind of risks are there?
24. What are some obstacles to the success of a plan for IS?
25. What is the role of a scenario in a plan?

PART II

The Information Services Environment

7

Leadership in Information Processing

There has been a great deal of research about leadership, but we seem unable to teach someone how to be a leader. Possibly those who are led have so many different expectations that no leader can accommodate all of them. Researchers in organization theory, psychology, and political science are all interested in leadership, and all view the problem from a somewhat different perspective. Leadership is very important for the CIO and other managers in information services.

We all observe leadership around us: the president of the United States, a prime minister, a governor, or a manager. For our purposes, it is the leadership role of the manager that is of interest. Management and leadership are not synonymous; management is a process in which work is organized, supervised, monitored, and controlled. Leadership involves one individual, the leader, exerting social influence over those who are led.

In many early industrial organizations and in organizations today that follow the military model, leaders are granted formal authority by the organization. In this kind of organization, like the army or navy, rank confers authority to lead. However, in most other organizations, leadership is a social influence process. The formal position of the leader requires this person to influence others to accomplish the tasks assigned to them. Possibly because of the formal position of the leader, subordinates are subject to influence. However, there are many cases in which leaders have had little influence on those who, in theory, should follow.

Modern organization theorists suggest that leadership does not flow from the authority of the organization, but instead comes from the consent of those who are led. A leader must understand subordinates and know what kind of leadership style is appropriate for a given situation. It is also helpful to consider what motivates individuals in organizations, since one role of the leader is to motivate subordinates.

Motivation

A model proposed by Victor Vroom (1964) is helpful in understanding motivation. This model, called the *expectancy model,* suggests that motivation is a force to behave in a certain way; the force is a function of the valence and expectation of an outcome. Valence measures the attractiveness of an outcome, and expectation is a measure of how likely we feel an outcome is, given our behavior.

Figure 7-1 is a diagram of the model and an example. Suppose that a manager is interested in motivating employees to complete a project early. As an incentive, the manager hints that they will receive 3 days of time off with pay if they finish early. How effective is this promise in motivating early completion?

The first part of the model is concerned with the valence of the outcome of time off. How attractive is the extra time off to the employees? Suppose they are new employees with no vacation time; 3 days off sounds good. On the other hand, if they are veterans with 60 days of vacation time "in

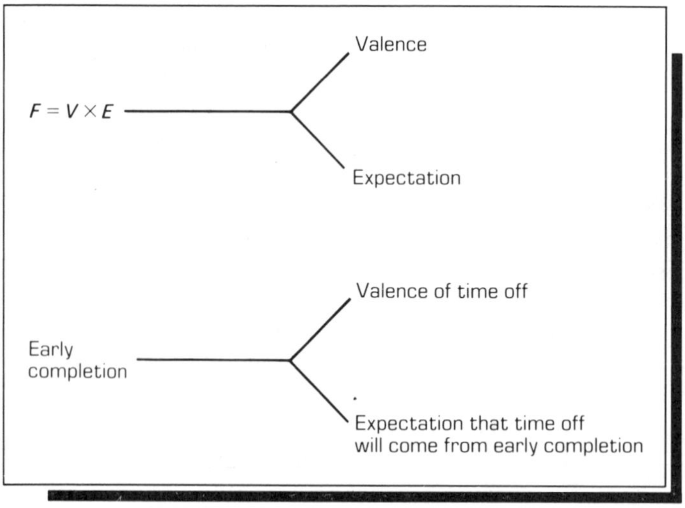

FIGURE 7-1 The expectancy model of motivation.

the bank'' carried over from past years, an additional 3 days is not that attractive.

Expectation is the belief that the manager really means that 3 days off will come from early completion and that the manager can grant the time off. The Vroom model hypothesizes that the force to act, that is, the motivation to complete the project early, is a multiplicative function of valence times expectancy. If valence is 0, time off is of no value to the employees, and offering 3 days off does no good because no matter what the expectation, valence is 0 so motivation is 0. By the same reasoning, if the employees doubt that the manager will give them the time off, expectancy is 0 and motivation is again 0.

We have suggested modifying the Vroom model to include numbers less than 0. One can imagine an outcome that seems so unattractive that persons are motivated to prevent it. Suppose that a user sees a new system as very unattractive; he expects its implementation will eliminate his job. The valence of being unemployed is highly negative. What is this user motivated to do? Probably the user will try to prevent the system from succeeding.

This simple model of motivation can help in understanding a great deal of behavior. It is important for leaders to be aware of what motivates subordinates and to think about their own actions. Something that appears on the surface to be an obvious motivator of human behavior may not be so at all. It is important for leaders to understand their subordinates and what rewards are highly valent. It is also essential to maintain one's credibility as a leader; if rewards are promised, they should be provided; otherwise, the impact on the expectancy of future rewards will be negative.

Theories of Leadership

We have mentioned that there are many different leadership theories. But why is leadership important for an organization or a function like information services? There are a number of reasons:

1. Organizations and their subunits face a great deal of uncertainty. It is very difficult to develop or follow procedures for coping with uncertainty; instead management has a responsibility to respond to and absorb uncertainty. One role for leaders is to locate and deal with uncertainty in the external environment and in internal operations.

2. Leadership is needed because organization design is not perfect. In Chapter 2 we presented some principles of organizational design; it was pointed out that a managerial hierarchy is needed because of exceptions that cannot be handled routinely. Leaders spend much of their time dealing with exceptions.

3. Leadership serves a linking role. This principle was first proposed by Rensis Likert. He viewed managers as linking different layers of individuals in an organization. In information services, this linking function is particularly important because the ISD has relationships with so many different departments and different layers of management.

4. Leadership is needed when the organization encounters an unusual opportunity or a major change in its environment. If an opportunity arises to merge with another firm, to acquire the rights to a new product, or to change the direction of the firm because of a new discovery, managers must lead the organization.

5. Leadership is also looking for improvement projects, according to Mintzberg (1973). Managers work at an unrelenting pace; even if all indicators are satisfactory, the manager is always looking for things that could improve the position of the firm.

In our earlier quotation from Mintzberg's book in Chapter 3, we emphasized that leadership permeates all of a manager's activities. Subordinates look carefully at a manager's actions to learn what is important in the firm. Mintzberg feels that the leader must try to integrate individual needs and organizational goals, a view consistent with our notion that leadership is an attempt to exert social influence.

The Great Man School

A significant amount of popular literature is written from the perspective of the "great man" school of leadership. The basic belief of this view is that an individual rises to a leadership position at a critical time for the organization. The talents of the great man fit well with the needs of the organization.

Because there are so few great men, and because the situation in which each finds himself (or herself) is unique, it is very difficult to generalize from these stories. Great men may also be very appropriate at the highest levels of the organization or government; however, there are also many senior- and middle-level managers on whom the firm depends. We need a more conceptual and insightful view of leadership to learn how to manage the firm better.

Behavioral Theories

There are a number of behavioral theories of leadership; these theories focus on the behavioral patterns and philosophies of managers. Filley, House, and Kerr (1976) summarize much of the research on leadership style. Three of their categories are of interest.

The first is *supportive leadership,* in which the leader gives great consideration to the needs of subordinates. The leader is concerned with the well-being, comfort, and satisfaction of subordinates. A supportive leader expresses appreciation when a subordinate does a good job; he or she does not demand more than the subordinate can do. Supportive leadership means not criticizing workers in front of others; leaders also provide rewards for jobs that are done well. A supportive leader treats subordinates as equals and is willing to make changes.

A second behavior category is *participative leadership,* in which there is a great deal of sharing of power, information, and influence between the leader and followers. In true participative leadership situations, the leader makes sure that all parties have an opportunity to influence the final decision.

The leader has to give up some formal power, and share information and influence with participants. The leader must prevent dominant personalities from having too much influence and must obtain input from reticent participants. The leader encourages the development of alternative solutions and guides the process of screening alternatives until a final solution can be selected.

A final category of interest is *instrumental leadership,* a category associated with the mechanics of a particular job. The focus here is less on personality characteristics than on the managerial tasks associated with leadership. Can the leader plan, organize, control, and coordinate the activities of subordinates? In a technological task, does the leader understand the technology well enough to manage the work? Instrumental leadership also involves the ability of the manager to acquire and marshall resources in the organization.

Contingency Theory

Contingencies are very popular in organization theory today; a contingency theory suggests that the appropriate behavior is contingent on some variable. For example, a leadership contingency theory states that the managerial style of a leader depends on the type of organization in which the leader is working. A leader who is a general in the army faces a different situation than the head of volunteers for the local Red Cross.

What kinds of contingencies influence leadership? The first are the personal characteristics of subordinates. Consistent with our earlier discussion of motivation and with preceding discussion of supportive and participative leadership styles, we would expect the characteristics of those being led to influence the leader. Are the needs of systems analysts the same as those of computer operators?

A second contingency factor is the environment or situation. Continuing the preceding example, the systems development environment is a creative one characterized by uncertainty. The environment in computer operations is more frenetic and is characterized by deadlines and pressure to meet operating standards.

Combining the two contingencies suggests a different approach to management based on the characteristics of individuals and the environment in which they work. The systems analyst has to reason conceptually and deal with a great deal of ambiguity; the operator has to execute tasks and respond quickly to problems. As a result, there tends to be a great deal of participation in the design of information systems; project managers are supportive and encourage a design team to solicit input from a variety of users in the firm.

Operations tends to be more instrumentally managed. There is concern with schedules, meeting targets, and monitoring the hardware and software environments. Because operations jobs have tight deadlines, supervisors want to be notified quickly if there is a problem; they tend to supervise closely.

Summary

Is there one theory of leadership? Probably not; there appear to be a number of suggestions on how to lead, each of which may be appropriate in a given situation. If we believe that leadership is contingent, we must pay attention to the personal characteristics of those who are led. Theories of motivation, supportive, and participative leadership are quite relevant to a contingent approach.

Since the situation is important, leaders must be aware of the situation and environment in which they are working. In information services, there are many different kinds of situations, just as there are many different types of firms.

Does this discussion entirely discredit the great man theory? There are examples of dynamic managers who have "turned around" an ailing information services function. Hopefully, these managers have considered the contingencies previously described and have developed an appropriate approach to leadership. In the next section, we shall see how some of the contingency factors influence leadership styles for information processing.

Leadership in IS

Chapter 3 described a number of management positions in information services; we shall discuss five key leadership roles, including those of the CIO, the manager of systems and programming, the manager of operations, project leaders, and the manager of end-user support. Our objective is to think about the different contingency factors and management tasks associated with these IS positions and to reason about their implications for the style of a leader. Table 7-1 summarizes the management positions under consideration and their characteristics.

CIO

The CIO and/or the manager of the ISD have the most complex leadership task in information services. This individual interacts with senior manage-

TABLE 7-1 Leadership in IS

Manager	Contingencies: Character.	Contingencies: Environment	Management Task	Leadership Style
CIO/ISD	Senior management users; task- and service-oriented IS professionals	Change; uncertainty; boundary spanning; multiple roles	Lead, develop; provide operations; set policy	Variety; supportive of staff; participative with users; consultative with senior management; instrumental with operations
Manager of systems and programming	Users need systems staff	Uncertainty, R&D	Manage project; develop staff	Task oriented for project; advisor to groups; manage resources; collegial and participatory
Manager of operations	Users as demanding customers; staff is in production environment	Deadlines; operational uncertainty routine	Provide reliable, high-quality service	Task oriented; consideration for subordinates; some participation
Project leaders	R&D team project	Uncertainty; user lack of knowledge	Create system; install	Team, participatory, advisory, consultative
End-user support	Random requests; unknown demands	User-driven learning, frustration	Render assistance	Advisor, consultant, teacher

ment and users, a constituency generally interested in service. At the same time, the CIO needs to be a visionary, matching opportunities in the firm to new technological developments. Given the nature of modern technology and its importance to the firm, the word *service* includes a great deal.

We have mentioned that not only must the ISD provide a service in the tradition of all information processing activities, it is also important for IS to contribute to the firm's objectives. This latter role will often involve the CIO with top management and strategy formulation for the entire firm.

Also, due to the pervasiveness of information processing, management and users are concerned with how information services are delivered and by whom. Chapter 2 describes a number of alternatives for structuring information services. Certain structures result in user management having a great deal of responsibility for hardware, software, and systems development activities. The CIO may be called upon for advice and asked to set policy on how all information services in the firm are to be managed.

In addition to users and managers of the firm, the CIO deals with information services professionals. These individuals have a different orientation than many other employees. The systems development group creates abstract designs; programmers convert the designs into a functioning system. Operations staff members are task oriented; their time frame is quite short compared with that of systems developers.

The CIO faces a highly uncertain and changing environment; he or she confronts constant changes in the technology and possibly in the nature of the firm's business. The CIO spans a number of organizational boundaries, interacting with many divisions and departments in the firm.

The manager in the Ives and Olson (1981) study described in Chapter 3 spends about half of his or her time in scheduled meetings; unscheduled meetings take another 20 per cent of the day. These meetings include a variety of individuals, sometimes a mix of ISD and user or management personnel. Ives and Olson reported that in 1981 the ISD manager spent 61 per cent of the time with individuals in the ISD. Today one would expect individuals outside of the ISD to consume a great deal of the CIO's time.

What is the nature of the CIO's management tasks? In some firms, the CIO will have direct line responsibility for information services. In others, like CMI, the CIO serves in a staff position, with ISD managers having a dotted line reporting relationship. Whether vested with line responsibility or not, much of what the CIO needs to accomplish will be done in an advisory and consulting role. The CIO has to help develop the structure of information services and then establish policy so that the structure functions effectively. The CIO is a change agent, bringing technology to the organization. This individual contributes to strategic planning for the firm and for technology.

What leadership style is appropriate for the CIO? An easy answer would be "all." Certainly the CIO will have to exhibit a variety of leadership styles, depending on the individuals and subunits of the organization involved. The CIO may turn out to be instrumental if he or she is responsible for operations. What hardware and software knowledge, and what personal skills, are needed to operate the firm's information systems?

For the ISD staff, especially those involved in systems development, the CIO will be supportive and probably participative. The CIO will be instrumental in bringing in design tools and techniques to improve design productivity.

With users, the CIO should be participative and consultative. It is important to learn what users are thinking and to understand their problems; a participatory style should help users provide information. The CIO is a consultant, suggesting solutions to problems for users and for senior management. In consultative and advisory positions, leadership is mostly a social influence process. Individuals may listen to the CIO because he or she has the position or is a vice president, but the quality of the advice and the competence of the individual will determine the success of the CIO's leadership.

Manager of Systems and Programming

The manager of systems and programming deals primarily with users and with the ISD staff. The user wants a particular system, though he or she may have very limited knowledge of how systems work or what the alternatives are for developing the system. The ISD staff working with the manager of systems and programming constitutes a group of professionals. These individuals, as we shall see in the next chapter, confront a difficult environment. They face a great deal of conflict, and their work cuts across a number of departments.

The manager of systems and programming works in an environment with long time horizons and great uncertainty. The development of a custom information systems is often an R&D project. There is uncertainty about the best alternative for a system (e.g., a package or a custom application) and about how to implement the chosen alternative. The management task here is clearly stated but difficult to accomplish. The manager of systems and programming is concerned with project management and the development of the ISD staff.

In terms of leadership style, we would expect to find the manager of systems and programming instrumental and task oriented for the details of projects. For example, the manager might insist on the use of a certain design tool such as dataflow diagrams and formal project management techniques, and might establish documentation standards.

The manager of systems and programming also has to be an advisor to various project groups. He or she may be called upon to resolve differences between analysts and users or to make final decisions on a resource issue or design points for an application.

This manager must control resources, primarily people and their time. He or she worries about assigning individuals to projects and about the performance of each project team. Since analysts and programmers see themselves as professionals, this manager often adopts a collegial and participatory leadership style. Unfortunately, this type of style may be in conflict with some of the instrumental duties of project management and resource allocation. It is difficult to be collegial and solve the problems of a system that is 6 months late.

Manager of Operations

The manager of operations faces a group of demanding users. He or she operates a utility. Consider another utility as an example. We take service from the electric company for granted unless something goes wrong and we lose power. How does an electric utility provide excellent service? We probably would say that from the customer's standpoint, the utility is good if power is always available, we never have a "brownout" or a complete outage, the company sends maintenance workers quickly if there is a problem, and costs are reasonable. Many users would provide the same description for information services.

Unfortunately, our success in generating and distributing electrical power far exceeds our success in designing and operating information systems. The manager of operations has to live with the quality of the systems produced by the development group. Usually operations is responsible for maintenance and sometimes for systems programming, a much different task than applications programming.

The ISD staff in operations functions in a production environment characterized by routine and rigid time deadlines and operational uncertainty. Will a particular piece of hardware suddenly develop a malfunction? If so, how long will it take for the vendor's service personnel to respond and fix the problem? How long will the system be down? What about software? Will a program that has operated for the last 3 years suddenly fail? Will the programmer be able to fix it? Will a user suddenly provide erroneous input data that no one thought to check in developing the program?

The IS management task is to provide reliable, high-quality service. The problems in providing this service are numerous and are little understood by non-IS managers and users. Many managers of operations also are unable to empathize with users; the manager needs to understand that users depend on systems to do their job. Any failure or outage creates extreme pressures and uncertainty for the user, as well as for the ISD staff.

We would be surprised to find managers of operations who are not task oriented. The operations task is the most structured one in information processing. A good operations manager will be supportive of his or her staff and will probably encourage some participation. In factory settings, we are learning that individuals making the product have many good ideas on how to do the job better. The manager of operations needs to create an environment in which the staff sees it as in their interests to be successful in offering reliable information processing services to users.

Project Leaders

Information services projects are typically undertaken by a team. The development of a computer system is a creative task that requires input from a variety of sources. Project leaders and managers in the ISD usually try diligently to obtain as much user participation as possible. The design team is a formal vehicle; users and ISD staff are assigned to it. The team is given the responsibility to develop the system and provided with resources for the project.

In the development of a new application, there is a great deal of uncertainty. The team encounters the same uncertainty as the manager of systems and programming. What alternative should be adopted for the system? Should we develop the application through a package or a custom system?

The project manager is concerned about these questions and about the management of the team itself. One ISD kept holding meetings about a key system; users received invitations well in advance, but for three consecutive meetings, no users attended. Uncertainty about the project is compounded by users' lack of knowledge about what they want and about technology in general.

The project leader's task is to create and install a system successfully. The most appropriate leadership style here is participatory; the leader wants all members of the team to contribute. The project leader must also be a consultant and advisor to the development team.

In first discussing participation, we observed that the participatory leader must be sure that one individual does not dominate the group and that reticent members are given a chance to express their views. For a systems development project team, the leader has to restrain the enthusiasm of the professional designer and encourage users to volunteer information, no matter how uncertain they feel about it.

Manager of End-User Support

End-user support is a relatively new activity in most ISDs. This manager faces random requests and unknown demands for services. He or she is expected to be knowledgeable about new products that can support end users and to provide direction for end-user computing.

The environment is driven by users; it is characterized by learning and frustration. Users need help in learning how to work with end-user tools, and they will encounter frustration when tools do not work as advertised. In addition, the ability to use the tool does not mean that the organization's database can support it. For example, consultants in end-user computing can teach users a 4GL. However, if users want to access data that are not in machine-readable form, they will be frustrated with the 4GL and the ISD.

Despite the problems, the leadership style for end-user computing is probably the easiest in information services to describe. It is clearly advisory and consultative. The manager of end-user support must have empathy; he or she must be able to think like a user and provide help. This management position is not a good one for a former manager of systems programming or of operations. In many firms, end-user computing is becoming so important that this manager actually works in and reports to a manager in the user area; this individual is not a part of information services.

Some Thoughts on Leadership

Multiple Styles

One observation drawn from the previous discussion is that for many managers in information services, multiple leadership styles seem appropriate. This conclusion is not surprising, since IS spans many boundaries in the organization. If the technology is pervasive in a firm, individuals from every part of the organization will encounter information services.

The typical IS manager, then, must interact with a number of different individuals in varying circumstances. There is nothing dishonest or hypocritical about displaying different leadership styles, depending on the individuals involved or the situation. It was once observed that a good athletic coach knows which players need a quiet, private word and which ones need to have a huge sendoff when they go into the game. A leader must be able to apply the appropriate style of leadership to the situation in the same manner as the coach.

Developing IS Leadership

One important role for a manager and a leader is development of the staff. Information systems professionals are interested in furthering their careers and enhancing their knowledge. Given project and operating deadlines, it is important for management to make sure that employees devote time to expanding their knowledge and professional qualifications.

Managers should also develop the next generation of managers. Individuals expect to advance in their careers; there is also a great deal of mobility among IS professionals. Part of leadership is identifying and preparing new managers for the organization.

Marketing IS

A leader in any position in the IS organization needs to be sensitive to the importance of marketing IS services. For too long the IS function has performed its tasks without making the rest of the organization aware of its contribution. Newsletters and annual reports can help to inform others in the organization about the services provided by IS. One company has been particularly effective with its newsletters by producing an annual report on how a particular business function (e.g., the production department) is using information processing technology. The focus of the report is on the business function, but the description clearly demonstrates the role of information technology in helping the function meet its objectives.

Leadership at CMI

Tom White, the CIO at CMI, described some of the leadership problems he faces at the firm.

"My biggest role is as a leader of change; nothing stays the same in systems or in the firm. We buy a business or sell it, and there is a new cast of characters and set of problems. The vendors bring out new hardware and software, and the whole business gets turned upside down."

He continued, "Let me give you an example. When I started, we used to be called EDP; then it was MIS, and now we are Information Services. During the days of EDP, the vendors gave away free software and made a bundle on hardware. Today the key is software; everyone looks first for a package to avoid the high cost of custom programming."

Mary Watson, ISD manager for Charleston, joined the conversation: "Not only that, but there are always exceptions to the trends. Suppose we wanted to develop a new system to give us an edge on the competition, say a manufacturing equivalent of the Merrill Lynch Cash Management Account. Where do we get a package for that application? Yet senior company management reads about the trend toward packages and wants to know why they can't have a system tomorrow."

Tom added, "Everyone reads about some great new application at the XYZ Company that is really state-of-the-art. Then they use one of our 7- or even 10-year-old systems and want to know why it's so clumsy. Well, the answer is that we can't afford to replace every system every year. Users are just going to have to learn to live with some advanced and some not so advanced applications."

"In some areas of the business," said Mary, "like financial strategy, the lead time on new ideas seems to be about 5 months. How do we accommodate that? How can we develop systems that quickly to support a new financial or business strategy? We just don't have the tools today to do that kind of job."

Bob Carlin, vice president of finance in Charleston and Mary's superior, stopped by. "I heard that," he said. "You think we keep changing our minds—you're right, we do! But that's business. We're not totally unreasonable around here, and you two are pretty good managers."

He continued, "I've been here for quite a few years and the changes are dramatic. But the biggest difference is having people around in IS like you two, who know more than how to program a computer. We have to lean on you for advice and for helping us to manage all of this equipment and software. I get the feeling that we have technology coming out of our ears; my concern is, how does CMI get the most out of it without going broke in the process?"

Tom White interjected, "That's another major change. The head of ISD used to be a technician who was promoted. My job is 90 per cent management. Sure, I've got to know something about the technology because we make a lot of decisions with a technological component, like what 4GL to choose for the information center. However, what I can do best for senior management is to provide guidance on how to manage and coordinate computing and keep them aware of what opportunities exist. I believe in the "electronic firm" concept. If that's the way it works out, everyone will be using the technology and we have a massive job ahead to help them do it right."

Recommended Readings

Daft, R., and R. Steers, *Organizations: A Micro/Macro Approach.* Glenview, Ill.: Scott, Foresman, 1986. (A good text on management and organizations.)

Filley, A. C., R. J. House, and S. Kerr, *Managerial Process and Organizational Behavior,* 2nd ed. Glennview, Ill.: Scott, Foresman, 1976. (A readable text on organization theory; see the two chapters on leadership.)

Ives, B., and M. Olson, "Manager or Technician? The Nature of the Information System Manager's Job," *MIS Quarterly,* vol. 5, no. 4 (December 1981), pp. 49–62. (A description of the work involved in managing systems shortly before the explosion of micros and end-user computing.)

Mintzberg, H., *The Nature of Managerial Work.* New York: Harper & Row, 1973. (Contains excellent insights into managerial and leadership roles.)

Vroom, V., *Work and Motivation.* New York: Wiley, 1964. (A classic book on motivation; a full explanation of the model discussed in this chapter.)

Discussion Problems

7.1 Don Johnson is executive vice president of Hi Energy Electronics. Two years ago, he promoted the manager of systems software and technology, Sid Harris, to be manager of information services. The firm interviewed a number of external candidates, but the ISD staff and an external consultant all recommended Sid for the position.

The major problem that everyone recognized in this promotion was Sid's technical background. He was very good in dealing with the technical staff, but had little experience with managers and users. Most of his technical work focused on the operating system and tuning the mainframe computer system.

Sid was experiencing a number of problems with users. "These guys want me to investigate four or five alternatives. That's stupid. I don't have the time or staff to do that kind of research. Users should rely on our knowledge to tell them what's best."

The users were not entirely happy with Sid's performance, and Sid was unhappy because he thought he should be made a vice president of information services. "Some of the users we've helped get out of hot water are now VPs, and I'm not."

How can Don deal with this problem? He wants to influence Sid's approach to work and still provide service to users. Don said, "I leave IS alone until the noise level from users gets too high, and then I do something."

7.2 Mike Sanders is vice president for information systems at Consolidated Chemicals. He has described his position as follows: "I see the president at least once a week for an hour. At headquarters I have a staff of 10 people; most of the action is; in the field, and I travel a lot. I don't have any illusions; my budget is peanuts compared with that of the other VPs. In addition, we're a service. No one sees us as essential in running the business, at least not yet."

What approaches can Mike use to provide leadership in information services, given his relatively isolated position at headquarters? In what way might he influence information processing more than he expects? What role does Mike play for the IS staff working in the divisions and plants?

Questions

1. What is motivation?
2. Why is motivation an important concept for a manager?
3. What is valence? Expectancy?
4. Explain the Vroom model of motivation.
5. Can an outcome have a negative valence? Give an example.
6. What does negative valence do to motivation?
7. Describe at least three roles of leadership.
8. Why do managers sometimes feel they have little influence in the organization?
9. How do subordinates pick up leadership cues from their managers?
10. How does a participative leader behave?
11. What is supportive leadership?
12. What is the difference between participative and instrumental leadership?
13. What is leadership contingency theory?
14. Describe the leadership tasks of a CIO.
15. What creates uncertainty in a CIO's environment?
16. What are the leadership challenges of the manager of systems and programming?
17. How does the manager of operations provide leadership?
18. What are the leadership responsibilities of the project manager?
19. How can a manager exhibit multiple styles of leadership?
20. As a CIO, how can one develop leadership skills in other IS managers?

8

Management of IS Personnel

One major task for managers in the ISD is the management of IS personnel. Despite the fact that we are dealing with machines, the success of information processing depends to a large extent on the people who work in information services.

Is management of IS personnel any different from management of other individuals in the organization? In some respects, the answer is "yes" because of the variety of tasks found in information services. Analysts and programmers regard themselves as professionals, while individuals in operations may feel more like line production workers than office workers.

Most of the research on IS personnel has focused on programmers and analysts, possibly because the educational and training requirements for these positions are greater than those for a computer operator, for example. (We include systems and maintenance programmers in the category of professionals even though they may report to an operations manager.) We shall review some research on the management of IS personnel and then offer guidelines for this part of the IS manager's job.

Survey of Research

Couger and Zawacki

One of the best-known research studies of programmer and analyst jobs was conducted by Couger and Zawacki (1978). This study focused on the motivations of IS professionals. Couger and Zawacki concluded that IS professionals have a stronger need for growth and personal development than other professionals. One of the potentially most significant findings is that IS personnel have a lower need to interact with others (low social need) than other professionals.

Goldstein and Rockart

Goldstein and Rockart (1984) extended the research of Couger and Zawacki to look at a constellation of factors associated with programmer and analyst job satisfaction. Whereas Couger and Zawacki focused on job characteristics associated with satisfaction, Goldstein and Rockart added two other classes of variables: those related to role perceptions and those related to supervisory and peer leadership. These latter researchers found that role perceptions and leadership, as well as job characteristics, are important in evaluating satisfaction.

It seems reasonable to expect that the environment in which the programmer or analyst works will have an impact on satisfaction and job attitudes. Why are we interested in satisfaction and attitudes? There has been little evidence linking worker satisfaction with job performance; however, the results of research suggest that job satisfaction is negatively correlated with the intention to leave the organization. That is, the less satisfied an individual is, the more likely he or she is to quit. Since turnover in information services is 15 to 20 per cent per year, anything management can do to retain good staff members is important. It can be very costly to recruit and prepare new employees to contribute to the IS department.

Bartol and Martin

A 1982 review by Bartol and Martin surveyed a large number of papers on IS personnel. The authors concluded that information processing professionals are similar in many ways to other professionals. IS personnel have high needs for achievement and growth, possibly higher than those of individuals in other professions. IS staff members place less emphasis on money than is often believed; individuals with a high need for achievement often value money as an indicator of their achievements rather than for its own value.

Individuals with a high need achievement function better when their goals are challenging but possible to attain. A manager creates a great deal of frustration for IS programmers and analysts by continually asking them to meet impossible deadlines or take on excessive workloads. IS personnel should function well when given realistic goals and regular feedback on their progress.

Bartol and Martin reviewed studies that included computer operators; these individuals did not find their jobs particularly motivating. Management needs to consider how to make these tasks more interesting and less routine.

Consistent with our discussion in the last chapter, research indicates that there is no one best way to manage IS; the best leadership style depends on the situation. Research suggests that management can be more directive in operations areas, where tasks are structured, and less directive in the unstructured area of systems development.

Bartol and Martin argued that human resources are the critical variable in information processing today. There simply are not enough professionals to develop the systems that users demand. New technology—tools like 4GLs, query languages, applications generators, and end-user programming —will help. However, none of these tools, even all of the tools together, will result in the order of magnitude or better improvement needed in systems development productivity.

The quality and talents of IS personnel become even more important as the role of IS changes in the firm. Managers and others in information services now expect to participate in setting the strategy of the firm; the emphasis is on the strategic use of technology. ISD staff members will have to be better versed in the functions of business and in the concerns of senior management.

The ISD manager has to consider personnel development as a high-priority activity; a turnover rate of 20% a year means that every 2 years almost half of the staff changes. How does one develop IS personnel? One way is to plan for education and training for the staff. Every professional in the department should be expected to spend 2 to 3 weeks a year on professional activities, including conferences and courses. The IS field changes rapidly, and there is a constant need to update IS professionals.

An IS manager may also want to consider job rotation. If an applications programmer is tired of this work, perhaps he or she would like to try maintenance programming for a while. The IS manager must also make sure that the best tools are available for the staff; this means investigating programmer/analyst workstations, aids to documentation, DBMSs, and the use of 4GLs for at least part of the development of new applications.

Baroudi

Baroudi (1985) conducted a study of IS professionals that focused on the determinants of an employee's stated intentions to leave. (An intention to leave is significant because actual resignations may depend on economic conditions; the intention to leave expresses negative feelings about one's job.)

Baroudi began with an elaborate model of the factors associated with intentions to quit; he built a causal model using a statistical technique called path analysis. The model that resulted after eliminating insignificant findings is shown in Figure 8-1.

Boundary spanning is one of the major variables in the model; it occurs when an individual crosses intradepartmental and interorganizational lines to perform the job. In information services, boundary spanning is part of almost every position, especially systems development. Given the pervasiveness of the technology, however, managers, designers, and operations

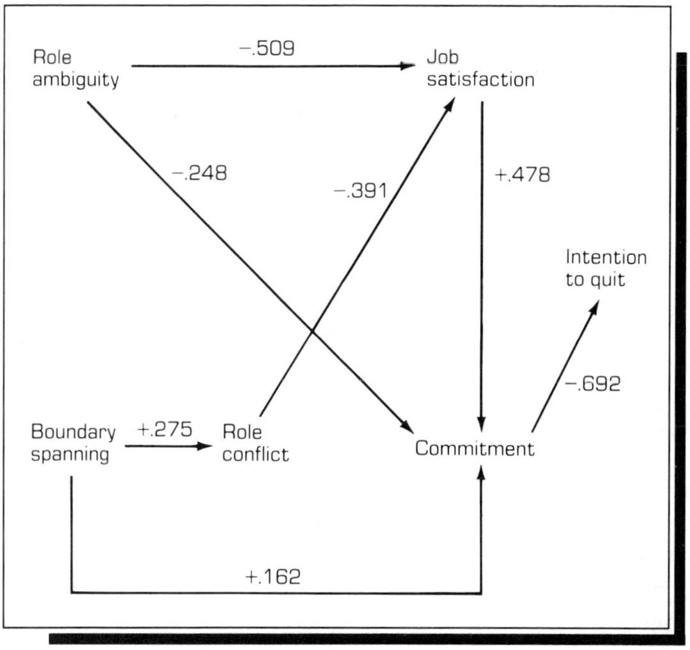

FIGURE 8-1 The Baroudi model. The numbers are path coefficients. The higher the number, the stronger the relationship. A minus sign means that the variables are inversely related. (From Baroudi, 1985)

staff are likely to come in contact with individuals from many different areas of the organization. As more intraorganizational systems are developed, boundary spanning by IS personnel will increase even further.

In the Baroudi model, role conflict exists when an individual receives conflicting job performance information or is overloaded. If a project manager tells an analyst to choose one alternative and the user in charge of the design team demands a different alternative, the result is conflict.

Role ambiguity is the lack of clear, precise information on what someone is expected to do. Since systems development work involves a great deal of creativity and autonomy, there is an opportunity for role ambiguity.

We can interpret the results of this study by looking at Figure 8-1. First, contrary to the researcher's expectations, job satisfaction was not directly related to intention to quit. Instead there was a negative path from commitment to intention to quit. We can interpret this finding to mean that the greater one's commitment, the less the intention to quit. (Of course, we cannot claim a causal relationship; it is equally likely that someone who has little intention of quitting has commitment.)

As expected, job satisfaction is positively related to commitment; we would expect to find that individuals who are satisfied are also committed to their work, and vice versa. Role ambiguity is seen as a negative factor in this study; it is negatively related to job satisfaction and commitment.

The variable of boundary spanning is an interesting one; it is positively related to role conflict, which, in turn is negatively related to satisfaction.

However, boundary spanning is positively related to commitment. It appears that boundary spanning is not viewed as a negative, at least by the programmers and analysts in this study. Boundary spanning has the potential to make a job more interesting; IS professionals may also feel that their work has a more significant impact on the firm if it encompasses several departments or divisions.

Role conflict, as expected, is negatively related to job satisfaction. The more conflicting demands are placed on a programmer or analyst, the less satisfied the person appears. In general, Baroudi concluded that role conflict and role ambiguity are dysfunctional.

How does one manage better, given the results of this study? One way is to reduce role conflict and ambiguity. For example, the manager can make sure that reporting structures are clear. Assuming that the systems development staff has a matrix organization, one could implement a policy that clearly defines the role of the manager of systems and programming and the role of individual project managers. One could indicate that the manager of systems and programming has the final word on performance reviews. He or she will solicit input from project managers, but raises and promotions will not come from the project manager. (The opposite approach is possible, too; the objective is simply to make the policy clear to programmers and analysts.)

Baroudi also found that in his sample of firms, profitability was low. The results were low raises and bonuses, but the reasons for lower than expected rewards were not explained. Programmers and analysts could not read a clear signal from their raises, creating ambiguity.

Some degree of role conflict is probably a result of boundary spanning and therefore may be unavoidable. IS serves so many constituencies that there will always be a need for boundary spanning. The manager can make it clear that boundary spanning is expected, and can provide an environment in which conflicts can be discussed and resolved.

The Changing IS Role

We have stated that the role of the IS professional, from manager to programmer, is changing. How do these changes affect the management of IS personnel?

First, the ISD is losing power, a loss that worries some CIOs. On the other hand, if managed properly, the loss of power can be turned into a gain in influence. Computing is being distributed to users, both hardware and the control over systems development.

CIOs will have less reporting to them, and hopefully will replace that reporting relationship by becoming more of an advisor to senior management. How should the firm organize information processing? How does it coordinate diverse divisions with different information needs? How does it avoid developing the same application over and over again at different locations?

The systems analyst now has a much wider range of alternatives to suggest to the user, both in terms of the way in which a system will be developed and in the technology for developing it. (We shall discuss these points further in Chapters 9 and 10.) This kind of change in technology for executing and developing systems transforms the systems developer into more of a consultant and advisor as well.

How do these changes influence the variables discussed in this chapter that are associated with IS professionals and their jobs? There is certainly an opportunity to satisfy high needs for achievement, since the task of managing IS is becoming infinitely more complex. There are many more options for organizing information processing and developing systems.

Unfortunately, all of these options probably contribute to greater role conflict and ambiguity and to greater boundary spanning. With users or division management in charge of information processing at the local level, what is the role of the CIO? How does the CIO exert influence? How far can he or she go in trying to convince management to encourage coordination of information processing in the firm?

For programmers and analysts, what kinds of conflicts will occur if they recommend that users work with a package instead of developing a custom application? Will there be more problems if they leave most of the development to a user or if they develop the system for the user? What is their role with respect to the user?

The programmers and analysts who report to a local division may feel dissatisfied because there is no group of IS professionals with whom they can interact. Will division management be able to establish clear reporting relationships and reduce role ambiguity?

Managing IS Personnel

In reviewing individual studies, we have discussed some recommendations for managing IS staff members; we shall integrate and expand that discussion in this section. See Table 8-1. The manager plays a number of roles in

TABLE 8-1 Managing IS Personnel

Develop clear reporting relationships.
Establish a well-understood reward structure.
Be sure that a superior is responsible for each individual in a matrix structured unit.
Provide feedback to the IS staff.
Communicate with the IS staff; discuss problems and management objectives; share the plan.
Monitor systems development projects and provide resources.
Provide the staff with a good environment (e.g., programmer workstations, program development tools)
Provide resources for staff development.
Prepare the staff to cope with change.

the organization. As a resource allocator and leader, he or she supervises IS staff members.

Remember that direct and indirect actions influence subordinates. The leader should be sure that reporting relationships are clear and that employees know for what behavior they will be rewarded. Even if reporting relationships are matrixed, they can be clear. At CMI, Tom White is the CIO. The managers of the ISD at Fremont, Omaha, Chicago, and Charleston know that they report to the local division/plant managers. The local plant manager may ask Tom for his evaluation of the ISD manager's technical skills and contribution to overall information processing at CMI, but it is the local plant manager who provides promotions, rewards, raises, and bonuses.

The local managers have a dotted line reporting relationship to Tom White. He, in turn, reports to the chief operating officer of CMI. Tom will try to persuade the local ISD managers to follow policies beneficial to the firm; if that fails, he can talk to their direct superiors, the plant/division managers. If all else fails, he can turn to the chief operating officer and try to convince him that the policy he wants to implement should be instituted. Hopefully, what Tom wants to accomplish will be seen as beneficial, and an appeal to the chief operating officer will not be necessary.

A good IS manager will provide adequate feedback to the staff. Since it appears that due to high need for achievement, IS personnel may require more feedback than other professionals, feedback and the reward structure are two ways in which managers can influence staff behavior.

Related to feedback and clarity of reporting relationships is the entire area of communications. None of the studies presented mention communications directly, but we have found it to be very important in managing professionals. The IS plan should not be a secret from the IS staff. Staff members should be informed about what is happening in the organization. If information services is to contribute to corporate strategy, staff members have to know what that strategy is. All of the managers in IS are linked to the levels above and below them; that link is a communications path for what is happening in the organization. We advocate quarterly or semiannual meetings of the IS staff; these meetings provide an opportunity to communicate what is happening in the firm. We believe that keeping the staff informed will help to generate creative ideas and foster commitment to the firm.

Managers in ISD also influence subordinates' behavior by the way they organize work. Analysts and programmers are assigned to different projects; operators perform different jobs on various shifts in the computer room. A manager has discretion in assigning staff members and in deciding what role staff members play in a particular assignment. The manager must listen carefully to what subordinates say about their progress and determine whether or not more resources are required.

Managers also provide the tools to be used by the IS staff. A number of systems development tools are available, including 4GLs, workbenches for analysts and programmers, and systems for computer-aided systems analysis and design. There are also a number of tools to improve the operations of a computer center. Packages to help manage tape and disk libraries have existed for a number of years. There is software to track changes in systems and to maintain source code for programs. All of these tools need to be considered as ways to improve the ability of the IS staff to do its job.

We have also discussed staff development. The CIO and ISD managers need a long-range perspective on the staff. How can they improve the skills of their employees? How can they develop commitment and make employees real professionals? The manager creates an environment for the development staff that is collegial and professional.

Change

A key theme throughout this book and in the studies previously reviewed is change. At first, the IS profession lived with technological change as computer generations advanced rapidly. New computers featured increased speed and storage; the rules of programming changed from maximizing hardware efficiency to getting the job done. Applications moved from batch processing to on-line interaction with the user.

Now the ISD faces change that is organizational as well as technological. The greatest challenge for the IS professional is to adapt to changes in user control over processing and user contributions to the systems development effort. The systems developer may no longer be in charge of applications development. Users with a microcomputer may create a dangerous situation when they try to generalize from Lotus to a multiuser, on-line system serving thousands of terminals. The computer professional has to accept all of these changes and somehow guide the organization toward effective information processing.

Managers in ISD have to prepare the staff for its role. We have presented a simple model for change that includes the steps of unfreezing, moving, and refreezing. What is the role of management in this process? Managers can facilitate unfreezing by showing their support for changes. Staff meetings, periodic meetings with all ISD professionals, and even casual encounters offer an opportunity for managers to indicate what changes they expect to see.

The manager can sketch a view of the firm in the future. CMI plans to become an electronic business. Tom White needs to tell the IS staff about this vision; he has to indicate that he and management support a pattern of processing in which local managers are in charge of information services. He must set the tone for the contribution expected from users and the approach to be taken by the professional.

The unfreezing process is combined with moving. On a design team, the manager of systems and programming might pair an analyst who is enthusiastic about user design with one who is opposed to giving up control to users. The exercise of designing the application will help to move the control-oriented analyst toward to the current style of the firm.

Refreezing occurs as the manager rewards those who have changed. Rewards may be monetary, but public recognition should also be considered. The analyst who has successfully functioned on a user-managed design team might become the next project leader.

Change is very hard to produce with no help. A key responsibility of management in today's IS environment is to develop the staff, and that means helping the staff change to keep up with the pace of change in information processing.

IS Personnel Management at CMI

Tom White was in Chicago at the quarterly meeting of information services managers for CMI. "I think we are getting somewhere with the plant managers. They are beginning to see the need for some coordination, especially when we pointed out that Chicago and Fremont were both developing similar accounts payable systems."

Mary Watson asked, "At the next meeting, we will have all of the professional staff from across the country, won't we?"

Tom responded, "Yes we should do that. We want to talk about the long-range plan, which should be ready for publication by that time."

The manager of the ISD at Fremont added, "Are you sure you want to do that? It may make everyone nervous, since they already have so much to do."

Tom thought and then spoke. "You may be right, but I would rather take a chance on scaring them in order to get them on board. We have a major problem to get analysts and programmers to accept all that is happening. We will try to get some group support at our semiannual staff meetings.

"I want to communicate to everyone that the game is changing, but that we know it and the changes are planned. I was thinking of getting a couple of outside speakers to talk about what is happening in the industry, and maybe follow that up with a panel so that the audience can ask questions."

"Tom, are you going to come right out and tell everyone what they should do to change?" asked Mary.

"No. I wish I could, but I'm not sure I understand all of the changes required yet myself," replied Tom. "I know that we will have to give up some control; we've been doing that anyway, since all of you now report to the plant managers. But it will go further than that; we have to get ready for users taking more responsibility for all of information processing."

The Omaha ISD manager spoke. "Some of that is happening already, but I suppose it would be good to talk about it with the staff. Some of my folks are taking it all in stride; others seem quite disturbed by what is happening. Maybe if we share some of our feelings, it will make it easier on the staff.

"That's what I'd like to get out of the next get-together of all our staff members. We have to let them know that we are aware of what is happening and that we support it. There is nothing wrong in deferring to a user; in fact, I would like to see if all of you can move to putting a user in charge of a design team. Your project leaders then become coordinators and guides on what to do next."

The Fremont ISD manager shook his head. "That will be hard to sell at our shop. We have a terrible time just getting the user members of a design team to show up; my project leaders run things, and they run a pretty tight ship."

Tom said, "That may be part of the problem; the users don't see that they contribute much. Try getting a user to be in charge, and then be sure to talk to your designers about how to make it work. You still can't run everything; instead, your guys have to structure the process and present alternatives to users for them to choose."

The Chicago ISD manager spoke next. "I've got a more immediate problem. We lost 25 per cent of our analyst staff last year, and I can't keep going that way. It takes us a year to make a new employee productive, and I'm taking two steps backward for every one forward."

Mary Watson asked, "Do you have any idea why? Is there something in the local labor market? Are you not paying enough?"

"Our salaries are competitive. My own guess is that the manager of systems and programming is not doing his stuff. I think he keeps most of the staff in the dark; they really don't know where they stand or what he thinks of their projects. One person who was leaving complained to me that we were in the dark age of systems development."

Tom White responded, "Fremont is evaluating a couple of nice tools that will help an analyst draw structure charts and define the database contents. Why don't you make a trip out there with your manager of systems and programming to look at them? If they are good, we'll talk about making one of them a company standard."

Mary added, "Along the way, why don't you talk to your manager of systems and programming about staff development? There isn't much feedback on a 2-year design project; we have to provide it. Everyone in my operation gets a formal evaluation of performance once a year, and if a major project ends, that calls for another performance appraisal before going on to the next assignment."

Tom White stated, "We can't afford even 15 per cent turnover every year. Each of you has to be aware of what your analysts and programmers are thinking and what their problems are. One of the keys to your jobs is staff development; don't forget that what you say and do is pretty important to the staff. They want recognition when they do something good, and they need your help in resolving conflicts they get into because of the business we're in and the way the environment keeps changing. Let's see if we can lay out an agenda for the next meeting with all the staff to talk about the issues we think concern them the most."

Recommended Readings

Baroudi, J., "The Impact of Role Variables on IS Personnel Work Attitudes and Intentions," *MIS Quarterly*, vol. 9, no. 4 (December 1985), pp. 341–356. (An excellent paper on the factors affecting IS professionals' jobs.)

Bartol, K., and D. Martin, "Managing Information Systems Personnel: A Review of the Literature and Managerial Implications," *MIS Quarterly*, vol. 6 (Special Issue, 1982), pp. 49–70. (A good survey of studies on analysts, programmers, and other IS staff members.)

Couger, D., and R. Zawacki, "What Motivates DP Professionals?" *Datamation* (September 1978), pp. 116–123. (One of the most widely quoted studies of analyst/programmer satisfaction and needs.)

Goldstein, D., and J. Rockart, "An Examination of Work-Related Correlates of Job Satisfaction in Programmer/Analysts," *MIS Quarterly*, vol. 8, no. 2 (June 1984), pp 103–115. (A paper that expands on the variables considered by Couger and Zawacki in looking at IS job satisfaction.)

Discussion Problems

8.1 Jay Thomas is manager of systems and programming for the United Bank. Prior to joining United, he was a systems engineer for a large computer vendor and was assigned to the bank. After several years, he decided to accept an offer to work for the bank.

As a systems engineer, Jay had spent most of his time researching and solving problems, often with the computer vendor's software or its interaction with a customer's applications software.

In his new role of systems manager, Jay had to supervise others for the first time and also had to be concerned with projects that ran for a long term compared with those of his systems engineering days.

Jay's manager was highly complimentary about his knowledge of the system and his ability to solve problems. "The only problem I have with Jay is keeping him going. Once he has solved the basic problem that requires a system, he tends to drop the rest of the project as uninteresting. He developed one important special report for a user, and after it ran for the first month, he lost interest in it. Jay was supposed to follow up to see that operations produced the report and the user liked it."

What can Jay's manager do to help him make more of a contribution to the firm? How have the demands on Jay changed since he left the computer vendor?

8.2 Mary Anderson is in charge of systems at the Beneficial Insurance Company. Mary's primary background is in insurance; she began as an actuary with the firm. Soon she was developing Fortran programs for actuarial analysis on a time-sharing computer.

As she gained experience, Mary became the user expert on programming for the actuarial department. When senior management became dissatisfied with information services, it began looking for ways to move the IS staff closer to the user. Mary was asked to work in systems and to introduce a greater degree of user orientation.

Mary is a capable manager, but she has had some problems within ISD. A number of the systems analysts have criticized her in two main areas. First, they say that she has only programmed in Fortran, which is not a "real information processing language." Second, they ask, how can Mary be in charge of systems when she has not really designed a business system?

Which of these criticisms is more valid? What can Beneficial do to help Mary gain the respect of the systems staff? What can Mary do?

Questions

1. Why might programmers and analysts have lower social needs than other professionals?
2. Is programmer and analyst satisfaction important? Why?
3. Do you think that satisfaction leads to productivity? That productivity leads to satisfaction? Both? Explain your reasoning.
4. Can you give too much of a challenge to someone who has high needs for achievement? What might be the result?
5. Why is there such a high turnover rate among programmers and analysts?
6. What is boundary spanning? How does it apply in IS?
7. Do you think boundary spanning will increase or decrease in the future for IS staff members?
8. What is role ambiguity? How can it be dysfunctional?
9. What management actions do Baroudi's research suggest?
10. What is role conflict? What harm can it cause?
11. Is a loss of power a serious problem for the ISD?
12. How does a loss of power change the way IS professionals operate?
13. What steps can management take to help the IS staff change its orientation?
14. How can technology create more role conflict and ambiguity for the IS staff member?
15. Why is it important for a manager to provide feedback to subordinates?
16. How does IS management support the staff?
17. Does the IS manager need to take any action to reorient the staff, or will it happen naturally as the role of the end user changes?
18. What kinds of technological tools can management supply to the IS staff?
19. What role do meetings with the IS staff play in management?
20. How can distributed processing reduce the morale of the IS staff, especially local staff members?

9

Systems Development

One of the most important tasks undertaken by the ISD is systems development. Until the advent of minis and micros, systems development tended to be tightly controlled by computer professionals. The typical system ran on a mainframe computer and served a number of users. The primary justification for a system was often cost savings.

Cost reduction led to the development of a large number of transactions processing systems; these systems handled the basic business of the firm, including order entry, production control, shipping, invoicing, accounts receivable, accounts payable, and accounting. Over time, some firms recognized that the computer allowed them to undertake applications that were previously impossible, such as a passenger name reservation database for an airline, rental car firm, or hotel chain.

Today there are many transactions processing systems that demand substantial processing power. These systems often build large databases that are of interest to various users in the firm. Instead of trying to determine what these users want, many ISDs are providing tools that allow users to extract their own information from a database.

In addition, many users feel that they can meet some of their processing needs independently of the ISD, for example, by using a microcomputer. Good candidates for this type of system are applications in which the user has complete control over the data or imports the data from an external information provider. For the most part, multiuser systems should be designed by computer professionals. In addition, systems that affect critical company operations should be designed at least with the advice of information services personnel. It is unwise to allow a user to design a critical system if the user is unaware of issues like data editing, data integrity, backup, controls, and similar concerns of the computer professional.

Role of the Professional

The changing role of the information processing staff member is evident, then, in systems development. First, the ISD no longer controls the systems development process in the firm. Second, given the high cost of developing a system, it is necessary to dramatically improve the systems building process. Chapter 10 is devoted to a discussion of some alternative approaches to systems analysis and design. Finally, systems developers should consider changing the way they guide the design process for large multiuser systems.

Multiuser Systems

There has been a conspicuous lack of success in the development of large information processing systems. Typically designers compromise on the original specifications in order to complete a project. Even then, the project is often completed well beyond the promised delivery time and with a considerable cost overrun.

Consistent with the developing advisory role for information processing professionals, there are a number of advantages to having the systems analyst become a consultant as opposed to a strict project leader. Too often users find it easy to abrogate their responsibilities in design and leave all decisions to the systems designer. Unfortunately, systems designers do not use systems after they have been completed; users do. It is vitally important for the ownership of a system to reside with users rather than with the ISD.

In Chapter 11 we shall discuss the implementation process for new systems in great detail. The objective is to obtain user involvement in the design process and user ownership of systems. If the design team leader is a user rather than a professional analyst, it should be easier to achieve these goals. The designer then becomes more of a "tour guide," showing the design team what steps have to be taken next.

When it is necessary for the team to make a design decision, the analyst structures the problem and suggests various alternatives. The design team makes the final choice. Since there are usually many alternative ways to design a system, the skill of the analyst is needed to choose an appropriate subset for the design team to consider. The analyst also has to explain the advantages and disadvantages of each alternative.

In this process, users are learning about systems and the technology. The professional designer is more than an advisor; he or she is a teacher as well. As users learn more about the technology, they should become more skilled in its use. Maintenance requests should be reduced, as greater user input should result in a better design. Users should also understand better the implications of their maintenance requests.

Microcomputer Systems

The development of an application on a microcomputer for a single user is the extreme opposite of a large multiuser application for a mainframe. It is quite likely that users will develop their own system under these conditions. First, users want independence from the ISD. Second, the organization probably does not have enough resources to provide systems analyst support for individual users.

It is important, however, to provide consulting support for individuals trying to develop applications. The first type of support ISD can offer is classroom instruction in developing applications. A course in systems analysis and design would probably not be too popular. However, courses in specific development packages like spreadsheets and 4GLs are of interest to users.

Beyond classroom support, the ISD will need to provide consulting help to users. After users have developed their first application, the need for support will probably be reduced. We have consistently failed to realize how little users understand about systems analysis and design and computer technology in general. Therefore, it is important to have some staff members devoted to consultation with users about their own development efforts on micros.

4GL Applications

Another approach for users seeking a solution to a problem is to use a 4GL on a mainframe computer. (See Chapter 10 for a discussion of these languages.) The application may be trivial from a systems analysis and design standpoint, such as the simple retrieval of data for a report. However, supporting this kind of retrieval can be a real problem.

To access data on a mainframe, the user must know the following:

1. The structure of the data elements desired on the mainframe.
2. The name of the file where the data are stored and the file's parameters.
3. The commands required to retrieve the data on the mainframe.
4. How to process the data using the 4GL.

Users can gain knowledge of 4GLs through classes and practice. However, a user must depend on information services for information on how to access the data on the mainframe, such as the structure of records and the location of the files.

The information center, a consulting office for users, is one vehicle for providing this kind of consulting help. The center is staffed by consultants familiar with the 4GL being used in the organization and with the structure of the databases on the mainframe computer. They should also be able to advise users when the application planned is so large that it should be undertaken by a design team.

Mixed Applications

In the future, the types of systems development efforts described previously will blur; users will work with microcomputer-based workstations connected to a network. They are likely to extract data from the firm's transactions processing computers and from various databases of data made available to them.

What is an application in this environment? There are multiuser applications running on the mainframe that build databases. In addition, users have their own applications that provide them with personal information and DSS. Finally, there are small multiuser systems running on micros and mainframes.

In this mixed environment, another variable complicates the design process: the interaction of the user with the network. Now the user has to know more than before, or else all of the following considerations have to be made transparent to the user:

1. How do you connect with the network?
2. How do you address the machine with the data of interest to your application?
3. What is the structure of the data on the machine you are accessing?
4. What is the query required to extract the data of interest?
5. How does one route the data to the workstation?
6. Once at the workstation, how do you massage the data to be processed by the user's local programs?

In this mixed, networked environment, systems analysts have a variety of tasks to perform. They must help the user accomplish all of the tasks previously described. In addition, they must help design the network and the requirements for software at the user interface. Finally, they must be able to offer consulting advice on a variety of problems so that users can obtain the processing they desire.

Choosing Alternatives

Table 9-1 summarizes the various types of systems previously discussed. When will ISD be asked for assistance? We hope that users will request help

TABLE 9-1 Some Types of Applications

System Type	Characteristics
Multiuser	Conventional application used by many people in the organization
Micro	Developed on a personal computer by the user or a professional designer
4GL	Developed using a 4GL or very-high-level language, possibly by the user but often by an IS professional
Mixed application	Characteristics of all of the preceding types (e.g., a reporting system accessing data from a conventional system; data are downloaded to a personal computer that runs a 4GL

from professionals whenever an application they are planning will require more than a day or so of user time. If the application is to serve multiple users or involve complex retrieval from a mainframe system, ISD personnel can help. In some projects, the ISD may provide considerable resources, for example, the development of a large multiuser system. In other instances, the ISD may simply help clarify users' thoughts about choosing a particular alternative.

The earliest opportunity for ISD involvement occurs when a user is first thinking about a computer application. In the early days of computing, the computer department undertook a feasibility study when a user requested a new system. The study sought to determine if the requested application was feasible and advisable. Often the primary criterion for the application was cost savings. Some firms required tangible cost reductions, while others allowed the inclusion of intangibles like "better customer service."

In today's environment, the question of feasibility is much less important. *Given the powerful technology available, there is probably some way to help a user.* The problem today is to determine how best to provide assistance.

Alternatives

The various ways to design a system described previously present options for the development of a basically custom-designed system. In addition, there are options based on the technology to be employed. For example, one can think of the following matrix:

	Mainframe	Minicomputer	Microcomputer
Custom			
On-line			
Batch			
Package			
On-line			
Batch			

The question of feasibility how focuses on what alternative is most appropriate for the request. Feasibility becomes important only if helping the user with a certain alternative is infeasible. For example, it is possible that a microcomputer cannot handle the volume of transactions predicted for a particular application; here the micro is infeasible.

Choosing an Alternative

It is likely that a user and designer can generate four or five alternatives for a given project. How do they choose which one to undertake? One approach is to use a simple scoring model. See Table 9-2. The design team must first agree on a set of evaluation criteria. Good criteria include the following:

- Percentage of user needs met
- Cost
- Development time
- Resources required for development
- Impact on existing projects
- Probability of success
- Priority of the application to the business

It is probably sufficient to use five to seven evaluation criteria in choosing among alternatives.

The problem with the criteria is due to the lack of a common unit of measure. User needs met is measured as a percentage, cost is usually stated in dollars, time to develop in months or years, and so on. How does the analyst convert these various measures into a common unit? There are a number of approaches; given our purpose of providing guidelines to the decision maker, we shall select a simple method. First, select a score range, like 1 to 7. Then ask users to consider other systems and give the current proposal a score based on their prior experience. For example, if the current system is expected to cost about 60 per cent of the average application, score it as 7×0.6 or 4. Since a low cost is better than a high one, reverse the scale to give $7 - 4 = 3$.

Proceed in a similar manner for the other criteria. If an organization adopts this approach to evaluating alternatives, it is a good idea to maintain statistics on projects. Historical distributions can then be substituted for a

TABLE 9-2 Analysis of Alternatives: The Data for a Scoring Model

Criteria	Weight	Mainframe	Micro	Package
Percentage of user needs met	0.40	75%	60%	50%
Cost	0.15	$150,000	$25,000	$95,000
Probability of success	0.15	0.7	0.8	0.6
Development time (months)	0.10	18	5	12
Priority	0.20	7	5	6
Score (sum weight × criteria)				

TABLE 9-3 Analysis of Alternatives: The Data for a Scoring Model

Criteria	Weight	Mainframe	Micro	Package
Percentage of user needs met	0.40	5	4	4
Cost	0.15	1	7	4
Probability of success	0.15	5	6	4
Development time (months)	0.10	1	6	3
Priority	0.20	7	5	6
Score (sum weight × criteria)		4.49	5.15	4.10

user's judgment on each criterion. For example, an analyst might decide to convert each criterion score to a common unit by mapping the user's rating to a historical distribution centered on the mean, with interval widths of half a standard deviation unit.

The next task is to weight the criteria. Which ones are the most important? Generally, individuals involved in the decision develop a consensus on the weight. Table 9-2 shows three alternatives for a project and five evaluation criteria. Each project is evaluated on each criterion. This kind of decision analysis is supported nicely by a spreadsheet package. Table 9-3 shows the results of multiplying the weights by the scores of each alternative on each project to get a score for each alternative.

The design team should not become a slave to the numbers, however. Instead, the numbers should force the team to ask questions about their assumptions. In Table 9-4, we change the percentage of user needs met for the microcomputer package and see the impact on the ranking of alternatives now. This kind of sensitivity analysis should lead to a consensus on what the best alternative is for the organization at the present time.

The Portfolio of Applications

Several authors have suggested that an organization look at its applications like a stock portfolio. This is an interesting analogy and can be useful in certain instances. However, there are a number of dissimilarities between a stock portfolio and a collection of information systems.

First, almost every item in a stock portfolio has a price at a given time. Second, one is buying a security, not developing it over an extended time

TABLE 9-4 Analysis of Alternatives: The Data for a Scoring Model

Criteria	Weight	Mainframe	Micro	Package
Percentage of user needs met	0.40	5	2	4
Cost	0.15	1	7	4
Probability of success	0.15	5	6	4
Development time (months)	0.10	1	6	3
Priority	0.20	7	5	6
Score (sum weight × criteria)		4.49	4.27	4.10

period. It is easy to determine the impact of buying x shares of stock in company 1 and selling y shares in company 2.

In the case of information systems, the value of a partially completed application is usually about 0. There is also little demand for a system that has not been finished. In fact, custom systems are usually of no value to someone outside of the firm developing the application.

It is very unusual to remove a system from the applications portfolio, much less realize a gain for doing so. Systems disappear only when replaced by a more up-to-date version. The applications portfolio keeps growing through the development of new applications and the maintenance on old ones.

Where is the portfolio concept useful? Examining the types of applications in the portfolio can show management the extent to which high-priority areas of the business are receiving attention. How balanced is the portfolio? Are aging systems concentrated in one area? Compared to competitors, are the applications providing a competitive edge?

The Life Cycle Model

Most books on systems analysis and design present a life cycle model of development. This model is helpful in showing how a system develops and the different roles of those involved in creating it at different times in the development process. The life cycle model is also a good way for managers in the ISD to monitor progress on systems development projects and to plan resource allocations. See Figure 9-1.

Inception

In the inception stage, a user determines that the potential exists to solve a problem using a computer-based system. Users, probably with some help from ISD personnel, conduct an analysis of needs to see whether the idea is worth pursuing.

Feasibility Study

As discussed previously, the life cycle model includes a feasibility study. Some organizations require a formal study to determine if there will be a payback from a system. Today management is more likely to be interested in whether it is feasible to do the requested processing through a number of different alternatives. The most important part of feasibility involves choosing which alternative to pursue. (Of course, one alternative is to do nothing, that is, to stay with the status quo.)

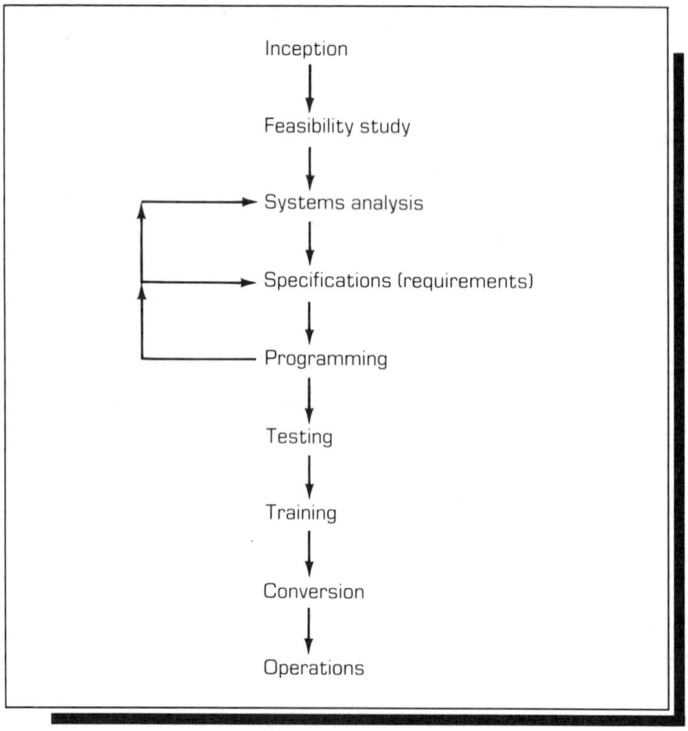

FIGURE 9-1 The systems life cycle model.

Systems Analysis

The first task in systems analysis is to understand the present processing procedures. Once the current method of processing information is clear, the requirements are analyzed. During this phase, users and systems professionals determine the requirements for a new system. They must specify the logic of processing and the necessary inputs and outputs.

Specifications

The requirements analysis gradually evolves into a series of specifications for a new computer-based system. Specifications must show processing logic, database contents, and input and output for the system. Specifications will also describe the structure of major programs and the manual procedures associated with processing.

Programming

If the alternative chosen for the application involves custom programming, it is undertaken at this point. It is important to emphasize that careful development of specifications is of immense value in programming. If programmers have to redesign the system because the specifications are incomplete, a great deal of time will be lost. Management must monitor programming carefully because this task has proven very difficult in the past.

Testing

The system must be tested. Programmers will first test their programs and then the interaction of programs with each other. Users should also provide test data and review the results of tests. Testing can only show the presence of errors; it cannot guarantee their absence. It is also customary to conduct a parallel test in which a new and an old system are run together, using the same data, to see if the results are the same.

Training

Systems require new procedures. If changes are major, effort must be devoted to training the users, who will have to learn new ways of working.

Conversion

When the system has been adequately tested and users are ready to work with it, it is time to begin using it for regular processing.

Operations

When the computer operations staff accepts a new system, it becomes operational. The actual acceptance may come from a quality control group, which will review the tests and the overall quality of design and documentation before accepting the new application. Maintenance on an operational system involves some fixing of errors, but generally it consists of enhancement of a system to add new features. The better the system is designed, the less maintenance is required.

Table 9-5 shows some of the responsibilities of various parties involved in systems development. In particular, users and their management initiate the request for a system. The ISD staff responds with ideas; its management encourages a rapid response. The feasibility study involves all groups; systems analysts suggest alternatives and user representatives evaluate them. All parties cooperate in choosing an alternative.

Users have the responsibility for describing how information is currently processed during systems analysis. The ISD staff guides the analysis and helps document the results. ISD management should review the results and act as a consultant for the ISD staff.

During the development of specifications, users should be involved in

TABLE 9-5 Responsibilities During the Life Cycle

Stage	User/Management	Information Services	ISD Management
Inception	Initiate	Respond with ideas	Encourage rapid response
Feasibility study	Evaluate alternatives; choose one	Suggest alternatives	Review; consider resource requirements
Systems analysis	Describe existing processing, procedures; collect data	Guide analysis; help document; analyze data	Review results; consult for ISD staff
Specifications (requirements)	Design logic of system, reports; plan conversion	Provide guidance on options; review specifications	Review results
Programming	Monitor	Manage programming	Manage project; allocate resources
Testing	Generate data; examine results	Review; conduct actual tests	Review adequacy
Training	Develop materials; conduct sessions	Participate as requested	Review
Conversion	Provide resources; convert	Provide assistance	Monitor
Operations	Provide input; use output; use system	Monitor	Include in operating plans

the design of processing logic, as should user management. The ISD provides skills here in showing how to develop specifications and documenting the results of a design. Often systems have major implications for corporate policy, and senior management needs to review each application. In one case, a system had six major policy implications, but management had not brought these policies to the attention of users, who bitterly resisted the system.

There is little that users can do during programming except monitor the results and prepare data for later testing. The ISD manages programming, and IS managers allocate resources and monitor projects.

Programmers test their modules with their own test data; an independent member of the staff should also develop test data, since programmers are notoriously poor at generating data that cause their programs to fail. Users develop realistic data, as well as data that test the system at its extremes. One insurance company, under time pressure for a system, skipped testing of the system with large volumes of data. When the system began operations, it rejected hundreds of thousands of transactions for editing violations.

It is best for users to be in charge of training; other users will respond far better to their colleagues than to someone from information services. Conversion should also be planned by users with help from the ISD staff. Finally, during operations, users should work with the system as it becomes a part of their job.

Problems

The life cycle model is an appealing way to think about the development process. It does, however, suffer from a number of problems. First, it implies that development proceeds in a sequential fashion through the various stages. In fact, that kind of progress rarely occurs. Steps are repeatedly revisited during the design process. Programmers have to go back to users to determine what a particular specification means. Changes by users or even changes in the environment require redesign and reprogramming during development.

Second, the life cycle model was developed at a time when most systems were large, multiuser, mainframe applications. It does not describe nearly as well the steps that might be required in developing an application using a database management package on a micro. For the management of large software projects, the model is quite useful; it has less to offer for individual user applications on micros.

Understanding

Many articles and books have been written about the problems of systems analysis and design in large programming projects. Design is hypothetical and abstract to many users; they do not know what to expect or how to determine their needs. Systems development is somewhat of an art, which makes it very difficult to manage. Unfortunately, there is no consensus on a single factor that is to blame for time and cost overruns, as well as failure to meet specifications.

Later in this chapter, we shall discuss some promising approaches to software development. However, we should look well before the programming stage to see at least one cause for systems failure: lack of user understanding of a new system. Figure 9-1 shows the steps in the traditional life cycle model. Note that in a typical organization, users are far less involved in the design process than was previously suggested.

The user may obtain some idea of what the system is to do during the feasibility study. If the user is relatively uninvolved in analysis and design, leaving everything to the systems professional, the user may get very little feedback on the system until asked to approve the final specifications.

In one instance, a design team took complete responsibility for developing the system; they interviewed users, but the users did not really understand the application. After more than a year of work, the users received a 3-inch-thick binder of specifications, which they were asked to approve in less than a week. The specifications were very difficult to read and contained extensive detail. Needless to say, they were unable to give users and managers a picture of the system.

Suppose they had made a mistake and simply approved the specifications; what would have happened? The project was ambitious and would take several years to complete. Not understanding the specifications meant

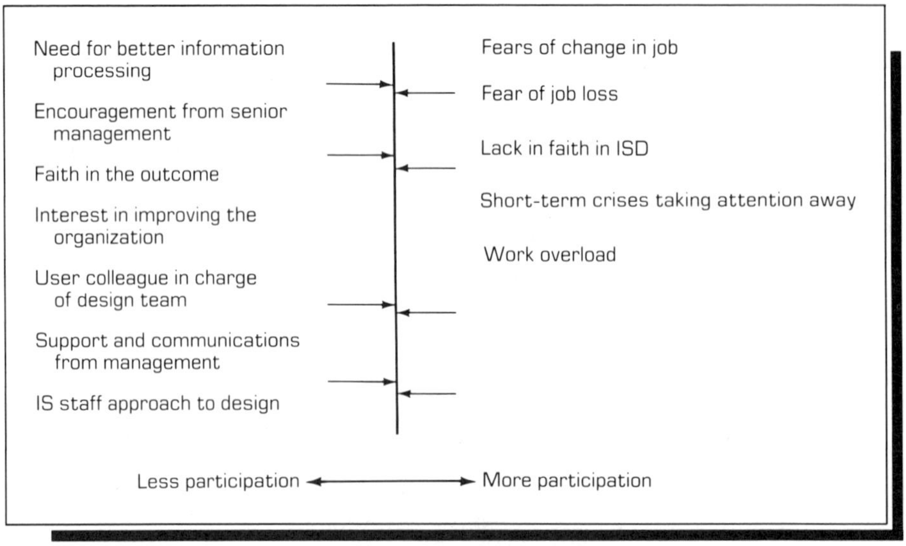

FIGURE 9-2 Forces affecting user participation in systems development.

that at least until testing, and possibly until conversion, users would not have a good idea of what the system did. If users finally understood the system near the end of the project, it would have been 2 years or more since the inception of the design effort!

How, then, can the ISD prevent unpleasant surprises at the end of a project? How can it encourage users to understand what a system is going to do? One ISD kept scheduling meetings on a system for master production scheduling; each time, only ISD personnel came to the meeting. Do users not care?

User-Led Design

In Chapter 7 we presented a model of motivation. How can users be motivated to take a more active part in systems development? (See Figure 9-2.) What forces are working against user involvement? In the case of a typical multiuser system, there are many forces that discourage user participation:

1. Fears about changes in one's job or even job loss.
2. Lack of faith in the ISD based on poor past performance.
3. Short-term crises that demand immediate attention; a system is seen as something in the future.
4. Work overload.
5. Lack of knowledge and understanding; computers and systems become intimidating.

This list could be extended almost indefinitely, especially when placed in the context of a specific organization. What factors tend to encourage users to work on the system?

1. A need for better information processing.
2. Encouragement from senior management.
3. Faith that something will come from their efforts.
4. Interest in improving the organization.

These encouraging forces are quite broad and even a bit patriotic compared to the specific and immediate nature of most of the inhibiting forces.

To encourage users to gain a real understanding of a new system and to participate in building it, it is necessary to increase the encouraging forces. One way to accomplish this is to put a user in charge of a design team; now the user has the responsibility for the system. Suddenly it is "our" system rather than a system belonging to the ISD.

Another encouraging force is management. If user management communicates that a project is important and encourages users to spend time on it, users will be motivated to participate more fully. This approach means that senior management must attend review meetings and strive to understand the high-level logic of the application.

Finally, the ISD can help encourage users by being more conscious of their problems. For example, systems analysts who concentrate on teaching users how to specify the logic of a system rather than doing the job themselves will encourage user participation. Similarly, if the systems professional genuinely wants to help users make their own design decisions, users will feel more responsibility toward the design project.

Review Meetings

In the 1970s the field of software engineering emerged. We shall discuss some of its ideas later in this chapter. The basic premise of the field is that software development should be treated like any other engineering endeavor; it is subject to standards and procedures, design rules, and management. This view contrasted with the opinion of many programmers that programming is a craft and that it cannot be managed.

One suggestion made by software engineers was the structured walkthrough. The walkthrough involves a programmer who presents part of a program or a group of program modules to an audience. The audience is generally a peer group of programmers, who are expected to critique the code presented. The objective is to make assumptions clear and to hunt for errors in specification and logic.

There is little evidence to support many of the practices suggested by software engineers, since it is hard to experiment with actual, large-scale systems. However, the idea of a structured walkthrough, like many other recommendations of software engineering, is very appealing.

If this technique has any value in programming, why not use it much earlier in the design process? In fact, a review walkthrough of a system is quite appropriate from the systems feasibility study stage on. In a system review meeting, one individual acts as the narrator, presenting the information at the appropriate level of detail. The narrator might be a consultant or a project manager in the ISD or even a user manager.

What is an appropriate level of detail? The answer to this question depends on what stage of the project is being reviewed and, to some extent, on the audience. At first, when the project is at a conceptual design level and the audience includes senior management, the level of detail will be quite high. The narrator will discuss the policy implications of the system and how management policies will be implemented. As the systems design progresses, reviews are held with different groups at a level of detail needed for their jobs. For a production control module with an audience of production schedulers, detail will be great.

Many individuals feel that review meetings consume time and produce very little benefit. In the case of systems development, however, reviews are crucial to building user understanding of a system. Time after time, we have seen individuals respond in a group setting and learn the functions of the system. Not only do they see for the first time what the system is supposed to do, they contribute to its development.

The narrator of the meeting must allow some discussion of each point, but if a consensus is not possible, the problem should be written down for further study. At the end of the meeting, the narrator assigns specific tasks to individuals so that any issues raised can be resolved.

Where is a review meeting used? Is it appropriate only for a large-scale system? Reviews of varying degrees of formality can be held even for the design of a user's own application on a micro. The effort devoted to preparation and the length of time spent will be less than for a large system, but the review can still help the user test the logic of the design.

Prototyping

We shall discuss prototyping in more detail in the next chapter. A prototype is a model of all or part of a system. Its purpose is to show users early in the design process how the system will appear. It, too, can contribute to users' understanding of a system.

Responsiveness

One of the major complaints about systems professionals is their perceived lack of responsiveness. In part, this complain is due to the fact that users do not understand what is required to develop or modify a system. Some lack of responsiveness, however, is real. It may be caused by overload, by too many user requests, and/or by too small an ISD staff. Whatever the reasons, this problem is extremely harmful to the credibility of information services.

A perceived lack of ISD responsiveness has been compounded by microcomputers and 4GLs. The user-friendly software of the personal computer makes it relatively easy for users to be very productive. If the user can develop a system so quickly on a personal computer, why does it take a professional so long on a mainframe?

Users do not understand that multiuser systems require a great deal of negotiation to resolve conflicting opinions as to how the system should work. The design team must come up with a database to support many different users. The professional designer is also very concerned with data integrity, editing, and documentation.

Whatever information services management can do to improve perceived responsiveness will help the organization and the systems effort. Keeping users and user management informed of activities in information services will help, as will fulfilling the liaison role of management.

Role of IS Management in Design

Table 9-5 outlines the role of ISD management in the design of a specific system through its life cycle. However, the CIO and other managers in information services have a broader role in systems development. These managers must serve as a liaison with management and users in other areas of the firm.

The CIO should be a member of key management committees; in this way, he or she is aware of the firm's strategy. The CIO also learns about the key concerns of various senior managers in the firm. In turn, these senior managers learn about the capabilities of the technology, as well as the problems of implementation.

ISD management can also help make review meetings work. By attending the reviews and encouraging peer managers in other departments to participate, ISD managers set a model for the reviews.

Similarly, action from ISD management may be required to arrange for design teams with significant user representation. If the firm adopts the practice of placing a user in charge of a design team, ISD management will probably have to provide the stimulus.

Finally, ISD management must monitor systems development. One evaluation mechanism for senior management is to see how well information services performs on systems development projects. Management must plan projects and see that they proceed as planned. Management has control over resources and may have to reallocate them when a project is in trouble. Chapter 12 will discuss project management in more detail.

Structured Design and Software Engineering

Concern over the problems of systems development has led to the creation of new approaches to design. These approaches have a number of advan-

TABLE 9-6 Approaches to Improving Systems Development

Structured design
Top-down design
Dataflow diagrams
Structured programming
Stepwise refinement
Modularity
DBMSs
Programmer teams
4GLs
Workstations
Documentation

tages; they also fit nicely with the recommendation that designers strive to help users understand systems. See Table 9-6.

Top-Down Design

When an architect designs a building, a series of drawings are usually prepared for the client. The first page of the drawing is usually a perspective of the exterior of the building. The next page contains different elevations; subsequent pages contain a floor plan. Near the last page are foundation, electrical, and heating plans.

Imagine what the drawings would look like if they were all on one page! The tremendous amount of detail would be overwhelming. Unfortunately, many systems analysts either provide no drawing or present a one-page version of the system. Top-down design is intended to bring the discipline and explanatory power of the architect's approach to systems analysis and design.

The analyst first prepares an overview of the system, which should fit on one page. Each part of this high-level design is represented in more detail on a subsequent page. These pages with more details, in turn, are broken down into greater levels of detail. The individual reading the documentation can always return to a higher level if clarification is required.

Dataflow Diagrams

The dataflow diagram (DFD) offers one form of notation that encourages top-down design. There are relatively few symbols in a DFD; see Figure 9-3. Basically, symbols are used for transformation of data, data flow, and data storage.

Figure 9-4 shows the first DFD for an inventory control system. The system features microcomputers at retail stores that are connected at different times during the day to a main computer at a warehouse. The micros order replenishment stock and report sales to the warehouse computer.

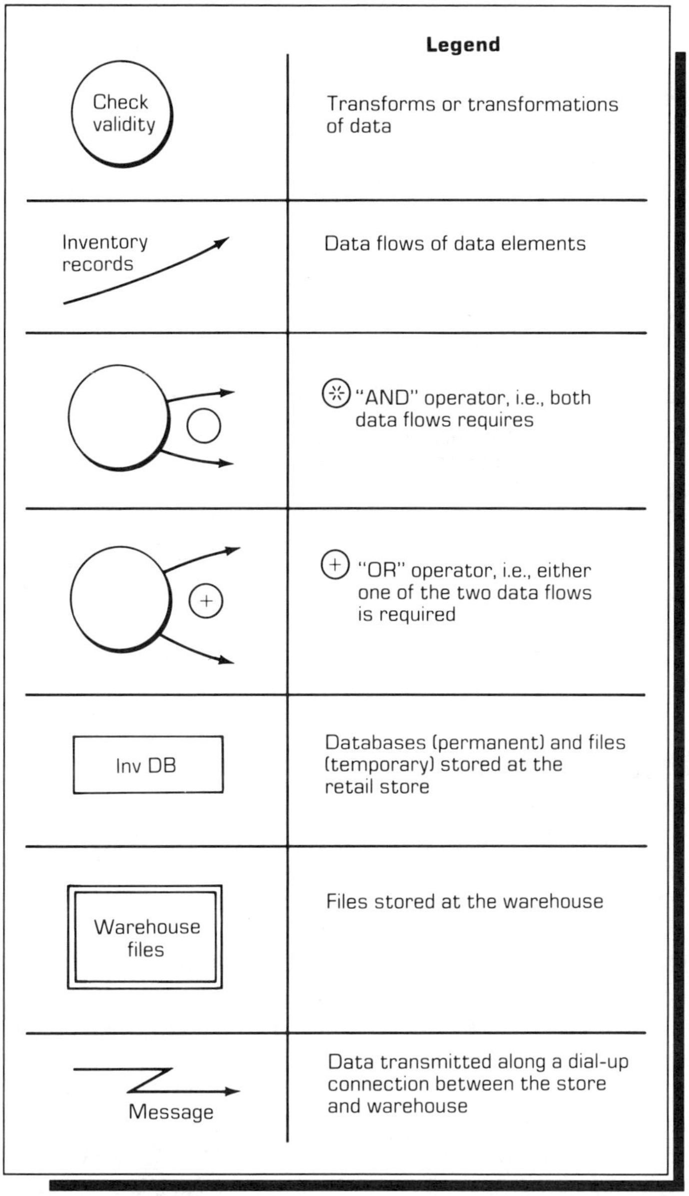

FIGURE 9-3 These symbols will be used throughout the chapter.

Figure 9-4 shows the main menu for the system on the personal computer and a DFD for processing it. Figure 9-5 presents the main menu for inventory control, which is the heart of the system. Notice in Figure 9-5 how the DFD clearly points out each choice for processing and shows how that symbol will be further exploded. For example, the first choice from the inventory control menu in Figure 9-6 is record sales. The DFD for that selection is shown in Figure 9-7.

The DFD presents a simple picture for the designers, both professional

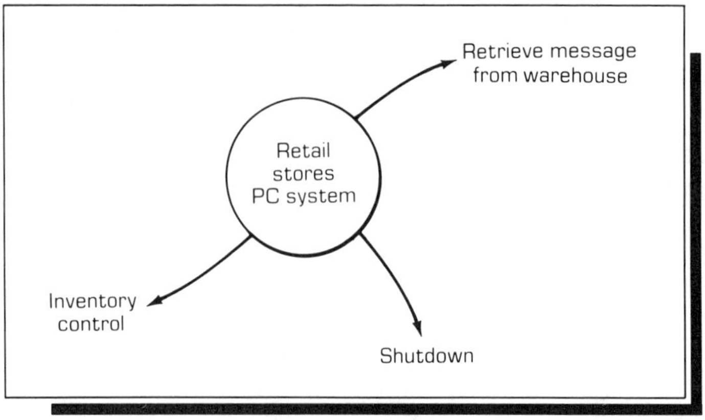

FIGURE 9-4 The system at its highest level shows the inventory control application and the options to retrieve warehouse messages or shut down the system.

analysts and users, to follow. It also makes it natural to employ top-down design because it encourages a structured, disciplined approach to the design task. DFDs are a good communications vehicle to use in the review meetings discussed earlier.

Structured Programming

Structured programming was one of the first software engineering techniques advocated for improving programmer productivity. Structured programming is also associated with the idea of stepwise refinement, a concept quite similar to the top-down design process previously described. The idea is to move to successively lower levels of detail in designing a program. At the highest level, the outline of a program is abstract. At each stage, the programmer breaks the program down into more detail. The last of these refinements is the program in a computer language itself.

At the most abstract level, the programmer might take the systems specification and write a cryptic English language description of it. This version is then refined, using a high-level program design language (PDL). Finally, when satisfied with the PDL version, the programmer begins to code parts of the program in an executable computer language.

Modularity

Top-down design applies to programs as well as to a system. In the case of a system, each major level is broken down into a series of smaller pieces. In the case of programming, a program is broken into a series of modules to make the programming task easier. The programmer is reducing complexity, since it is necessary to specify what the module does and how it interfaces with other modules, rather than deal with the entire program at one time.

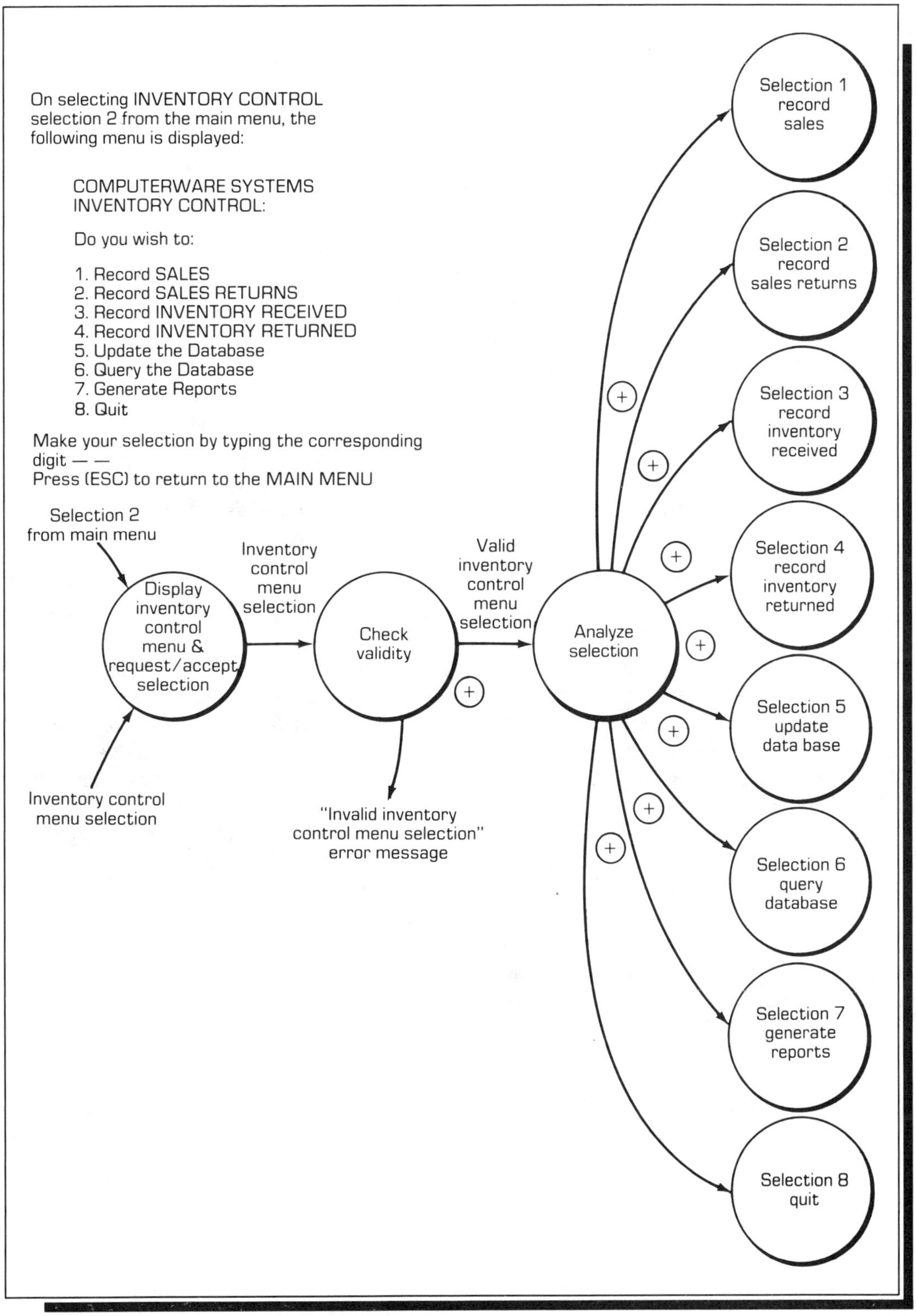
On selecting INVENTORY CONTROL selection 2 from the main menu, the following menu is displayed:
COMPUTERWARE SYSTEMS
INVENTORY CONTROL:
Do you wish to:
1. Record SALES
2. Record SALES RETURNS
3. Record INVENTORY RECEIVED
4. Record INVENTORY RETURNED
5. Update the Database
6. Query the Database
7. Generate Reports
8. Quit
Make your selection by typing the corresponding digit — —
Press (ESC) to return to the MAIN MENU
Selection 2 from main menu
Display inventory control menu & request/accept selection
Inventory control menu selection
Inventory control menu selection
Check validity
"Invalid inventory control menu selection" error message
Valid inventory control menu selection
Analyze selection
Selection 1 record sales
Selection 2 record sales returns
Selection 3 record inventory received
Selection 4 record inventory returned
Selection 5 update data base
Selection 6 query database
Selection 7 generate reports
Selection 8 quit

FIGURE 9-5 The main menu and DFD.

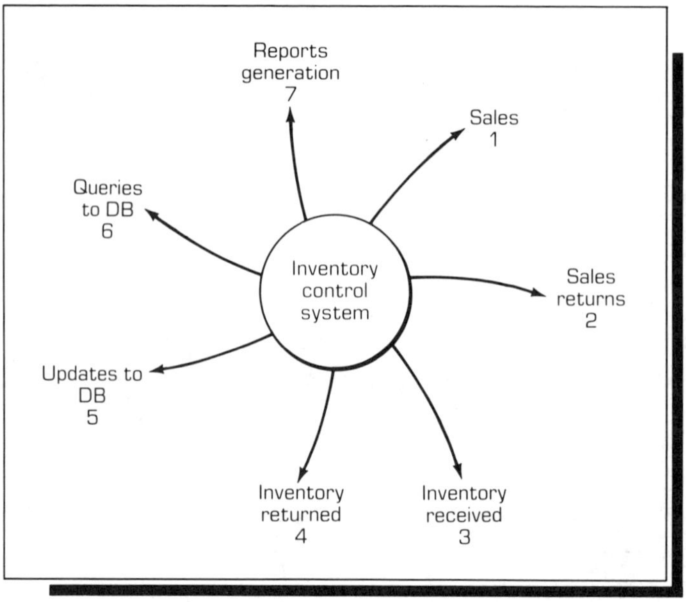

FIGURE 9-6 DFD for an inventory control system.

A module should be relatively small so that a programmer can read it and keep its functions in mind. It is best to avoid obscure or clever couplings among modules (coupling is the passing of data from one module to another). The worst case is when one module refers to data inside another. Modules should be kept as independent of other modules as possible. In fact, one criterion for modularization is *information hiding,* developed by Parnas. He argues that a module should hide what it does from other modules.

One objective of modular programming is to make it possible to change a system more easily. Imagine the situation if every routine that accesses a file has its own Read statements. What happens when it is necessary to change the format of a file record? Each module has to be changed. Instead, the programmer should create a single module that interfaces with the file. The single module is called by modules needing data. If the structure of the file has to be changed, only the one interface module needs to be modified. (In fact, this is a DBMS).

Database Management Systems

A DBMS is another approach to improving systems development productivity. A DBMS should help do the following:

1. Create more independence of data from programs that access them, facilitating changes. This feature is known as the *database concept* or the separation of data and programs.
2. Reduce the duplication of data.

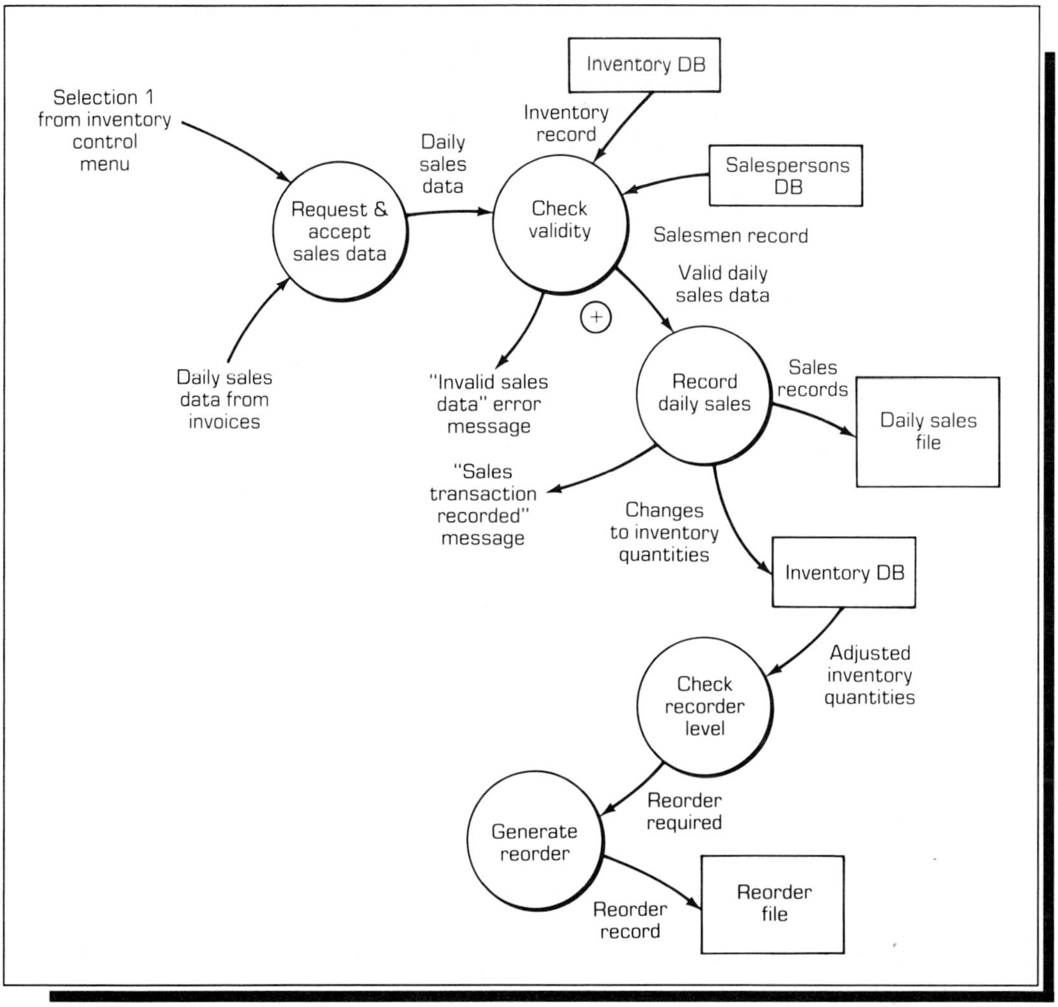

FIGURE 9-7 Record sales. The daily invoices filled out for each store sale provide the data for accumulating sales information and subtracting the items sold from the computer's inventory records.

3. Provide a facility for defining the logical and physical characteristics of data.
4. Provide a file access facility.
5. Provide facilities to protect the integrity and security of data.

A DBMS should provide the following components:

1. A data definition language (DDL) that the DBA uses to define the records in the database and the relationship among them.
2. A data dictionary, which is a repository of all data elements in the system. The DBA defines the data and places them in the dictionary, which becomes the central record for information about the data-

base. Many data dictionaries operate on-line, and some are linked dynamically to the programs as they execute.

3. Query languages provide a logiclike language for the user to employ in making ad hoc requests for data from the data base.
4. The DBMS itself, which generally is designed to support one or more models of data, either hierarchical, network, or relational.

It is very costly to bring in a mainframe DBMS and to learn how to use it. However, subsequent systems should benefit greatly as programmers and analysts learn how to improve their productivity by using this tool. There are also a number of DBMSs for minicomputers and micros, some of which provide very-high-level languages and generators to speed the development of applications.

Programmer Teams

In addition to the various approaches to better program construction, some software engineers advocate the use of programmer teams managed by a senior programmer. The idea is to obtain a collaborative effort in writing programs so that the programmer does not develop an unhealthy attachment to his or her code. Programmers review each other's programs and help each other when there are problems.

Fourth-Generation Languages

A 4GL can be very useful in systems development in at least two ways. First, it can often be used to develop a fast prototype of the system under development. Second, it can be used as a permanent part of the system for report generation.

One strategy is to carefully document the contents and structure of the database and to let users work with a 4GL to design their own reports. Of course, ISD personnel will have to provide some consulting assistance, but this approach is one way to offload some of the development work to users and to eliminate the difficult job of designing a report for someone else.

Workstations

The computer is now being applied to the development of information systems themselves. There are at least two commercial products that herald the arrival of the programmer/analysts' workbench. These systems feature a microcomputer that has software to aid the analyst. In particular, the software contains a graphics package to facilitate the creation and modification of DFDs. The software is hierarchical; a symbol at a high level can be exploded to create a lower-level diagram.

One of the systems also includes a data dictionary so that the analyst defines and enters data elements during the design of the system. The workstation can convert these dictionary entries into some of the final program components for a completed system.

These workstations provide management with one way to enforce structured design and to support systems analysts at the same time. They offer the prospect of dramatically improving systems development productivity. See Chapter 10 for examples of how one of these Computer Aided Software Engineering (CASE) systems works..

Documentation

One of the least liked jobs in information processing is the development of documentation. Programmers and analysts are notoriously remiss in documenting their work. Fortunately, some of the techniques previously described produce documentation as a by-product. For example, DFDs and a data dictionary provide satisfactory documentation of a system, though a good narrative helps too.

Documentation is important for two reasons. First, it allows the ISD to maintain and enhance the system. Typically the individuals who originally worked on a system are not the ones who end up modifying it. Maintenance programmers need well-documented systems.

Second, user documentation is needed so that users will understand how to work with the system. While individuals do not like to refer to bulky notebooks, simple documentation is needed, along with examples of what to do in a given situation. On-line systems frequently feature help keys that provide the user with an explanation and, hopefully, an example.

Since ISD professionals do not like to prepare documentation, management will have to provide some stimulus and incentives. We know of one CIO who hired unemployed English majors from college to prepare user documentation. These individuals did not understand computers, so they repeatedly queried the professional staff for clear explanations that they could incorporate in user manuals.

In an insurance company, we tried to find out the accounting rules for treating a particular type of policy. The actuary sent us to the controller, who in turn said that he had long ago forgotten the rule, since it was "on the computer." He advised us to seek out the program documentation. Naturally there was none, so the rule was found by reading COBOL code. It is probably a bad idea to have program statements constitute the only documentation of important business procedures.

Summary

Systems analysis and design is one of the most important and visible activities undertaken by the ISD. If a mainframe computer system is to last for 7 years and takes 2 years to develop, the design process, including operations and maintenance, will take nearly a decade! The systems developed today may determine how the organization processes information 10 years from now.

Like other facets of information resource management, systems development is far more complex today than in the past due to the proliferation of computers and software. Users are designing their own systems and participating to some degree in the design of multiuser systems. We have advocated nontraditional roles for the development staff—those of consultants, advisors and teachers.

The approaches to development described here are intended to improve productivity and user satisfaction with completed systems. Even they, however, are not enough. We need to consider some alternatives to traditional approaches to systems analysis and design. That is the subject of the next chapter.

Recommended Readings

DeMarco, T., *Structured Analysis and System Specification.* Englewood Cliffs, N.J.: Prentice-Hall, 1979. (An important book describing the basics of structured design.)

Gane, C., and T. Sarson, *Structured Systems Analysis.* Englewood Cliffs, N.J.: Prentice-Hall, 1979. (This book covers systems development from the conceptual overview to considerations in programming; it is highly recommended.)

LeBlond, G., and D. Cobb, *Using 1-2-3.* Indianapolis: Que Corporation, 1983. (A good example of documentation for users.)

Lucas, H. C., Jr., *The Analysis, Design, and Implementation of Information Systems,* 3rd ed. New York: McGraw-Hill, 1985. (A general textbook on systems analysis and design.)

Discussion Problems

9.1 The executive vice president of Magic Carpets was concerned as he regarded a 3-inch-thick binder on his desk. The binder contained preliminary plans for a new application. In fact, the new system consisted of a number of individual applications; when completed, they would dramatically change the way the firm operated.

Magic produced a variety of carpets in different grades, colors, and patterns. The firm was a leader in the industry and had used computers for many years. A desire to replace and update the present on-line order entry system led to the present concept of a completely new information system from forecasting to production management.

The notebook containing the design was the result of a year's effort by a design team. The vice president was concerned because he did not understand its contents, and yet the design team assured him that users had been heavily involved in the project.

What can the vice president do to ease his anxiety?

9.2 The Metals Mining Corporation generally designed systems at and for its largest division, and then took them to its local divisions for installation. A comprehensive spare parts inventory system was the latest such application. Before beginning installation at the largest division, the design team decided to review the specifications at other locations so that any unique problems could be included in the design.

At one remote mining site, the review meeting went very badly. The manager of the mine would not talk about the new inventory system; instead he wanted to talk about current service levels. He said in anger, "How can I worry about some system that's coming in a few years, if at all? Last month you guys couldn't process the payroll checks and transmit them to me by Friday afternoon. Have you ever had 150 miners outside your door on a Friday night wondering where their money is? Don't talk to me about inventory until I can pay my men."

Is the manager's problem a design problem? How does it affect design? What can the systems development team do to move the discussion to the new inventory application?

Questions

1. How is the role of the systems analyst changing?
2. What are the problems in developing large multiuser systems?
3. Why are users so excited about microcomputer applications?
4. How does the professional IS staff help with micro applications?
5. When does a micro application become sufficiently complex to involve systems professionals?
6. What kind of support is needed for users who want to develop their own custom applications?
7. What does a user with a micro need to know in order to be able to access data on a mainframe?
8. What services are provided by an information center?
9. What kinds of applications will be developed in the future when most computers are on a network?
10. Why is the feasibility of an application less important today than it was 10 years ago?
11. What procedure should users and the IS staff follow in deciding what alternative to choose for a new application?
12. What is the role of the final numerical result when using a scoring model to choose alternatives for a system?
13. How is a group of applications like a stock portfolio? How does it differ?
14. What are the steps in the life cycle model?
15. What are the limitations of the life cycle model?
16. Why is it important for users to understand a system?
17. What steps can be taken during design to foster user understanding?
18. What factors discourage user involvement in design?
19. What factors encourage user involvement in design?
20. What is the role of management in securing greater user input in design?
21. What is the role of a design review meeting?
22. How does the CIO promote systems design in the firm?
23. What is software engineering?
24. Describe top-down design.
25. What are the advantages of DFDs in representing a system?
26. What is structured programming and why might a firm adopt it?
27. How does modular programming contribute to a systems development project?
28. What are the advantages of using a DBMS in systems development?
29. Describe some of the features that might be offered by a systems analyst workstation.
30. Why do we need to consider alternatives to traditional design practices?

10

Systems Development: Alternatives to Tradition

As we have seen, the development of a custom programmed information system is a labor-intensive task. It involves users, professional systems analysts, programmers, user management, and the management of the ISD. We have also described the general dissatisfaction with the systems development process. Users are unhappy because it takes so long to design a system and because the system often does not meet their requirements. User dissatisfaction is frustrating for the ISD.

How can some of these problems be ameliorated? One solution is to attack some of the bottlenecks in systems development. The following problems contribute to both user and computer professional dissatisfaction with the design process:

1. Lack of user participation in the design process.
2. Lack of user understanding of the system.
3. Poor documentation and representation techniques to facilitate user and analyst understanding of the system.
4. Belief that technology will be difficult to apply.
5. Poor programming productivity.
6. Difficulties in project management.
7. User resistance because of uncertainty and change.

The techniques discussed in this chapter modify the traditional approach to

TABLE 10-1 An Overview of Design Alternatives

Packages
Very-high-level languages
Systems software
Problem-oriented packages
Dedicated packages
Generators and nonprocedural languages
End-user programming
Report generators
Query languages
Generators
Prototyping

design, which focuses on the development of a custom application, following the systems life cycle. These techniques are applicable to various parts of the systems life cycle and, where suitable, can help improve productivity in systems analysis and design. See Table 10-1.

Packages

A package is a set of programs developed by one organization to be sold to others. Today the package may also be a combination of hardware and software; it is easiest to think of a package as a problem solution that is partially or completely ready for installation. The package almost always includes computer programs and may also include hardware.

The purpose of the package is to reduce the time required to install a system by saving part of the design effort and most of the programming. While desirable, it is not always possible to achieve these savings because organizations often want to modify the package to fit their particular situation.

The advantages generally attributed to packages include the following:

1. The total development time for a system should be less because of reduced programming and design.
2. The total costs of a package should be lower than those of a custom system because one piece of software is sold to a number of firms. In one sense, all customers share the cost of development.
3. A package may have more functions than a custom system.
4. If the package has already been sold and is in use, the customer is buying programs that already execute. There should be fewer errors in them because of this experience that in new programs that the organization writes for itself.

However, packages also have disadvantages:

1. A package may not have all of the functions the organization needs.
2. The package may have to be extensively modified. Sometimes ven-

Package Type	Characteristics	Example
Very high level of 4GL	Easy to use; user solves own problem	Focus NATURAL, RAMIS
Systems software	Computer-oriented task like terminal management Possibly DBMS	CICS ADABASE, DBASE,
Problem oriented	Language fits problem type like statistical analysis	SPSS, SAS, LOTUS 1-2-3 MULTIPLAN
Dedicated	Focused on one application area	Production control COPICS, accounts receivable

FIGURE 10-1 A framework for classifying packages.

dors do not want to alter their packages; it can be hard for an internal ISD staff to understand the package programs and make changes.

3. Companies sometimes have to change their procedures in order to use a package because they do not want to try to change the package.
4. The customer must depend on the package vendor for support.

The vendor has to construct a general-purpose program that will fit many customers. Usually the package comes with many input parameters, data values that customers must supply to prepare the package to work in their environment. For example, the user has to enter the numbers used to label accounts in order to use a general-purpose ledger package.

Some packages have different modules for the same task, and the buyer selects the one that is appropriate. For example, there may be an accounting package with modules for two or three types of depreciation. The customer chooses the depreciation module that reflects the way in which the company handles depreciation.

Types of Package

There are many different kinds of packages intended for different purposes. Some packages resemble languages; the user works with the package to build an application. Other packages are dedicated to a particular application, like material requirements planning, accounts receivable, or inventory control. See Figure 10-1.

Very-High-Level Languages

These programs are also called 4GLs. They contain statements that are higher in level than those of BASIC, COBOL, or FORTRAN. A 4GL has single statements that would require many individual statements in a compiler-level language. Compilers are the third generation of programming languages after machine and assembler languages; these very-high-level languages are the fourth generation.

This kind of package is used not for a specific application, but to solve a particular problem. Some 4GLs are designed for special types of problems, such as financial modeling, while others are more general purpose. A growing number of these languages are available for a wide variety of computers, ranging from mainframes to micros.

How does a 4GL differ from a query language that might come with a DBMS? The statements in a query language are often at the same high level as those of the 4GL. The 4GL must offer much more than retrieval statements. This language must make it possible to process data that have been retrieved, to process transactions against data files, to define input forms, and to define and format output reports. A 4GL should contain many of the features of a query language, plus many additional capabilities. A 4GL is a very attractive option for developing an application quickly; it competes with the purchase of a dedicated applications package.

Systems Software

Some packages exist to control the interaction between a computer system and its terminals. This particular terminal-handling program is called a *telecommunications monitor.* This kind of package is classified as systems software, since it provides services similar to those provided by an operating system.

Some would also include database management packages in this category of systems software. A program for the microcomputer that managed diskettes and a hard disk for a personal computer would also be examples of systems software packages.

Problem-Oriented Packages

A problem-oriented package is like a very-high-level language, but is aimed at a specific problem. A good example of this type of package is the Statistical Package for the Social Sciences (SPSS), a program used widely by nonprogrammers to analyze data statistically. The user of the package does write a program, but in a very-high-level language that is oriented to someone with a knowledge of statistics rather than computers.

Two of the most popular packages in this category are Visicalc and Lotus 1-2-3. The latter has displaced the former as the leading microcomputer spreadsheet package.

Dedicated Packages

Problem-oriented packages like Lotus are used to solve a particular processing problem. The packages we call *dedicated* are very different because the buyer is focusing on a single task. The package is not used to create a solution; it *is* the solution, according to the vendor.

Consider a function like accounts receivable. A firm must keep track of the funds owed by its customers. The vendor of a package for this function will try to create a system that appeals to a large number of firms.

There are companies that sell many small items repeatedly to the same customers, such as a sweater manufacturer selling to various kinds of clothing stores throughout the country. The package vendor would like to sell his product to a different type of firm, possibly one that manufactures airplanes. Such a company probably has customers who do business with the firm only every few years, if that often.

Each of these firms has a different kind of accounts receivable. It is possible that one dedicated package with different options could satisfy each of them. The sweater company will have a large number of transactions listed for each customer; it will want to match each payment with the different invoices it has sent to customers. The aircraft firm's receivables will be fairly simple but will represent a large amount of money. Here, financing, working capital, funds flow, and late payments will be of concern because the manufacturer must be able to finance production and meet its payroll with large, irregular payments from its customers. It sells far fewer airplanes than the garment manufacturer does sweaters.

On the surface, it probably seems that all accounts receivable applications are the same. However, the preceding examples demonstrate that all applications for the same function, such as accounts receivable, are not identical. For this reason, the user should define the requirements of the system before looking at a package. One cannot assume that because the package is designed to handle accounts receivable, it will necessarily work in the user's environment.

There is an important difference between packages intended for the user to construct a solution, to a problem and packages that purport to be the solution. The packages used to construct a solution are general purpose and will usually not be modified by their vendors. The user is expected to figure out how to apply the package to his or her problem. Implementing a dedicated package may involve modifications in the software and/or changes in the buyer's procedures.

Acquisition

Selecting packages is not easy. Often in the excitement of finding that something exists so that a custom system does not have to be programmed, one forgets to determine the requirements for the application. In choosing any kind of package, it is very important to determine the requirements of the application. In the case of a problem-solving tool like Lotus, the buyer should consider the features that will actually be used before selecting a product. This specification will be fairly simple because certain generic functions are performed by all packages in this category.

Where do we find information about packages? There are numerous industry magazines that report on new microcomputer software; in addition, a prospective customer can visit one of the many stores that sell computer hardware and software. For larger computers, it will probably be necessary to contact the vendors of the computer to see if they have or know of a package for the application under study.

The preparation for acquiring a dedicated package is even more demanding than for a general-purpose package. It is necessary to develop a preliminary systems design at a high level before actually looking for the package. Why bother? Because users need to think about the kind of system they want before being influenced by the package vendors.

The buyer needs a benchmark, a plan with which to compare the features of various packages. With such a plan, it is possible to estimate what modifications will be required to use the package. It is unusual not to make some modifications in a dedicated package, at least for large organizations with established procedures. It may be simpler and certainly less expensive to accept a package as is and change the firm's procedures.

Whatever is decided about changes, it is important for users to be heavily involved in the selection of a dedicated package. Users should be sure to see the package work and understand what it will and will not do. Experience has shown that it is very difficult for users to see a package demonstration and apply the package's functions to their own job.

For the actual selection of a package, the procedure advocated for selecting alternative systems in the last chapter is appropriate: rank and evaluate the various packages and then choose the one that appears to be the best. This choice can be compared with alternatives such as a custom system using the same criteria.

Implementation

Figure 10-2 is a model of the implementation process for a dedicated package. The processing needs of the adopting firm are one of the most important considerations in the model. These needs should be delineated in a systems design document showing the logic of the proposed application.

The needs of the adopting organization have to be carefully compared to the characteristics of the vendor's software package. This analysis concentrates on the discrepancies between the needs of the customer and the features of the package. If the discrepancies can be resolved, the firm can consider the package as one option for developing the proposed application.

Assuming that the package is selected, the next stage is to develop an implementation plan. This plan must resolve the discrepancies in one of two ways. Either the firm and/or the vendor must modify the package, or the firm must change its procedures to conform to the logic of the package.

Throughout this implementation process, the users of the package should be heavily involved. Especially during the evaluation of the package's features, it is vitally important for users to understand their own needs and to understand how the package works. For this reason, we emphasize the development of a high-level specification for the system to act as a benchmark when evaluating the package.

Because the package is already coded, the implementation process can proceed more rapidly than for a custom-developed system. However, though shorter in time, the implementation process may require a more intense effort with a dedicated package. Because packages are so attractive today, a design team should always try to determine if one is available for the application under consideration.

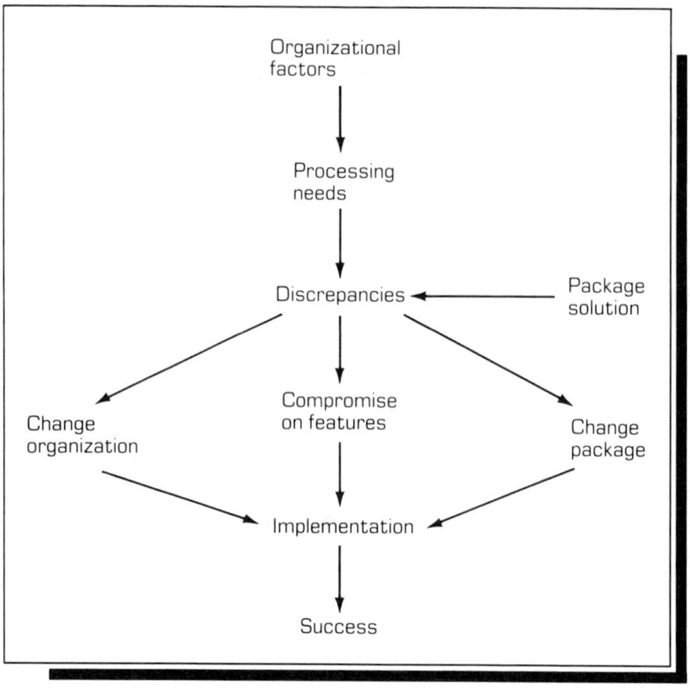

FIGURE 10-2 The implementation of dedicated packages.

Generators and Nonprocedural Languages

The kind of language described in this section is higher in level than a language like COBOL or FORTRAN. Basically, the higher the level of a language, the fewer the statements required to accomplish a task. Many statements in assembly language are required to perform a computation that in FORTRAN requires only one statement.

Very-high-level languages accomplish tasks with fewer statements than a language like COBOL. For example, to sort a series of data records into a new order—for example, to change from an order by social security number to one by last name in BASIC—requires a number of statements. In a very-high-level language we could say something like:

SORT EMPLOYEES BY LAST NAME

Compiler-level languages are considered procedural because the programmer has to specify detailed procedures for solving the problem. A nonprocedural language requires far fewer details. Of course, even with very-high-level languages, users are still not able to say "Compute the Payroll," but some of these languages are still very powerful.

End-User Programming

A major trend is toward more programming by end users. This programming, however, does not closely resemble the traditional code produced by professional programmers. Instead, users work with a variety of special languages and packages on different types of computers.

With an electronic spreadsheet package the user works with a particular model of the world, a spreadsheet, to solve a problem. A great deal of microcomputer software is available for end users. One of the great appeals of these computers is that, for the most part, a systems professional is not required to make them work.

For mainframes, the packages described later make it feasible for end users to develop some of their own solutions. These tools may approach conventional programming, but they are employed for such tasks and in such a way that the end user can rapidly learn how to work with them. It is probably more accurate to say that end users are solving their own information processing problems than to say that they are programming.

Report Generators

Some of the first attempts to develop easy-to-use languages resulted in report generators. Specifying a report in a conventional programming language is a very tedious process. These report generators help the user to define the layout of a file, to extract records based on logical criteria, to manipulate the data, and to format a report.

Some report generators have evolved into languages and include the ability to update files. Theoretically one could develop an entire application using just a report generator. The popular mid-range IBM computers like the System 38 are extensively programmed in RPG, a report generator language.

Report generators first appeared for sequential files. They are particularly good for extracting data from different files. In one instance, an insurance company used a generator to combine a master record on losses by policy and another file of details for each claim for its auditors. The report generator sorted both files into the same sequence (policy number), and produced a report of each policy's total losses and a detailed history of claims.

Report generators have been provided with more capabilities to take advantage of the widespread use of direct-access files and DBMSs. Sometimes they are called *retrieval languages* and are employed by users to develop reports quickly, without the need for a professional programmer.

Query Languages

A DBMS usually comes with some kind of query language for retrieving data from the database without the intervention of a programmer. Remember that a query is a question the user wants to ask of the database. The user enters statements that the query language processor interprets.

To use a query language, users must have knowledge of the database. They must know the structure of the various files or relations in the system. Most DBMSs feature some type of query language. Computer vendors also offer query languages of their own. Although using them requires some training, as well as an awareness of the contents of the database, these languages are a good example of how the power of a computer can be extended to an end user.

4GLs in Information Services

It has been estimated that over one half of the mainframe sites in the United States have 4GLs. Query languages and 4GLs are often described as designed primarily for end users, while report generators may be employed by end users but are typically used by the professional programmer. What is the role of these tools in the ISD? The objective of using any kind of tool in systems development is to increase productivity and/or the quality of the resulting system.

The 4GLs enhance quality because they encourage the design team to develop prototypes. Later in this chapter, we discuss some of the advantages of prototyping; improving quality is one of the main reasons. The 4GLs have also been associated with productivity improvement claims ranging from 10 to 1 to about 5 to 1. Bank of America has employed Nomad2, a 4GL, for about 10 years and has trained over 10,000 employees to use it. About a third of this number are professional programmers, and the bank claims about a 10 to 1 improvement in programming productivity resulting from the use of this tool.

All of the techniques described in this chapter can be used by ISD staff members in developing prototypes. However, does it make sense for computer professionals to use 4GLs for custom systems development? The answer to this question is a qualified "yes." One investment banking firm in New York has achieved impressive productivity increases in systems development by using a DBMS and a 4GL for all of its development work.

However, consider the case of a major accounting firm that used a new 4GL to develop a motor vehicles system for the state of New Jersey. All modules were written in this language. The response time for the system was terrible, and there was not enough computer time overnight to complete batch processing. State police were instructed not to cite motorists for expired registrations because the system was so far behind!

The vendor of the 4GL explained that certain parts of the system had to be written in COBOL for efficiency purposes. New Jersey hired another consulting firm to fix the system, and had to rewrite the most frequently used modules in COBOL.

It appears that 4GLs can now be used with discretion and will become even more appealing in the future. Hardware is becoming more and more powerful, and prices are dropping. The next generation of computers might execute the New Jersey system without any problems. At the present time,

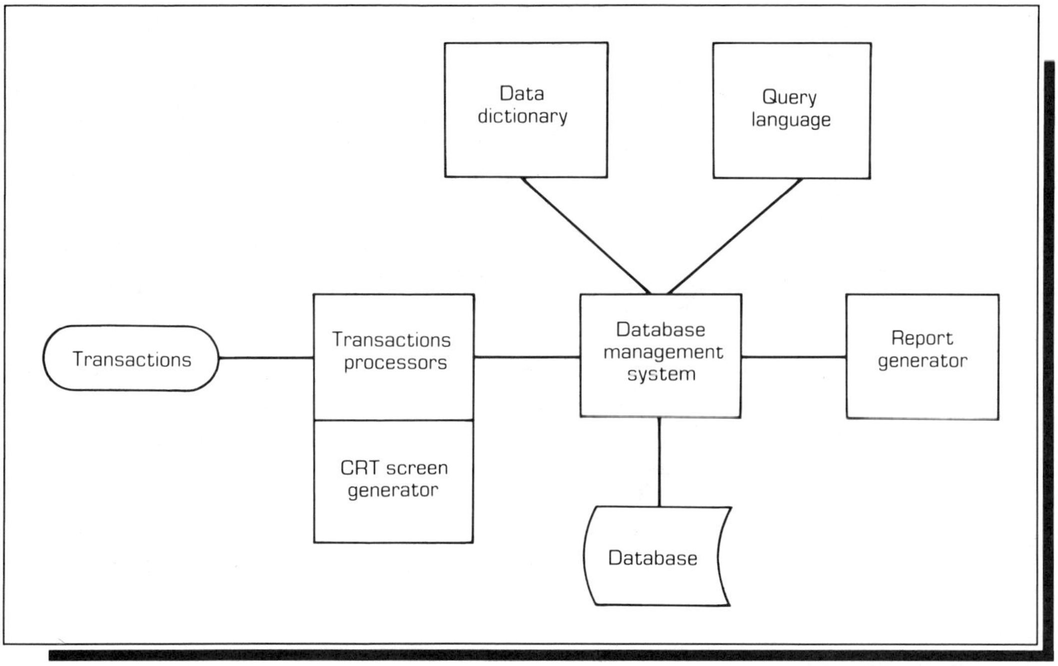

FIGURE 10-3 Applications generator. An applications generator is often built around a DBMS. A transactions processor generates code that processes input transactions and updates the database. A report generator is also a part of the package.

however, ISD professionals should consider using a 4GL for development as long as they are sensitive to run-time requirements, especially for on-line systems. A 4GL is an excellent tool for providing reports, prototyping a system, and developing many parts of an application.

Generators

The generator programs of today are generally used by professional systems analysts or programmers to create new applications. The analyst describes the desired system to the generator program, which, in turn, creates the database and the programs necessary to operate the application. Although this process sounds simple, a great deal of information must be put into the generator. The generator is actually a number of very complex programs that the firm must purchase if it wishes to adopt this approach to building applications. We should also remember that programming is only 15 to 20% of the system life cycle. Tools like generators will help, but it is unlikely that they will halve the time needed for developing a system.

A complete generator should assist the definition of input transactions, the editing of transactions, the creation of a database, file updating, report generation, and query processing. See Figure 10-3. Most of these programs are constructed as part of a DBMS because the definition and creation of a database are critical in the design process.

The generator is aimed at reducing the time required for the programming and testing stages of systems development. One organization reported reducing the time needed to develop transactions-oriented applications by a factor of four to five, using a generator available for a popular DBMS. With this time savings, users quickly see the results of the design; they do not have to wait for the laborious coding of programs in a language like COBOL.

Even with a generator, however, it is still necessary to design a system. A specification is needed before a generator can be used. The generator cuts down on programming time and can give users feedback on a preliminary basis. One has to know what the application is supposed to do, however, before generating a system.

What are the prospects for users to generate their own systems with this software? The mainframe generators are sufficiently complex that they are best left to professionals. However, at least one micro DBMS package now comes with a generator that facilitates the development of complete applications. It is possible that users will gain some experience with this program and then move on to more complex generators. However, until generators become much easier to use, they will probably remain part of the repertoire of ISD tools.

Prototyping

It is common in many fields to build a model of a product, or prototype, before assembling the finished version. Prototypes of automobiles are almost always constructed, and an architect often builds a scale model of a building before developing the final plans. In creating a system, some experts advocate building prototypes where possible. The prototype may not be for the entire application, but for only a part of it. A developer might prototype just the input screens for a new system so that users can understand how they will interact with the application.

The objective of a prototype is to reduce the time before the user sees something concrete from the systems design effort. Too often in custom development, users do not understand system specifications when approving them. As a result, the first real picture they get is during testing. A long time, at least 1 year, has elapsed between the idea for the system and the first tests.

With a prototype, which is produced fairly soon after design has started, the user can give the designer rapid feedback. The prototype becomes a focal point for discussing the system and completing its design. Examining the prototype can force the user to become involved in the design process.

Time-sharing systems and microcomputers are excellent tools to use in developing prototypes. One company used a microcomputer DBMS to develop a comprehensive personnel system. Using the DBMS, the original development effort on the micro took a week; during that time, a sample was produced to which managers could respond. The prototype became a living specification that programmers then converted to run on the firm's mainframe. When satisfied that the system worked as desired, the company had its computer staff reprogram it in BASIC to make sure that it would run at an acceptable speed on the mainframe.

Another firm is trying to use tools like report generators and applications generators to make prototyping a part of every development project. The idea is to produce a sample system for a user within 2 weeks of a request. It remains to be seen if this approach will succeed, but it is certainly worth trying. The IS field must find ways to reduce user frustration over systems development and be more responsive to requests for new computer applications.

Designer Workstations

Systems designers have very little automation to support their tasks. A designer workstation gives the systems developer the same kind of support that a designer workstation provides an engineer. These workstations are usually based on a powerful microcomputer and provide graphics-based design tools.

The tools provide an easy way for the analyst to enter flowcharts like DFDs and edit them. One of the packages, illustrated in Figures 10-4 through 10-8, provides the analyst with graphics for charting, a data dictionary, screen reports, and documentation. The system is based on a data dictionary, and an analyst can use the workstation to define the database. The graphics diagrams are based on a top-down approach to design; a high-level chart can be exploded into a lower-level chart with more detail. See the examples in Figures 10-6 and 10-7 for a firm selling software products.

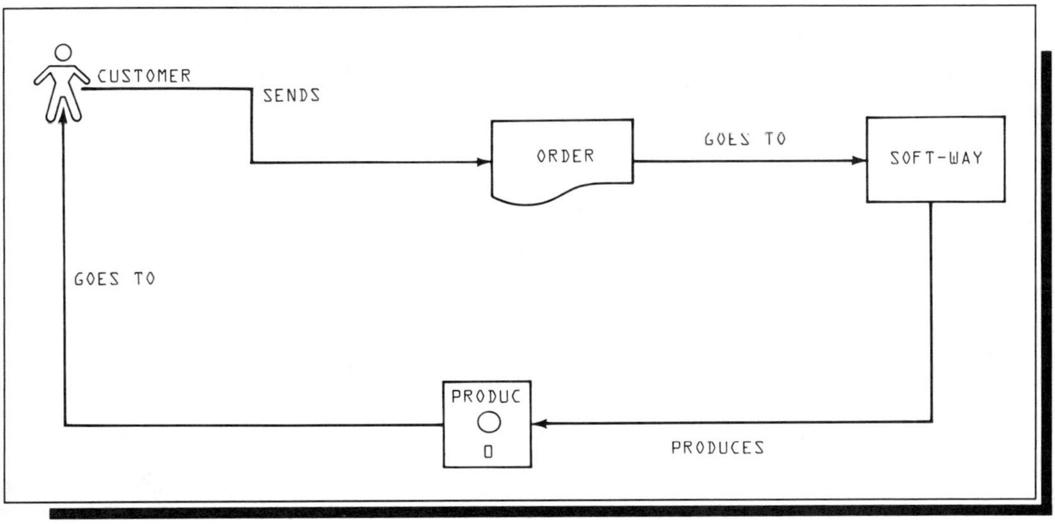

FIGURE 10-4 Soft-Way: The software fulfillment system.

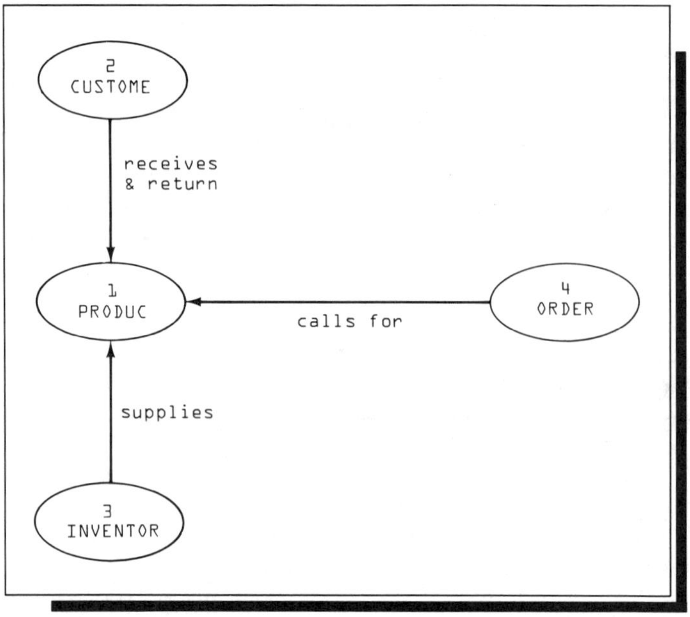

FIGURE 10-5 Important entity and relation classes. This is the logical data model of this operation.

Some of the workstation systems can be run on a network, so that a project team is able to work on different parts of the project under the coordination of a chief analyst. As well as providing design support, a workstation design aid helps maintain documentation when a system is

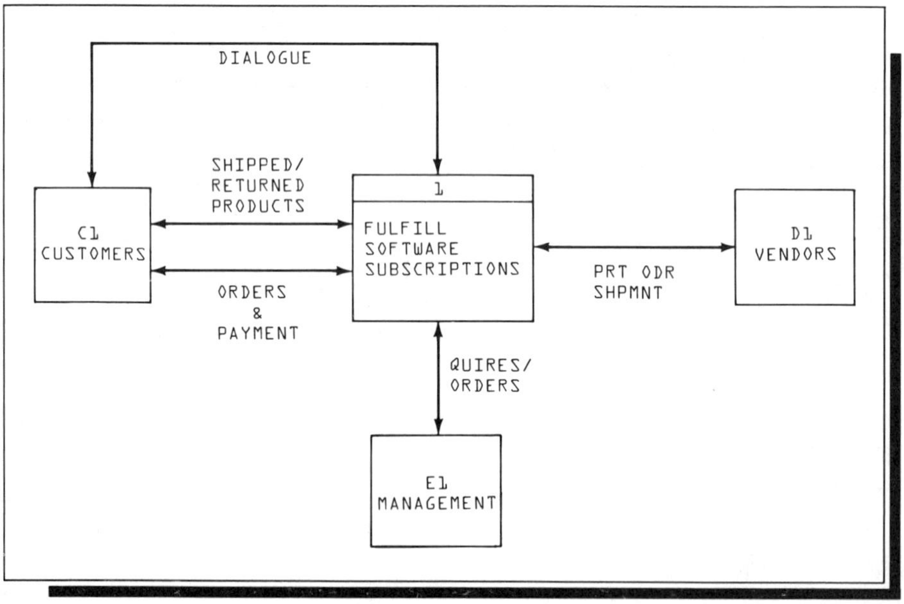

FIGURE 10-6 Fulfill Software Subscription. This is a zero-level data flow diagram.

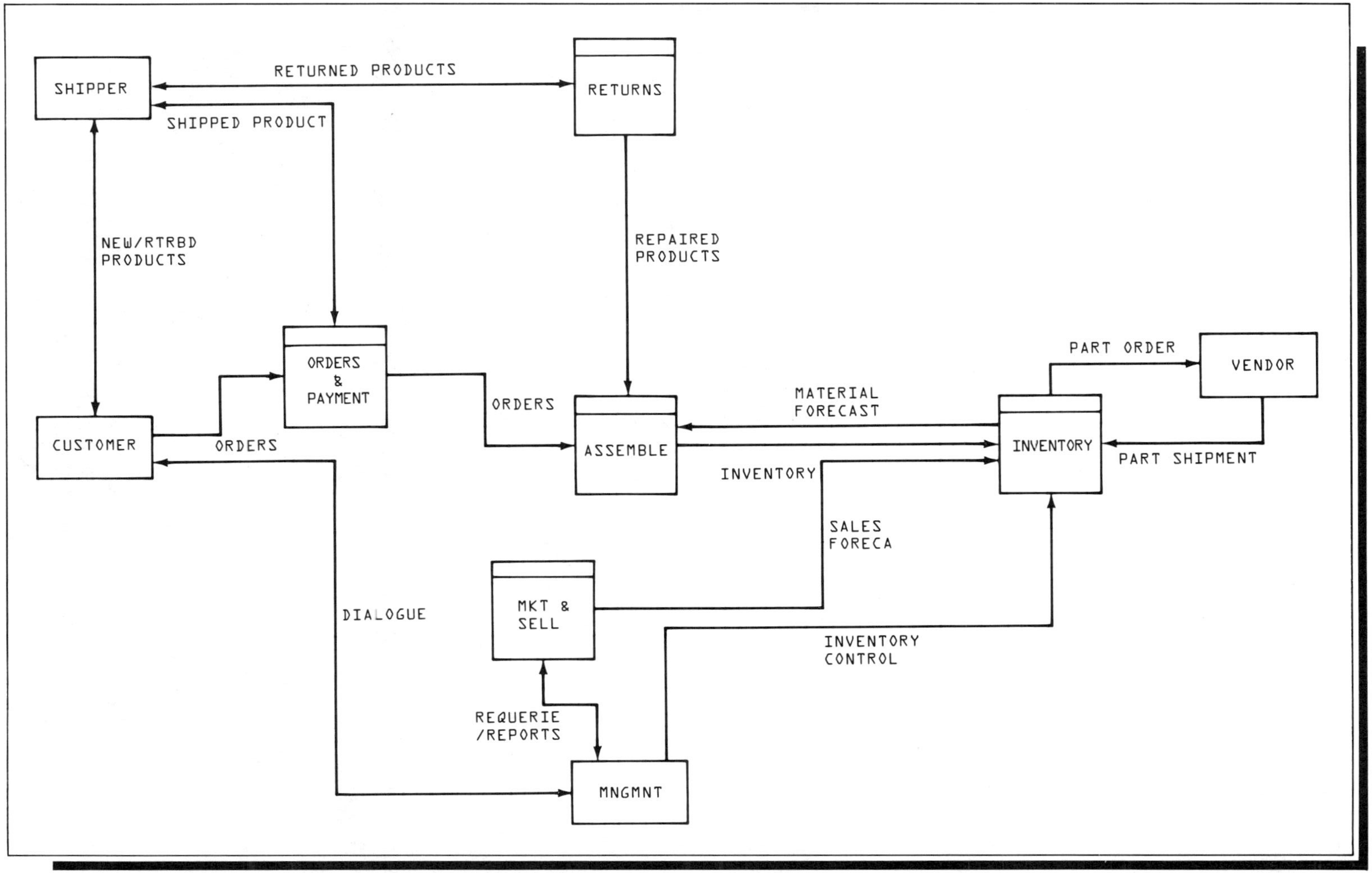

FIGURE 10-7 Example of first-level DFD: Order process. Note: This is the explosion of ''Fulfill Software Subscription'' (Process 1) in the previous DFD-level-0. It would be recognized as DFD-level-1.

```
                                                                  PAGE      1
DATE: 27-MAY-1986      ELEMENT - OUTPUT                           EXCELERATOR
TIME: 15:04            NAME: CODE

TYPE Element                                 NAME CODE

  Alternate Names

Definition          UNIQUE IDENTIFIER FOR A PARTICULAR PRODUCT

Input Picture       9{9}
Output Pic          9{9}
Edit Rules

Storage Type        C
Characters left of decimal 9   Characters right of decimal 0
Prompt
Column Header
Short Header
Base or Derived     _
Data Class
Source
Default


Description

Modified By         user          Date Modified    860527      Changes 1
Added By                          Date Added       860527
Last Project        demo
Locked By                         Date Locked      0           Lock Status __
```

FIGURE 10-8 COMMAND: XLDICTIONARY/DATA-ELEMENT/OUTPUT. This is an output of elements. Users are allowed to specify the format (underlined or not underlined) and the element. The contents include name, type, definition, I/O picture, creator name, project name, and the date created.

changed. We expect to see the widespread use of these tools as ISDs attempt to reduce one of the largest bottlenecks in the life cycle: systems analysis and design.

Systems Development at CMI

Tom White and Mary Watson were having lunch with the vice president of finance at CMI, Bob Carlin. The topic of discussion was a general ledger system that would be used by all divisions in the firm. Tom and Mary proposed a task force with members from each division's controller's office and a representative of the ISD to look for a package.

Carlin responded, "I don't see why you are jumping immediately to the conclusion that there is a package out there that is right for us. I remember that package we tried to install 5 or 6 years ago for accounts payable; what a disaster!"

Tom replied, "I wasn't here then, but I've certainly heard about that experience. Things have changed a lot in the last few years. Mainly, it's gotten so expensive to program a system from scratch that we always try to see if there is a package around first."

Mary added, "That's getting to be standard industry practice. Also, the general ledger is a very good candidate for a package."

"Why is that?" asked Bob.

"Almost every firm has a general ledger. In addition, most general ledgers are alike from a functional standpoint; they are hardly unique to the business."

"Ours is. I'll bet no one else has exactly the same chart of accounts or account numbering scheme," responded Bob.

"What Mary is driving at is that the uniqueness that companies have with respect to the general ledger is one that can be taken into account in the design of a package. It is not hard to build a package that lets a user define his own chart of accounts and to leave enough room in the data field for any kind of unique account number."

Bob thought for a minute and then said, "Okay, I guess it makes sense to look for something, but I'm skeptical based on our past experience."

Tom said, "I understand your reluctance, but packages have gotten a whole lot better. Two things have happened. First, a lot of packages are in their second, third, or even tenth release; they have been improved tremendously as users and the vendors have gotten experience with them. The second thing is micros; the packages that people build for micros are really outstanding. They knew that it was impossible to offer a consultant and training course with a $300 piece of software and still make a profit. As a result, the user interface with micro packages has set new standards for all types of packages."

Mary added, "A lot of companies just go out shopping. Here we require a systems definition at a high level so that we know what we are looking for. It gives us a benchmark to shoot for in evaluating packages. The design team we are asking for would do this high-level design and then be sure that it fits what each division needs. All of this would be finished before we looked at our first package."

"What you're saying sounds reasonable. I'll talk to the division controllers at our meeting next month, and we'll get a team organized. I'd like to be kept informed of progress and review the features the task force ends up recommending for the system."

Summary

This chapter has presented some methods for supplementing the traditional approach to developing a system. The goal is to reduce the labor-intensive, time-consuming task of systems analysis and design. Through the intelligent use of packages, nonprocedural languages, generators, and prototyping, many organizations have been able to achieve impressive results. The use of these modern techniques need not be mutually exclusive; one can envision using a generator to prototype an application quickly. Because the traditional approach takes so long and requires many scarce human resources, it is a good idea to use whatever alternatives can improve this process.

Recommended Readings

Martin, J., *Applications Development without Programmers.* Englewood Cliffs, N.J.: Prentice-Hall, 1982. (An excellent book with a number of alternatives to traditional methods.)

Mason, R. E. A., and T. T. Carey, "Prototyping Interactive Information Systems," *Communications of the ACM,* vol. 26, no. 5 (May 1983), pp. 347–354. (A good discussion of the reasons for prototyping.)

Nauman, J., and M. Jenkins, "Prototyping: The New Paradigm for Systems Development," *MIS Quarterly* (September 1982), pp. 29–44. (A good discussion of prototyping.)

Discussion Problems

10.1 Marion Bradshaw is director of marketing for Blue Bell Clothes. She would like to develop a database application on her microcomputer to keep track of key client contacts, when she last talked with them, and the nature of the conversation. Marion has read about two DBMSs that are in use at the firm, Paradox and DBase III+. She has actually produced a small application on Paradox, but has decided that she wants a menu-driven system.

"Now I have tried the thing out and I can see that it will be valuable for me. It is a bit tiresome to work with the commands. My needs are well defined and the system is now stable. All I want to do is to make it more automatic."

What kind of support from the ISD does Marion need in order to develop menus and make this end-user application more sophisticated? Can she do the job herself? Should she?

10.2 Good Foods is evaluating 4GLs for an information center. However, the manager of the ISD also wants a product that her programmers can use, too. The problem is that the 4GLs favored by the users on the selection team are not liked by the professional programmers.

The ISD manager feels that her position is correct: "It will be so much easier if we all use the same 4GL. I don't know why we can't reach agreement. I'm even willing to buy a whole new DBMS so that we can consider any of the 20 or so products available."

Suggest a procedure for resolving this dispute and moving the evaluation forward.

Questions

1. What are some of the major problems in the design process?
2. What are the different types of packages?

3. Why is it important to distinguish between systems software packages and dedicated packages?
4. What is the objective of a 4GL?
5. How does a 4GL differ from COBOL or FORTRAN?
6. What is a problem-oriented package?
7. What is unique about dedicated packages?
8. How does one implement a dedicated package?
9. Why are discrepancies important in the selection of a dedicated package?
10. What is a generator?
11. How does a generator contribute to productivity?
12. Why is it unlikely that a generator will improve productivity by 200%?
13. What are the differences in language requirements for an end-user versus a professional programmer?
14. What is a query language?
15. What is prototyping?
16. How does prototyping contribute to systems quality?
17. What is the role of a 4GL or a generator in prototyping?
18. What is the reason for using a systems analyst workstation?
19. What are the tools typically provided with an analyst workstation?
20. What can the manager of the ISD do to improve systems development productivity?
21. What can user management do to improve systems development productivity?
22. Should an organization use a 4GL for programming custom systems? If yes, under what conditions?

11

Implementation

What is implementation? Textbooks often describe it as the stage in systems development that begins 2 weeks before conversion to a new system. Implementation, however, begins long before the end of a project; it is the process of developing a system in such a way that the system will be used and well regarded by users. Designers should start to think about implementation when a system is first suggested. Too often, systems have been a technological success and an organizational failure: intended users are dissatisfied and the system does not achieve its potential.

How do we know if a system is a success? There are many different possible measures of success, including the following:

1. The extent to which the system is used. This measure requires that use of the system be voluntary. There are many systems in which the user is required to work with the computer as part of the job, such as when a clerk enters data on the movement of items through factory. Forced use of a system is not a good measure of success, but voluntary use is.

2. User satisfaction. When use is voluntary, we can analyze users' satisfaction with a system.

3. The extent to which a system meets its original goals and specifications.

4. The contribution the system makes to the organization, either in

terms of cost savings, ability to do a job that could not be performed without a computer, competitive advantage, higher-quality products or services, and so on.

5. Payback. It has proven extremely difficult to assess the payback of an information system. Systems are always partially justified by intangible returns; exercises to quantify such returns tend toward fantasy. One consultant in England feels that he can show very attractive returns on 80% of a large number of systems studied by his firm. We have also seen systems that provided a substantial payback. However, there are many applications where payback cannot be assessed or where the system has to be justified on faith. For example, many strategic applications defy payback analysis.

Implementation Factors

Management Action

A manufacturer of home furnishings developed an on-line order entry system in the 1970s; the system was the first one in the industry. When a customer went to a retail store, the salesperson could call the order entry clerk and determine instantly if the quantity, model type, and color were available. If so, the system sent orders to the warehouse, and that afternoon the warehouse staff had the order on a truck headed toward the retail store.

This system gave the manufacturer a competitive advantage because it was easy for the customer to substitute a similar item from another vendor if the item wanted was not available. This manufacturer knew what was in his inventory and could ship it to customers quickly.

By the 1980s, the on-line system was suffering from old technology; the user interface was crude by modern standards. The firm decided to redesign and reprogram the system. The new design would include forecasting, order entry, and factory floor scheduling. The firm hired a new lead systems analyst and formed a design team to work on the project.

After about a year's work, the design team issued preliminary specifications for user review. The specifications took the form of a 3-inch-thick notebook full of diagrams, file definitions, and report samples. The team distributed the notebook widely. The president and executive vice president of the firm became nervous when they could not understand anything in the book.

They hired a consultant, who was also unable to understand the specifications. The consultant interviewed a dozen users who had contributed to the design and found that they had very little understanding of the system. He organized a review meeting with widespread participation and presented the system at a conceptual level.

Management presented six policy decisions that it had made and that would influence the system. For example, management wanted a unified forecast so that all parts of the company used the same sales forecast. It wanted to merge customer services into one department so that a customer did not have to call two separate places to find out about an order. Many of these policy decisions were unpopular; because it had not been made clear that the decisions were management's, users associated them with the system. As a result, there was a great lack of cooperation with the design team.

When senior management clearly stated the reasons for the policy decisions and its commitment to them, the review meeting was able to proceed and concentrate on the system. The consultant presented the objectives and logical flow of the system; the audience identified problems and design questions that had not been resolved. At the end of the meeting, the unresolved issues were assigned to various subgroups, and progress on the system continued.

This story shows that a project that seemed to be proceeding well was, in fact, in deep trouble with respect to implementation. Users did not understand the system and were resisting it. *Management action* in hiring the consultant, verbalizing management policy decisions, and participating in the review meeting helped change the direction of the project.

Technical Characteristics

A money center bank developed a microcomputer-based workstation for client treasurers which was described in Chapter 5. The bank developed the first version of the system itself, but then purchased a system developed from an outside vendor when the development group found the programming and systems group unresponsive. While use of the outside system was risky, the developers thought it was better technically than the in-house system and that its designers were more responsive.

A competing bank also bought a third-party system, but in this case did not get the source code for the system. The third-party vendor went into bankruptcy, so that the competing bank was unable to modify or maintain its system. Another competitor developed a system itself, but used a nonstandard microcomputer that none of its customers wanted to purchase.

The money center bank in this example went through a somewhat turbulent development process, but it was careful to consider the *technical characteristics* of the systems it was offering to customers. *Technical success is a necessary but not a sufficient condition for successful implementation.* A system has to work right before it will be accepted by users and before it can make a contribution to the organization.

What is the contribution of the cash workstation? Bank officers feel that it draws the customer closer to the bank. Since the treasurer then uses the workstation to enter wire transfers and to manage the firm's investments and debts related to cash management, the bank derives fees for these services. It also has a better idea of what the customer is doing and can propose more services to the treasurer.

Attitudes

We all have attitudes toward various people, ideas, and objects. Often these attitudes determine how we act; they are important in shaping our behavior. Knowing attitudes, we can often predict someone's behavior. The more specific the object of the attitude, the easier it is to predict behavior. For example, even if we know the political party to which someone belongs, it is hard to predict how that person will vote. If instead we know the person's attitudes toward the party's candidate, prediction is easier and more accurate.

We have found that attitudes toward information processing systems and toward the ISD staff are often an indicator of how well the ISD is doing in the firm. In addition, these attitudes can be a good predictor of the system's use and/or user satisfaction.

In one firm, users had long complained about the perceived incompetence of the ISD staff. ISD professionals complained that users did not participate in design and did not understand information processing. The results of this kind of conflict are unfortunate; unhelpful behavior creates more problems and conflicts. Users do not participate in systems development, and the result is poor systems. Users take these poor systems as proof of the incompetence of information services is, and as an excuse not to cooperate with the ISD staff. Management within ISD needs to concentrate on creating credibility for the department and on taking actions to create favorable *user attitudes.*

Decision Style

There is some evidence that people have different ways of approaching problems. Some individuals like to see textual reports; they prefer not to be bothered with numbers. Other, more quantitatively oriented decision makers want to see data and come to their own conclusions.

A consulting firm developed a computer system to assist the portfolio managers in the trust department of a bank. The trust officer manages a number of portfolios and must decide how to invest the money in the portfolios according to the objectives of the individual for whom the trust is administered. Portfolio theory suggests that a manager should look at the entire portfolio in making investment decisions rather than examine a particular stock.

Because most information is about individual securities, it is typical for a portfolio manager to study the stock of one firm and then to review each of the portfolios containing that stock. This approach to investing might be called *security oriented* rather than *portfolio centered.*

The new computer system allowed the managers to review the status of portfolios much more easily than under the previous manual system. The managers could now follow a portfolio-oriented strategy. However, the managers tended to use the system at the beginning of the day to obtain an up-to-date printout of their portfolios' status.

Why did the managers not change their approach to investing? They were successful when operating in a security-oriented mode; it would have been very risky for them to change. The designers of the system provided no real reason to adopt the new approach, and management offered no incentives to change. The portfolio managers' *decision style* was security oriented, so that the new system did not achieve its full potential.

Personal/Situational Variables

In the home furnishings case described earlier, there was one key man in the design process: the manager of production. This individual scheduled all production. In fact, he even made his own forecast of what to produce after throwing away the forecast made by the marketing department! This man was nearing retirement and was, at first, very antagonistic toward the new system and the idea of combining the two places now providing customer service into one department. He had been with the firm for many years.

There were lengthy debates and discussions among management and the design team about what to do with this individual. The options considered ranged from firing him to making him a vice president! Eventually he was designated as the chief user on the design team. During the review meeting, he began to assume ownership of the system. He used terms like "our system" and said, "We will develop it this way."

The designers and management were worried because they needed input from this individual and because he could have sabotaged the entire development effort. His unique *personal and situational characteristics* were important in determining the success of the design effort.

A Model

Figure 11-1 is a model of how the factors previously described are hypothesized to influence successful implementation. Management actions are hypothesized to influence implementation through attitudes toward a system. We have mentioned several times the important role that management plays in influencing subordinates in the firm. When senior management in the home furnishings case took an active interest in the system, users realized that the firm was serious about developing this new application, and they began to cooperate with the design team.

Technical characteristics are extremely important; a system must work technically to be successful. Technical characteristics also influence user attitudes. A system that has many errors or a clumsy and displeasing user interface, or that fails to meet users' needs, will create poor user attitudes.

Decision style, as we saw in the portfolio case, can directly influence implementation. Particularly in voluntary systems like those developed for decision support, decision style problems may result in the system not being used at all. Decision style can also influence a person's attitudes toward a system.

Finally, personal and situational factors may influence implementation. The chronic change resistor may sabotage a system. The situation may be so unfavorable that a system should not be developed at this time.

Implementer Influence

Given these factors, what can the implementer do to enhance the chances for success? Figure 11-2 shows the factors arranged on a continuum of implementer influence. Implementors have the most influence over the

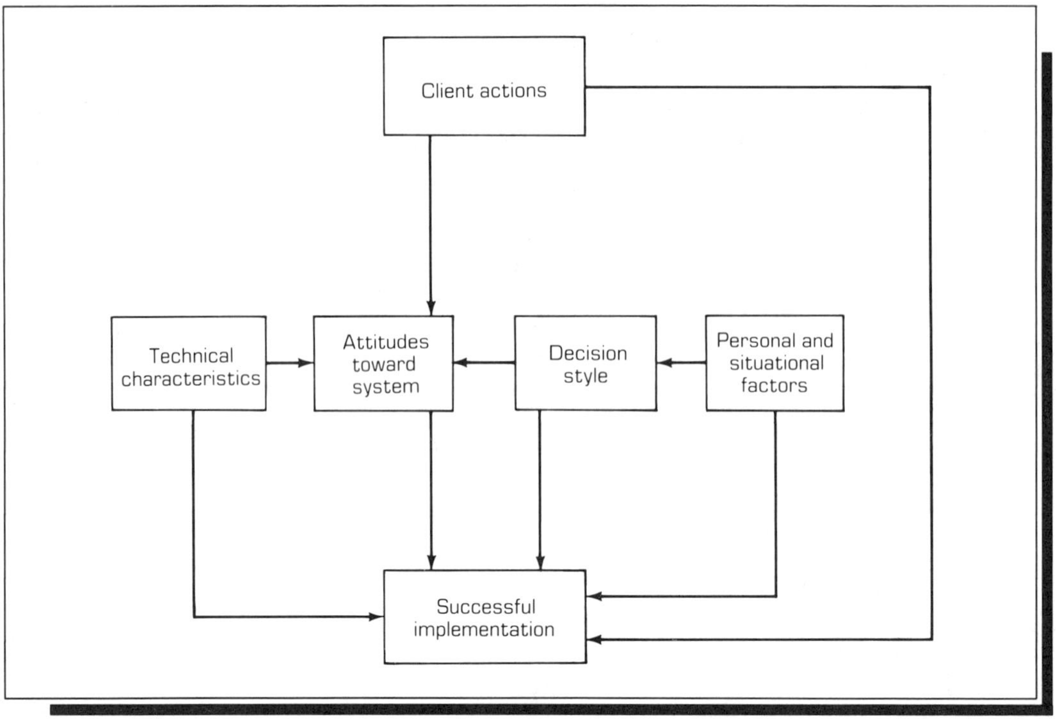

FIGURE 11-1 Hypothesized relationship among implementation forces. (From Lucas, 1981)

technical characteristics of a system; after all, designers are supposed to be experts in the technology.

In some instances, implementers can influence management actions. In fact, this is probably their greatest opportunity for leverage in the short run. It may be possible to influence attitudes toward a system or the ISD, but attitudes take a long time to change.

Decision style is rarely amenable to change by the implementer. In the portfolio example, management might have been able to change the way portfolio managers approached their job. However, the designers of the system would have had great difficulty making this change themselves.

Personal and situational factors are a given. It may be possible to influ-

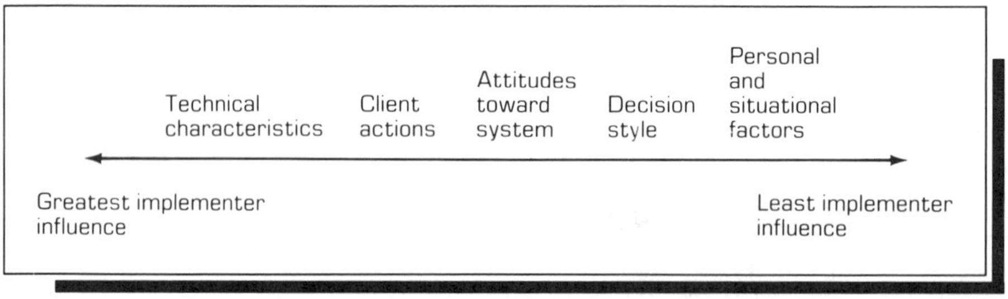

FIGURE 11-2 Implementation factors and implementer influence. (From Lucas, 1981)

ence them, but probably only through management action. For example, the furnishings company put the production control manager on the design team.

Relationship Considerations

The factor model has some support from research; many of the factors described have been found to be associated with successful implementation. However, there is something lacking in this model; it does not consider the relationship between the designer and the user of the system.

Figure 11-3 presents the Kolb-Frohman model for organizational development. This model applies nicely to the relationship between the users of a system and its designers.

In the first stage of the model, the systems staff member is scouting the environment. Who is really requesting the system? What is the motivation for the system? What is it to accomplish?

The next stage is crucial; the designers have to find an entry in the user organization. Who will sponsor this project? Usually the higher the entry point in the organization, the greater the chances for success. Senior managers generally have influence and resources to apply to the system.

Diagnosis is where the designer and, hopefully, a design team undertake systems analysis. They also develop a schedule and estimates of the resources required to complete the system. During action, a new system is defined. The bulk of the technical work occurs during this stage. The team develops specifications, which are turned over to a programming group (assuming custom development as opposed to a package). The design team and users convert and install the finished system.

During evaluation, the designers assess the impact of the system; there will probably be modifications based on evaluation. Termination means that the design team is finished; the system is now turned over to users.

A key activity during the entire procedure is the transfer of ownership of the system from the designers to the design team to users. There is some

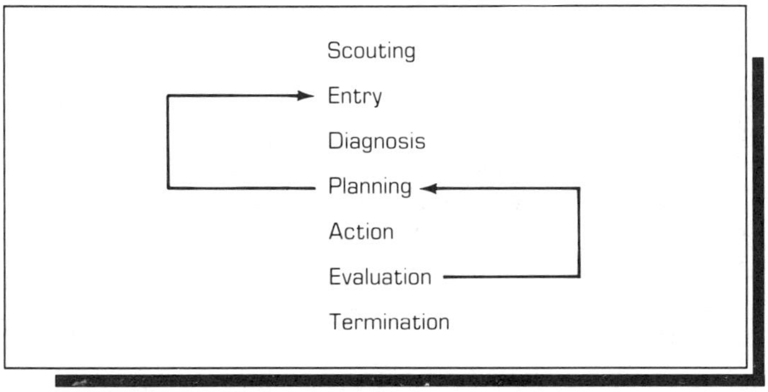

FIGURE 11-3 A process model. (From Lucas, 1981)

research evidence that termination is the most important stage; as a result, it should be planned for from the start.

As one user department manager put it, "Designers don't use a system. They can help build it, but it is the user who makes it work." The designer disappears after the termination phase, and the user is left with the results. Thus it is vital for ownership of the system to reside with users.

A Framework

Table 11-1 combines the factor model with the Kolb-Frohman model to create a framework for the implementation process. The framework stresses the need to consider the relationship between the designer and the user, while simultaneously evaluating each of the factors associated with implementation success during each stage.

During the scouting stage, the designers assess the need for a system from a technical standpoint. During entry, the designer tries to determine the goals and boundaries of the application. In diagnosis, one looks at the feasibility of different technologies to support the application. In planning technical considerations, one turns to resource requirements and scheduling. The action stage involves developing the specifications for a new applications, and actual programming and conversion. During evaluation, part of the technical design may have to be modified. At termination, implementers hope to find high levels of use of the system.

In a similar fashion, the implementer can consider client actions, attitudes, decision styles, and personal and situational factors at each stage in the design process. While professional designers would probably all agree that the considerations in Table 11-1 are important, often they are not considered in an organized manner. The purpose of the framework is to help the design team develop a structured approach to implementation, just as they are expected to use a structured approach to the design task itself.

A Two-Stage Model

More recently, we have extended the ideas previously presented to provide a two-stage model of the implementation process. This model includes some relationship variables, along with the more static variables presented Figure 11-1. The major difference between this model and other implementation models is that this one envisions a two-stage process.

The models in Figures 11-4 and 11-5 represent a manager and a user. Frequently today the major user of a system is not the individual who requested the application. It is often the user's manager who has determined that a system is needed. In one firm, the only sponsor of a new system is the divisional vice president; it is difficult to find enthusiasm for the system in anyone else.

TABLE 11-1 An Implementation Framework

	Factors				
Stages	**Technical Characteristics**	**Client Action**	**Attitudes Toward System**	**Decision Style**	**Personal, Situational Factors**
Scouting	Need	Observe	Observe	Observe	Observe
Entry	Goals Boundaries	Enlist support involvement	Observe	Observe Assess impact	Delineate
Diagnosis	Feasibility	Formalize support involvement Form design team	Assess formally	Assess formally Reflect in goals	Assess formally Reflect in goals
Planning (project process)	Resources Schedule	Delineate resources needed for change Management action	Expected reactions	Incorporate alternatives, different styles Assess impact	Plan for different conditions
Action Unfreeze Change Refreeze	Delineate system Specify program Convert	Management action User teams Added resources Reward structure	Costs/benefits of change Group influence Group commitment	Include different styles in plans Different alternatives in system Tailored training Conversion	Design contingent Reflect in specs Tailored training and conversion
Evaluate	Modify	Through design plan Required management action	Assess and reinforce	Contingent on styles relative to goals	Contingent on factors relative to goals
Termination	High levels of use	Diffusion to others Continued management support	User commitment Ownership High satisfaction	Widespread user ownership	Widespread user ownership

The presence of the manager as the initiator of the system creates implementation difficulties, particularly if this manager is very senior and is unwilling or unable to participate in the design process. This two-stage model is intended to draw attention to the added problems that occur when the sponsor of the system is not involved in the development process.

Manager Model

Manager acceptance is the central variable in the manager model in Figure 11-4; it is also the link to the user model. The model suggests that a system's developer should concentrate on gaining manager acceptance of a new system. Acceptance is a variable that measures the extent to which a manager wants a system to be developed, accepted, and used by others. The following variables are also included in the manager model; they are hypothesized to influence acceptance either directly or indirectly.

1. Acceptance—predisposition to use the system.
2. Knowledge of the system—understanding of the system and its capabilities.
3. Assessment of the system and support—the manager's evaluation of the quality of the system.

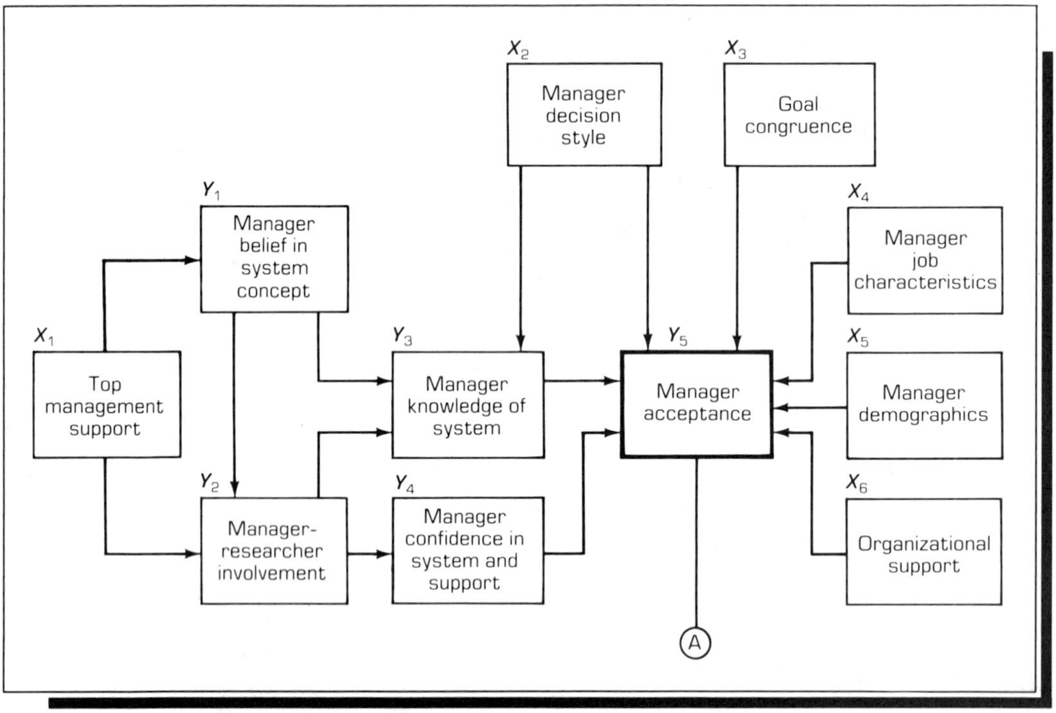

FIGURE 11-4 Manager model. (From Ginzberg et al., 1984)

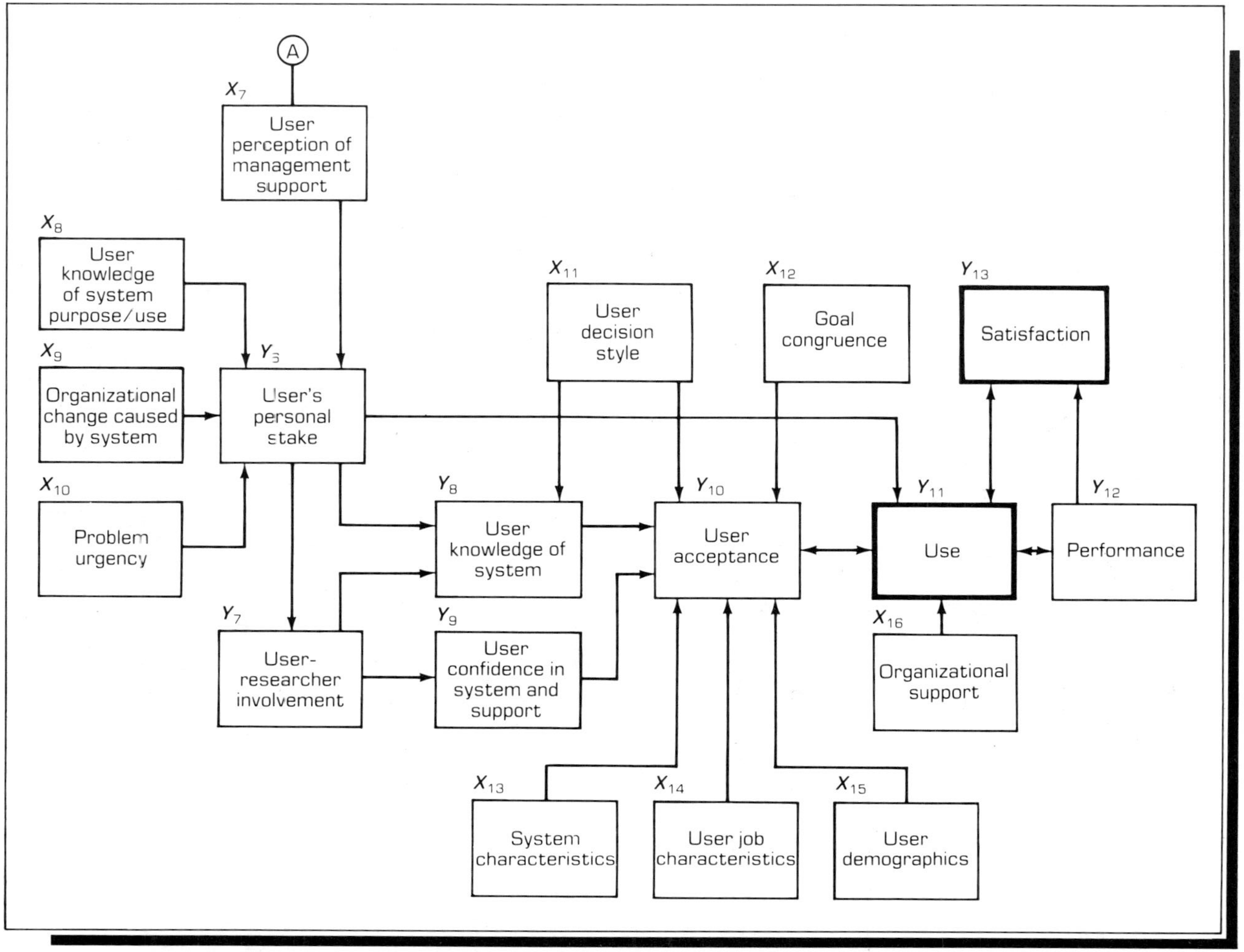

FIGURE 11-5 User model.

4. Manager's decision style—his or her characteristic way of approaching a problem.
5. Goal congruence—fit between the manager's and the organization's goals.
6. Job characteristics—the tasks of the manager.
7. Demographics—personal and situational characteristics.
8. Organizational support—structural support for the system, such as having adequate equipment.
9. Belief in the system concept—the extent to which the manager believes in the underlying approach taken by the system.
10. Manager–developer involvement—quantity and quality of the interaction between the manager and the systems designer.
11. Top management support—support exhibited by top management for the system.

User Model

The user model in Figure 11-5 closely parallels the manager model, but it contains a few more variable. The developer wants to encourage high levels of use and user satisfaction with a new system, as shown in the figure.

1. User acceptance—the users' predisposition to use a system.
2. User knowledge of the system—the extent to which the user understands the system.
3. Assessment of system and support—evaluation of the system.
4. Decision style—the user's way of approaching problems.
5. Goal congruence—the fit between the user's goals and those of the organization.
6. Job characteristics and demographics—the nature of the user's tasks and personal and situational variables.
7. System characteristics—features and capabilities of the system.
8. User–developer involvement—degree and quality of interaction between the user and the systems designer.
9. Personal stake—the degree to which the user's future rewards are tied to the system.
10. Management support—assessment of the manager's support from Figure 11-4.
11. Knowledge of the system's purpose and use—degree to which a user understands the reasons for the system.
12. Organizational change—changes in the task and the working environment, communications patterns, and organizational structure that users anticipate from the system.
13. Problem urgency—the significance of the problem.
14. Use—the degree to which the system is used.
15. Organizational support—the degree to which the organization provides support, like terminals.
16. Performance—the performance of users and the organization.
17. Satisfaction—user reaction to the system.

There are many variables in this model, and the model has not yet been extensively tested with data. However, based on past research, the implementer may want to keep some of these variables in mind when confronted with what appears to be a two-stage implementation problem.

Who Should Design Systems?

Earlier we suggested that there should be extensive user representation on a systems design team. Why stop at this point? Why not have the users actually design the system, instead of the professional analyst? Users are being encouraged to work with 4GLs, and there appears to be no way to discourage them from making extensive use of micros. Why not have users actually design systems?

The hope is that user control over the design process will have a number of payoffs for the firm. The new system is more likely to be used because the user will be the owner. If the user is in charge, this should help achieve the goal of the termination stage: user ownership of the application. Because of their exposure to the system, users should be well trained and conversion should proceed smoothly.

Users will also be more knowledgeable about the system if they control its design; they will be forced to understand the design in order to contribute to it. We would expect to find fewer errors and a better design because users understand their information processing problems better than the ISD does.

This stress on user-controlled design does not mean that users actually write programs. In fact, the systems professional must still provide a tremendous amount of input in the design process. As we have seen in other places, however, the role of the systems designer is changing.

Now the systems designer is acting as a consultant to the design team; being a tour guide is a good analogy. The designer must explain to the team what has to be done at each stage in the design process. During analysis and design, the computer professional analyzes the many alternatives and selects a reasonable number to present to the design team. The analyst also helps the design team evaluate different alternatives.

By providing this kind of direction, the analyst is placing decision-making responsibility with users while still furnishing technical assistance. Since the aim is for the user to own the system, and since it is the user who will ultimately work with the completed system, this new role of the analyst is consistent with all of the implementation objectives. The analyst will still provide advice and consultation; his or her comparative advantage is in this knowledge of the design process and the technology.

We have seen several cases in which this approach has succeeded. Since ISD personnel are relinquishing power in so many areas due to the proliferation of computers, the role described here in systems analysis fits nicely with current trends. It should also benefit the organization in general and information services in particular.

What responsibilities does user-controlled design place on management within the ISD? First, managers must help and support the change in approach. It is not easy for professional systems analysts to change their behavior. It is far more expedient to be in charge of the design; the analyst does not have to wait for users or explain things when allowed to make arbitrary decisions. It may be necessary to provide seminars or special training for analysts in the consulting process to prepare for this new role.

In addition, management in the ISD will have to work with users and their managers. Often ISD staff members try to involve users, but the users seem too busy and/or uninterested in the project. Of course, some of this lack of interest may be due to the fact that projects have traditionally been controlled by the ISD staff. If the user clearly has responsibility for the success of a project and that responsibility has been communicated by his or her superior, the interest level should be higher. ISD management has to be the catalyst to make the relationship and the design team work.

Summary

Just as the role of information services is changing with respect to the structure of information processing, the placement of computers in the organization, and the kind of support it must provide to users, the role of the systems analyst should change.

We have stressed the importance of looking at the relationship between the designer and the user. In particular, the systems analyst is becoming of a consultant to a user-led design team rather than the person who controls the design.

It is also important to think about the sponsor of a systems development project. Is it really the user on the design team who wants the system? What can be done to improve the chances for success if a senior-level manager is the sponsor and is unable to participate in the design?

Management within information services should be concerned about implementation and the relationship between designers and users. Management will have to counsel ISD employees and will also have to be a liaison with user department management to secure user input and involvement in the design process.

It is not enough to design systems that are technically sound; too many other factors and relationships influence the systems development process. Systems analysis and design is a key activity; performing well in this endeavor is an important part of managing a successful information services department. Implementation is as important a consideration as using the right design tools, setting the proper system boundaries, and completing the technical design. In the next chapter, we look at a final part of systems analysis that must be successful for a system to succeed: project management.

Recommended Readings

Ginzberg, M., R. Schultz, and H. L. Lucas, Jr., "A Structural Model of Implementation," in *Applications of Management Science: Management Science Implementa-*

tion. Greenwich, CN: JAI Press, 1984. (A discussion of the two-stage model presented in this chapter.)

Lucas, H. C., Jr., *Implementation: The Key to Successful Information Systems*. New York: Columbia University Press, 1981. (Describes factor and relationship models of implementation.)

Mumford, E., and D. Henshall, *A Participative Approach to Computer Systems Design*. London: Associated Business Press, 1979. (An excellent book on the design of a system using very participative approaches.)

Discussion Problems

11.1 A major manufacturer of electronic components maintains an extensive marketing database. The database records the purchases of all of the firm's customers, and various planners can obtain a wealth of information from the system. A product planner might look at the existing base of a certain part to see who might be interested in an enhanced version.

The retrieval system may be classified as a general data analysis DSS. Planners are the most frequent users, though managers often have staff members prepare special reports. The system was designed over 10 years ago and is showing its age. Two researchers studying the system thought that its use was voluntary, but were surprised to find out that users felt they had to work with the system.

Can you explain why users might have felt that way? How can the firm go about designing a new version of the system without creating major disruptions for the hundreds of users who work with it daily?

11.2 A large company was in the habit of designing a system at its largest division and then taking the system to other locations for installation. In the early days of computing, there were few problems, as the local sites were happy to have help. However, as minicomputers were developed and offered freedom to local managers, this top-down implementation process grew more problematical.

How can the firm's management help the systems staff in the largest location adopt a different perspective on implementation? What kind of freedom should be given to local managers with respect to information processing? Are there certain types of systems that have to be developed centrally? Are there some systems that are naturally developed by local divisions?

Questions

1. What is the implementation process?
2. Why is implementation a concern of IS management? Is it a concern of IS management alone?
3. Describe two measures of systems success. In what ways are the measures good and bad?
4. Why is it hard to use payback to evaluate a system?
5. What kind of action can management take to improve the chances for successful implementation?
6. How do the technical characteristics of a system influence implementation?
7. What are attitudes? How do they play a part in a user's reaction to a system?
8. What is decision style? Do you think it is a valid concept?
9. How do personal and situational variables influence implementation?

10. Over what variables in the model in Figure 11-1 does an implementer have influence?
11. What is the difference between the task of systems design and the relationship between the designer and user?
12. Why is entry an important stage in the Kolb-Frohman model?
13. Why is it important to turn ownership of a system over to users?
14. What role does the termination stage have in the Kolb-Frohman model?
15. What does the two-stage model in Figures 11-4 and 11-5 add to our understanding of implementation?
16. Why is the role of the manager who asks for a system sometimes overlooked in implementation?
17. Why might a user's personal stake be important in determining acceptance of a system?
18. What are the arguments in favor of users designing their own systems?
19. How have technological trends in the last decade encouraged greater user design?
20. What burden does user design place on the professional systems design in ISD?

PART III

Managing Information Services

12

Project Management

Information systems development projects seem to be chronically behind schedule and over budget. Lack of success in managing projects is a source of user and management dissatisfaction with the ISD. Is the ISD unique in this characteristic?

Many industries and many types of projects have experienced serious time and cost overruns. Are there similarities between these examples and the task of developing an information system? Table 12-1 shows the original estimates for developing the Concorde supersonic airliner and the revised estimates at each stage.

It is clear from this table that the early estimates for the development of the plane were wildly optimistic. The designers' first estimate was that the plane would be in service by 1970. In fact, it first flew in 1973 and then entered regular service in 1976. The plane now shows an operating profit on the New York to London and Paris runs only if one writes off all of the capital investment costs. Britain and France developed the plane jointly; only their state airlines operate it. The current route structure is considerably smaller than the one envisioned when the plane was first proposed.

Table 12-2 shows the history of nuclear power facility construction by the TVA. Many of the cost (per kilowatt) estimates are off by a factor of two or more. The completion time overruns range from 1.09 to 2.5. The entire construction of the nuclear power stations was forecast for completion by

TABLE 12-1 The Concorde Cost Overrun

Original estimate = 100		
Spent	**Cost of Remaining Work**	**Revised Estimate**
100	150	250
150	120	270
200	140	340
250	150	400
300	120	420

the late 1980s but has been set back by at least 10 years. In fact, there is now new management at the TVA, partially because of the agency's nuclear construction problems.

Project Characteristics

What characteristics of these two projects, and other information systems development projects, explain some of these difficulties? In the case of the Concorde, the new airplane represented an R&D effort. Of course, the manufacturers had had experience building airliners and military aircraft that flew faster than the speed of sound. However, it turned out to be difficult to combine the characteristics of a commercial airliner with those of a supersonic fighter.

In the case of the TVA, R&D does not appear to be the issue. After all, there are many commercial nuclear power plants. However, the U.S. power industry has been criticized for demanding custom-designed power plants. Instead of adopting an "off-the-shelf" design, utilities have asked for power plants to be designed with unique characteristics. The utilities also complain about the fact that regulations for the plants are constantly changed by the government during construction. As a result, the entire industry, and not just

TABLE 12-2 The TVA Nuclear Power Stations: Cost and Time Overruns

	Cost Estimate—$/kw		**Completion Time (Months)**		
	Original	**January 1980**	**Original**	**Latest**	**Factor**
Browns Ferry	113 (1967)	263	46	81	1.75
Sequoyah	138 (1968)	598	47	117	2.50
Watts Bar	200 (1969)	581	55	78	1.40
Bellefonte	271 (1970)	770	55	63	1.15
Hartsville	274 (1971)	1127	54	71	1.30
Phipps Bend	615 (1974)	1146	62	67	1.10
Yellow Creek	731 (1974)	1082	66	72	1.09

Note: The latest estimate of cost assumes completion of the program by the late eighties, but it has now been set back by a further ten years.

Source: Data reproduced by kind permission of the TVA.

the TVA, has been in great difficulty. The huge cost and time overruns, combined with questions about the feasibility and safety of nuclear power after the Three Mile Island and Chernobyl accidents, may lead to radical new designs and more "packaged" plants.

Information Systems Development

To a large extent, information systems development projects can be characterized by both of the problems just presented. While developers have designed other systems, no two seem to be exactly alike. Since the organization probably has not designed a system with all of the features of the one currently being undertaken, there is an R&D flavor to development.

The degree of R&D, and its attendant uncertainty, depend on how far the organization is trying to increase its own experience with the technology. For example, when American Airlines and IBM developed the first-generation SABRE reservations system, there were huge cost overruns, even though the project was reportedly finished slightly early. Developing a new accounting application probably involves less R&D than trying to use computers to automate a factory.

The custom design problem is similar to the one experienced by the nuclear construction industry. While we have stressed the need to provide a range of alternatives, including packaged systems, many custom system development efforts are still underway. To the extent that each of these systems is unique, the design team has a more difficult task. Also, as in the power industry, users and designers are constantly changing the requirements and the design, which complicates the development process.

In this chapter, we shall explore what management can do to help reduce the risk of information systems development projects. First, we shall concentrate on systems that are custom designed. Then we shall consider the challenges posed by package implementation, end-user computing, and the development of systems on micros.

Design Considerations

What steps can be followed to make a project easier to manage? Is there a design methodology that contributes to management? Following are some suggestions for the overall structure of the design process to facilitate project management:

1. Use structured design techniques. Complexity is difficult to manage. If a system is designed as one large, complex entity, it will be more difficult to manage than if it is divided into smaller components. The design methodologies suggested earlier will help here. For example, the idea of top-town design encourages the designers to break down each complex process into a series of smaller processes. As well as being conceptually simpler, each smaller process can be managed as an entity.

In discussing the structure of the organization, we presented Galbraith's information processing view of the organization. He suggested that one approach to management is goal setting. In fact, that observation came from a study of Boeing's aircraft manufacturing approach. Each team for a part of the aircraft was given targets; as long as they met the targets, there was little need for coordination. For example, the team designing the wing of the plane had targets for weight, fuel capacity, engine mounting, and so on.

In information systems project design, if one can define interfaces and goals for various components of the system, each component or module can be managed without having to worry about its interaction with other modules. Of course, this approach requires the designers, in breaking the project into pieces, to minimize the interaction among the components. In fact, independence should be one of the design team's primary objectives. The principle is the same as the one for software modularization: to develop subsystems that are as self-contained as possible.

2. Use clear, easy-to-understand notation. We have suggested the use of various types of structured design symbols like DFDs. If the design team, users, and programmers are all consistent in their use of diagrams and symbols, there will be less confusion and fewer errors.

3. Set the boundaries for a system and adhere to them. It is very tempting, particularly when developing a custom application, to allow the boundaries to creep outward to encompass more and more functions. Systems can quickly become too large for the resources of the firm. It is important to set a boundary on a system; if necessary, break the system into a series of subsystems and schedule the sequence in which they will be developed. With limited resources, one cannot hope to design all parts of a large, complex system at once.

4. Use good design tools. We have talked about packages that assist the analyst and about tools for prototyping. At a minimum, the design team should use whatever features the organization offers, like a DBMS to record data elements during the design process. Beyond a DBMS, consider developing programmer and analyst workstations to be used for all major design work. These workstations combine local intelligence with software tools to help programmers and analysts develop systems.

5. Manage the project. Historically, project management for systems development has been lacking. The project team leader is usually heavily involved in design work; he or she often fails to shift from doing the design to managing it. If we ask users to become the project manager, the information services team leader should function as the manager of project resources. Later in this chapter, we discuss project management techniques in detail.

6. Involve others in project management. It is important for individuals working on the project to know that an effort is being made to manage it. In addition, these individuals must provide estimates of how long their assigned tasks will take and notify the manager about completion. The results of reporting must be used to help the project, not evaluate the performance of the person giving the report. It is important to have the best information possible, not information that is biased to protect the provider.

7. Monitor the project and take action. It is not enough to set up a

formal project management scheme; one must also determine when problems occur and move to solve them. The project manager has some options for solving project problems, which are discussed later in the chapter.

Obviously there is no guarantee that efforts devoted to project management will lead to project completion on time and within budget; there are too many uncertainties. However, if the project is well managed, there should be fewer surprises and more credibility with management.

Estimates

One reason that information systems projects are often over budget and over cost is lack of success in estimating what is required to complete a project. There are two facets to estimating: determining what is required and how long it will take to complete. An estimate may be accurate for the task as understood, but what happens when the task suddenly is found to have a whole set of requirements that had been overlooked? The estimates will now be wrong.

How does one arrive at a reasonable estimate? The first thing to realize is that an estimate is a forecast. The individual making the estimate is using past experience as a guide to determine how long it should take to perform a task. Since one is usually forced to make estimates before detailed design is complete, a high level of uncertainty is involved.

One firm does not have the project manager make the estimates; instead the project manager assigns tasks to different individuals, who are responsible for completing them. These individuals are asked to provide time estimates. The advantage of this approach is that the estimates come from the person who is responsible, rather than from a third party who is trying to forecast how another individual will perform. Hopefully, the person making the estimate will also become committed to that estimate and work to complete the tasks within the time provided.

The manager of information services in another company followed a life cycle model for systems development. He had a policy of not making a time or cost forecast for the next stage in the life cycle until near the end of the preceding stage. Of course, this policy meant that company management did not have a very good idea of the total cost of a project before authorizing its development. It is not clear whether this method of estimation could be sold to all managements, but it is an interesting approach.

Estimating Techniques

There have been a number of studies of project performance to see if forecasting tools can be developed to predict how much labor and time a project will require. Usually these studies are conducted by a researcher who collects data on project performance and analyzes them statistically, often fitting a curve of some type to the data.

The difficulty with this approach is that one is gathering data that are specific to a single organization. A few studies have included multiple organizations, but then one worries about comparability of measurement. Some of the models are macro in scope and seem dangerous to apply to a project of three to five individuals.

One model for person loading in systems development and programming that has been mentioned frequently in the literature is the Rayleigh equation:

$$y = 2Kat\ e^{-at^2}$$

where y = personnel utilized in each time period t
K = total cumulative personnel on the project
a = parameter determining the shape of the curve
t = time period in months
e = the base for natural logarithms

A plot of the Rayleigh curve is shown in Figure 12-1; the plot shows the effect of changing the parameters K and a. The model consists of two components. The term $2at$ increases in a linear manner over time, while the exponent $K\ e^{-at^2}$ decreases exponentially over time. This particular model has been tested on several hundred medium- to large-scale software projects and on some smaller ones.

Wiener-Ehrlich et al. (1984) applied the Rayleigh curve to four medium-scale projects (each under 80,000 lines of code) at Bankers Trust Company in New York. The authors concluded that the model fit the actual experience fairly closely except for the maintenance phase of the project. Estimates of maintenance were consistently below actual expenditures.

Applying the Model

How can a project manager use a model like the Rayleigh curve in planning a project? Unfortunately, using this forecasting approach requires a considerable amount of effort. First, the organization must fit the curve to some of its past projects in order to determine what the ranges are for a and K. Then the manager must estimate how the project being planned compares to past experiences to estimate a and K for the project under consideration. Both parameters are very important: a determines the duration of the project and K changes the total effort, the area under the curve.

Then the manager uses the best estimates of a and K to plot the Rayleigh curve, which is the prediction for the project being planned. The curve suggests the personnel requirements and the duration of the project. Such estimates should be compared with others, for example, estimates made by the individuals who are assigned to work on the project.

In the Bankers Trust case, the fit to the Rayleigh curve (except for maintenance) was good for projects with teams of 10 to 15 individuals. As the organization gains experience, it will develop a history of project data and find it possible to select a and K values more easily and routinely for estimation purposes.

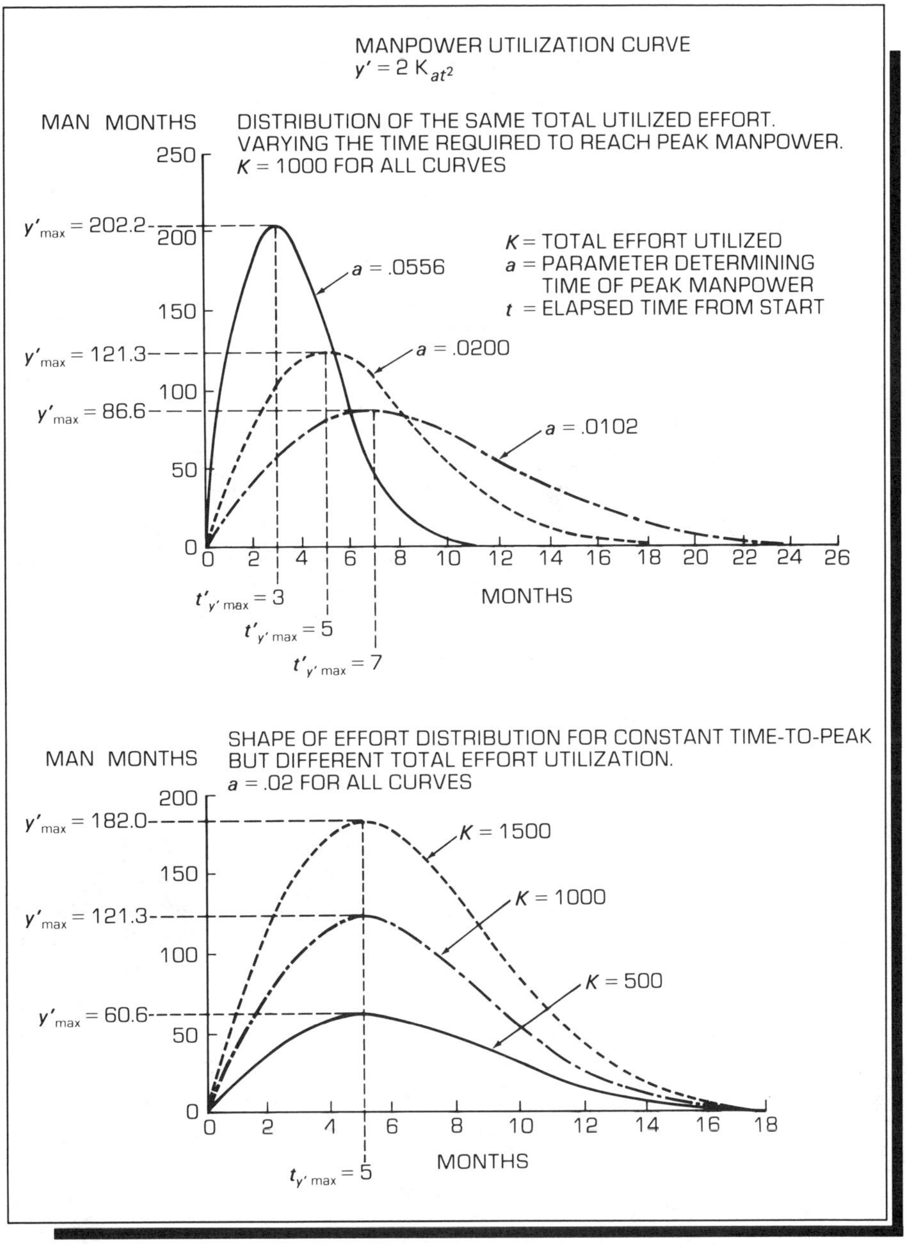

FIGURE 12-1 Effect of changing parameter values (K and a) on the Rayleigh life cycle curve. The top panel illustrates the effect of varying a given a constant K. The bottom panel shows the effect of varying K given a constant a. (From Wiener-Ehrlich et al., 1984)

It is not essential that the organization use the Rayleigh curve; however, an important part of project management is estimating resource requirements. The use of multiple methods, such as a forecasting technique based on data in addition to estimates by individuals working on the project, will help to reduce uncertainty in forecasting.

Project Management Techniques

Networks

Most project management approaches today are based on a network representation of a project. A project is viewed as consisting of a series of tasks and milestones. A task is any activity with a well-defined beginning and end, such as "finish specifications for module c." A milestone is a significant mark identifying an important completion of one set of tasks and the beginning of another.

To use a formal project management technique, the project manager must be able to define tasks and milestones. There are few rules for this requirement, and most managers seem to work from experience. One successful project manager found that it was best to ask the individuals working on the project to define their own tasks. The project manager had first broken the project into major components, which he assigned to the staff. Then staff members were asked to divide their assigned portions of the project into individual tasks, generally adhering to the guideline that a task should (1) have a measurable finish and (2) take no more than 10 person-days to complete.

Since various tasks in the development process cannot all be done at once, they are completed in sequence. In a network model, the network reflects the required sequence of tasks. Suppose we are undertaking a project to develop an information center as a consulting facility for users of a mainframe computer. The center will need a new room and some software; we also have to train consultants and probably should run some tests with users.

Table 12-3 shows the tasks, which have been identified in the left column. Figure 12-2 is a rough sketch that was drawn before constructing the table to determine the sequence in which tasks had to be performed. Figure 12-2 begins with the point labeled "Start." Remodeling the room does not have much to do with the tasks of ordering software, training consultants, and so on, so we can remodel in parallel with the other tasks.

While the room is being readied, we order software and install it; we also train consultants. However, before we test this concept with users, we

TABLE 12-3 Tasks for an Information Center

Task	After	Before	Duration
Start			
1. Remodel room	Start	5	10
2. Order software	Start	3	5
3. Install software	1, 2	4	5
4. Train consultants	3	5	3
5. Test users	1, 4	End	3
End	5	—	

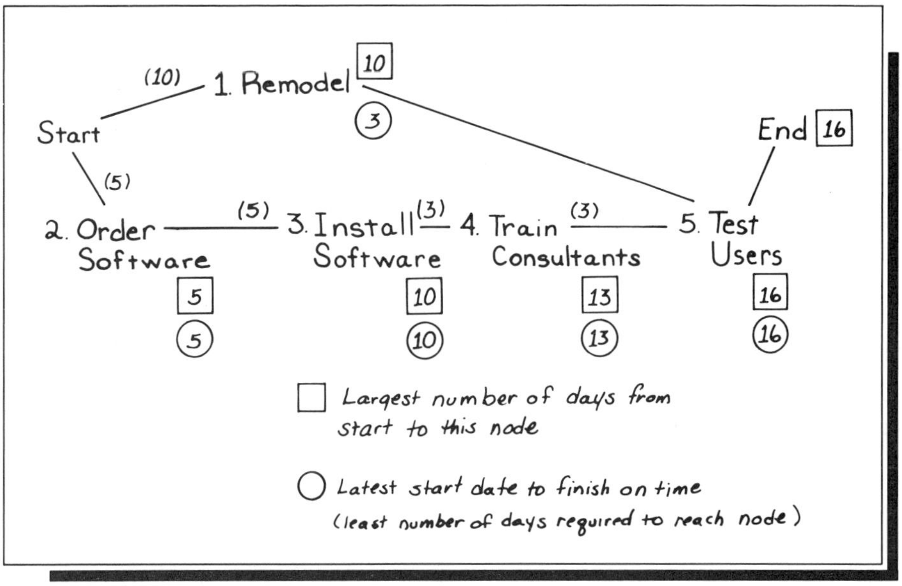

FIGURE 12-2 Sketch of a network for an information center project.

want to have the room ready. Therefore, the remodeling tasks must be completed before undertaking the task of testing with users.

Table 12-3, with the columns labeled "After" and "Before," reflect this task precedence; the "After" column indicates after what tasks a project can be started. Normally we list a series of tasks and develop the table and network together.

The Critical Path

One of the major contribution of network management is the identification of the critical path, the path through the network that has no slack. What does this mean? There is one sequence of activities, one route through the network, that takes longer than all of the others. This path is critical; any slippage on it will result in slippage in the whole project. On the other hand, if there is slippage somewhere else, it may not cause a problem with the project.

There is a simple algorithm for computing the critical path in a network, though today most managers use packaged computer programs for this purpose. To compute the critical path manually, first find the earliest possible start date for each project (shown by the number in a square in Figure 12-2). This number is the longest time required along any one path from the beginning of the network to that point. For example, to get to task 5, we can take the path through task 1, which requires 10 days, or we can follow tasks 2, 3, and 4, which takes 5 + 5 + 3 + 3 or 16 days. Thus, we write 16 days, the longest path, in the box by node 5.

TABLE 12-4 CMI Order Entry Project

Task	Start After	Finish Before	Duration (Days)	Assigned to
1. Input screen 1	Start	2	6	Nancy
2. Input screen 2	1	4	5	Nancy
3. Commun. module	Start	5, 8	6	Bob
4. Inquiry screen	2	5	4	Nancy
5. Test 1, 2, 4	4	12, 13	8	Nancy
6. Order WATS line	Start	7	1	Bob
7. Install WATS line	6	8	2	Bob
8. Test WATS line	7, 3	12, 13	5	Bob
9. Logon changes	Start	10	4	Jane
10. Function restrictions	9	11	8	Jane
11. Test 9, 10	10	12, 13	5	Jane
12. Field test	5, 8, 11	14	8	Nancy
13. User training	5, 8, 11	End	5	Jane
14. Install at distributors	12	End	15	Bob

Next, we find the latest start date to finish on time. Start at the last event and work backward. This time, record the smallest rather than the greatest number of days required to reach each node and place it in a circle by the node. To get to task 1, we can only go from the end node, and the shortest time required to reach it is 16 days minus (10 + 3), so we put a 3 in the circle by node 1.

What is the critical path? It is the path through the network for which the latest start date and the earliest start date are the same. In Figure 12-2 it is the path from tasks 2, 3, 4, and 5 to the end. If any of the tasks on this path is delayed—for example, if it takes 7 days to install software—the entire project will slip. On the other hand, since task 1 is not on the critical path, it does not necessarily have to be started on day 1. It could slip until day 3 and still not affect the completion time; task 1 has a slack of those 3 days. If we begin to remodel after 3 days have elapsed and it takes 10 days, remodeling would be done in 13 days, which is when the critical path indicates that task 5 is to begin.

Another Example

This example involves setting up a network to manage a modification to an existing system. CMI has decided to place terminals in distributors' offices for the Fremont operation. (Distributors are firms that buy parts and then resell them to final customers.) The order entry system already exists, but until the development of the modification described here, customers phoned order entry clerks in Fremont, who used terminals to enter orders.

For a relatively large volume of its transactions, CMI feels that it can place a terminal directly in distributors' offices. The distributor business, while high in volume, involves only 10% of CMI's most popular parts.

A lead systems analyst, working closely with a user in the sales department (sales is responsible for the order entry operation), has defined the requirements for the modification to the existing order entry system. The present order entry system used by CMI employees is too complex for customers; it also contains information that CMI does not necessarily want to show all of its customers.

Working together as a team, the systems analyst, two programmers, and the user from sales have determined what has to be done. First, the distributors will only need to access two input screens; both of these screens must be designed and programmed. A program the developers are calling a communications module must be written to take the screen formats and interface them to the existing order entry system; the desire is to add an interface for the distributors without having to make changes to the existing system. Finally, in addition to the screens for input, the distributors are to have an inquiry screen so that they can (1) check availability before placing an order or (2) respond to a customer's questions.

CMI has decided to install Wide Area Telephone lines to link the dial-up terminals at the distributors' location to the computer center. Since security is viewed as important, some changes will be made to the application's logon sequence to be sure that legitimate distributors are accessing the system. A module is also necessary to be sure that the distributors are able to access only certain functions within the order entry system. The requests will be passed through the function restriction module to be sure that the limited number of functions supplied for the distributors are the only ones being used.

Table 12-4 shows the tasks for this major addition to the order entry system, along with the lead systems analyst's assignment of tasks to individuals. He and the others working on the project have prepared a network showing task precedence relationships as they see them now; it is shown in Figure 12-3. Each of the individuals assigned to the project has thought about his or her task and has responded with an estimate for the amount of time they expect will be required.

The project leader for this simple project could probably compute the critical path himself. Instead, CMI at Fremont has a policy of using a project management system on a microcomputer to manage projects. The company has found that if project leaders prepare a network manually, they rarely take the time to modify the network when something changes. If the network is on a computer, changes can be made easily and the manager is encouraged to make them.

Figure 12-4 shows the results of entering the project data into a project management package, using a start date of June 1 and a completion date of August 1. The package has produced the network representation in the figure. In this particular package, tasks are shown by short mnemonics like "WATSord" and events are shown in a box. This particular package allows only one task in and one out from a task. In order to bring several paths to the same point in the chart, one must use an event node. The package also indicates that there should be a task between two milestones; therefore there are a few dummy tasks of 0 duration in the figure.

The package shows several things about the project. First, an option in the package has been used to display slack; how much slack time is there for each task? For the critical path, which is shown by the double line, there is negative slack. This means that the project cannot be completed given the requirements for each task in the time allowed. Note the slack in the tasks that are not on the critical path.

Figure 12-5 shows what happened to the network when Bob found out that there is a big delay on the WATS lines; it will now take 20 days instead of 1 to arrange for WATS service. In order to provide a better completion target, the lead analyst also changed the completion date to August 5 while entering the change of task duration for task 6. Note in Figure 12-5 that the critical path is now different; ordering the WATS lines is now on the critical path, and even with the change in target completion date, there is negative slack on the critical path. (Note that there is more than one critical path; any path with negative slack is considered critical.)

Figure 12-6 illustrates another feature of the package: the ability to print a project schedule. Note that the schedule shows the presence of slack in terms of when tasks can be started (dotted lines). Figure 12-7 also shows a resource allocation graph for Nancy, one of the programmers. This feature of the system is not too helpful for computer projects because a programmer's time cannot necessarily be supplemented by adding another programmer. However, one can look at allocations at the beginning and change some task assignments to make the workload smoother.

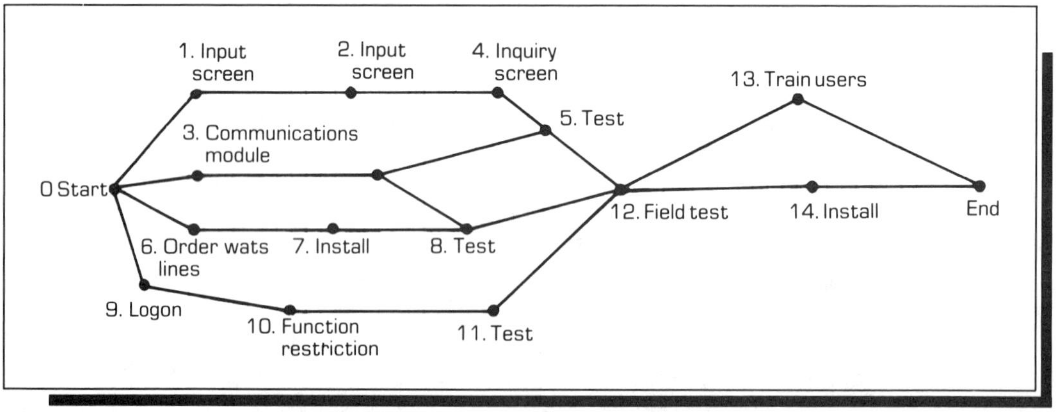

FIGURE 12-3 CMI order entry network.

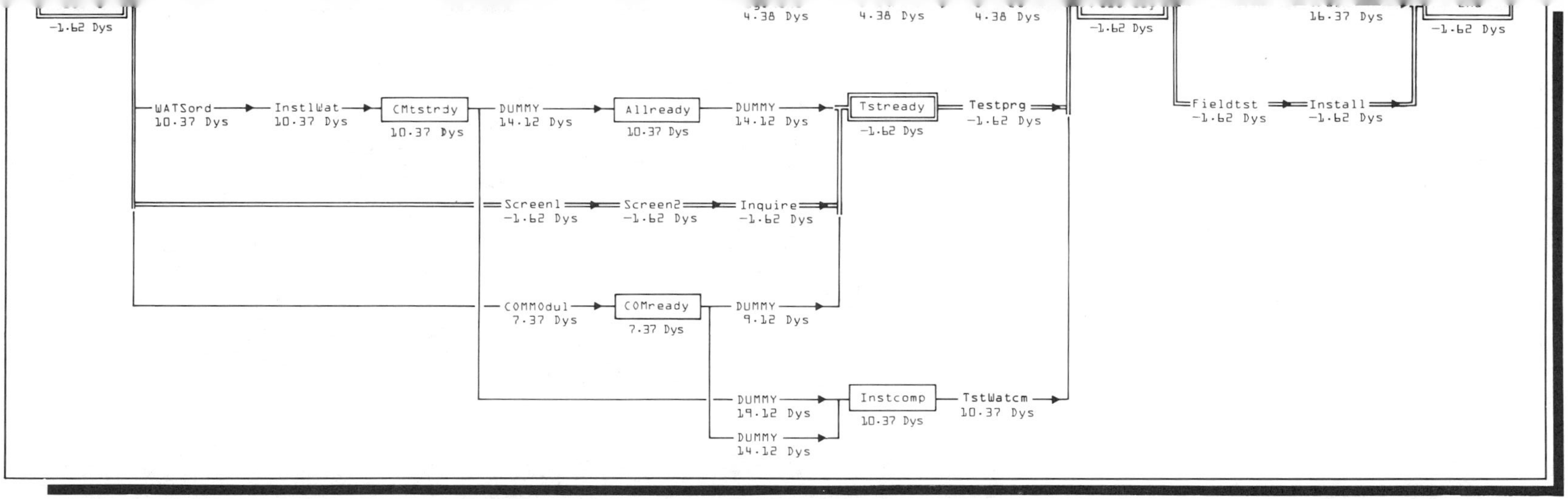

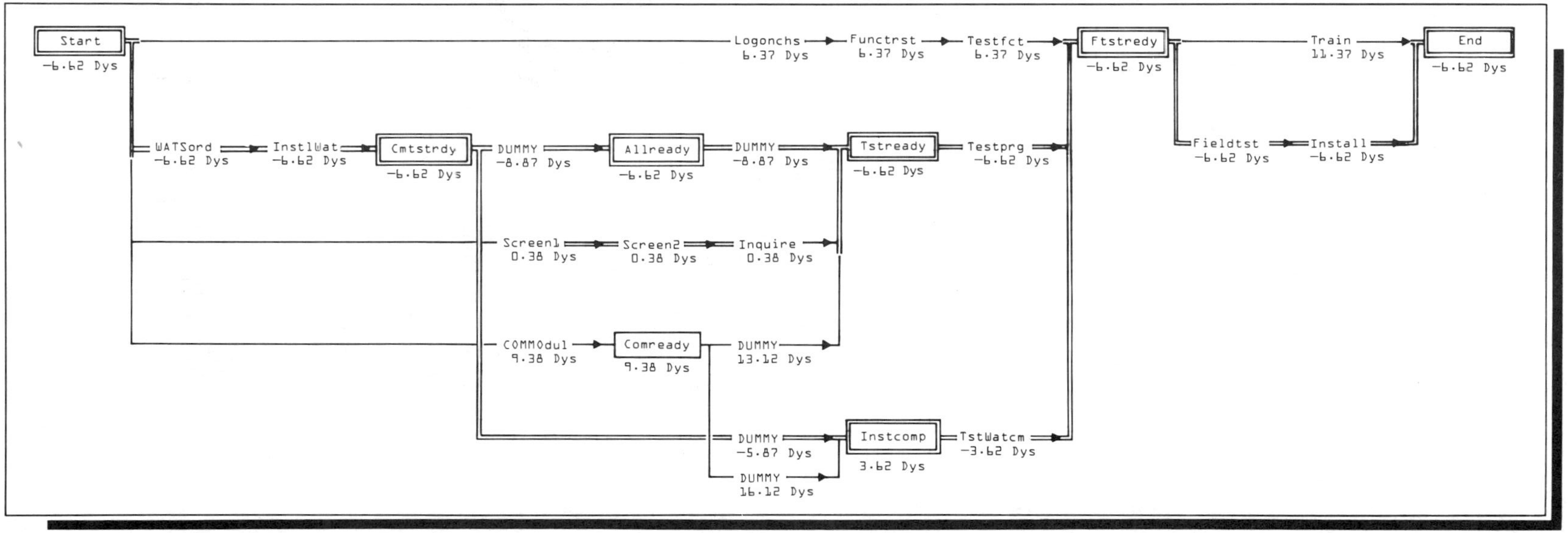

FIGURE 12-4 (top) CMI project management program output 1.

FIGURE 12-5 (bottom) CMI project management program output 2.

Top-Down Management

The preceding example is fairly simple; a one-level network will probably suffice for monitoring this project. However, many custom information systems development projects are so complex that the network soon becomes unwieldy. The project management package used in these examples facilitates top-down management.

This package provides the ability to define a broad project plan compared to the first level of a DFD. Then each component of the high-level plan can be broken down into a set of subprojects with as many levels as needed. This modular structure nicely fits the use of a structured analysis approach to design itself. The aim is to follow stepwise refinement in systems design, programming, and project management.

Monitoring

Developing a project network and plan is important in beginning the project; project managers are often reluctant to devote the time needed to monitoring the project. However, it is in the monitoring process that the real benefits of a formal approach to project management are attained.

The first thing the project manager wants to do with a plan is to check the critical path. What assumptions have been made for the tasks on this path? Have enough resources been allocated to the tasks? Can we add people or break a task into parts that can be done in parallel to reduce total project duration?

Next, what tasks are most likely to become critical? Are there tasks with very low slack? If so, are the estimates for them realistic? It is possible that one of these tasks might slip and change the critical path.

The project manager also wants to review resource allocations. As previously mentioned, there may be imbalances in the demands placed on individuals. The manager can always move some tasks with slack early to try to level resource demands. He or she may also have to consider changing task assignments in order to smooth resource utilization. Sometimes a task can be split in two and assigned to different people.

The developers of the package used in this example suggest that the manager first give resources to tasks with the least slack. If two tasks have the same slack, resources should be given to the one that is expected to take the longer time or the one that uses more of the resource.

Given a final plan for the project, the project leader must enter completion data and changes in task durations. It is important to have defined tasks in such a way that completion is measurable. In the early days of computing, the construction of a large program was sometimes broken down into parts such as flowcharting, coding, compilation, testing, and completion. Unfortunately, since no one could tell how far along a program was, some programs were 90% complete for years. In fact, one programmer worked on a huge master file update program for over a year and finally had it flowcharted

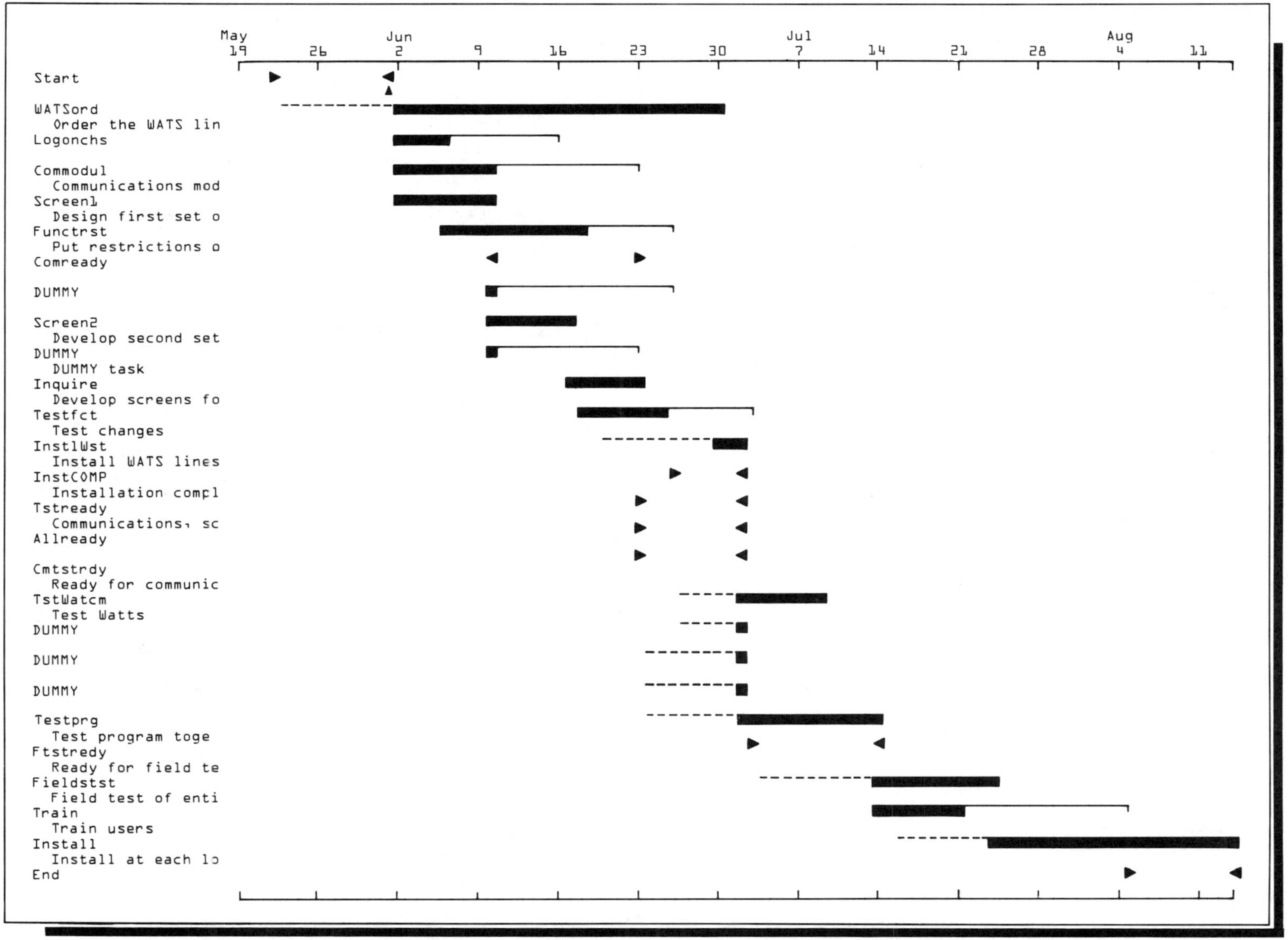

FIGURE 12-6 CMI project schedule.

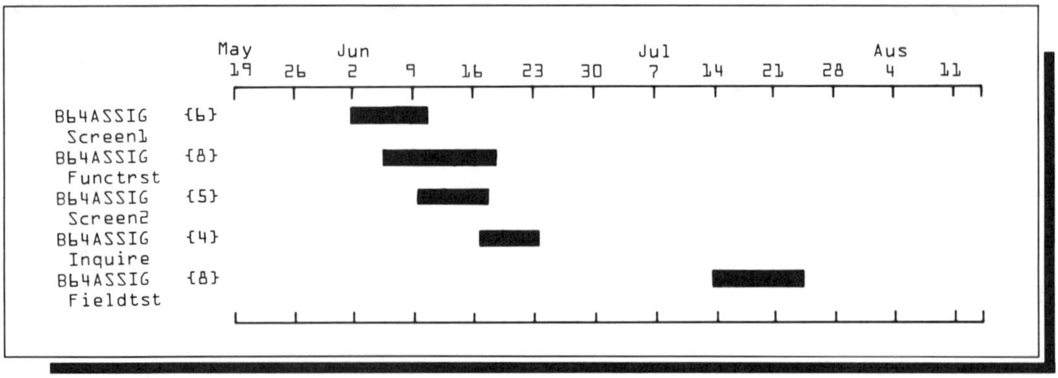

FIGURE 12-7 Resource allocation graph for Nancy.

when he moved to another company. All of his work had to be repeated because no one could understand his documentation.

If a program module is made small enough, it is not necessary to ask for reports on the percentage complete in coding. Instead, there should be verifiable milestones such as first compilation and testing completed. Try to keep task durations to 5 to 10 days, if at all possible.

If members of the project team know that they will be helped and not punished for accurate reporting, the manager should obtain the input necessary to manage the project. The same options as those at the beginning of the project are available if something begins to slip. The manager can alter the schedule, bring in more resources (if appropriate), and try to accelerate tasks on the critical path.

It is not always possible to add a person to a task, but it may be possible to reassign a task. Maybe a task can be split into two parts, one of which can be assigned to a different person. If an individual is working on a program module, it is unlikely that a new programmer will be able to contribute much to that program. The new programmer might be able to take over some other task, but to learn about an existing program and try to work on it with the original programmer might actually slow progress.

Conclusions

Few project managers will voluntarily make the effort required to use a formal project management methodology when developing commercial information systems. It is up to management to encourage and even require the use of project management tools like a package for project management. The lack of success we have experienced with project management suggests that formal techniques are needed. Try using an approach such as the one suggested here on a small- to medium-size system and then evaluate it for use as a standard on all systems. Given a rather dismal past history, it seems likely that any approach that encourages project management will help.

Managing the Alternatives

Does it make sense to develop custom systems, given all that seems to go wrong with them? Why not stick to a 4GL or make users develop their own systems on micros? There will always be a need to develop custom systems, and these projects have to be managed.

Packages

The techniques previously discussed have been illustrated with a custom system; what changes if a package is used? Dedicated packages often have to be modified before being installed. Even if there are few software modifications, the implementation of a dedicated package is a major undertaking. There are many design steps, including setting up the package with parameters for the firm, configuring it for a particular computer, developing data files, conversion, training, and so on.

With so many aspects to the implementation of a package, the approaches previously suggested for formal project management are most appropriate. Compared to a custom system, there may be less programming. However, since we can often install a package in less time than it takes to develop a custom system, it is necessary to manage the project carefully in order to meet the schedule for completion.

Prototyping

A prototype changes the way specifications are developed, but it does not alter the need to monitor a project. The development of a prototype may become a task or may consist of several tasks in the network. Prototypes should facilitate project management by making better estimates possible. The prototype reduces some of the uncertainty associated with requirements analysis and therefore should result in a better-specified system. Specifications that do not change constantly lead to more accurate task estimates and fewer changes, making project management easier.

Fourth-Generation Languages

The choice of a programming language does not alter the need to monitor and manage a project. The real issue is not what language is chosen but how extensive the development effort is. If we are developing a small modification or adding a few reports to a system, it does not make sense to use elaborate, time-consuming project management techniques.

However, there is often a great deal below the surface of information systems projects. A simple request for a change may generate a large amount of redesign and programming. Experience is the best guide in deciding when formal project management techniques are appropriate.

User-Developed Systems

At the level of user-developed systems, either with a 4GL or on a micro, guidelines become less clear. We cannot expect a user to incur the overhead of using a project management system. After all, one reason for user-developed programs and one motivation for micros has been to get away from the overhead of the ISD.

Consultants to users, however, may suggest that they seek assistance when projects become too large. One type of assistance that can be rendered is project management. For the most part, however, it is likely that user-developed systems will be done on an ad hoc basis. We can only hope that if and when these projects grow out of control, the user will seek assistance.

Conclusions

There has been great reluctance on the part of project leaders to apply formal project management techniques to information systems development projects. However, given the poor record to date in delivering systems on time and within budget, project management is badly needed.

Senior ISD management will have to establish standards for project management. These managers will also have to review project plans and the status of projects. Senior management within the ISD can contribute to project management by encouraging it, participating in reviews, and making suggestions on how to solve problems. Senior management may also be able to supply added resources to increase progress.

There are dozens of project management packages that run on microcomputers. We have advocated the development of a systems analyst workstation using tools for systems design. One piece of software for this workstation should be a project management package.

Recommended Readings

Benbasat, I., and I. Vessey, "Programmer and Analyst Time/Cost Estimation," *MIS Quarterly*, vol. 4, no. 2 (June 1980), pp. 31–43. (A review of some models for estimating tasks.)

Harvard Total Project Manager Handbook. 1984. (The manual for the project management software used in this chapter.)

Lucas, H. C., Jr., *The Analysis, Design and Implementation of Information Systems*, 3rd ed. New York, McGraw-Hill, 1985. (See especially the chapter on project management.)

Wiener-Ehrlich, W., J. Hamrick, and V. Rupolo, "Modeling Software Behavior in Terms of a Formal Life Cycle Curve: Implications for Software Maintenance," *IEEE Transactions on Software Engineering,* vol. SE-10, no. 4 (July 1984), pp. 376–383. (The study of software development at Bankers Trust discussed in this chapter.)

Discussion Problems

12.1 McKay Industries has an active ISD that has developed a number of systems over the years. Unfortunately, the ISD has a reputation for being late and over budget. Users complain that the department never seems to be able to estimate the time required to complete a system properly. Users have been vocal in urging more end-user computing to avoid having to deal with the ISD.

The manager of systems and programming always prepares a Gantt chart, showing the tasks required to complete each system as a line on a schedule board. The chart might show that program 5 should be started the second week of May and finished at the end of the first week in June. The manager is aware of other project management techniques but feels that they are too time-consuming. "I need to spend time working on the project, not on a group of fancy charts," he said one day.

What do you recommend to McKay to improve its project management practices? How do network representations differ from the Gantt chart described here?

12.2 Major Electronics was faced with a problem. Many of its products contained rare metals, and the price of these metals was fluctuating wildly each day. Management finally decided that it was losing too much money by pricing a product at the time the order came in. The price of components at order entry might be far below their price when the product was actually built.

Management decided that it would now price products at the time of shipment, not at the time of order entry. This decision required a great deal of reprogramming. The order entry programs had to be changed so that they did not price the product; they also had to generate an order confirmation stating that a final price would be set at the time of shipment. Then the shipping system had to be modified to compute prices rather than to simply accept prices from the order file.

The changes took a month to make, during which time almost all progress on new systems stopped. Users, however, still complained that their projects were late. The ISD manager felt there was little he could do, since the new pricing scheme came from the chairman of the company.

How does one handle such emergency changes to minimize disruption on existing projects? What action should the manager of ISD take? What is the impact of the month's delay on a project management cpm chart?

Questions

1. Why are so many estimates for projects like the Concorde wrong?
2. What do the Concorde and TVA nuclear power plants have in common with information systems projects?
3. How does structured design contribute to project management?
4. What does one gain from using DFDs in managing a project?
5. What is a system boundary? How are boundaries established and why are they important?

6. Describe the components of a programmer workstation.
7. What software should be included in a systems analyst workstation?
8. Why do so many organizations fail to devote effort to managing information systems projects?
9. What is the role of users in project management?
10. What is required to monitor a project?
11. Why are resource requirement estimates hard to make?
12. What does a model like the Rayleigh equation contribute to project management?
13. What are the practical difficulties of using something like the Rayleigh curve in a firm?
14. What steps are required to use the Rayleigh model?
15. What is a network model?
16. What is meant by precedence relationships?
17. Define the critical path in a network.
18. What is the significance of slack in a network model?
19. Why should one update network models as tasks are completed or time requirements change?
20. Why should a network package provide the ability to explode activities into further levels of detail?
21. How does modularization contribute to project management?
22. Who should prepare the estimates for the tasks in the network?
23. Should one use network project management techniques with a system a user develops using a 4GL?
24. Should one use a network project management technique when implementing a dedicated package?
25. What rules of thumb can you suggest for when it is appropriate to use a formal network model to manage an IS project?

13

End-User Support

In the information processing field, we often hear of computer generations and the revolution that has taken place in computer technology. Concomitantly with the revolution in technology, has been a revolution in the role of users of information processing. In the early days of computing, users were passive clients of the professional designer; the design process, by and large, was left to systems analysts.

Several factors combined to make this approach to systems development unsatisfactory:

1. Users were too willing to delegate design to professionals; as a result, systems reflected what the designers thought appropriate, which was often not what users wanted.
2. The demand for new applications grew far beyond the capacity of most ISDs to undertake systems analysis and design.
3. Professional systems analysts and programmers experienced great difficulty in completing projects on time and within budget.
4. User desires for enhancements, combined with the need to change systems because they had not been designed well in the beginning, led to large maintenance backlogs.

These problems are responsible for some of the user dissatisfaction with information processing. Combined with the service problems that invariably occur in running computer systems, the ISD is often held in rather low esteem in the organization. Trends in technology have provided users, and to some extent systems professionals, with new options.

1. Distributed processing and minicomputers have become extremely popular, since departments and divisions find that they can separate themselves from a centralized, professional ISD and control their own processing.

2. Microcomputers provide independence for users; as long as users do not need data from a mainframe or do not need its calculating power, they can be independent of the ISD.

3. The 4GLs make it possible for the user to access mainframe data (with some consulting help) without waiting for a professional programmer to write a program for retrieving and formatting the data.

4. Package programs have matured to the point where they often offer a satisfactory solution to a user's problems without the need to develop a custom application.

As a result of these trends, more and more responsibility for information processing is being transferred to end users. This process changes the traditional relationship between end users and the ISD staff, and the roles of each.

The New Roles

The User

The user is becoming more involved with the technology, partially because information systems are increasingly important to most organizations. Also, the user has begun to realize that it is often faster to do the processing personally rather than wait for a professional from information services. Finally, there are more and more computer-based tools that provide direct support to workers. Many of the packages that run on microcomputers simply help one to do a job; they are personal support systems, as opposed to a traditional information system that generates numerous reports.

How skilled should the typical user become in working with microcomputers and 4GLs and participating in systems development? At what point does learning more about computers and information processing interfere with the tasks normally associated with a user's job? These questions are puzzling many managers and organizations today.

We have stressed that a user should be heavily involved in systems analysis and design, yet that is not the user's primary job. Should an office professional be so intrigued by microcomputers that he or she becomes the systems expert for a user area? These questions will have to be answered by each organization.

One pharmaceuticals firm assigns individuals with no computer background from its laboratories to develop information systems for quality assurance. In this case, the information systems are sufficiently important that the firm is willing to allocate individuals trained as scientists to systems development.

General Electric reports success in having existing department members become "personal computer coordinators" for their work units. One engineer who developed microcomputer expertise on his own became the coordinator in his department. Over half of this engineer's time is spent advising colleagues on the use of the personal computer; the central information services group provides support and consulting for coordinators. GE is a large company with many separate businesses; the role of personal computer coordinator appeared to be the best solution to providing help to users in such a dispensed organization. It remains to be seen how long these coordinators will want to remain in their roles and when, if at all, they will want to return full-time to their regular jobs.

As information systems become increasingly important, the organization may find that it needs to add positions like end-user computing advisor to bring expertise to departments. Existing members of a department who are interested in information systems may be the best candidates for such positions.

In summary, a transition is occurring in which users are becoming more involved in and knowledgeable about information processing. As with other endeavors, some end users will be satisfied to use a computer as a tool when it helps them; other users will become fascinated with the computer and want to change the focus of their activities to work with it.

The Systems Professional

Just as user roles are changing, so must the role of the systems professional. In the case of users, the change is probably seen as positive: users obtain better results by doing some computing themselves. The microcomputer helps the professional develop budgets, prepare materials for presentations, write memos and reports, and so on. With a 4GL, users can obtain results much more quickly than they could by waiting for a programmer to understand the problem and write a program.

What is the new role for the systems professionals, and is it likely to be viewed as positive? The new role for systems staff members is to act more as a consultant than as the person in charge. Historically, systems analysts and programmers ran projects. Users depended on the information services staff for anything they needed, from a new system to a special report.

In developing a custom application, the systems analyst will experience the least amount of change, though there are now many more options and alternatives to be presented to users. The realm of micros and 4GLs is new to systems professionals. Often the ISD opposed micros when they first appeared in the organization. Supporting micros and end-user programming makes the systems professional a consultant; he or she relinquishes control over users and their projects.

Rendering advice and consulting assistance is very different from being in charge of a project. A consultant succeeds by influencing others; he or she cannot make decisions or implement plans for the client. An advisor seeks to influence the behavior of the client by making suggestions. A leader or manager is able to give instructions to subordinates, who carry them out; the consultant is in exactly the opposite situation.

Are these changes positive or negative for systems professionals? At first, they will probably be perceived as negative. It is more expedient to be able to give instructions that others follow than to work at developing influence. Certainly one has a greater sense of control and power in a leadership rather than an advisory role. One of the challenges for ISD management is to help the staff make a transition to a more advisory role.

Over time, if being an advisor results in greater success for the ISD, the systems professional should find work more satisfying. The traditional model has not been a spectacular success; it is hoped that the new role for the systems professional will result in an improved contribution from ISD to the organization.

Management Demands

We have already mentioned one demand on management: the need to ease the transition for the staff. Management must also be concerned about making the consulting role work. Users, reacting against all of the problems they have had with information services, may not be willing to ask for assistance. On the other hand, for many of the things managers might like to accomplish, help from a systems person can greatly facilitate progress.

ISD management has to sell its advisory and consulting services. The change in roles for the ISD does not affect individual systems analysts alone; it affects all levels within information services. In Chapter 2 we discussed different organizational structures for information processing; ISD management needs to consult with the management of the firm to help create an appropriate structure for information processing. The consultative role for information processing extends from the CIO through operations.

The Coming End-User Environment

Figure 13-1 shows a likely computer configuration in the next few years. There is a mainframe complex that has large databases and processes a high volume of transactions on-line. The databases contain information that is of corporate interest and therefore must be accessible to many employees. The ISD and computer professionals will operate the mainframe complex and will be responsible for networks in the organization.

Various departments, and operations like a factory, will have minicomputers to meet their specialized processing needs. These minis will be able to access the mainframe database, and other computers, in turn, will be able to access their data. Individual users will have powerful workstations connected to LANs. The LANs will have gateways to other networks so that the workstation user will be able to access data from a variety of computers. In

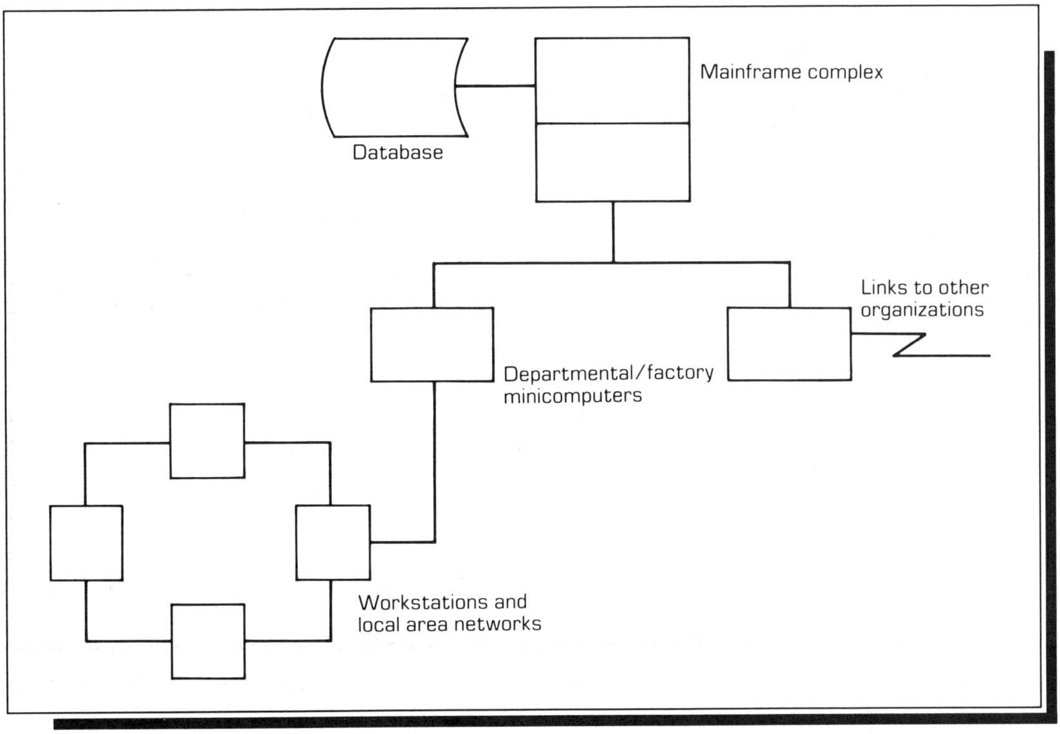

FIGURE 13-1 A future computer configuration.

addition, local users will be able to execute jobs on other machines; for example, they will be able to run a 4GL program on a mainframe.

Where does this architecture for computing originate? The process of developing a 3- to 5-year plan for information systems should lead to the specification of a target architecture for the firm. How does one decide whether a job is to be run on a mini or on the mainframe? On a micro or a mini? These decisions should be made on an individual basis, application by application. Later in this chapter, we shall discuss some guidelines for systems development that suggest how one decides whether to develop an application on a mainframe or a micro.

The Age of the Workstation

Individual users have enthusiastically adopted microcomputers to support their work. Leading firms like Travelers Insurance and IBM are all planning to have more than one microcomputer or terminal device per professional and clerical worker. Today many of these micros are used for a few tasks; a frequent application involves a spreadsheet program like Lotus 1-2-3, which is used to evaluate a new investment, prepare budgets, or perform a similar task. A second popular application of the micro is word processing.

Another group of users also works extensively with computers: engineers are involved in design work that requires extensive computations.

```
Run File Directory Edit Option Application Compose Log XDOS PathMinder
Run highlighted program

 Filename               Ext      Size  |        System Status
                                       |
                                       | Tue 1 Jan 1988            12:02:35a
                                       |
                                       |          Drive C Status
                                       |
                                       | Volume Label          No Volume Label
                                       | Bytes of Storage Total    21,225,472
                                       | Bytes of Storage Used     16,195,584
                                       | Bytes of Storage Free      5,029,888
                                       |
                                       |          Memory Status
Root Dir                     Directory | Bytes of RAM Total           655,360
  AUTOEXEC              BAT        172 | Bytes of RAM Used             39,120
  COMMAND               COM      17792 | Bytes of RAM Free            616,240
  CONFIG                PDX         22 |
  CONFIG                SYS         27 |
  AMGTBOOK                   Directory |           Log Status
  AWORDBIN                   Directory | Current User
  BASIC                      Directory | Current Account             Personal
  CONDOR                     Directory | System Log is currently          Off
  DGRM                       Directory |
```

FIGURE 13-2 A DOS shell. (From PathMinder v3.00. © Copyright 1984, 1985, 1986 Westlake Data Corporation)

Vendors offer a variety of engineering workstations with programs to support different types of engineering tasks. These workstations run on more powerful computers than the micro found in a typical business office. However, the new generation of 32-bit microcomputers is much faster and features the larger memories needed for a workstation.

A workstation for a manager or office worker is built around a microcomputer and an interface program to manage all of the user's programs on a hard disk. The workstation can execute several programs at once and can connect to a network. Why would anyone in an office or factory want a workstation? Is there really a need to run more than one program at once on a micro? The concept of a workstation involves more than a minor addition in features to a micro on which one has been running stand-alone programs in an ad hoc manner. The workstation should become an integral part of the way professionals do their job.

Design Considerations

To reach a high level of integration with a user, the workstation needs an interface program that hides the operating system. A good example of such a program is shown in Figure 13-2; however, it does not handle more than one program at a time. It is a utility that hides DOS commands on a personal computer from the user. It also lets the user define an applications menu,

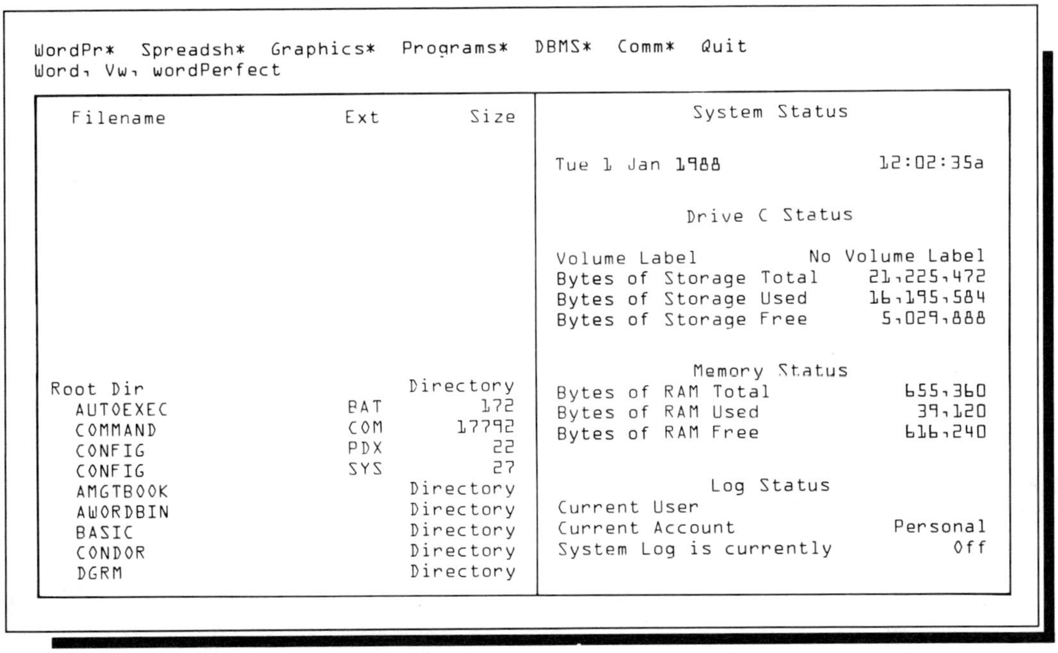

FIGURE 13-3 A DOS shell. Note the applications menu across the top. Each choice leads to a menu with programs for that function (e.g., DBMS). (From PathMinder v3.00. © Copyright 1984, 1985, 1986 Westlake Data Corporation)

shown in Figures 13-3 and 13-4, where the user first selects a database application and then chooses a particular database management package.

The advantage of this kind of utility is that the user does not have to remember the names of programs or how to start them. Of course, the workstation requires a hard disk to provide this facility. One would not build workstations from machines that have only diskette drives.

The designer of an engineering workstation is preparing it for a particular class of employees; the consumers are already technologically inclined. What kinds of applications packages will an office professional want? What will the manager in a production environment need? It is difficult to predict exactly what software will be included in a workstation, and undoubtedly there will be many special-purpose applications. However, an examination of today's popular software provides some ideas of what should be included in a workstation for information workers.

Spreadsheet

The most popular application for professionals is still the electronic spreadsheet. An example of this problem solving model is shown in Figure 13-5. Using the package, users may build something as mundane as a budget, or they may construct a sophisticated decision support system (DSS). The major advantage of the electronic spreadsheet is the ability to construct the model using formulas that link different cells in the worksheet together.

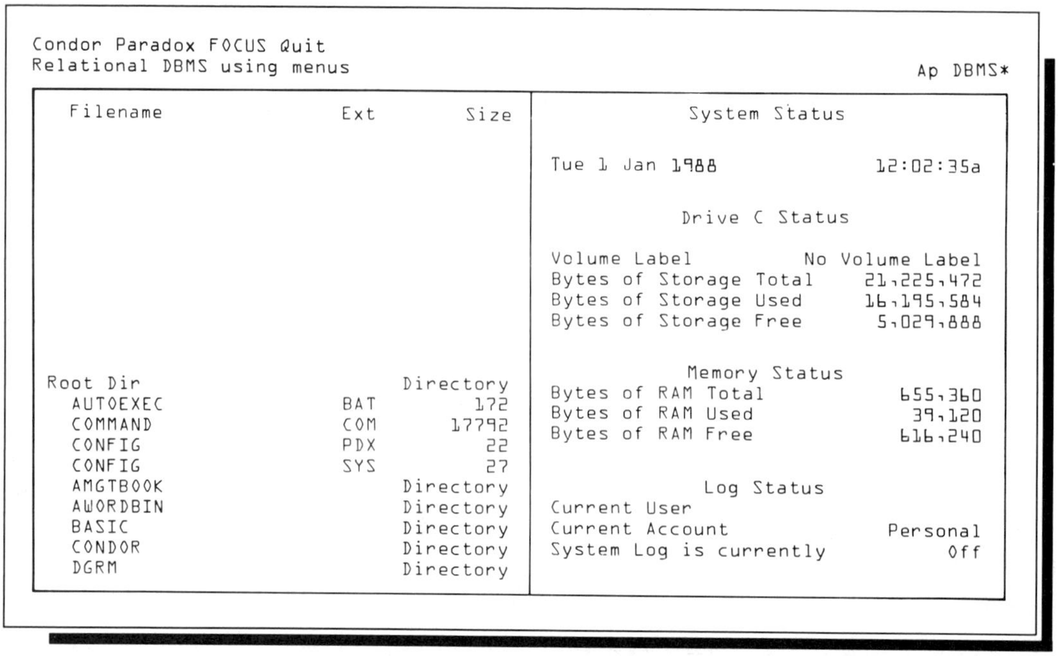

FIGURE 13-4 A DOS shell. The applications menu now shows the choice of DBMS. (From Path-Minder v3.00. © Copyright 1984, 1985, 1986 Westlake Data Corporation)

By making changes in the assumptions, the user can generate different scenarios to assist in making decisions.

Word Processing

In an increasingly information-intensive society, the work of many individuals involves the preparation of written documents. Another extremely popular use of micros is for word processing. There are many packages for this task; thus the choice of a word processing package is a little like the choice of a painting.

It is quite possible that the current interest in desktop publishing systems will merge with word processing so that the author of a document will also arrange its layout for printing. Another, possibly more appealing, possibility is to route the document to a specialist in graphics design, who will use a desktop system to prepare it for production. A popular word processing package is illustrated in Figure 13-6.

Database

A DBMS, even on a micro, requires a higher level of user training than a spreadsheet or word processing package. Word processing is similar enough to typing that one simply learns to use it and to appreciate the advantages that a word processor provides. Spreadsheet programs provide a model that is familiar to many individuals; the electronic spreadsheet looks like many business documents and reports.

A database, however, is a more computer-oriented concept. The user, of course, can work with a simple system that presents an electronic version of

PROJECTED ANNUAL FIGURES FOR THE COMPUTER STORES BUSINESS: 1986-1990

****

YEAR	1989	1990	1991	1992	1993
Estimated sales	1000000	1100000	1210000	1331000	1464100
Cost of Goods Sold	500000	550000	605000	665500	732050
Gross Profit	500000	550000	605000	665500	732050
Selling Costs	50000	44000	42350	39930	37335
Administrative Costs	100000	120000	144000	172800	207360
Net Profit	350000	386000	418650	452770	487355

FIGURE 13-5 A spreadsheet example.

a stack of notecards. However, the power of the computer is much more effectively utilized with a fully relational DBMS. Figure 13-7 is an example of a DBMS with a user interface that is similar to the interface of the most popular spreadsheet package. This interface featuring menus is much more easily learned than are the commands for a command-driven DBMS.

Some of the DBMS packages come with complete or partial applications generators. While the concept of a generator is very appealing, the generator program requires a strong computer background. The generator automatically produces code in a programming language that usually comes with a relational DBMS on a micro. The designer works at a high level, the level of the specifications, and the system generates the code for the system. However, it may be necessary to modify the generated code, so that more than a casual knowledge of computers is required to use the generator. In the foreseeable future, generators will probably be much more heavily used by professionals than end users.

Communications

To be fully effective, the workstation must be connected to the networks envisioned in Figure 13-1. There are several types of connections. At the lowest level, the workstation is a dumb terminal accessing data and pro-

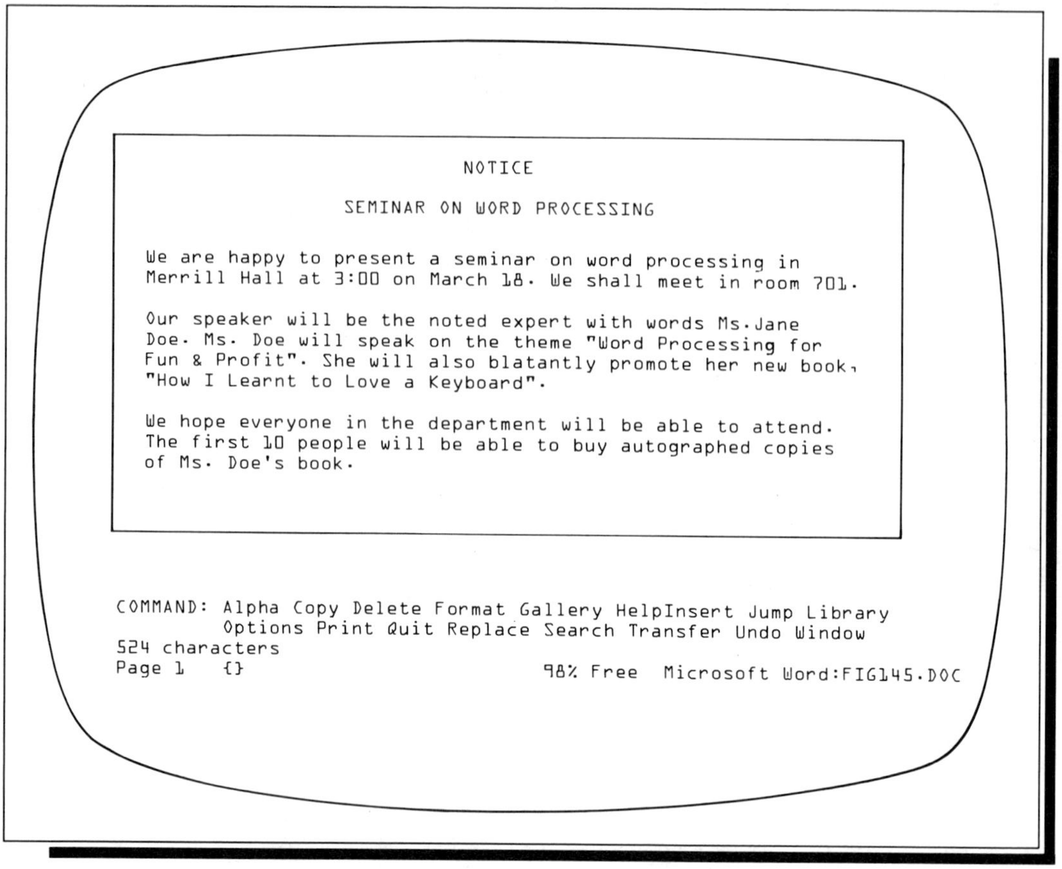

NOTICE
SEMINAR ON WORD PROCESSING
We are happy to present a seminar on word processing in Merrill Hall at 3:00 on March 18. We shall meet in room 701.
Our speaker will be the noted expert with words Ms.Jane Doe. Ms. Doe will speak on the theme "Word Processing for Fun & Profit". She will also blatantly promote her new book, "How I Learnt to Love a Keyboard".
We hope everyone in the department will be able to attend. The first 10 people will be able to buy autographed copies of Ms. Doe's book.
COMMAND: Alpha Copy Delete Format Gallery HelpInsert Jump Library
Options Print Quit Replace Search Transfer Undo Window
524 characters
Page 1 {}
98% Free Microsoft Word:FIG145.DOC

FIGURE 13-6 A word processing example.

grams on the mainframes or minis on the network. Such a level of access is adequate, say, to run a 4GL such as the one shown in Figure 13-8.

The next level takes advantage of the capabilities of the workstation for file transfers with other computers on the network. A final feature is to have the network connection maintained in a multiprogramming workstation while the user runs other programs to work with data downloaded from other computers.

The software requirements for the scenario just described are quite demanding. The user must know how the data on, say, a mainframe are stored. What query language commands are required to access these data? The user then must have the appropriate network software to transfer the data to a micro. Finally, the data from the mainframe will probably have to be converted in order to be processed by programs on the micro. ISD professionals will have to create this network environment.

Electronic Mail

A network and widely available workstations will encourage the use of electronic mail. A number of organizations have implemented electronic mail systems, but few of these encompass the entire organization. A network

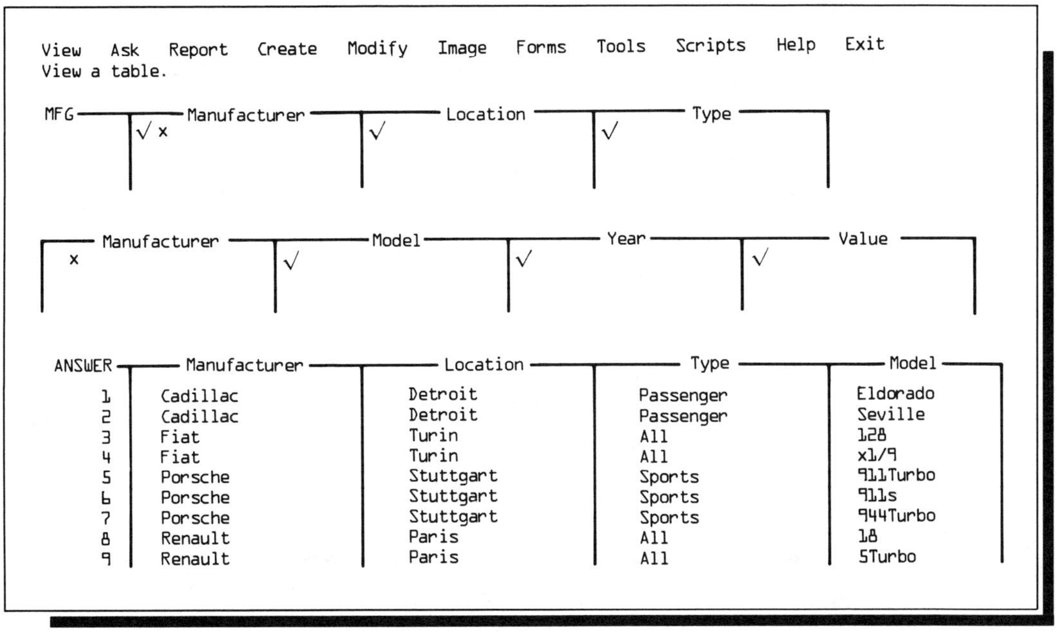

FIGURE 13-7 A DBMS.

and the presence of numerous workstations should result in far greater use of this communications medium.

Presentation Graphics

Information workers are frequently required to make presentations to various groups. Presentation graphics programs assist the individual in producing transparencies and slides for meetings. Figure 13-9 is an example of one such program, which is oriented to the production of text in various formats and styles. Figure 13-10 is an example from a popular drawing program, showing the kind of output that is possible. Of course, these black-and-white drawings can be produced with a plotter in color on transparencies or with a special camera device on 35-mm slides.

Special-Purpose Applications

One of the most fascinating results of information processing has been the tremendous creativity shown by users and designers in applying the computer to solve problems. Firms have developed systems that give them a competitive advantage, save tremendous amounts of tedious labor, and improve the quality of products and services. We would expect to see a large number of special-purpose applications on a workstation suited to the needs of individual users in the firm.

Decision Support Systems

A DSS helps a decision maker utilize data and models to solve a variety of problems. When most processing was done on mainframe computers and professionals developed the applications, the decision maker was dependent on an IS or operations research staff member to develop a DSS. With the

```
                 SALES FILE

FIELD NAME       MEANING

REGION           Marketing Region Code
SITE             Store Code
PONUM            Purchase Order Number
DATE             Order Date
NAME             Customer Name
AMOUNT           Total Amount of Order
TAX              State Tax on Order
FILLCODE         Indicator of Shipment Status
PRODUCT          Product Number
UNITS            Quantity Ordered


                SUPPLY FILE
PRODUCT          Product Number
DESCRIPTION      Product Description
COST             Wholesale Cost
RETAIL           Retail Price
VENDOR           Supplier Code Number
QOH              Quantity on Hand Warehouse
```

FIGURE 13-8A Two files for a FOCUS example.

advent of time sharing on minicomputers and with the proliferation of micros, many users are now developing their own DSS. In fact, one could argue that many of the spreadsheet models developed to date are a type of DSS.

DSSs bring the power of the computer to the manager; no longer is the machine used just to improve productivity or process transactions. Now the computer actually supports a manager who must make a decision. End-user computing is one vehicle for encouraging and supporting the development of DSS in the organization.

Supporting the End User

If the forecast of the coming computer environment is correct, and even to support end-user computing as it exists today, the ISD is faced with a tremendous challenge. IS management must both support end-user computing

```
TABLE FILE SALES
PRINT NAME AND AMOUNT
    AND DATE
BY REGION BY SITE
IF AMOUNT GT 1000
ON REGION SKIP-LINE
END
```

FIGURE 13-8B A program to create a simple listing from the sales file.

PAGE 1

REGION	SITE	NAME	AMOUNT	DATE
MA	NEWK	ELIZABETH GAS	$2,877.30	82 AUG
	NEWY	KOCH RECONSTRUCTION	$6,086.23	82 APR
	PHIL	ROSS INC	$3,890.22	82 JUL
		LASSITER CONSTRUCTION	$1,120.22	82 SEPT
MW	CHIC	BAKESHORE INC.	$5,678.23	82 OCT
		ROPER BROTHERS	$2,789.20	82 AUG
	CLEV	BOVEY PARTS	$6,769.22	82 MAY
		ERIE INC	$1,556.78	82 JAN
NE	ALBN	ROCK CITY BUILDER	$1,722.30	82 JUL
	BOST	HANCOCK RESTORES	$8,246.20	82 FEB
		WANKEL CONSTRUCTION	$2,345.25	82 JUN
		WARNER INDUSTRIES	$3,155.25	82 OCT
	STAM	ACORN INC	$2,006.20	82 MAR
		KANGERS CONSTRUCTION	$2,790.50	82 JUN
		DART INDUSTRIES	$7,780.22	82 MAY
		ARISTA MANUFACTURING	$4,295.90	82 FEB
SE	ATL	RICHS STORES	$1,345.17	82 AUG
	WASH	CAPITOR WHOLESALE	$3,789.00	82 JUN
		FEDERAL DEPOT	$2,195.25	82 MAR

FIGURE 13-8C The report requested in Figure 13-8B.

and provide sufficient control to prevent serious incompatibility, sharing, and IS support problems.

Just facing the issues raised by personal computing creates a number of problems. Guimaraes and Ramanujam (1986) surveyed 173 U.S. companies to determine their trends and problems with microcomputers. The top 10 problems as prioritized by the sample were:

1. Lack of user education about personal computing.
2. User requests for assistance that overwhelm the IS department.
3. Lack of user knowledge or concern about microcomputer data integrity control measures such as file backup.
4. Lack of integration in micro–mainframe data exchange and control.
5. Poor maintainability of user-developed systems.

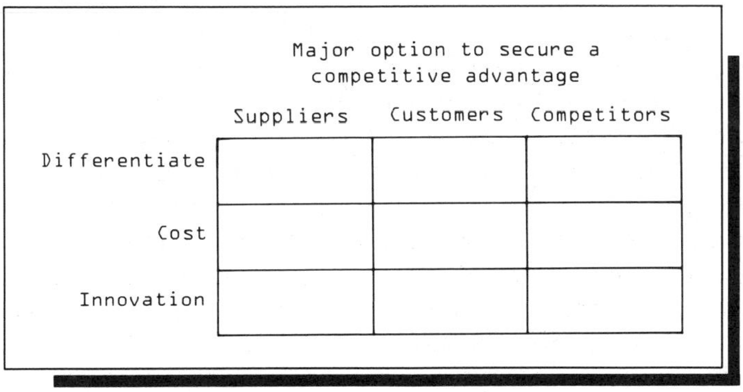

Major option to secure a competitive advantage
Suppliers
Customers
Competitors
Differentiate
Cost
Innovation

FIGURE 13-9 Presentation grahics for text.

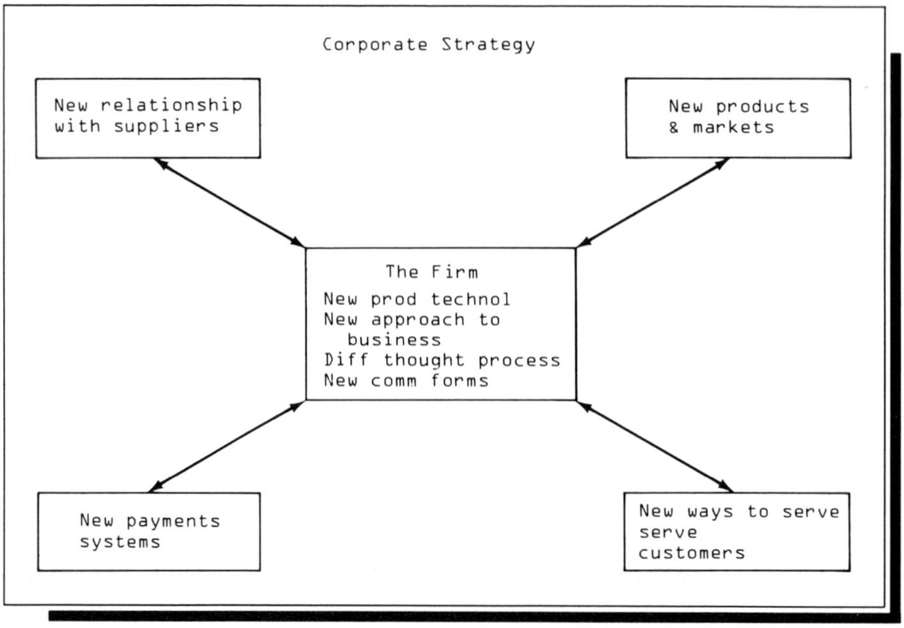

FIGURE 13-10 Example of a microcomputer drawing program.

6. Mismatching of user problems and computing alternatives (personal computing, mainframe packages, etc.) for systems development.
7. Lack of centralized management of corporate data resources that support personal computing.
8. Lack of integration in IS management of personal computing and mainframe end-user computing.
9. Lack of user concern about equipment security.
10. Lack of user-friendly mainframe software to compete with microcomputers.

Note that the respondent for each company was in the ISD and was asked to fill out a structured questionnaire indicating the extent to which each of 32 items was a problem. The preceding list represents the top 10 choices as rated by the ISD. We do not have comparable data for users.

It is interesting to note that many of the issues ranked in the top 10 reflect management issues rather than technical ones. Some of these problems could probably be remedied by information services, except that many view personal computers as a way to escape from the ISD. Even so, the second most significant problem reported by information services is user requests for assistance overwhelming the department.

The 10th item reflects an interesting perception: information services is concerned that mainframes do not have user-friendly packages to compete with micros. One ISD manager scoffed at Lotus and said that it would be trivial to develop a package like that for the mainframe. Unfortunately, this manager missed the whole point of a personal computer. The user does not have to confront a time-sharing operating system; with a hard disk, the user simply turns on the computer. The machine belongs to the user; no one else can cause it to "crash," and the user cannot hurt another user. There is no need to depend on a systems analyst, programmer, or computer operator.

The Nature of Support

Implied in the 10 points previously listed and stated directly by some IS managers is the desire to control personal computing just as the ISD has traditionally controlled mainframes. It seems clear at this point that no one will be able to control micros directly in the firm. There is probably no use trying, since extensive control would reduce the benefits users obtain from their personal computers.

Instead, the aim is to influence the way micros are acquired and used. The best support will come if IS can exercise *limited* advisory control. Totally uncontrolled end-user computing will lead to so many computers and languages that IS will not be able to provide support. Keen and Woodman (1984) argue that the key is coordination rather than control. But how does one coordinate users who all seem to be going in different directions? We shall discuss some kinds of support mechanisms for end-user computing and for micros; these mechanisms, as a by-product, influence the direction of this kind of computing.

The best mechanism for coordinating computing is the long-range plan for information processing. That plan should describe a hardware and software architecture for the future. The plan makes it easy to develop a policy for the acquisition of hardware and software of all types, from mainframes to micros and from 4GLs to spreadsheet processors. Following a strategy aimed at achieving a specified architecture at some point in the future should solve some of the problems ISD has had with lack of management of micros. The important issue for ISD management is to recognize that micros, minis, and end-user computing should be integrated with the tools of the computer professional to produce an overall strategy for information processing in the firm.

Information Centers

In the late 1970s, IBM Canada began experimenting with a consulting program for users that ultimately developed into the information center. The information center has become a key suggestion for IBM's customers as a way to make computing more responsive to users. A computer vendor would like to eliminate the antagonism that exists in many organizations toward mainframe computers.

The information center exists in a physical location reserved for its use. Internal consultants staff the center and offer advice to users. In the days of the first information centers there were no microcomputers, so center consultants focused on tools that would help the user answer requests for information from a mainframe.

One of the first tasks of the consultants is to choose a 4GL if none is already available in the firm. Sometimes this choice also involves the selection of a DBMS that has a friendly query language for end users. Then the consultants have to install whatever software tools are being used and learn how to use them.

The next step is to open the doors to users; the center sponsors classes for users in how to work with the tools it is making available. The last stage in development is for the consultants at the center to begin advising users when they have specific problems.

The user requests most amenable to the use of a 4GL usually are for reports from existing databases. Depending on the software, it is quite likely that the consultants in the information center will have to arrange for data to be extracted from one or more existing files and loaded into a special file for access by the user. Consulting help will be needed especially when the data the user wants are located in more than one file or system. The consultant will also have to help users at first with their programs in the 4GL; later users should become more self-sufficient.

The individuals who staff the center should not be dedicated systems analysts or programmers; this task clearly calls for consultants. Individuals are needed who want to help others solve their own problems rather than those who view it as their responsibility to solve everyone's problems for them. By the time one includes software costs and salaries, information centers can be expensive. However, they seem to be the best mechanism devised so far to support end-user computing on minis and mainframes with 4GLs.

Micro Laboratories

The survey described earlier suggests that there are many problems in supporting micros, especially since users may not see the ISD as a source of support. In the case of a 4GL, users know that the ISD holds the keys to the database; if they want certain data, they will require help from information services.

It is possible to put a microcomputer consultant in an information center, but if the center is successful, it is probably a fairly busy place. To demonstrate a real commitment to the support of micros, it might be better to consider a separate micro laboratory and even a personal computer store. The micro lab is also staffed by internal consultants, who have expertise in microcomputers and software packages for them.

The micro laboratory has typical configurations of the micro(s) recommended for purchase in the company. A user can visit the lab and use different machines and software. If the lab is a store, he or she can order the equipment that seems best for the job. The lab/store should then help the user set up the computer and start using it.

From the user's standpoint, the lab/store has made it easier to get started. As the user sees more applications for the computer, there will be return visits to the lab for consulting assistance. The user may have started with a spreadsheet package; what does the lab now recommend for database management?

From the standpoint of the organization, the lab and store have helped implement the firm's policy for micros. The store probably has volume purchase agreements and thus can offer prices that are competitive with those of outside vendors. Even if the prices are higher, the store makes it convenient for the user. By recommending the products included for purchase under the firm's microcomputer policy, the store helps to enforce that policy. The store provides coordination through support. This concept of *coordination by support* is the key to end-user support in general; those providing support need to be aware of their dual role in providing help and in making adherence to company plans and policies the easiest choice for users.

Micromanagers

Several firms have established a new position called *microcomputer manager.* As the name implies, this individual has the responsibility for supporting all types of micros in the firm. He or she might install a LAN, a disk drive in a user's computer, or a new software package. The manager might run a micro store or laboratory. The existence of such an individual is a clear sign that management supports microcomputing.

User Groups

User groups have existed in the computer industry almost since its inception. Their purpose has been to advance computing by sharing experience and ideas. Some members of user groups routinely exchange programs that might have general-purpose use.

Why not consider user groups within a single company? The micromanager might start such groups oriented to particular applications like spreadsheet packages. If the firm is willing to sponsor an occasional lunch or dinner, the user groups can get together to hear about interesting applications or learn new techniques of working with a package. A user group can also help the micromanager advertise his or her services and keep this individual aware of what users are doing with the package.

As an adjunct to the user group, the micromanager might consider publishing a newsletter about micros in general or about specific packages such as the word processor used in the firm. The newsletter could contain ideas about new ways to use the package and might focus on a particular application. It can also advertise classes and special events related to microsoftware.

Research and Development

We have stressed the need for R&D within information services. In a rapidly changing technological field, it is important to see what new technology is available to help the firm achieve its objectives. R&D for end-user computing and micros is also one type of support.

As users become excited about micros, they will read about new products. The micromanager must be aware of these products and how they might help individual users. The micro support staff needs to acquire new packages and evaluate them so that when users come to the micro laboratory, consultants can work with them to determine if a new package is suitable.

It is difficult and costly to convert to new products and systems, but as software is improved, there will be strong pressures to adopt the best package for the task at hand. We have converted to three different database management packages within about 4 years. Existing applications run in the package for which they were designed; new applications are generally making use of what we think is currently the best micro DBMS for our purposes. It takes considerable effort to evaluate these packages, however, and make a selection.

Which Alternative?

With so many options available now, what is the best approach to a particular system: a traditional custom system, a micro system, a system developed by a user, or some combination of these approaches? To some extent this issue was covered in Chapter 9, where we advocated presenting a design team with a number of alternatives for developing a particular system.

Is there an easier way to choose an alternative than studying each one in depth? Are there dominant criteria? One possible criterion that might automatically determine the development alternative is size. If an application is sufficiently large, it will run only on a mainframe computer. For example, it is inconceivable that one could operate an airline reservations system on micros.

One aspect of size is the number of users who must have simultaneous access to the same database. With today's technology, an airline system requires thousands of terminals and a single database at one location. These characteristics suggest a mainframe without bothering with much further analysis.

At the other extreme, when a user wants to develop a budgeting application for his or her department that requires no data from any existing systems, it seems most appropriate to recommend a spreadsheet package on a micro. What about the cases that fall between these extremes?

The ISD in Hennepin County, Minnesota, developed an interesting questionnaire to be completed jointly by users and an ISD consultant. Questions ask about the characteristics of the application. The nature of the answers determines how many points each of three alternatives scores: the traditional method, user design, and a micro. For example, the first two items on the questionnaire are:

	Traditional	User	Micro
1. Number of concurrent users			
A. 1	N/A	10	15
B. 2–3	2	10	N/A
C. 4+	15	1	N/A
2. Number of locations			
A. 1	5	5	5
B. 2–3	5	5	N/A
C. 4+	5	1	N/A

If the application under consideration would be used by two to three users in one location, the traditional approach would receive a score of 2, user design a score of 10, and a micro a score of 0 on question 1. On question 2, each alternative would receive a score of 5.

The number of points allocated to each question reflects its importance in the profile. At the completion of the questionnaire, the user sums the points for each alternative and the user and consultant test the sensitivity of the analysis. If there is a clear choice, the decision is fairly easy. If two or three choices are very close in numerical score, there should be more analysis and consideration of the best way to undertake the system. If close, probably both options should be included in a final choice matrix.

The remaining questions from the instrument deal with the following issues:

3. Number of workstations.
4. Output characteristics: can the job be scheduled?
5. Processing characteristics: scheduled versus on demand.
6. Data recovery required: automated to manual.
7. Application support: service from user or ISD.
8. Audit requirements.
9. Security requirements: extreme to nonexistent.
10. System transferability: section, department, or county.
11. Data importance: section, department, or county.
12. Processing access: immediate or sporadic.
13. Life expectancy in years.
14. Data volume.
15. Source and currency of data: existing file to nonautomated data.
16. Data retention requirement.
17. Number of employees updating data.
18. Complexity.

The questions in the Hennepin County instrument reflect careful consideration in the county about what characteristics are important in determining how a user request should be handled. Each organization has unique characteristics, as well as some that are probably common across organizations, like the number of users, system complexity, and so on. Another organization might also want to expand the number of alternatives to consider a package that runs on a particular computer versus a custom-developed system. It is not necessary to use a questionnaire approach, but the Hennepin example should help both the user and the analyst get a feeling for the appropriate technology to be considered further in the analysis.

An Information Center at CMI

Mary Watson was explaining her request for an information center at Charleston to Bob Carlin.

"I would like to encourage more end-user computing here," began Mary.

"What's that?" asked Bob.

"The idea," explained Mary, "is that users learn enough about a very easy-to-use language to request some of their own reports."

"Why do we want to spend this much money on something like that when we've got all of these micros floating around? Half of them never seem to be turned on."

"The micros address one type of computing, the kind of application that one person wants to do on his or her own. We plan to make it possible for users to get at data on the mainframe. Some of them, though, will want to run the data on the mainframe rather than trying to download it to the micro. This kind of user is interested in generating a report from the data on the 4300."

"I guess I'm not following; we have Lotus and other stuff on the micros. Why won't that do?" asked Bob.

"Lotus is good for a certain type of problem where the user wants to do a lot of analysis. However, it is very clumsy to extract data from the 4300, change the format, and put it on a micro for Lotus when all you really want is to add up sales for the month of July and break them down by product and by region. That is not the kind of task for which Lotus was designed."

"That makes sense. I've used Lotus once or twice and I don't see how to generate the sales report you described."

"The answer to the sales report is something called a fourth-generation language that lets the user write a program to solve a problem."

"Wait a minute," Bob interrupted, "I don't want users becoming a bunch of programmers. That's not an effective use of their time."

"I agree for the most part," said Mary, "but consider the following example. Suppose someone in sales really wants that report. Under today's practice, he has to make out a maintenance request and send it to the ISD. The request goes to the maintenance priorities committee to be scheduled. Suppose that he is lucky and it has a high priority. Probably about 4 weeks after he gets the idea, a programmer begins work. Since we have only COBOL, the programmer spends 2 days writing and debugging a program."

Mary continued, "Suppose instead that we buy a 4GL, as they are known. The information center I propose gives classes in how to use the 4GL and provides ongoing consulting help. Now the man from sales decides to do the report himself. He has attended the class, so the first stop is the information center to find out if the data exist. The consultant determines that they do and fills out a description of the file with the user."

"Our man in sales goes back to his desk and works on the program; maybe he visits the information center once or twice to get help. After 3 or 4 hours of work, the program runs. Within a day or so of starting, he has the report."

Bob thought and asked, "Okay, but why not just buy the 4GL and let the programmer use it instead of COBOL?"

"That's one possible solution and one that we may want to use for some requests. The problem is that we just don't have enough people to develop new systems and be responsive to maintenance requests. We are pushing some of the maintenance load off onto the users."

"All right," Bob responded, "let me read your proposal and think about it. Two additional people and a couple of hundred thousand dollars for software is a big addition to the budget . . ."

Recommended Readings

Guimaraes, T., and V. Ramanujam, "Personal Computing Trends and Problems: An Empirical Study," *MIS Quarterly*, vol. 10, no. 3 (June 1986), pp. 179–187. (Contains the complete results of the study described in this chapter on personal computing problems.)

Hennepin County Case. Boston: Harvard Business School, 1984, Case #0-185-005. (An example of how a progressive county is working with micros and end-user computing.)

Keen, P., and L. Woodman, "What to Do with All Those Micros," *Harvard Business Review* (September–October 1984), pp. 142–150. (A good article describing the micro policy of an insurance firm; suggests strongly that control of computing be exercised through support rather than by rules.)

Discussion Problems

13.1 Giant Foods is a major manufacturer of food products that are sold through grocery stores. The firm has a large centralized computer operation in Illinois. In the years preceding the installation of personal computers, the center provided batch, on-line, and time-sharing service to Giant employees. Staff members from the factory to marketing all made use of the large mainframe computers at the center.

When personal computers were introduced, users were quite interested in adopting this technology. Many users were intimidated by the time-sharing operating system and the learning time required to use the computer. Personal computers seemed the answer for them.

Within the ISD staff there was much dissent over personal computers. One group of managers did not want to allow them in the company. "If we buy 50 or 60 of these computers, that money would allow us to make a large expansion of the mainframe."

Another group felt that personal computer were just toys. "Wait until the users find there isn't any software and realize just how limited those machines are. They'll be back to the mainframes soon enough."

Even with this negative reaction, managers in different parts of the ISD all felt that their area should be made responsible for personal computers in the organization. What is your reaction to Giant's thinking on personal computers? What do you predict is likely to happen? What is the role of the ISD in managing microcomputers?

13.2 A business school at a major university decided that it could not wait for an all-university solution to information processing problems in administration. The school bought a dedicated VAX computer and hired a staff for purely administrative processing.

The school decided to use INGRES, a relational DBMS that has some advanced tools, like a forms-generating language, to speed systems development. The school wants to extend the use of this system to end users so that they can query files and set up simple reports themselves. What kinds of support services does the administrative computer center need to provide for end users?

Questions

1. Why are there so many problems with traditional approaches to systems development?
2. What trends make possible end-user computing?
3. What is the new role for the user in computing?
4. How does end-user computing affect the systems analyst?
5. How does end-user computing affect the CIO and/or the management of ISD?
6. What is the pharmaceuticals firm that takes laboratory staff and trains them to become analysts trying to accomplish?
7. What is a managerial workstation?
8. What are the major components of a workstation?
9. What are the most popular applications packages for micros today?
10. What are the major problems with personal computers found by Guimaraes and Ramanujam?
11. How should the ISD provide user education on micros?
12. What is an information center?
13. What kinds of services does a typical information center offer?
14. What are the duties of a manager of microcomputing?
15. What kind of R&D is necessary to support end-user computing?
16. What are the advantages of the Hennepin County questionnaire in choosing processing alternatives? What are the potential problems with this technique?
17. How does one control personal computers through support?
18. What is the purpose of having a microcomputer store or laboratory in a firm?
19. What kind of service do you think a typical end user wants?
20. What are the differences between the help required by a user of a 4GL and a microcomputer-based workstation?

14

Managing Operations

Managing operations, the actual computer processing in an organization, is considerably different from other IS management tasks we have discussed. Systems analysis and design are team oriented. A design project has a set of general goals, yet it leaves room for a great deal of creativity. Operations has goals that are quite specific; it must see that computers operate and that processing is successful. There are immediate operational deadlines for processing, in contrast to the long-term nature of design.

The individuals who work in operations generally have different experiential and educational backgrounds from those performing systems analysis and design. There is a fairly large number of clerical jobs in operations, though some of the jobs are skilled, like those of a computer operator.

The nature of operations depends a great deal on the philosophy of the firm and on the types of applications being run. If a firm is extremely decentralized, with minicomputers in various locations, there may be very little to operations. Some locations with small computers will not have a full-time operator. Others will have only one or two people running the computer; their jobs consist of being sure that there are supplies, loading the printer, and creating backup files on a regular basis.

In a centralized operation with large mainframes, or as distributed processors become larger and require more attention, one finds a staff of operators, data librarians, input/output clerks, and possibly maintenance and systems programmers. In this kind of environment, the task of managing operations is much more involved than in the one with a small system; there are likely to be several layers of management. Regardless of the configuration, the operation of computers has to be managed.

Characteristics of Successful Operations

We have suggested that successful applications (1) meet their design objectives, (2) contribute to the goals of the organization, (3) are used, and (4) have high user ratings. What are comparable measures of success for operations? See Table 14-1.

Availability

The first objective for users is a computer system that is available when they need to use it. The frustration of having a computer unavailable is something we have all experienced. How many times do individuals respond that they cannot help us because the "computer is down?"

The manager of operations needs to track availability carefully. In addition, it is important to check availability when someone is interested in using the computer. Failures during the day are far more serious than those at 2:00 A.M. for most organizations. Reports of percentage availability always look good because the denominator is typically 24 hours per day. One should also monitor the availability of computers during each shift, with particular attention to the time when most users will be trying to work with the system.

Response Times

Most systems today feature some type of on-line processing, if only to accept and edit input for later file updates. A significant number of systems update files on-line as users enter data from terminals. The response time is the time from the moment the user presses the enter key on a terminal to the moment the computer responds with a message or indicates its readiness for the next input.

Users express considerable displeasure over long response times. When response times become too lengthy, users can forget the next input, and their

TABLE 14-1 Some Criteria of Success for Operations

Availability
Rapid response times
Meeting schedules
Accuracy

work can be seriously affected. In one study, we found that for a complex data entry job, response times of more than 12 seconds led to a complete breakdown in data entry.

Response times in the 2-second range are excellent; some firms feel that 5 to 6 seconds is adequate. As times lengthen beyond this interval, users become unhappy and the computer center will hear complaints. Of course, response times must be expected to fluctuate because of widely varying loads on a computer. Again, one should look at both average response times and the distribution of response times during the day. Averages tend to hide periods of slow response times, which may be indicative of the need for more capacity.

Meeting Schedules

There are many jobs that run according to a schedule. For example, the general ledger program may be run after users have entered data on-line for accounts receivable, accounts payable, factory data, and so on. Individuals in accounting must provide the final data in the form of manual journal entries for accounts that the computer system does not post to the general ledger. However, once all input is in, the accounting department depends on information services to process the ledger and return the output so that they can complete their part of general ledger preparation.

The accounting department is interested in having the general ledger completed on schedule. Operations may not be at fault, for example, if input is late. However, operations is the group that will be blamed for late reports. Therefore, it behooves the operations staff to follow up on missing input and to make sure that the people on whom it depends for input provide it on schedule.

One chronic problem in meeting schedules is the need for reruns. When there is a problem in a computer run (primarily in a batch environment), the operator frequently backs up to an earlier stage and starts the processing again. One internal measure of operations, then, is a record of the number reruns. If a manager notes that a particular system seems to require reruns frequently, that system probably needs some maintenance or better documentation for operators to follow.

Accuracy

Users are also interested in accurate results. The responsibility for errors belongs to many people involved with a system, but again, operations is often the group that ends up getting the blame when data are inaccurate. Users may have provided erroneous input data that met all editing checks. It is very easy to key the wrong amount in to a system that accepts dollar amounts, as the system can only edit for reasonable figures. Suppose, for example, that the user enters $55 instead of $44; it is very unlikely that an edit check can be devised to catch this error.

There can also be errors in the way program are run. It is quite common for complex systems to require the execution of dozens of programs. Using job control language to a large extent allows one to automate the execution of each job in sequence. However, there are times when operators are required to perform certain actions, such as mounting a file or even running a program. Operator error has introduced a number of errors into systems.

What is the impact of errors? First, there is the problem of wrong data, which can cause unhappy users and customers. Second, the incorrect data may not be detected for some time. As a result, further processing builds on incorrect information. Finally, incorrect data corrupt files, so that the integrity of the database is in question. Nothing destroys user confidence in a system like errors in data.

Providing accurate data, given the dependence on users for input and on systems designers for developing "bullet proof" systems, is a difficult task for operations. It may be impossible to operate a poorly designed system, one that has no edit and error checks or one that provides such little motivation for input that users do not bother to provide data.

Data Center Operations

What is included in data center operations? See Table 14-2. The easiest way to get a feeling for operations is to spend a few days in a data center. Most systems today are mixed, containing both batch processing and on-line work. First, consider an operation that is all batch processing. Here the operators must respond to a schedule that tells them when certain jobs have to be run. They must be sure that they have the input and that there is adequate computer time to run the job. Since modern computers process a number of jobs at one time, the operators will be responsible for a mix of jobs.

In this batch environment, operators are busy providing input, mounting files for data that are not on line, and monitoring the printing of reports. This kind of operation resembles the classic factory job shop. The data center has a number of computers and jobs; the objective is to finish the jobs on schedule. The computer room is a bit like a factory producing information.

TABLE 14-2 Some Data Center Management Activities

Scheduling
Documentation
Library maintenance
User services
Quality assurance
Problem handling
Hardware and software inventory
Disaster planning
Backup
Security
System maintenance and fixes

The on-line environment is considerably different. Operators have very little to do in terms of providing input or generating reports. Files are on-line so that they do not have to be mounted. Operators tend to watch the communications network and the computer itself for any signs of problems. On the surface, the computer room appears far more calm than the batch processing shop just described.

In today's environment, we are most likely to find a combination of on-line and batch processing at a single data center. There may be a computer devoted to each type of operation, or on-line applications may be processing while batch jobs are being run.

There are a number of management considerations in operating a data center; the objective is to have a center that is successful according to the criteria previously described.

Personnel Management

Even though we are talking about managing machines, the key to making the computers and systems operate is people. Therefore, the manager of operations, like other managers, has to be skilled in personnel management. His or her task is to motivate and develop staff members.

What does an operations staff member want? There are many different types of individuals in a large data center:

1. Clerical personnel.
2. Computer operators.
3. Systems programmers.
4. Maintenance programmers.
5. Quality assurance staff (possibly).

As one might expect, these individuals have different objectives and are motivated by different rewards.

For clerical personnel and operators, one positive reward is personal development and the possibility for advancement. In addition, clerical workers and operators need training in their current jobs. Systems and maintenance programmers want resources and influence. They see many opportunities to improve operations and/or specific systems. The manager has to balance their enthusiasm for change with the costs of change and the resources available to the data center.

Scheduling

If there are any jobs to be run with specified times for completion, the data center must be concerned about scheduling. As previously described, batch or time-dependent jobs in a data center are analogous to the job shop scheduling situation. There are a number of jobs and a number of machines; how does one route the jobs through the shop?

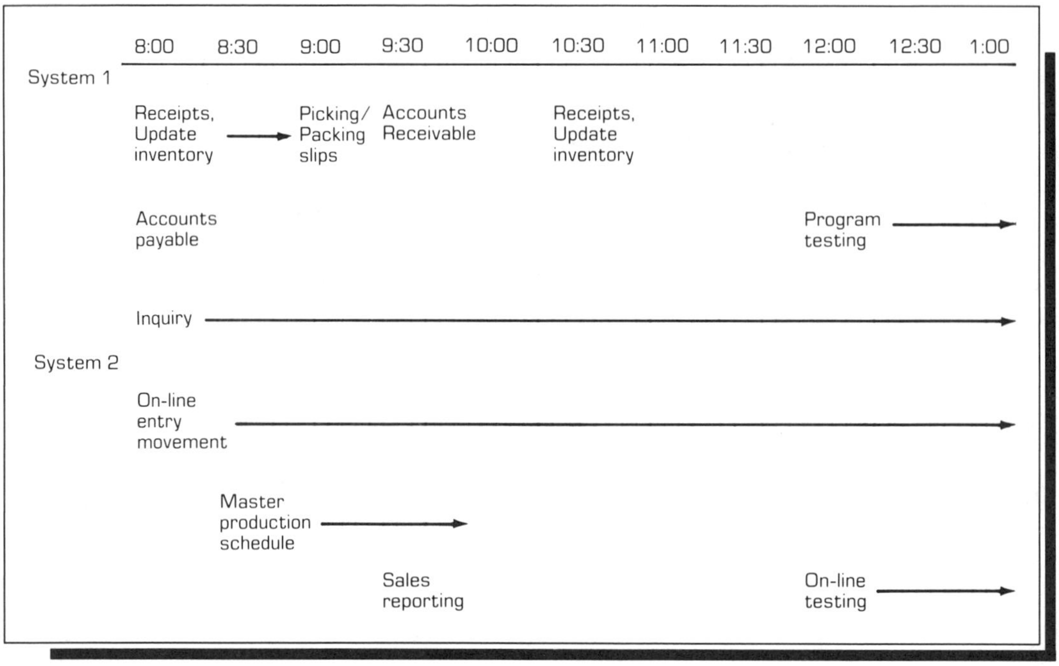

FIGURE 14-1 Gantt chart for scheduling.

The job shop scheduling problem is a very difficult one to solve. In the case of computer systems, the task is a little easier because generally a job runs to completion on one computer. In the job shop, a job needs the services of several machines in a specified sequence. Also, there tend to be relatively few computers in the data center compared with a factory. Finally, certain jobs may run only on certain computers.

In the computer scheduling case, the Gantt chart, a tool used by schedulers for many years, may be helpful. Figure 14-1 shows a Gantt chart for a typical data center with two computers. The chart schedules activity at half-hour intervals during the day. The company makes a product and ships it to customers.

System 1 processes receipts of finished goods and updates book inventory. Then it generates picking and packing slips for the warehouse to ship orders. (These systems are being converted to on-line updating, but for now, they run in batch mode.) At 9:30 the system is to start an accounts receivable run to generate statements, while accounts payable runs at 8:00. Inquiry is "up" all day for users who need to determine what goods are in inventory.

System 2 handles an on-line application in the factory; it records the movement of material as a batch of products leaves one of 25 work centers in the factory and moves to another one. At the same time, it runs a master production schedule program at 8:30, along with sales reporting. This machine is also available all day for programmers who need to test new programs they are developing.

There are other approaches to scheduling; the important point is that a manager of operations has to ensure that jobs with deadlines are scheduled.

Then it is important to monitor the results of the schedule to be sure that service is acceptable.

Documentation

Good operator training is important in assuring good operations. However, the operator needs help beyond training, and the purpose of operations documentation is to provide this assistance. Documentation will vary depending on the type of application; some documentation will actually be programmed into the system, so that certain errors will result in messages telling the operator how to solve the problem, particularly in an on-line system.

For a more batch-oriented system, the operator should have a run book for each application. The run book should contain the following information:

1. A systems flowchart that shows each program in sequence and the files that it accesses.
2. A structure chart showing the various modules of the system and how they are interconnected.
3. For each program the input required, files or databases accessed, output produced, error conditions, messages, and operator responses. A narrative of the program's processing is helpful as well.
4. Who provides the input and when it is to be completed.
5. Who receives the output.
6. The name of the programmer responsible for maintenance.
7. A user contact for the system.

The run book is the first place the operator looks for help when there are problems with a system or when a new operator is learning how to process different applications.

For an on-line system, the documentation task is more complicated. There is probably less that an operator can do here before having to call a programmer. However, it is still a good idea to keep documentation on various programs and their functions and to have very good documentation on the database.

In any environment, the data center needs clearly defined procedures on whom to contact when a problem reaches a certain level. At one airline reservation system data center, there is a chart with the names and phone numbers (work and home) of managers to be notified as the system goes down for an increasing length of time. After each hour passes with the computer down, a higher-level manager is called.

Data Libraries

In the early days of computing, files were generally kept on magnetic tapes. In a large data center, there may be thousands of tapes, which can be difficult to manage. A number of computerized tape management systems are available, and any installation with a large volume of tapes should use programs to help organize them.

Removable disk packs were the next form of storage, though there were fewer of them than tapes. Thus, the packs were more easily managed than tapes. The trend today is toward nonremovable disk drives, which means that there is no-off line disk library.

However, it is standard practice to back up disk drives by making copies of the data on tape. Therefore, there will still be a tape library for on-line systems. Also, since we often find mixed batch and on-line systems, there are likely to be production tapes as well. Thus, we should expect to find tape libraries in most mainframe and minicomputer centers.

As information systems have become more crucial to the operation of organizations, there has been growing concern with backup for critical files. There are a number of services available that will store files in protected and controlled environments away from a customer's data center. It is the responsibility of operations management to be sure that key files are backed up off site on a regular basis.

User Services

Users will have operational questions as they work with computer systems, particularly when systems are on-line. A simple communications problem might result in a terminal's being unable to access the computer. When the computer is down for some reason, the user will want to know when service is to be restored.

A user's services phone desk is one way to answer these questions and to be responsive to users. In addition to operational problems with equipment, users will call this number for help that is applications specific. The individuals taking calls on the help desk will have to know how major applications work, as well as the hardware, software, and network in the firm.

Quality Assurance

Some organizations have formal quality assurance groups. One of their tasks is to test and accept new applications for production. Their agreement means that operations is willing to accept responsibility for the system and that development has completed its work.

Quality assurance is also involved in change management. Because so many changes are made to information systems, it is important to have a process for managing the changes. The first step is to look over the proposed change and to agree that it will accomplish its objectives. Since one change to a system's function often involves multiple program changes, quality assurance must be certain that there is no unforeseen interaction among the changes.

Many organizations have the ability to run test versions of systems before they are placed in production. Quality assurance tests the changes independently of the programmers who made the changes to certify the new version of the system before it replaces the production copy.

Quality assurance should also track changes that are made. There are software products that keep back copies of production programs, so that it is possible to retrace the path of changes easily or even to return to an earlier version if errors are discovered. Quality assurance, then, is intimately involved in the maintenance process, which is discussed in more detail later.

Quality assurance should also have input into the standards used for modifying packages. One firm purchased a very expensive Materials Requirements Planning System and made numerous changes to customize the system for its environment. Unfortunately, in the haste to install the system, programmers did not follow any conventions or identify the code they modified in the programs. As a result, this firm will not be able to take advantage of any updated version of the package that the manufacturer might offer.

Quality assurance needs to set up standards for package program modification, as well as for the modification of custom programs written in the firm. While the existence of a quality assurance function may seem like a luxury, it is one way of providing better service to users.

Problem Reporting

Problems are to be expected in computer operations. Many different things that can go wrong, and it almost seems guaranteed that at least one will! To control the operations process, it is important for management to keep track of problems and their disposition. Problems may be directed to the operations area or to systems. The cause of a problem may not be obvious, so the first step is to find it.

One method is to delegate problem resolution to quality assurance. A written form should be available to anyone who has a problem, though possibly someone at the user services desk should fill out the report for users. The problem report identifies the person reporting the problem and describes the nature of the problem. If it is possible for the person reporting to identify the source (e.g., hardware or software or even a particular program), this is helpful in solving the problem.

If quality assurance does have the responsibility for dealing with problems, it works with the appropriate staff to diagnose and resolve the problem. The firm may want to develop codes for problems, making it possible for management to review the types of problems encountered to see if there are general operating or systems development problems. A problem reporting form also has room so that the person who develops the solution can indicate the nature of the repair.

Given the large number of problems that surface in computing, it is a good idea to assign priorities to problems. A problem that causes the system to stop working is more serious than one with the format or printing of a single report. Another task for management is to monitor how problems are resolved and to see if low-priority problems are ever solved. If not, this is evidence that there are too many problems or too few resources assigned to their resolution.

Inventory

In this age of end-user computing and distributed processing, a major task is to keep an inventory of equipment and software. It is important to know what computers exist and where they are located in the organization. This information is useful in planning and in keeping track of the firm's assets.

An inventory of software in a large firm may result in purchase economies. If different parts of the organization need software, one can consult the inventory to find out if there is software that can be shared. Keeping track of hardware and software is a good application of a DBMS on a micro.

Disaster Planning

We have talked about file backup; what happens when a major data center is destroyed? Is there any need to worry about such an event? Every year, fire, hurricanes, earthquakes, and other disasters strike computer centers. A disaster plan is a guide to what the organization can do if all of its computers at a given location are unavailable.

One of the first things needed are the files that have been backed up and stored off site. Since the computer has been destroyed, it is necessary to have a backup tape of all the software used, from the operating system to individual production programs. What about copies of key documentation?

Disaster recovery occurs after the disaster has struck. If the data files and software exist in backup storage off site, a computer center is needed to run them. Part of a disaster recovery plan is the arrangement made with some other organization to back up each other's critical processing in case of a disaster.

While mutual backup sounds like a good idea, it involves many problems with it. First, applications are unique to their configurations; the mutual backup site needs to have virtually the same hardware and operating system as the organization. Second, the other site still has its own processing to do. How much computer time can it provide to another firm? In an environment with communications, there may be no network in place to connect the organization's terminals with the backup site's computer.

Many firms have backup arrangements with other companies, but few of them have tried to run their software and key systems at the backup site to see if they work. Another strategy has been for an industry group to set up a backup site with a large capacity. The site is dedicated to backup, and it is easy for members of the group to test their systems on it. Such a solution is expensive, but for organizations like banks, which are highly dependent on their computers, it may be necessary insurance. For most firms, however, the disaster recovery plan looks far better on paper than in reality and probably inspires much false confidence.

Security

In the days of batch computing, security in the data center probably amounted to a locked door, and those seeking to penetrate security resorted to special programs on punched cards. In an on-line environment, particularly one with access to a firm's computers by individuals outside the firm, security is a more significant problem. There have been a number of reports of individuals "cracking" computer systems simply as a challenge. Fortunately, there has been little malicious damage, though one security penetration did involve dosage records for cancer radiation therapy. A change in files in this case could have been quite serious.

The classic way of keeping on-line systems secure has been to use passwords known, in theory, only to the user. There is a great deal of research on security now, and various schemes have been proposed to improve on simple passwords. (A person broke into our university computer center recently and printed a copy of all account numbers and passwords.) Some organizations, concerned about data interception, encrypt their data communications so that someone intercepting the data will not be able to understand its meaning. Encryption does cost time and effort, but it is probably the most secure form of transmission.

Encryption, however, does not stop individuals from breaking into systems. If passwords are inadequate, what other alternatives are possible? One solution is a scheme in which a user dials the computer for access; the computer checks the supposedly valid account number and ID on a file, hangs up, and dials the telephone number associated with that ID. This system is more difficult to implement when individuals use different phone numbers to access a machine on a regular basis.

None of these schemes protects the system from legitimate users who have some grievance against the firm. Probably the best solution today is to monitor threats to the system by keeping track of refused access, checking output and systems regularly, and maintaining good backup in case someone does damage a database. Penetration is a growing problem and new solutions are needed.

Systems Programming

It is typical for larger data centers to have a systems programming staff. These individuals are responsible for the installation and maintenance of systems software like the operating system, DBMSs, and telecommunications monitors. Their efforts affect everyone who uses a computer, from the programmer to the user to the operator. However, most of these people are unaware of what the systems programmer does.

Vendors of systems software, especially computer manufacturers with their operating systems, continually improve and fix known problems in their programs. Every so often, the vendor issues a new release of the software and customers have to decide whether or not to install it. Eventually the vendor stops supporting old releases, so while one does not have to install each release in sequence, at some point there will be a need to upgrade. The systems programmer has the responsibility for installing these new releases.

The systems programmer is also a consultant for programmers on the operating system and other systems software. When a problem arises that relates to the system, the systems programmer is likely to be the one asked to solve the problem. Eventually one would like to reach a point where the software works so well that systems programmers are not needed. For the near future, however, the employment prospects for systems programmers remain quite bright.

Maintenance

The problem of maintenance is a critical one for information services. We expect machinery in a factory to need maintenance after it is installed; we expect to spend funds to maintaining equipment like automobiles. Why should software be different?

It is probably the magnitude of maintenance that seems excessive. Lientz and Swanson (1981) surveyed firms concerning their maintenance practices. They found the following in regard to annual personnel hours:

Maintain and enhance current systems	48%
Develop new systems	46%
Other	6%

The firms in their survey allocated almost half of their discretionary resources to maintenance. About 20% of the firms allocated 80% of their resources to this activity.

What is maintenance? Lientz and Swanson report:

Errors and emergencies	17%
Changes to data, input, files, hardware	18%
Improve user enhancements, increase efficiency	60%
Other	4%

The errors and emergencies category reflects what is normally defined as maintenance, that is, something has broken and has to be fixed. At least this category required only 17% of the effort of responding firms.

The 60% category, improvements, should be considered enhancements. We usually do not spend 60% of our maintenance budget enhancing machines on the factory floor or enhancing our automobiles. However, because applications are creative and involve a variety of users, computer systems require a great deal of enhancement as users work with them and come up with new ideas for features and functions.

Better systems design should reduce enhancements. However, if a system is being used, we must expect users to come up with suggestions for improvements. For most organizations, the demand for maintenance will exceed the resources that are devoted to it.

Managing Maintenance

One way to allocate resources to maintenance is to use the maintenance priorities committee discussed earlier. Individual users on the committee represent their departments. A manager from the ISD chairs the committee and helps it to prioritize requests. This manager also provides information on the past month's activity, including the number of requests resolved, the person-days expended, the estimated backlog in person-days, and the number of requests. The management of ISD can review these reports to determine if additional maintenance resources are needed.

Reducing the Need for Maintenance

We have suggested that an actively used system is bound to generate requests for changes, but that good systems design can help reduce the need for maintenance. What kinds of design practices will accomplish this goal?

First, involving users heavily during design to the point where they understand the system should produce specifications that are closer to what the user wants. Too often today, systems are designed after they have been programmed and installed, an expensive way to develop applications.

Prototyping can also help reduce maintenance requests because the user will be able to see key parts of the system before it is complete. The objective here is the same as previously: to help the user understand the system so that suggestions come before rather than after its installation.

Can programmers and analysts do anything to help reduce the maintenance burden? Not surprisingly, the number of errors in programs seems to be related to the size of a system in terms of the number of lines of code, at least according to a study by Gremillion (1984). Others have suggested that the number of bugs is related to the complexity of a system, but lines of code may be a reasonable measure of complexity since complexity is associated with the number of states of a system. In most cases, the larger the number of program statements, the larger the number of states and the greater the complexity of a program.

Systems analysts can use top-down design and automated aids that maintain the documentation for the system. Top-down design makes it easier for those responsible for maintenance, who are unlikely to be the staff that developed the application, to understand and make changes to the system. Having the documentation for the system like DFDs available on a workstation should facilitate changes.

Elshoff and Marcotty (1982) have also suggested ways of writing programs to make them as maintainable as possible. Of course, one would expect programmers to design the system with modules and to use structured programming. What else can be done to enhance program readability?

1. Add comments; comments make it easier to read programs.
2. Maintain a consistent format for program statements.
3. Add an "else" clause to every "if" to explain the conditional better.
4. Make program loops and loop terminations obvious.
5. Do not allow multiple exits from loops.
6. Use status variables to track execution.
7. Use "on" units such as "on end of file."
8. Put common code sequences into procedures.

Planning for eventual maintenance is helpful when changes have to be made in systems and programs. Maintenance and enhancements are a major part of information processing. The maintenance requirement grows continually as new systems are implemented and few systems are discontinued.

In addition, we are in the age of "permanent systems," applications that are so large and expensive that they will probably never be reprogrammed entirely at once. Instead, there will be continual modifications and enhancements until much of the system is changed in an evolutionary manner.

Aging Systems

A significant problem facing operations and the entire IS staff is what to do about aging systems. For the operations group, an old application may be difficult to run and hard to maintain when users make requests for changes. To users, an aging system may be a continual source of irritation, since it does not perform as well or have as pleasant a user interface as more modern applications. Because it is difficult to change, an older application may also appear inflexible to users.

At some point, the old programs will have been changed so many times that it becomes too costly to change them further. At this point, the operations staff and users will probably join forces to seek a redesign of the system. It is difficult to determine this point, however, because unless one is thinking of a complete redesign with major new features, the reprogramming of an existing application is not very exciting, especially when there are entirely new systems to undertake.

As the information processing profession matures, many more systems will fall into the "aged" category. Many of these systems will be redeveloped piecemeal because the organization cannot afford to develop them all at once. In addition, the disruption of trying to implement a new version would be too great. Examples of these systems on which firms have become dependent include airline reservations applications and integrated order entry systems. The decision on when and how to redevelop aging applications will be a recurring one for many IS managers.

A Distributed Environment

Much of our discussion in this chapter has focused on the single data center rather than on the distributed environment that characterizes much of today's computing. However, even in a decentralized environment, data centers will gradually grow and have to be managed. Some firms have large mainframe operations, as well as smaller data centers in different locations. Management may want to coordinate operations policy at different sites; for example, a common procedure for file backup might be specified.

CMI is a good example; it has multiple vendors' computers located in different subsidiaries. Because different makes of computers have unique operating requirements, one would expect to find differences at each location with respect to operations. However, the CIO will want to have some common procedures among the different subsidiaries, for example, for disaster planning and file backup. The degree to which other procedures can be standardized will depend on the extent to which there are operational problems that standard procedures will solve.

Certainly the central location will want to maintain an inventory of equipment and software, if at all possible. The inventory is one coordination mechanism and is a way to share information, especially about applications packages and new applications that are under development.

At a minimum in a distributed environment, the CIO will want to ensure that procedures to protect the firm are in place. The next step is to implement some of the standards and procedures described in this chapter so that operations can be managed as successfully as possible.

Recommended Readings

Dickson, G., and J. Wetherbe, *The Management of Information Systems.* New York: McGraw-Hill, 1985. (See especially the chapter on computer operations.)

Elshoff, J., and M. Marcotty, "Improving Computer Program Readability to Aid Modification," *Communications of the ACM,* vol. 25, no. 8 (August 1982), pp. 512–521. (A series of guidelines for making programs easier to understand and maintain.)

Gremillion, L., "Determinants of Program Repair Maintenance Requirements," *Communications of the ACM,* vol. 27, no. 8 (August 1984), pp. 826–832. (An examination of predictors for program errors.)

Lientz, B., and B. Swanson, "Problems in Application Software Maintenance," *Communications of the ACM,* vol. 24, no. 11 (November 1981), pp. 763–769. (Contains the results of the survey on maintenance discussed in this chapter.)

Discussion Problems

14.1 The manager of a time-sharing computer center was getting desperate. He was rapidly running out of disk space on his systems, and general messages to users to eliminate old files went unanswered. Finally, he decided that the only way to solve his problem was to take dramatic action. Any file that was unused for more than a year was deleted from each user's set of files. Following this act, the manager notified users that their files had been deleted, but that if they were needed, they were on an archive tape.

This action did not endear the manager to many users. Can you think of another way to accomplish the same goal, given the reluctance of users to take the time to review their files?

14.2 Forward Industries had never experienced much success with information processing. Systems were developed late and over budget; users complained that applications did not do what they needed. Management thought that too much money was spent on information processing, and the ISD staff thought that management did not know what it was doing.

The firm decided to split into three profit centers based on the different kinds of products manufactured at Forward. The manager of the ISD was frustrated enough to go along with a split of computer systems too, though he knew that it would be difficult to break up mainframe applications so that they could be run in three separate divisions.

He commented, "We can change the software, but I wonder if these guys know what they're getting into? Now there will be three data centers and three managers of operations. How will that be any cheaper? I don't think these managers are good enough to handle operations, either. They had better hire some good people in their centers for a change."

What do the division managers need to consider in setting up computer operations in their divisions?

Questions

1. How does managing operations differ from managing systems design?
2. Why is availability so important to users?
3. What is response time? What can cause it to vary during the day?
4. What is the impact of long response times on users?
5. What kinds of jobs can be scheduled?
6. Are accurate processing results the sole responsibility of operations? Who else is involved?
7. How do on-line and batch processing operations differ?
8. What is the role of maintenance programmers?
9. What are the duties of quality assurance personnel?
10. What is the purpose of operations documentation? What should it include?
11. What are the problems of managing a tape library?
12. What can operations do to enhance security?
13. What is encryption and how does it enhance security?
14. What is the role of a systems programmer?
15. What is the nature of most maintenance requests?
16. At what point does maintenance become a redevelopment or redesign of the system?
17. How does a maintenance priorities committee work? What is its purpose?
18. What strategies exist for reducing the need for maintenance?
19. How do operations in a distributed environment differ from those in a centralized ISD?
20. Do you expect to see many one-vendor computer centers in the future? Why or why not?
21. What problems are created for operations by having a variety of computers from different vendors in a single firm?

15

Control and Audit of Information Services

In November 1985 a computer malfunction at the Bank of New York essentially closed down the Treasury bond market delivery system for almost 28 hours. Apparently a software change in the bank's government securities clearance system limited a counter to 32,000. On November 20, the bank cleared over 32,000 securities for the first time. The program stored the additional securities incorrectly and destroyed the integrity of the database.

The exact details are not clear, but it is likely that the program continued to store data for one security by writing over the data for the last one. Two teams with about 55 people worked on the problem. One team developed a temporary solution and the other team started to redesign the entire system, consisting of some 700 programs. The short-term repair worked for a day, but it too failed. Shortly thereafter, the redeveloped system began to operate satisfactorily. It had been developed by an outside software firm that helped make the repairs.

What was the impact of this failure? The Bank of New York is the nation's largest clearer of government securities, so this function basically stopped. The bank felt that it had to pay the cost of carrying securities, so it did not demand payments for clearance until its records were corrected. As a result, *the bank had to borrow $20 billion from the Federal Reserve Bank of New York so that it could pay for the securities received;* this was said to be the largest loan from the Federal Reserve window. The loan cost the bank an estimated $4 million in interest.

Because the Bank of New York could not accept payments from banks that had purchased securities, these other banks were left with $20 billion on their hands. They did not need to borrow in the federal funds market, which created a cash glut; the excess cash in the system caused the federal funds rate to plummet from 8% to 5.5% in 24 hours. Rumors about bank problems often affect the commodities market. The price of a January delivery of platinum at the New York Mercantile Exchange surged $12.40 an ounce to $351.20 on a volume of 11,929 contracts, representing a 29-year record.

This control failure is one of the most dramatic and expensive ever reported, though there are probably other examples that have not been publicized. Controls within the computer system should have caught the problem. For example, assuming the processing was in batch mode, the system should have counted the number of securities and compared it with changes in the system's master files. Even if the designers had omitted the controls, testing with a large volume of transactions should have shown the problem.

This example illustrates just one type of control problem. Control is fundamental to the modern organization and is one of the primary responsibilities of management. In this chapter we shall discuss control theory and how it applies to different aspects of an organization, including information services.

Control Theory

Control is an important concept in many fields, including engineering. One engineering-oriented model of control is shown in Figure 15-1. It provides a useful framework for thinking about control in organizations.

Figure 15-1 shows an adjustable standard that is the objective of the control system. A sensor determines actual conditions, while the discriminator compares the conditions recorded by the sensor with the standard. The effector responds to the discriminator if some action needs to be taken; it initiates communications with some mechanism to change conditions so that they come closer to achieving the goal set on the adjustable standard. The activity consumes some type of energy in this control process. See Lawler and Rhode (1976) for a more complete discussion of this model.

If we apply the model to a familiar system such as the one for a furnace, it should help illustrate the principles of control. For the heating system, the adjustable standard is the setting on the thermostat. The thermostat also contains a sensor in the form of a bimetallic strip; this strip bends according to the temperature. If there is too large a gap between the standard set as the desired room temperature, the bending of the sensor closes a circuit, which constitutes the effector. The closed circuit sends an electrical signal or communication to the furnace, which is the activity in the model. The furnace uses oil or gas to change actual conditions to bring them more in line with the standard.

The advantage of the engineering approach to control is the degree of automation involved. The only manual intervention is to change the setting

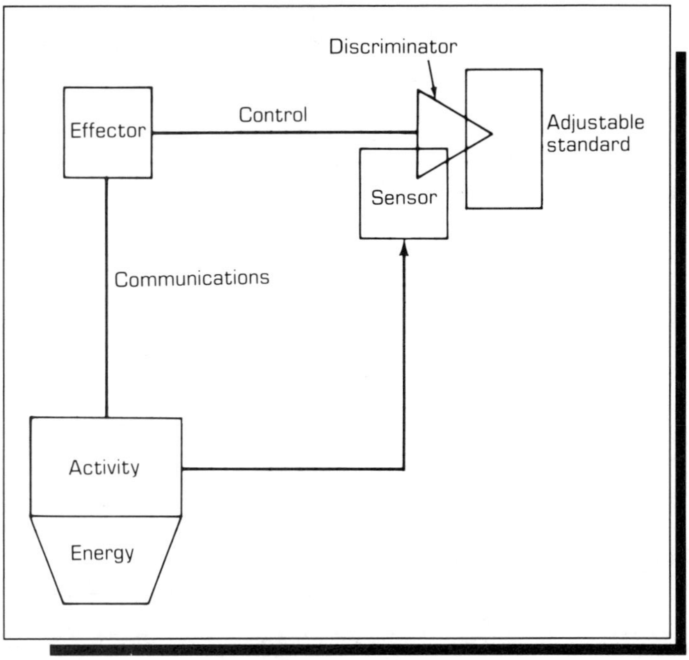

FIGURE 15-1 An engineering control model.

on the thermostat, that is, to set the standard. Such control systems are very common in different kinds of mechanical and electrical equipment, including automatic pilots for aircraft, automobile speed controls, and many similar applications. In organizations, unfortunately, control systems are much less automatic; they rely far more on humans to play the roles of sensor, effector, communicator, and action taker.

Control in Organizations

Figure 15-2 portrays three different types of control in the context of the often used pyramidal shape for an organization. The pyramid implies that day-to-day responsibility for a specific type of control lies with a particular level of management (e.g., top management is responsible for organizational strategy and control).

Organizational Strategy and Control

Organizational strategy is one form of control in the firm. The strategy offers one set of goals or a standard for which the organization should strive. Often, however, the goals inherent in a plan are not well publicized in the firm. Management also frequently fails to implement the plan or to manage according to its directions.

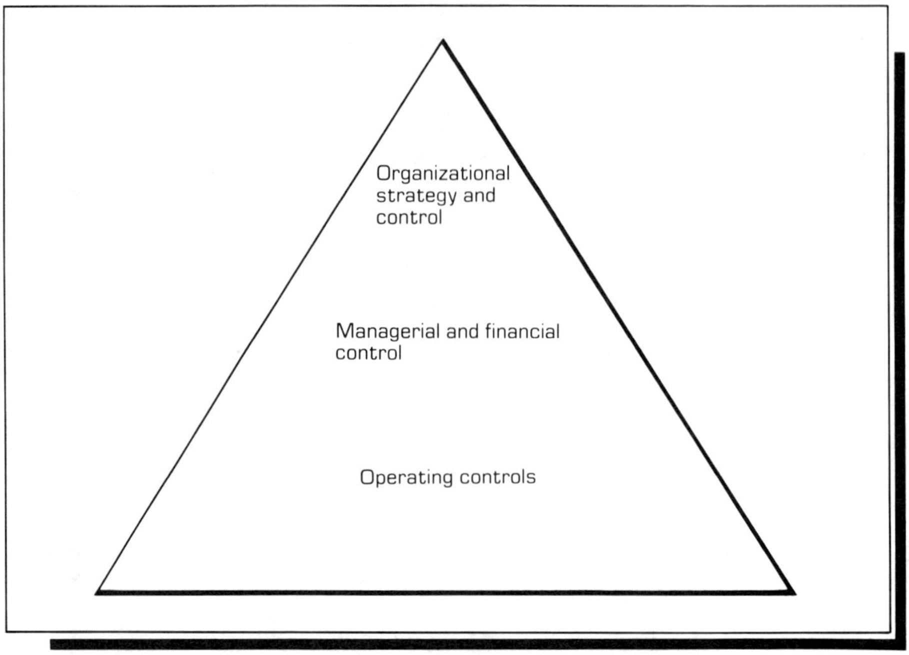

FIGURE 15-2 Organizational control.

Table 15-1 shows the control framework applied to a variety of control systems, including the heating example previously described. The second row of the table describes organizational strategy and control. The plan provides the standard, but management review is required to sense when things are not going according to plan. Management must notice and communicate performance problems in its role of discriminator and effector. Senior management communicates with lower levels of management, influencing them to take action that will bring the organization back on a course that meets the plan. Senior management can exhort others to take action and can influence them with various rewards and inducements. The only energy for this control system comes from human beings.

There is almost nothing automatic about the control system at the organizational strategy level of the firm. All aspects of strategy and control require individuals to play certain roles; the entire system must be orchestrated by senior management. In the absence of a plan, or in the presence of a plan that is not widely shared in the firm, managers often feel that they are operating in a vacuum. If senior management wants to control the organization, it must provide the standards in the form of strategic goals and a plan. It must then play the roles suggested in the control framework to ensure that the goals of the plan are achieved. Simply having a plan is not enough.

Managerial and Financial Control

The term *managerial control* has become popular in describing a middle level of control: that exercised between strategic goal setting and the control of

TABLE 15-1 Types of Control

System	Standard	Sensor	Discriminator	Effector	Communications	Activity	Energy
Heating	Thermostat setting	Bimetallic strip	Thermostat	Circuit closed	Electrical signals	Turn on/off furnace	Gas, oil
Organizational strategy and control	Plans	Senior management review	Performance	Senior management	Management	Actions; rewards	Human
Managerial/ financial control	Budgets	Management review; exception reports	Performance Actual versus planned	Management	Management reports	Actions; resource reallocation	Human, computer
Operating control	Standard operating procedures	Management review	Exceptions; audits	Management	Management	Control systems	Human, computer
IS planning	Plan goals, vision	Management review	Performance review	Management	Management committees, CIO	Actions; resources	Human
IS management	Organizational structure and policies	Management review	Management reviews	CIO, senior management	CIO, senior management	Actions; rewards	Human
IS operations	Standards	Management review; exception and trouble reports	Exceptions; errors; security lapses; audits	IS management	IS management	Revise standards; develop new control systems	Human, computer

day-to-day operations. Managerial control is usually associated with financial and budgeting controls, as well as with the management of personnel.

Table 15-1 describes a typical managerial control scenario. The standard for the control system is provided by a budget. The sensor is management, which must review budget and exception reports. Performance differences between the budget and actual experience provide the discrimination function. Management is the effector; it communicates directly with others and provides reports.

Managers can do certain things to bring the system back under control. First, they can take direct action; common ones include freezing hiring, banning many forms of travel, and instituting measures to cut costs in general. In more dramatic situations, managers can urge early retirement, sell off divisions, lay off employees, and so on. When less drastic actions seem appropriate, management may be able to bring the budget back under control by reallocating resources.

Again, with this system the energy source is human; key parts of the control system rely on managers to play their roles. However, this control system is more firmly embedded in organizations than is the strategic one. Budgets are an accepted form of financial management. Possibly because firms have to be concerned about their financial performance and statements, budgets are widely accepted as a necessary management control system.

Operating Controls

The lowest level of control in the organization consists of operating controls. Large organizations often have elaborate standards that must be followed by employees. Particularly in manufacturing, there are standards for what a machine operator should do and how long each task should take. Some of these standards are the basis for pay and productivity measurement. Procedures for handling accounting are usually specified, particularly for dealing with things like cash receipts and disbursements.

Management review is the sensor when there is an exception or problem with operating controls. There are also audits by internal and external auditors.

The discrimination function may be handled internally through exception reports or management observations; outside auditors may also act as discriminators. It is up to management to be the effector and to communicate with others in order to solve a problem. One possible method is to construct a new control system. The energy for such action comes from humans and possibly from a computer.

Managerial and operational controls are often well structured in the firm. Middle- and lower-level managers have the responsibility for specific tasks like accounts receivable, order entry, sales analysis, production scheduling, and quality control. Their tasks include controlling the processes for which they are responsible.

Many control systems in the organization rely heavily on computers for information processing. Consider a control system to ensure that only products meeting quality standards are shipped. Such a system often involves statistical sampling and the calculation of a number of statistics to see if products are within acceptable limits. It is likely that a computer will be used for this kind of task.

Information Systems Control

Figure 15-3 is a pyramid of information systems control which is similar to the organizational pyramid of Figure 15-2. Information services and its systems have an important role to play in helping to control the organization. Information systems themselves also need to be well controlled.

IS Planning

In Chapter 3 we discussed the need for a plan and a vision for information systems in the organization. This plan helps management control information services by providing a standard in the form of goals for IS. In Table 15-1, management review is the sensor in the planning control system; it undertakes a performance review against the plan to provide the discriminator function. Management must also be the communicator; communications might be directed at one of the various management committees discussed earlier such as a senior management steering committee.

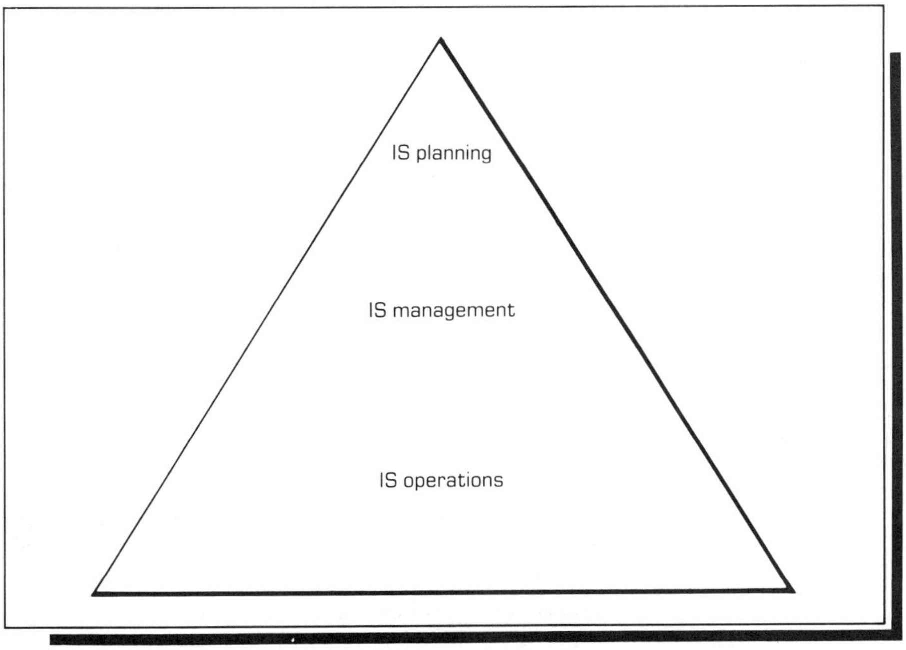

FIGURE 15-3 IS control.

Senior management and the CIO can take action to try to bring under control the accomplishments and objectives of IS—that is, bring IS back in line with the plan. Management options include allocating new resources to IS, changing systems development priorities, shifting resources to or from maintenance, purchasing outside services, and/or making changes in personnel assignments.

IS Management

IS management is concerned with the control of information processing in the organization. In Chapter 2 we discussed various options for structuring information processing. Whatever structure is chosen, management has the responsibility for control and especially for coordination.

For standards, there may be policies in the firm such as one describing what vendors' equipment may be purchased. There may be a requirement that all purchases of hardware and software above a certain dollar amount be reviewed by a central group. Another requirement may be that new systems development projects must be reported to a central review group so that someone in the firm can look for opportunities to share development costs and packages.

In contrast to the broader area of managerial control for the entire firm, the control of information systems is far less fully developed. Management reviews must act as the sensor and discriminator in this control system. It is possible that the CIO or senior management will be the effector; communications will flow to the CIO and/or senior management.

The available options are varied and will be tailored to fit the situation. Senior management or a steering committee may decide on a new policy when a control problem exists. Certain problems will be brought to a committee on an ad hoc basis because they are not expected to recur. Management control of information services requires human energy and motivation.

IS lacks the clearly defined procedures associated with budgets and financial controls. This is not to say that budgets are unused in information services, but they constitute only a small part of managerial control of this group. A major problem in information processing is the lack of attention given to the control of information services in the firm; the CIO needs to keep this issue visible so that the firm is confident that it is controlling processing, and not vice versa.

IS Operations

IS operational controls fall into a number of areas. They can be broken down into two broad categories: computer operations, and systems analysis and design. In each of these areas, the firm will have standards. Management reviews, trouble reports, and exception reports are the sensors in this control system. Typically, a lot of "sensing" will be done by managers in the operations area, when errors occur.

Audits, exceptions, and errors, such as the one at the Bank of New York discussed at the beginning of this chapter, provide the discrimination function. IS management is the effector and the target of communications. A variety of actions are available, ranging from a revision in standards to the development of complex, new control systems. The energy for these control systems will come from humans and the computer.

Lapses in controls during systems development may be caught during testing. However, control problems in systems design frequently are not manifested until a system is in operation and there is a dramatic failure like the one at the Bank of New York. These control failures are very damaging to information services and are frequently cited by senior executives as the reason they place little faith in the ISD.

IS Controls

An overview of controls in IS may be found in Table 15-2.

Planning

Little can be done to automate the control system for planning. Successful control at this level requires a systems plan and its acceptance by senior management. The CIO can use the plan actively in explaining decisions and as a basis for reporting.

As an example, the CIO might consider preparing an annual report on information services. The report is a part of the planning process for the coming year. The annual report discusses the goals for the year and what IS has accomplished; then it considers the goals for the coming year. The 3- to 5-year plan should be extended by 1 year; the annual report is a good introduction to a revised, longer-range plan.

TABLE 15-2 Some IS Controls

Planning
Budgets
Managers
Policies
Committees
User support mechanisms
Charging for services
Operations
Access controls
Systems design
Program controls
Database integrity controls
Operations
Security

This control system is not very automatic; it depends on senior management and the CIO to have faith in a plan and to use it for making decisions. If the plan is seen as something that must be done to satisfy senior management or as a burden, the firm will have lost one opportunity to gain control over information processing.

IS Management

It has been mentioned that control over the management of IS begins with the plan and budget. However, IS has more control problems than many other areas. Management-level control over IS involves coordinating processing in the firm.

The mechanisms we have recommended for managerial coordination also provide a form of control. First, there are policies and guidelines established for coordination purposes. Policies on what vendors' computers are approved for purchase help control the proliferation of computers in the firm. A policy that requires the CIO to approve the development of all new systems expected to cost over $25,000 and that requires the CIO to keep a record of these systems helps prevent duplication. The firm does not want two plants developing the same system independently of each other unless there are very good reasons for it.

Beyond policies, there are control mechanisms like steering committees and review committees. Visits by the CIO and his or her staff also serve a loose control function in addition to coordinating IS activities. IS staff meetings across distributed divisions and departments are another mechanism for control. These visits and meetings provide sensor inputs for the CIO's control system. The CIO must then decide whether the divisions and departments are out of control and, if so, what can be done about it.

Management control over IS is also exerted through user support mechanisms like information centers and personal computer stores. By learning users' needs and offering recommendations, these places help control processing in the firm. For the most part, this control is accomplished in a positive manner; the ISD is helping users while at the same time influencing them to follow policies that are designed to control processing in the firm.

Chargeout

One controversial method of managerial control is charging for information services. There are a number of ways to charge the costs of computing, and we will discuss three of them: (1) total charge to overhead; (2) a cost center charging approach, in which all costs are charged back to users; and (3) profit center charging, in which users develop their own budgets and IS operates to make a small profit.

Overhead charging basically avoids the issue of chargeback to users. The argument in favor of overhead charging is that users are encouraged to make use of information services. If users in the organization are naive and do not appreciate the potential of computers, overhead charging makes it easy for them to adopt the technology. Overhead charging is also inexpensive to implement because there is no need to develop algorithms for allocating costs.

Most organizations today probably use some type of chargeout approach in allocating information services costs. One reason for charging for services is to recover costs and to allocate computer resources. Pricing is used as a mechanism to allocate scarce resources. Pricing can serve another function as well: to regulate the demand for computing services. Of course, behind this philosophy is an assumption that individuals are aware of the costs and that the demand for computing is elastic; if the price is raised, the demand will fall.

Instead of viewing information services as a cost center, an organization can recover costs by establishing IS as a profit center. Some authors (Allen, 1987) have suggested that under this approach information services becomes a "business within a business." How does a profit center for IS differ from a cost center? As a profit center, information services sets its own prices for service; it bills other parts of the organization for the services it provides. Since it is considered an independent business unit, the information services organization can set its own prices and budget its own expenditures. Sometimes under this type of arrangement users are free to seek outside information processing services. In addition, the IS unit may be able to offer its services to external organizations.

Arguments in favor of this approach stress service and the efficiency that a profit center forces on the IS unit. The existence of IS depends on its ability to satisfy users and to offer a cost-effective service. A profit center should lead to a more dynamic IS organization, that brings new technology to the firm.

The disadvantage of the profit center is that users may not be able to judge the quality of the service or evaluate the alternative of going outside the organization for information processing. Users may also resent a unit like information services making a profit on the service it provides. If the IS unit sells its services outside the organization, internal users may believe that they are subsidizing external customers.

Of course, there are mixed strategies as well. A firm might charge users for operations, since the cost of operations is fairly predictable. Systems development is viewed as an R&D effort that is borne by the corporation as overhead. In this scheme, the firm is trying to encourage innovation and the development of new applications while controlling the operational use of computers.

McKell, Hansen, and Heitger (1979) have surveyed a number of approaches to chargeout; they state that a decision to charge to overhead in effect allocates resources by default. Many of the models they have reviewed are quite elegant, but they observe that measurement can be a discouraging factor in developing a chargeout algorithm.

If the purpose of a chargeout scheme is to allocate resources, what characteristics must it possess? First, chargeout should promote cost-effective use of information services. Second, it should be consistent. If a user runs the same job every week, charges for that job should be about the same unless there is a dramatic change in the volume of data processed. Third, a charging algorithm should be understood by the user. If the user does not know the basis for charging, it is hard for the charging algorithm to influence the user's behavior.

A charging scheme should also be easy to administer; it does not make sense to spend large amounts of money developing or computing charges. The charging scheme should be such that users can influence it by their actions. Often the expenses to be charged out are considerable because overhead is included; as a result, users see the rates for using computers as prohibitive. If the chargeout scheme is arbitrary—for example, based on the user's proportion of CPU use for the prior year—the user's actions will have little impact on charges.

Finally, the ISD should charge on the basis of long-term marginal costs. Truly fixed costs that cannot be controlled should not be charged—for example, the cost of the data center building. The ISD should submit a budget each year for fixed-cost items that are not controllable, and these charges should not be included in chargeback rates. Also, standard costs should be used for users so that the actual rates will be fixed for the year.

Differential charges for various types of services should be considered. Running a large job on a shift with little work should cost less than running it at a busy time. Even in an environment where chargeback is being used, IS may want to offer some services at no cost to encourage use. The first 6 months after opening an information center, IS may choose to offer consulting services free of charge.

At the level of individual users, chargeout is often not taken very seriously. A department manager may look at computer chargebacks, but individual users say that they use the computer to do their job and pay little attention to what it costs.

The question of whether to charge out to users or not is an emotional one. The CIO may have to abide by accounting customs in the firm. If the decision is to charge, the CIO should try to develop a plan that users can understand and that allows their behavior to have some influence on charges. If a plan does not have these characteristics, it will not provide much managerial control.

IS Operations

Control over IS operations has been a concern of IS management since the first computers were installed. The opportunities for processing problems are almost impossible to enumerate. Control problems come from a variety of sources, including systems design, programming, and operations. In addition, there are control system problems that occur due to intentional abuse of systems.

In the late 1970s there were two false missile alerts in the United States. Sensors in the warning system indicated that a large Russian missile attack had been launched. When not all of the sensors showed the attack after a few minutes, generals in the command centers suspected a false alarm and did not notify the President.

What happened? A technician mounted a simulation tape on a computer that was supposedly not connected to the on-line monitoring system.

Somehow a communications link was forged between the off-line and on-line computers, and the simulated attack showed up as real in a number of U.S. command posts. The simulation evidently did not include all classes of sensors, so that the data were not confirmed over time. What would the results have been, however, if the simulation had been complete, that is, had included data from all sensors?

A manager was working with two related spreadsheets with 15,000 different cells on his microcomputer to project the market for different types of equipment. He underestimated the size of the market by $36 million because he had the program round figures to the nearest whole number. The inflation factor, which had been entered as 0.6, was rounded to 1, so that it had no impact on the figures in the spreadsheet.

An operator in a medical institution forgot to remove the protect ring on a magnetic tape that contained the only records of $500,000 in cash receipts. He accidentally mounted the tape on the wrong tape drive, and it was erased. The organization hired additional workers to reconstruct the data; as the job was completed, the same accident happened again.

A group of teenagers in Milwaukee decided that it would be fun to gain access to as many different computers as possible. They dialed computers throughout the country and tried to log on to the account that the vendor had set up for the vendor's own service personnel when the operating system was shipped to customers. The account had the same password throughout the country; it was up to the vendor's engineers to change the password when they first worked on the system. Evidently, few of the engineers bothered, and the teenagers were able to gain access to computers.

Many of the machines were used for research, and the students accessed one computer at a major cancer research and treatment center. The interlopers' activities were spotted, but without realizing it, they could easily have changed data values on a file that contained the x-ray dosage for patients undergoing radiation therapy.

Why and how do these failures in control systems happen? We are not very optimistic about the ability of the profession to protect systems; there are too many threats and the systems are too complex. We will now describe some of the basic controls that are recommended; however, they do not provide adequate and complete operational control for systems. Figure 15-4 presents an overview of system vulnerabilities.

Systems Design

The first line of defense is the controls embedded in a system when it is first designed. Many of the controls used today in an on-line environment have been carried over from the days of batch processing.

The first concern is with amount of input. While not a control, is there an incentive for users to provide input? Designers should consider this question. Factory floor workers using one data collection system provided only about 60% of the input that should have gone to the system. As a result, the system failed and threw the factory into chaos.

Next, designers should be concerned with the quality of the input. For example, in a batch setting, programs check input fields to be sure that numeric fields do not contain alphabetic data. Batch programs also typically

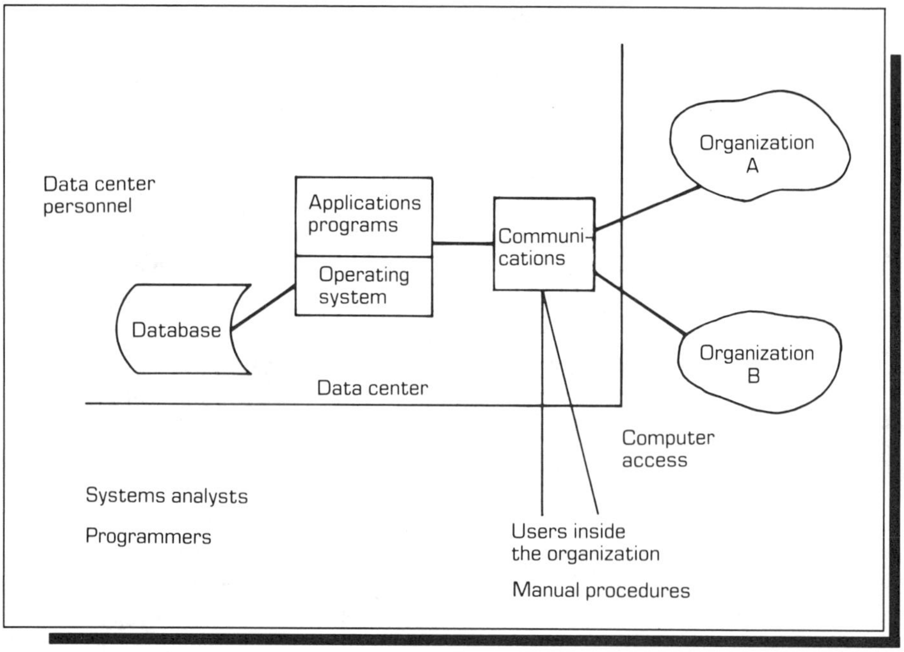

FIGURE 15-4 Some system vulnerabilities.

count the number of data records entered and compare them with a batch total to be sure that all data were entered. This batch checking is very common, with systems processing cash records like checking account applications for banks.

On-line systems can check each field carefully and can access data from master files to be sure that they are correct. For example, an order entry system might require the user to enter the first three letters of a customer's name, followed by the customer's zip code. The program looks up the customer's name and address and displays them on the screen for the data entry clerk to confirm.

In a similar manner, the program checks each field for valid data; its goal is to ensure that only accurate data enter the system. In the batch environment, all the editing program can usually do is to consider the reasonableness of each field. On line, the input program consults files and works interactively with the user to obtain good input from the start. The on-line program will also try to perform the equivalent of a batch control check. For example, during order entry, the computer might add up the total number of items ordered and ask for the input of the same number by the clerk who computed the total before beginning data entry.

Another input control is the use of a check digit to see if a key input field is correct. A check digit is a number added to a field, such as the customer number or the number of an item that the customer is ordering. The computer follows an algorithm that transforms the data entered and computes the check digit. The program compares the computed check digit with the one entered to see if the number keyed by the operator is correct.

Systems designers also have to guard against another common error:

duplicate entry of data. On more than one occasion, the same set of input documents has been entered twice despite manual procedures to prevent this from happening. With on-line input, it is customary to log transactions to tape as they are received. If it is necessary to recover because of a failure, the system can reload its latest database backup and replay the transactions tape against it.

Processing checks are an important part of a computer system. The designer is trying to anticipate sources of error and guard against them. Programs can compute various hash totals through processing, which are compared at the end of the run. As an example, it could carry a total of all debits and a total of all credits in processing for an accounting system. At the end of processing, the two totals should match.

Programs that are to be run in a sequence also need to check to make sure that they are actually being run in their proper location. If a program expects input to be in a certain sequence, the program must check each input processed to be sure that the sequence is correct.

Output reports must also be checked. The program might compute various figures two different ways to be sure that processing is correct. In batch processing, control totals are often used to be sure that each succeeding program balances. The first program in a sequence might add up the total value of the transactions it processes, including additions and deletions. The next program picks up this total and checks to see that after processing it agrees with the total. The second program passes an updated control total to the third program, and so on.

This discussion has covered only some of the major controls possible in the design of a system. Because each system is to some extent unique, controls depend on the nature of processing. In a typical commercial program, we would expect to find one half or more of the program statements devoted to error controls.

Database Integrity

A major control concern is the integrity of files and databases. When the organization is using files rather than a DBMS, programmers must take the responsibility for maintaining file integrity. One good check in batch systems is to be sure that the total number of records in the file before processing plus additions and minus deletions equals the total number in the file at the end of processing. A more rigorous check is to follow the same logic, but use a hash total by adding up the value of the datum in one field of a file.

In a database environment, the programmer will have to work with the DBA to determine what kind of error checking is appropriate for the DBMS being used in the firm. One common practice is to back up databases by copying them to a magnetic tape or another disk file. The organization should have procedures in place for this kind of backup. The information center and the IS staff should also encourage users to back up files when they are programming or using a package on their micros.

Operations/Data Center

There are a number of standards that one can establish for the data center. It is a good idea to have a schedule for jobs that are run on a regular basis. If users supply data in batch mode, an operations staff member should record their receipt on a log. Operators in a batch environment should log jobs, when they began, when they ended, and any problems encountered. In an on-line application, operators should record the time and nature of any anomalies.

The operations staff should establish procedures for off-line data libraries and should have a management system for them. There should be access controls for the data center itself. When programs need to be changed, the quality assurance group should see that proper testing is done and should agree that a change is ready for production. Old versions of systems should be maintained as well.

The firm should have backup arrangements for processing at another site and should keep backup copies of files in a protected location off the premises. There should be a written disaster plan and recovery plan for a data center.

Access Controls

The problem of unauthorized access to on-line systems is becoming more crucial as networks proliferate. Firms are also encouraging systems use by individuals who do not work for the firm, including suppliers and customers. As a result, people over whom the firm has little or no control can access its systems.

The classic access control is a password, but passwords are not very secure. A former employee of the Federal Reserve in Washington gained access to a computer so that he could obtain early information on economic statistics that influence the stock market. Though his account was closed, he used the account and password of a person still employed at the bank. A supervisor noted that the account was used on a day when its owner was absent; she alerted officials, who traced the former employee. One computer vendor does change its passwords every month, but in some firms passwords are taped to users' terminals!

Greater security at some expense in processing comes from encrypting data in transmission and on files. There is a national standard, the Data Encryption Standard (DES), which has been in use for a number of years. All encryption relies on a key to undo the encrypted data. The weak link in this control system is knowledge of the key. Various approaches have been suggested for safeguarding keys so that a would-be unauthorized user cannot obtain one.

In the future, firms will require greater security as they put more computers on networks. Currently there are few good controls against illegal access, and we expect to see more encryption in the future. The problem of unauthorized access will continue and will become more severe.

Source of Controls

There are books that list controls of various types, and an experienced staff will have many more in mind. How does one develop a control strategy? One approach is to give the assignment to a task force within the ISD. The task force should be charged with developing a plan for controls in the systems development process, for database integrity, for operations, and to protect access to the system.

This plan can be discussed and reviewed, especially by the quality assurance group. The objective of the reviewers is to come up with scenarios in which controls fail, and then to devise a new control so that the failure will be prevented.

Computer Audit

External auditors are concerned with the fairness of financial statements and with assurance that management has adequate control over the firm. Internal auditors are interested in all aspects of the organization's control. However, both of these groups will probably be uninterested in the levels we have called *strategy* and *control*. They will focus on operational issues and then on managerial control.

A key component of the Foreign Corrupt Practices Act of 1977 requires management in publicly held corporations to devise and maintain a system of internal accounting controls to provide assurance that transactions are properly authorized and recorded. The act also requires that access to assets be limited and that there be a periodic reconciliation of records with the assets they describe.

The Role of the Auditor

There are many possible roles for an auditor. We have mentioned the external auditor; after doing an audit, this individual states that the financial statements of the firm have been prepared according to accepted accounting principles. An audit by a certified public accounting firm is required in the United States for any publicly held firm, and most lenders require a certified audit before they will provide a firm with credit.

The external auditor is most concerned with systems that affect the financial statements of a firm, such as those that enter orders and keep track of receivables. The internal auditor is concerned with all systems and the entire set of controls in the firm.

A IS auditor is an internal auditor who works on the design of information systems as a consultant on controls. One firm estimates that a control costs 4 times more to add after system specifications are completed and 16 times as much if it is developed after the system is running The objective of the consulting auditor on the design team is to incorporate adequate controls so that few or none will have to be added after conversion to the new system.

The Audit Problem

Computer systems continually make the job of the auditor more difficult. The auditor interested in computer processing will focus on transactions. He or she wants to determine if recorded transactions are valid and if they have

TABLE 15-3 Errors in On-Line Systems

Transactions may not be recorded.
Fictitious transactions may be recorded.
Transactions may be processed more than once.
Transactions may be entered incorrectly.
Transactions may update the wrong file.
The correct file may not be updated.
Master file data may be destroyed.
Unauthorized users may gain access to files that contain private data.
Source documents may be destroyed.
A management (audit) trail may be destroyed or become subject to manipulation.
Transaction data may be processed incorrectly.
Automated decisions may be incorrectly invoked.

Source: C. Litecky and R. Rittenberg, *Communications of the ACM*, vol. 24, no. 5 (May 1981), p. 292.

been authorized. Are transactions actually recorded and are they classified properly? Is the effect of transactions found on the permanent records of the company?

Computers have introduced a large number of problems for auditors trying to accomplish these tasks. Computer applications provide a new level of complexity in processing transactions. One reason for developing a computer system is to reduce the amount of paper, yet the paper record represents a tangible record for the auditor.

Probably the most serious problem is that computer applications tend to eliminate the audit trail on which auditors traditionally rely. An audit trail is simply a series of documents that show the arrival of a transaction and, at each stage, what happens to that transaction as the organization processes it. Sometimes an audit trail exists electronically; in other cases, it may have disappeared entirely. Table 15-3 is a list of some of the things that can go wrong in an on-line system; try to develop an audit approach to verify that controls exist in the system to prevent them from happening.

If we combine these problems with the difficulty of finding individuals who are skilled in information processing to work with auditors, the level of auditing of computer-based systems leaves a great deal to be desired.

Some Audit Approaches

An article by Weiss (1980) summarizes some of the popular techniques used to audit the controls in computer systems. (It should be noted that a complete audit will also address data center controls, systems development procedures, and similar aspects of internal control.)

1. One approach is for the auditor to run the system being studied with test data. The transactions in the test data have both valid and incorrect data. This strategy requires the auditor to become very knowledgeable about the system being audited. He or she has to be sure that the program in the test is the actual production version. This approach is quite costly, since test data will be necessary for each system tested.

2. An auditor may create a parallel simulation, an audit program that simulates the software. The auditor's program processes the transactions files of the real system and compares the output of the simulated and production programs. This approach is quite costly in terms of labor.

Both of these techniques are static; they do not interfere with production programs in any way. There are also techniques that allow the auditor to test controls on a more continuous basis.

3. An integrated test facility involves the creation of an artificial entity and transactions that are processed against the entity; the auditor is creating a minicompany within the larger firm. Weiss calls this approach running test data in a live production environment.

4. A snapshot produces reports of key decision variables in a program at designated points in time. A snapshot requires the auditor to know a great deal about how a program works internally. Weiss recommends it especially when trying to understand questionable results in processing.

5. Standard programming languages usually offer some kind of tracing technique by which one can follow different variables in the program. Often the trace involves the auditor in reading and interpreting program code, a time-consuming task requiring an auditor who understands programming languages.

6. Mapping is used to generate a summary of how software was utilized—for example, a list of program statements not executed when the program was run. The auditor then relates the summary to the transactions file that the program processed.

Weiss argues that continuous techniques are better than static ones because they allow the auditor to become more involved with systems and to test them in a live environment. However, continuous auditing is more costly and requires greater knowledge on the part of the auditor.

Most computer-assisted auditing today is done using some form of parallel simulation. Major accounting firms have developed their own equivalent of 4GLs to allow auditors to sample data from computer files and to process these data in order to test the way production software functions.

Implications for IS Managers

The information services area will be audited; the auditor will focus on operational concerns and possibly will get involved in managerial control. The controls of interest to the auditor are quite important; the firm must process its basic transactions correctly if it is to stay in business.

From the standpoint of the CIO, control is a major problem at the strategic planning and managerial levels, especially in coordinating processing. External and probably internal auditors will not be of much help here.

An audit of application controls, systems development practices, and the data center itself will be helpful in pointing out areas where controls can be strengthened. IS management should act on these recommendations; disasters like those encountered by the Bank of New York are embarrassing and costly; they tend to undermine the credibility of information processing.

However, management cannot rely on the auditor; it must emphasize controls itself. Control is a key task of management; managers have the responsibility of controlling the organization in the broad sense discussed in this chapter.

Recommended Readings

Allen, B., "Make Information Services Pay its Way," *Harvard Business Review*, (January–February, 1987), pp. 57–63. (A thorough discussion of the arguments behind profit-center charging for IS.)

"Bank Blames Nightmare on Software Flop," *Computer World*, December 16, 1985. (An article describing the computer background of the Bank of New York clearing problem.)

Lawler, E., and J. Rhode, *Information and Control in Organizations*. Pacific Palisades, Calif.: Goodyear, 1976. (Presents Control from an organizational behavior standpoint.)

Markus, L., *Systems in Organizations*. Boston: Pitman, 1984. (See Chapter 2 on monitoring and control systems.)

McKell, L., J. Hansen, and L. Heitger, "Charging for Computing Resources," *Computing Surveys*, vol. 11, no. 2 (June 1979), pp. 105–120. (A comprehensive treatment of changing techniques.)

"A Computer Snafu Snarls the Handling of Treasury Issues," *The Wall Street Journal*, November 25, 1985. (An article on some of the financial effects of the Bank of New York's computer problem.)

Weber, R., *EDP Auditing: Conceptual Foundations and Practice*, 2nd ed. New York: McGraw-Hill, 1988. (An excellent textbook on information systems auditing.)

Weiss, I., "Auditability of Software: A Survey of Techniques and Costs," *MIS Quarteriy*, vol. 4, no. 4 (December 1980), pp. 39–50. (An important survey of techniques used for auditing computer systems.)

Discussion Problems

15.1 McTaggart and Company is a respected computer consulting firm located in Chicago. A few years ago, they were called by a CPA firm with offices in the same building. The CPAs had a serious problem. They had just been approached by a potential new client to conduct an audit.

The new client was an insurance firm, and most of its records were computerized. The CPAs had no computer background but badly needed the new account. Could McTaggart help? The CPA in charge of the new client described what was needed: "We have to be able to check outstanding computer systems like those for keeping track of policies and the ones used to pay losses. We will want to take random samples and then contact the policy holder to verify what we find in the records. How can we do all of this?"

The consultants at McTaggart agreed to help because they knew of an easy solution. What do you think it was?

15.2 Jason Williams was approached by an old friend and asked to help with a problem. Williams was an independent consultant in the information systems field. His friend, Lee Richards, was a brilliant and eccentric investor with a Ph.D. in mathematics.

Richards had found, through years of research, a way to perform nearly riskless arbitrage in the commodities futures markets. He had contacted a number of wealthy investors and managed several large funds. To actually implement his strategy, Richards hired three very bright programmers and bought a minicomputer for them to use in coding his "system."

Recently Richards had been audited, something that his clients required. The auditors were very concerned about the state of his computer system, and Richards wanted to hire Williams to help him. Williams reviewed the computer system and found the following situation:

1. The computer was located in an insecure wooden office building in an earthquake zone.
2. The building was not guarded and had no sprinkler system.
3. Because Richards was afraid that his strategy would be stolen, he did not allow programmers to make listings of their code; all debugging was done from the terminal. Only two people understood the computer code.
4. A backup tape for the computer was kept at the senior programmer's house.

What should Williams recommend to Richards?

Questions

1. What was the impact of the computer problem at the Bank of New York?
2. How could the bank have prevented the problem?
3. Describe the components of a control system.
4. What is the standard for management control?
5. What does control mean for senior managers?
6. What is managerial and financial control?
7. How do operating controls differ from senior management control?
8. Why do control systems often rely on computers?
9. How is planning for IS a form of control?
10. What is managerial control in the ISD?
11. Describe some operating controls in IS.
12. What are the advantages of a chargeout scheme for information services?
13. What are the disadvantages of a chargeout scheme for IS?
14. What characteristics should a chargeout plan for in IS have?
15. Why might IS not want to charge for some services?
16. Is there a way to prevent control failures in systems such as those used for missile warnings?
17. Why is systems design a part of control?
18. Is control easier in a batch or on-line system?
19. How can bad input corrupt a database?
20. How does an IS manager guard against unauthorized access? Is this problem likely to become more severe or less severe in the future?
21. How have computers made auditing more difficult?
22. What audit approach do you recommend for auditing computer systems?
23. Can an audit catch widespread fraud or collusion between information services and management, as in the famous Equity Funding scandal?
24. What is the role of technology like 4GLs in auditing information systems?
25. Why does management have to be concerned about control?

16

Capacity Planning

When computer systems are at their capacity limits, service to users generally declines. Poor service is added to users' frustrations with other aspects of information processing and contributes to the poor reputation of the ISD in many organizations. Managers responsible for the operation of information systems must be concerned with the capacity of their resources, the hardware and software systems that process information. Managers should also be aware of the fact that demand often seems to rise to meet new capacity!

There is some confusion among terms in this field. *Capacity management* is being aware and taking action to provide adequate capacity to operate systems at an agreed-upon level of service. A major part of managing capacity is planning; when will information services run out of capacity for processing? The manager of operations must always know how much capacity exists now, forecast how much will be needed in the future, and estimate when additional capacity will have to be added to existing systems.

Various performance evaluation techniques have been used for analyzing capacity problems and for projecting the capacity of a system. Each of these techniques has its strengths and weaknesses and, of course, has a different cost to the organization. In this chapter, we shall discuss some of the problems of capacity planning and offer suggestions for approaching this task.

Capacity Bottlenecks

Much of capacity planning and performance evaluation involves locating the bottleneck. What aspects of a computer system are likely to be saturated? Where can performance problems arise? Figure 16-1 attempts to identify typical points where a problem can reduce the capacity of the system or where a bottleneck can develop that limits capacity.

Figure 16-1 begins with terminals and a communications network. Communications networks are designed in a number of different ways, and the organization may have limited influence on their performance. For example, if a packet-switched common carrier is used, the organization is dependent on the carrier's network and interface equipment.

On the other hand, if the organization develops a private network with leased lines, the performance of the network is the organization's responsibility. The most likely problem for communications is not the line speed, but rather the volume of data and how they are processed by the computer.

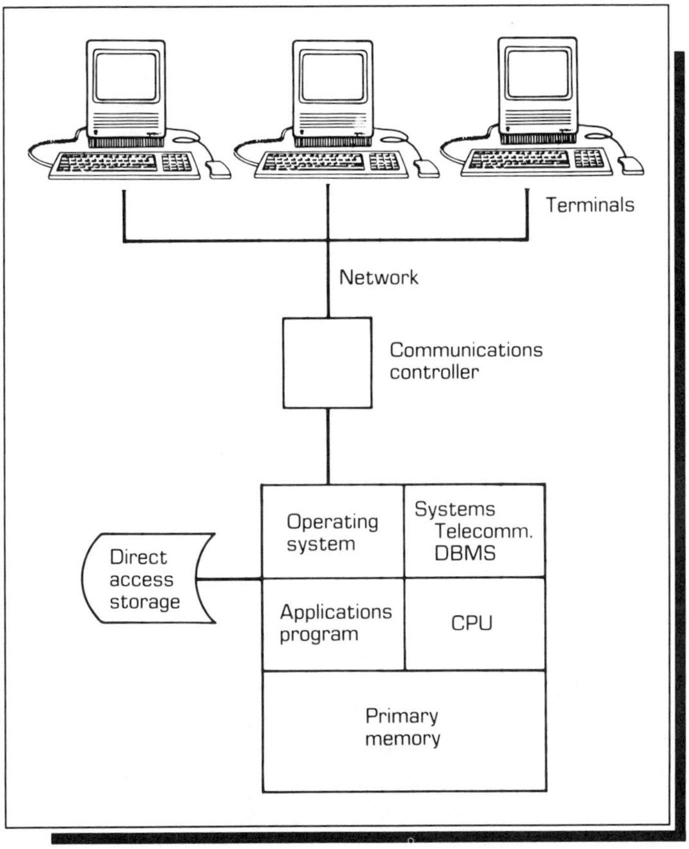

FIGURE 16-1 Potential capacity bottlenecks.

Between the network and the computer, there is usually some type of communications controller or front-end processor. This device is responsible for interfacing data between the terminals and the computer. It probably does some code conversion and to some extent manages the network.

The computer complex itself has two interacting components, which makes it hard to determine the reasons for capacity problems. On the software side, there is an operating system that manages the resources of the computer. There is also systems software—for example, a telecommunications monitor and a DBMS. All of this software interacts with applications software, the programs written by the organization itself (or purchased from a vendor), to accomplish a specific task. Software problems can lead to capacity constraints.

The software requires hardware in order to execute. The hardware system has three places where performance problems often occur: (1) the CPU, (2) primary memory, and (3) direct access storage. One way of looking at the hardware system is as a series of three queues. There is a queue at the CPU, at memory, and at direct access storage devices.

Since hardware and software are inextricably intertwined, a problem with the system is unlikely to involve just one of them. For example, many modern operating systems provide virtual storage. A combination of hardware and the operating system maps a very large virtual address space into a smaller physical address space. The operating system swaps pages of program code and data into and out of primary memory. If a system pages too much, it accomplishes little useful work; all of its efforts are devoted to moving pages from secondary to primary storage. Primary memory becomes the bottleneck because of this combined activity of hardware and software. Information services must be concerned about the interaction between hardware and software, as well as the effects of each component of a computer system alone.

Approaching the Problem

Figure 16-2 is a model showing how someone working on capacity planning might proceed. The first task is to identify the problem. How do we know there is a problem? What are the symptoms? Has response time decreased? Are runs taking longer than normal to complete? The analyst will want to collect data both to show that a problem exists and to help identify the cause of the problem.

Simple but very helpful data sources are the records maintained in operations. What has been the pattern of response times? Has it changed dramatically? How long are jobs taking to run to completion? What kinds of changes to the system are noted? Are there new applications? Is there a record of a new release of the operating system being installed?

The analyst may need to choose an evaluation technique to collect the data and help pinpoint the problem. A number of techniques are available and will be reviewed. Working with the data and an evaluation technique,

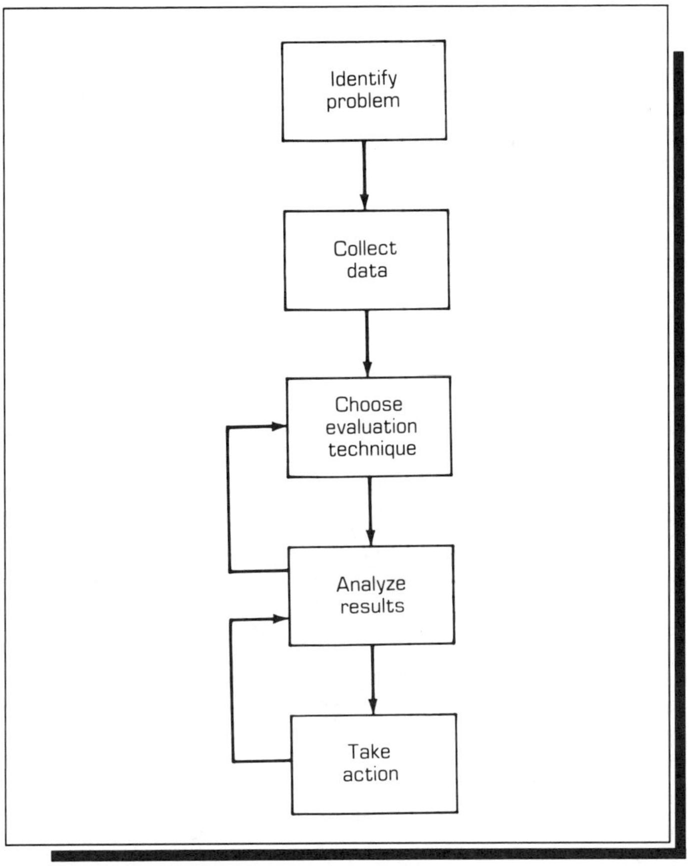

FIGURE 16-2 Capacity planning stages.

the analyst will look at the results to determine the cause of the problem. Finally, the analyst will take action and review the results.

This discussion suggests that the reason for capacity planning is to find a problem. Such is not necessarily the case; one may also look at the capacity of a system because one is planning to acquire it. In this case, the problem is one of assessing whether or not a planned system can meet the organization's needs. The data collection effort focuses on determining the requirements that will be placed on the system. The data and an evaluation technique are used to determine whether or not the proposed system has enough capacity for the organization.

Evaluation Techniques

Many techniques are used to evaluate the performance of computer systems. Each of them can be used for different purposes, though most are focused on one type of problem. In the next section, we shall map different evaluation techniques to the different types of situations that arise in capacity planning.

TABLE 16-1 Capacity Planning Options

Types of problems
System becomes overloaded
Sudden change in performance
Request for a new computer
New application being planned
Data collection sources
Operations statistics
Operating system statistics
Job accounting system
Software/hardware monitors
Applications characteristics
Evaluation techniques
Timings
Benchmarks/synthetic jobs
Models
Queuing
Simulation
Regressions/projections
Other systems

In this section, we shall look at data collection and evaluation techniques themselves. Table 16-1 summarizes the data collection and evaluation techniques that are most valuable in capacity planning.

Data Collection

One of the key tasks in capacity planning is to collect data on the problem. In many organizations, a great deal of data already exist to give the analyst a start.

Operations Statistics

It is hoped that the operations staff in the ISD keeps a record of certain performance statistics, like average response times during the day. There should also be data on problems that have occurred during processing and a record of changes to systems software. The analyst should be able to determine from operations what new applications are now being processed. If operations keeps a record of reports late and reports on time, this statistic over time can provide valuable information on how the system is performing.

Operating System Statistics

The operating system is likely to maintain statistics that can be used to determine what is happening in the system. For example, the analyst will be interested in whether paging rates have increased dramatically with some change in a systems program. A major change in input/output counts and/or the load on a data channel might indicate that there is a problem with an application accessing disk storage.

As an example, DEC provides a performance monitor for its VAX VMS operating system. The monitor keeps track of memory used, swap counts, average CPU modes, CPU and input/output overlap, and system and user paging rates per second. The monitor also records buffered input/output rates per second, file cache attempt effectiveness, lock rates, disk paging rates, disk queue lengths, disk server and paging rates, and disk server queue lengths. The user can display these data in tabular or graphic form as an aid to understanding how the system is performing.

Job Accounting Systems

A job accounting system is usually run for chargeback purposes; it also provides data that indicate the performance of the system. For example, the analyst can compare job accounting statistics for a mix of jobs now and in the past to determine if performance has changed. The accounting system can also provide data for evaluating the performance of some other computer system on the current workload.

Monitors

The analyst can connect a monitor to the system to gather statistics on performance. Hardware, software, and hybrid monitors are available. The software monitor interrupts execution of programs (thus creating overhead) to collect statistics on what is happening in the system. A hardware monitor comes with probes that the analyst connects to different parts of the computer to collect data. A hybrid monitor has both hardware and software features.

The difficulty with monitors is data analysis. A monitor can generate huge amounts of detailed data in a very short period of time. Summary programs are available and the analyst can use them, but one is left with a major data analysis chore. If we are trying to generalize to another system, a monitor is of limited value; monitors are most often used in tuning a system. Monitors are also limited because they can only show where a bottleneck exists. They have no way of demonstrating what will happen when that bottleneck is removed.

Application Characteristics

If the task is to determine how a new system will perform for the application, the source of data is the requirements analysis for the new application. The analyst will have to estimate things like the average and peak volume of transactions, the number of users on line at one time, file sizes and activities, and so on. These data will then be used to project or estimate the performance of a new system.

Evaluation Techniques

Given these data, the analyst may want to use an evaluation technique to help analyze the data. Some of the techniques are quite simple, while others require a major investment in time and funds.

Timings

Timings have been used since the first computers were marketed. There are two popular numbers in the popular press: MIPS and megaflops. *MIPS* stands for *millions of instructions per second* and is presented as a measure of raw speed. (One cynic also suggested that MIPS stands for *meaningless indicator of performance.*)

Megaflops is *million of floating point instructions per second* and is used for comparing the performance of supercomputers. Since supercomputers are used for scientific and engineering work, they are called upon to perform many floating point computations. Floating point arithmetic is more demanding than other types of instructions, so the megaflop reflects greater demands than a MIP.

A third measure is sometimes printed for micros: megahertz. A megahertz is 1 million hertz or 1 million cycles per second. Computers have clocks that govern the execution of instructions. A CPU on a chip that runs at, say, 8 megahertz should be faster than the same CPU run at 4.77 megahertz.

These timings are interesting for comparing computers if one is thinking of acquiring them. They are not very useful for evaluating the capacity or performance of a system that is already in house and operating. Timings are easy to obtain from published literature, but they are not very useful. A microcomputer's performance is determined by much more than the speed of its clock. A slower computer that fetches 32 bits at a time may turn out to be faster than a computer that has a higher clock speed but fetches only 16 bits.

In moving from micros to larger computers, there is much more that determines the performance of a minicomputer or mainframe that the number of instructions per second that the CPU is capable of executing. A supercomputer may be able to execute 500 or 1000 megaflops in a second, but this speed requires a very favorable program—for example, one that might have loops fitting within a high-speed vector processor on the computer.

Benchmarks/Synthetic Jobs

A benchmark is a program that is executed on a computer for comparison purposes. An advantage of a benchmark is that, if well developed, it offers information on the performance of hardware and software including the operating system. If we were planning to buy a new computer, we might take a benchmark program and compare its execution on the new computer with its execution on our existing computer. A synthetic program is like a benchmark, but it is not an actual production program. Instead the synthetic program is contrived to measure a variety of situations in the test.

Synthetic programs are used by different magazines to test new microcomputers. Since the micros generally execute one program at a time, the comparisons are reasonably valid in comparing speed on the synthetic jobs. However, if the computer will be used for purposes not well represented in the synthetic jobs, the results of the tests may not be useful.

For minis and mainframes, the task of testing with benchmarks of synthetic jobs becomes more complicated because multiple jobs are being processed at once on most of these machines. In one case, we were trying to evaluate a time-sharing computer that would run many jobs at once. We wrote a synthetic job typical of the kinds of tasks for which the machine would be used. The synthetic job was parameterized so that it could be made more demanding; for example, one part of the job was to invert a matrix; the size of the matrix could be increased easily.

We reserved time on a system similar to the one we planned to order and used a number of volunteers to start the synthetic job from a variety of terminals. We selected one terminal to use for timing and stationed an observer there with a stopwatch. We computed the time it took for the job to run to completion under varying loads and used this time to judge whether or not the system would be adequate.

For a mainframe computer running a large job mix, preparing an appropriate set of benchmarks or synthetic jobs is a major undertaking. Then the analysts must run the jobs under different conditions; they must also have enough jobs so that the operating system starts up and achieves a steady state, processing multiple jobs at one time.

Models

A model is a representation of reality. To some extent, the benchmark or synthetic job represents an empirical model. There are also more formal models that have been used successfully to evaluate computer systems. Models are particularly useful when one is trying to project the performance of a target system.

Mathematical models attempt to model the behavior of a system, frequently using queuing theory. In Figure 16-1 we discussed various queues that arise in a computer system such as the CPU, primary storage, and secondary storage. There has been some success in modeling these systems as a queuing network, or even as a sequence of independent queues.

Most organizations do not have a resident mathematician to develop a queuing model. However, there is at least one model that has been turned into a software package for commercial use. A firm provides parameters on its computer system and calibrates the model by comparing its output with a known workload. When the model's predictions match what actually happens on the system, it can be used for projecting performance. Of course, one always has to be careful in making extreme extrapolations; for small changes, the model is likely to be quite good. However, radical changes may perturb the parameters on which the model is based, so that the results will not be valid.

There are also simulation models of computer systems. For example, one computer vendor has a simulation model for its mid-range minicomputer line. This model accepts the characteristics of a planned application and predicts how different models of the computer will perform in executing that workload. The simulation happens to be based on several queues, and thus is a mixed queuing and simulation approach to predicting performance. Simulation models tend to require the analyst to collect a large amount of data, and their output can be difficult to interpret.

Sometimes simple statistical models are applied to data to aid in planning capacity. One might plot a regression line to fit response times for a system. If response times have been increasing, the extrapolation along the regression line might show the point at which response times will become unacceptable. For computer systems, performance tends to degrade exponentially. As a result, the analyst will probably use a logarithmic transformation in running the regression; the underlying model is an increasing exponential function.

Simple statistical models may be quite good for rough estimates of capacity. However, one has to be careful because the statistical analysis is responding to data; there is no underlying model of how the computer works. The model may be too conservative, since some hardware or software bottleneck could cause the system to run out of capacity well before the statistical analysis predicts a problem.

Other Systems

Other systems are not usually suggested as a method of evaluation. However, when buyers ask a vendor to size a computer, they often rely on that vendor's experience with other systems. An astute sales representative will attempt to locate other customers with a similar processing load and will use their computer as a guide in proposing a computer to the buyer.

An Example

A firm was considering the purchase of a software package for an on-line application involving order entry and customer service. There would be a large number of calls, and it was important for the system to perform well so that customers would not have to spend hours on the phone. The package would have to be modified, and the firm wanted to know if it should invest the money to buy and modify the system.

One major consideration, then, was the capacity of the system. Business was increasing, and a recent acquisition raised the possibility of combining computer systems. Could the package handle the processing load? When would the system run out of capacity?

The package ran on an IBM System 38. At the time of the evaluation, there was a relatively small line of System 38 computers, and their capacity was limited on the high end. There were many rumors about models that would increase the power of the line, but the firm did not want to make a commitment based on an unannounced product.

IBM engineers had developed a simulation model of the System 38 based on queuing theory. By providing the model with extensive data on transactions volumes, number of terminals, file accessing requirements, and so on, the model could be used to predict response time. The user of the model first parameterized it to ensure that the model accurately predicted present response times given the present load. It was then possible to run experiments in which the CPU was replaced with a more powerful version, added disk, and/or added memory.

A noncompetitive company was using the package and agreed to provide statistics for the IBM model. The other firm's environment was similar to the one of the company interested in buying the package, so the input for the model would be representative. The testing showed that the application package could run for the foreseeable future without demanding a computer with capacity beyond those currently in the System 38 line.

This analysis of response times and system capacity played a major part in the decision to acquire the package. An interesting aspect of this example is the variety of techniques employed. We would expect to find mixes of data collection and evaluation mechanisms used to solve a capacity problem. In this instance, the firm used its own application characteristics to decide that the other firm's use of the package provided adequate data for testing. Then the analysts utilized a performance evaluation model that included simulation and mathematical queuing theory. In complex situations, there should be considerable creativity in capacity planning.

An Overview of Planning

Figure 16-3 presents three different types of capacity planning problems. Remember that *capacity* is the ability of the computer software and hardware system to do work and provide service at some targeted level. *Service* usually means (1) acceptable response times and (2) a reasonable length of time to process jobs for users. Basically service levels reflect the ability of the

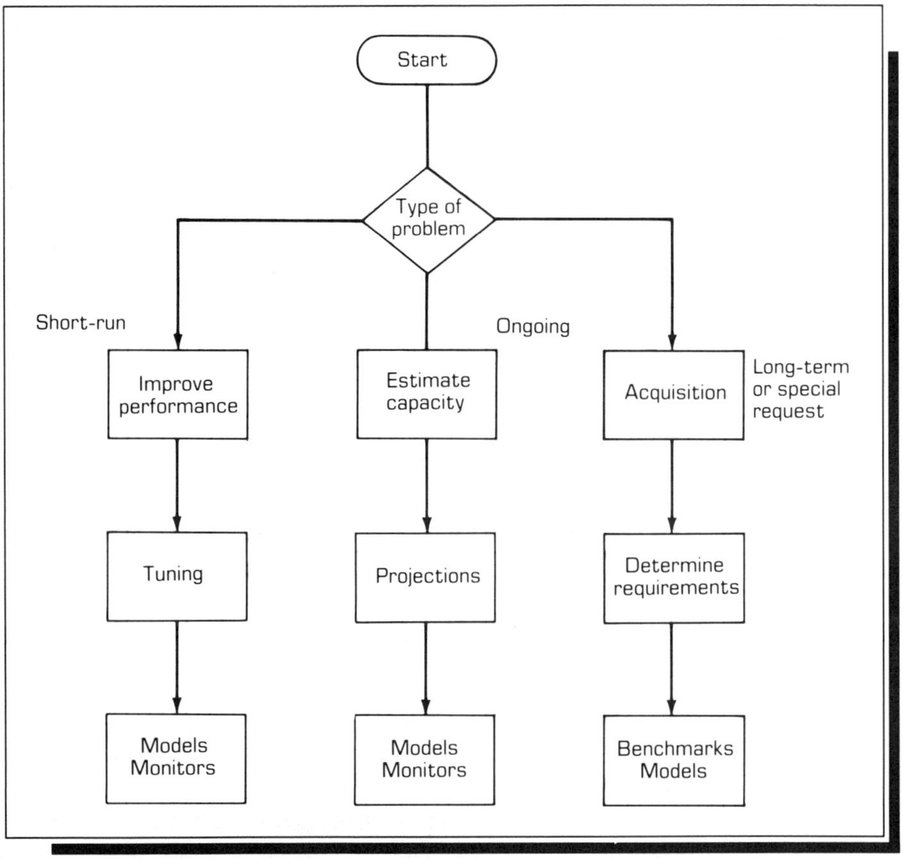

FIGURE 16-3 Capacity planning overview.

system to meet processing deadlines. *Adequate capacity* means not running out of space for data as well.

Short-Run Considerations

In the short run, IS may be trying to improve its performance because of the lead time to increase capacity. Alternatively, there may be no more budget for improvements, so it is necessary to increase existing capacity.

There may also have been a sudden drop in performance. Something has happened to reduce the capacity of the system. For example, a new application may have been added that takes a great deal of capacity; this application is responsible for reducing response times on the computer for all currently operating applications.

Much of this short-range work is aimed, then, at an immediate improvement in performance. Systems programmers may try to tune the system by changing various parameters for the operating system or by changing access patterns for secondary storage. How do they obtain data and ideas on what to tune?

For tuning, one could use almost all of the data collection sources described previously, including job accounting systems, operations statistics, operating system statistics, and even a software or hardware monitor. To analyze these data, the systems programmer might make use of statistical analysis. If the firm maintains a model of the system, it can check the model's projections against actual experience to see if what is being observed is predicted.

Tuning tends to be experimental and empirical. If the system is very sensitive to the mix of jobs, tuning will be quite difficult. The system will be tuned for one set of conditions and may not perform well when conditions change. Some people argue that with cheap hardware, it does not make sense to spend a lot of time and effort tuning a system. However, when one is about to run out of capacity and a new computer installation is months away, tuning may be the only way to salvage the system.

New Jersey Registration System

Could tuning and capacity planning during the development of the New Jersey auto registration and licensing system have prevented the disaster that occurred when the system was installed? A consulting firm had the contract for designing and programming the system. The firm chose to use a 4GL, Ideal, for virtually all of the programs in the system.

When the system was installed, response times were terrible and the computer was unable to complete overnight processing in the time available. With any on-line system, response time is a key consideration. First, the system should have been tested under a heavy on-line load. Second, volume tests should have shown that the overnight batch programs took too long to process.

Using simple statistics from the operating system or even a stopwatch at terminals should have shown that there were problems. The next task would have been to find the programs that were responsible. Some people suggest that the 80–20 rule is a law of nature. Usually 80 per cent of a firm's sales come from 20 per cent of its customers, and so on. It is likely that 80 per cent of the processing in the New Jersey system came from 20 per cent of the programs. The design itself should have provided some information on what programs were expected to be most active. Alternatively, simply monitoring the execution of the most frequently run programs would have identified candidates for rewrite in COBOL. If this procedure turned out to be difficult for some reason, a monitor could have been used to collect data.

Tuning can be used in a variety of ways to improve performance and stretch capacity. Capacity is an issue when a system is operational, but it is also important during design. Capacity planning begins with the development of the system.

Ongoing Capacity Considerations

One responsibility of ISD management is to avoid running out of capacity. Capacity planning on an ongoing basis is a requirement for good management in information services. In Figure 16-3, the operations staff should always know when systems will become saturated and should have an orderly plan for adding capacity.

This type of capacity planning involves both an analysis and a projection of current capacity and an analysis of the capacity offered by new equipment. The first task is to plot current workloads and project them into the future. Then the analyst must look at the capacity of the present system, probably in terms of data storage and processing power.

TWA has prepared such an analysis for the backup processor for its on-line reservations system. Since the backup processor is occasionally used on-line, TWA has good data on its performance. The airline has a graph (Figure 16-4) that shows approximately what year and month a new backup computer will be necessary.

Operations management will probably use relatively simple statistics for projecting performance; the job accounting system, operating systems statistics, and the operational statistics that the firm keeps are good tools to provide data for projecting performance.

The firm may want to keep a parameterized model of its systems as an aid to locating the point at which they become saturated. Particularly for a system with extensive on-line processing, a model will help show when response times become too long. In the absence of a formal model, statistical projections of current data can be used to judge when new capacity has to be added.

It is important for management to understand that additional equipment will always be necessary. Too often managers approve a computer with the feeling that it is the last one they will need. Two things combine to make new equipment purchases almost guaranteed. First, there is technological progress. New computers that are more powerful and less expensive are continually being announced. By raising maintenance prices and withdrawing support, vendors eventually force customers to move up to new machines.

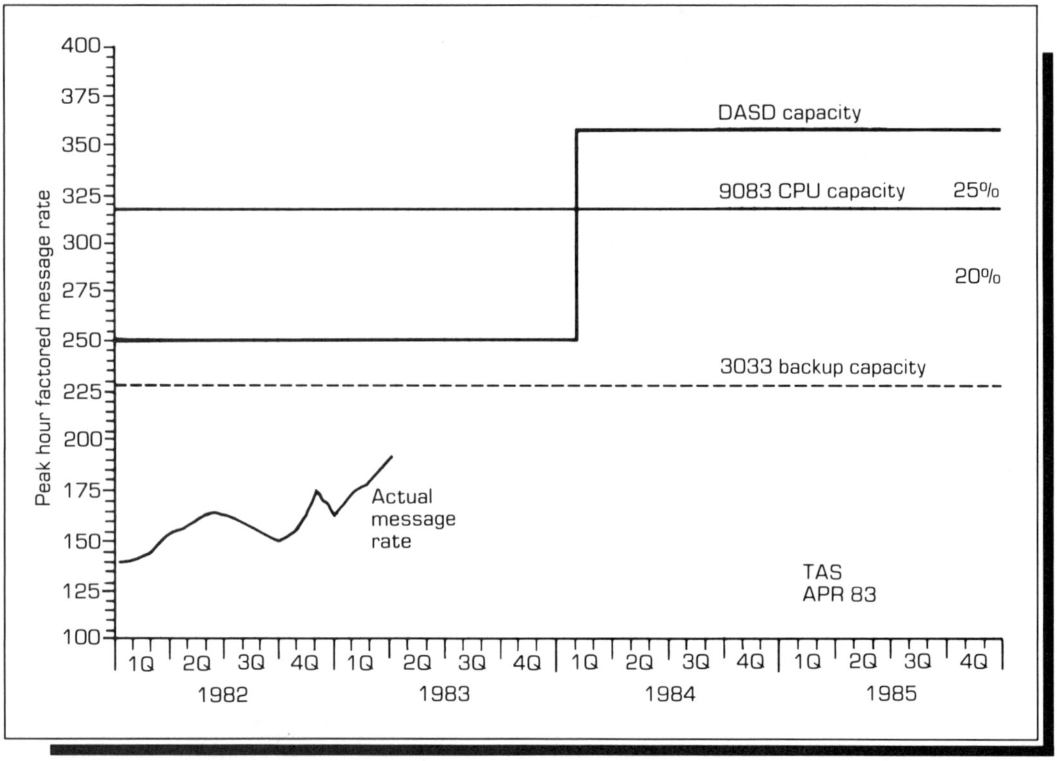

FIGURE 16-4 PARS system capacity and message volume projections. The graph shows the actual transaction rate (solid line) and the predicted transaction rate (dotted line) for the TWA system. The DASD capacity line indicates the maximum transaction processing rate that can be sustained by TWA's disk configuration. Note the anticipated disk configuration change in the first quarter of 1984. The 9083 and 3033 capacity lines indicate the maximum transaction rates that can be sustained by each of those processors. (From Gifford and Spector, 1984)

Second, even without the impetus provided by vendors, firms are continually adding computer applications. Rarely is a system discontinued, so the workload on the system constantly increases. Even if there are few new applications, a growing business generates more data for processing. An orderly plan for expanding capacity to keep up with demand should help senior management understand why it is asked to buy so many new computers.

Longer-Term/Special Request

A capacity plan will show upgrades of various types, for example, the purchase of more direct access storage. At some point in the plan, there will be a need to replace or add computer power. Information services may also receive requests from users to help evaluate computers for purchase.

Acquisition of equipment is a major part of capacity planning. The first task here is to define the requirements for the system. If a user who asks for help plans to use a micro only for word processing and an analyst can see no other use for a micro for this individual, recommendations will be very different than if the user really needs a multifunction workstation.

In the case of a mini or mainframe for a data center, the workload is probably known and is approximated well by the existing workload in the center. Under these conditions, one might make use of benchmarks. However, in the case of a replacement, it is fairly typical to simply take the vendor's next larger computer. The question that then arises is, how many sizes larger?

If a computer is being added to gain more capacity, how does one decide on its size? In the absence of capacity planning, the decision will be fairly arbitrary. With a capacity plan, the analyst can project when this computer will become saturated and determine if it is better to order a larger model now, or if the computer under consideration will provide adequate capacity far enough into the future.

A Capacity Plan

There are many ways to present the capacity plan itself. This section presents an outline of the contents of such a plan.

Service-Level Objectives

In this part of the plan, the ISD describes its objectives for service. An example might be average response times on line during the day of 3 seconds or less and a peak hour average of 6 seconds or less.

Another objective could be to have 98% of reports delivered to users on time. Batch job turnaround might be targeted at some figure, depending on the size of the program. There may be specific requirements for the firm, such as having all warehouse picking slips ready by 7:30 A.M.

Current Status

This part of the plan describes the current status of operations. What are the major demands for processing? Describe the key applications and what they require. For example, information services might include a graph showing that on the average, 85,000 on-line transactions per day were processed last month. The data might break down into the major systems, such as order entry and factory floor work in process tracking.

This section also contains a list of the resources available to process the data. The list should be presented in layman's terms, with details on models in an appendix, if they are needed at all. Keep the description of equipment simple; for example: "We operate an IBM 3090 mainframe, which is a very powerful computer. We run the MVS operating system, which provides users with a great deal of apparent memory. This feature makes the operating system very sensitive to the amount of real memory on the computer. We also have 25 billion characters of on-line data storage, of which about 19 billion are in everyday use. Some 250 terminals are connected to the computer over our own leased line network."

Project Demand

Next, describe significant new applications that are scheduled for completion. What demands will these new applications place on processing? Then, using the combined demands of existing and old systems, prepare a plot that shows workload against the projected capacity of the computer. The y axis is some measure of workload, like the number of transactions processed, and the x axis is time. A line parallel with the x axis shows the capacity of the computer; where this line comes close to the workload line, capacity is too low. It may be desirable to have a graph for different aspects of capacity—for example, one for the CPU and primary memory, one for direct access storage, and even one for communications.

Acquisition Schedule

The plan should conclude with a recommended acquisition schedule for the next 3 years. This schedule should be keyed to capacity bottlenecks so that the reader can see how the recommended equipment prevents a bottleneck from causing performance to deteriorate. It might also be useful to note the installation of new applications in the analysis, as it is these applications, combined with increasing volumes for existing applications, that create the demand for new capacity.

Capacity at CMI

Tom White has been working with all of the ISD managers at CMI to develop orderly capacity plans. He wants local management to know about and approve a schedule for capacity upgrades as demands increase on their systems. Lately he has been concerned about end users and their seemingly insatiable appetite for microcomputers.

"These things are proliferating all over the place, with no planning and no plicies on brands," he told a meeting of all ISD managers from the divisions. "What will happen when you want to network them?"

The ISD managers recognized the problem but had no solutions in mind. The Omaha manager suggested that they all assign at least one person as a personal computer coordinator. This individual would be a contact point for users.

White agreed, but wanted them to go even further. "If you don't have some kind of information center now, you had better set aside a room and have your consultant staff it. The room should have a variety of microcomputers that are on the corporate list for approval so that users can try them out."

The Fremont manager replied: "Where is the list of computers that meet with corporate approval? I've never seen it."

"We have to develop it, and if you all agree, we shall go to work and bring it back to you for approval."

Mary Watson from Charleston asked, "Tom, that's fine, but I don't have too much trouble keeping users to an approved list. However, how do we tell them what size and capabilities they need in a micro? I can't spend $25,000 worth of effort to evaluate the needs of a user and the performance of a computer that costs $3000."

Tom thought and said, "What would you all think of us at corporate headquarters coming up with some guidelines? We'll look at the popular magazines and get some timing comparisons on the machines. Given the reviews of products in the magazines, maybe we can come up with a series of profiles of users with a recommended computer and peripherals. If we have to, we'll set up a few simple benchmarks that come from our own people.

"We could do a big spreadsheet, say 8 or 10 operations on a big document in a word processor, and some kind of database problem where we join relations, update, sort, and print some big files.

"Then we could publish recommended computers for each of our profile users and publish the results of our benchmarks."

The other managers agreed that if corporate headquarters would do it, they would use the results. The rest of the meeting was spent developing four user profiles and soliciting requests for benchmarks to be used in the evaluation. From this, Tom White hoped to develop a policy on micros for the firm, along with a plan on how users might progress from a low-level micro to one with greater capacity as their needs grew.

Recommended Readings

Anderson, G., "The Coordinated Use of Five Performance Evaluation Methodologies," *Communications of the ACM,* vol. 27, no. 2 (February 1984), pp. 119–125. (An interesting paper that shows how one can bring more than one technique to bear on a performance problem.)

Dickson, G., and J. Wetherbe, *The Management of Information Systems.* New York: McGraw-Hill, 1985. (See especially the chapter on capacity planning.)

Lucas, H. C., Jr., "Performance Evaluation and Monitoring," *Computing Surveys,* vol. 3, no. 3 (September 1971), pp. 79–91. (An early article that presents a framework for when various performance evaluation techniques are most suitable.)

Discussion Problems

16.1 Cumberland Associates is a medium-sized consulting firm in Los Angeles. The firm at first rented computer time on a time-sharing system. When personal computers were first offered for sale, several partners bought them and noticed that their need for time sharing dropped dramatically.

Soon the firm had switched almost entirely to personal computers; there was very little demand for time sharing. However, several partners decided that it would make sense to install an electronic mail system, so Cumberland began to look at an in-house time-sharing system. At first, the firm thought that it might subscribe to a common carrier. However, a few of the newer associates were used to having the extra power of a minicomputer from their college days.

Thinking about new uses for time sharing plus the interest in electronic mail, Cumberland decided that it would acquire its own time-sharing system for mail purposes and general computation. However, the firm wondered how, after so many years without using a computer in house, it could determine what capacity it needed for a machine. What can you recommend?

16.2 A major investment bank and brokerage firm decided that it was taking far too long to develop all of its applications in COBOL. As a replacement, the bank invested in a DBMS that came with its own 4GL. The bank began to use the 4GL for almost all of its new development work.

Programmers and analysts were pleased with their enhanced productivity. However, operations management was faced with a real problem. "We know how to predict the rate of applications development when COBOL is the language; however, it's a different world now. Not only are we unfamiliar with the demands of the 4GL, but the systems group is now turning out so many more systems in a shorter period of time."

How can the bank anticipate the demand for computing hardware and provide adequate capacity in this changing environment?

Questions

1. What are the major bottlenecks in a computer system?
2. How does the operating system affect overall performance?
3. What is capacity management?
4. Where does the analyst expect queues to develop in a computer system?
5. What is paging, and how can it affect performance?
6. Where does one look for statistics on systems performance?
7. How does a job accounting system provide data on performance?
8. What kinds of monitors exist? How are they used?
9. What is the drawback with timings?
10. What is a benchmark? How does it differ from a synthetic job?
11. What are the problems in using a queuing model for performance evaluation?
12. How can one learn about performance from looking at other systems?
13. What were the major problems with the New Jersey registration system?
14. How could the consultant have solved the New Jersey system's problems before the system was installed?
15. What are service level objectives?

16. How should the firm project the demand for computing?
17. Why does there always seem to be a demand for more computing capacity?
18. What capacity planning approach applies to evaluating personal computers?
19. What special problems does evaluation of the performance of a software package present to a potential customer?
20. Of what use are the benchmarks published for microcomputers in popular trade magazines?

17

The Acquisition of Hardware, Software, and Services

The nature of the computing industry has changed dramatically as it has passed through various stages of technological development. Vendors of computer equipment, software, and services have had to change the way they do business and the types of products and services they offer.

In the early days of computing, one could rent or buy a computer from a vendor. Most early mainframe computers were rented because of fears of technological obsolescence. Later, firms began to buy the CPU and primary memory, while renting peripherals. (The CPU and memory became known as the *mainframe* at that point.) Companies entered the leasing business so that a firm could obtain the benefits of lower monthly payments for a computer, and the leasing firm could gain the benefits from depreciating the computer.

A few companies entered the package software business; they looked for applications that were common across an industry, for example, systems in banking that a bank might be interested in buying instead of developing itself.

In the 1960s, the most exciting business was time sharing. Most ISDs were interested in batch processing and large transactions-oriented systems. If a manager wanted a system to use on an occasional basis interactively, there was little interest on the part of ISD in providing service. Managers of operations did not want unreliable time-sharing systems bringing down the mainframe.

Outside service vendors took advantage of this situation to offer time-sharing systems to a variety of users. The user gained access to some programs but was primarily interested in raw computing power. Batch processing service bureaus continued to offer services to firms with too little capacity or no computer at all. Package vendors also continued to the development of software, but there was great resistance to buying a program written by someone outside of the organization. Users feared that the program would not meet their requirements, and ISD staff members did not want to maintain someone else's code.

As minicomputers began to appear, time-sharing vendors had to change their approach. A minicomputer with a time-sharing operating system could support a number of users in house for a fraction of the cost of external time-sharing services. Aggressive time-sharing bureaus began to develop proprietary programs and databases to secure their customer base. These problems for time sharing were exacerbated by the micro; few people today want to buy raw computer time from a time-sharing vendor.

During this period, the package industry changed dramatically. Early package vendors sold to the ISD; the packages improved with each new release. Companies' interest in packages has been increasing steadily due to the high cost and lengthy time required to develop new applications.

The micro opened a mass market for software vendors. New companies have arisen that deal exclusively in micro software. Since the micro package is relatively inexpensive, say from $100 to $800 on the average, a vendor cannot afford to teach the customer how to use the package or to offer on-site consulting. As a result, the packages have been designed with elaborate help screens and manuals; for the most part, they are self-taught. Support consists, in most cases, of telephone consultation.

User-friendly micro packages have set new standards for software packages; they have also helped convince users to look for a package as opposed to a custom design when considering other applications. All of these developments and trends have led to the situation today, in which there is great interest in avoiding custom programming—just the opposite of where the field began.

Because of the proliferation of computers throughout the organization and widespread interest in distributed processing, a large number of individuals are involved in decisions on the acquisition of computer hardware, software, and services. Policies and procedures for acquisition differ in each organization; in this chapter, we approach the acquisition problem from the standpoint of an ISD and the firm as a whole. Many of the concepts presented in the chapter can be applied to the case of a departmental computer center or even an individual user of a microcomputer.

Alternatives for an Application

First, we shall look at an application alone; the next section deals with the acquisition of equipment, software, and services. In this section, we assume that a computer already exists on which to run the application.

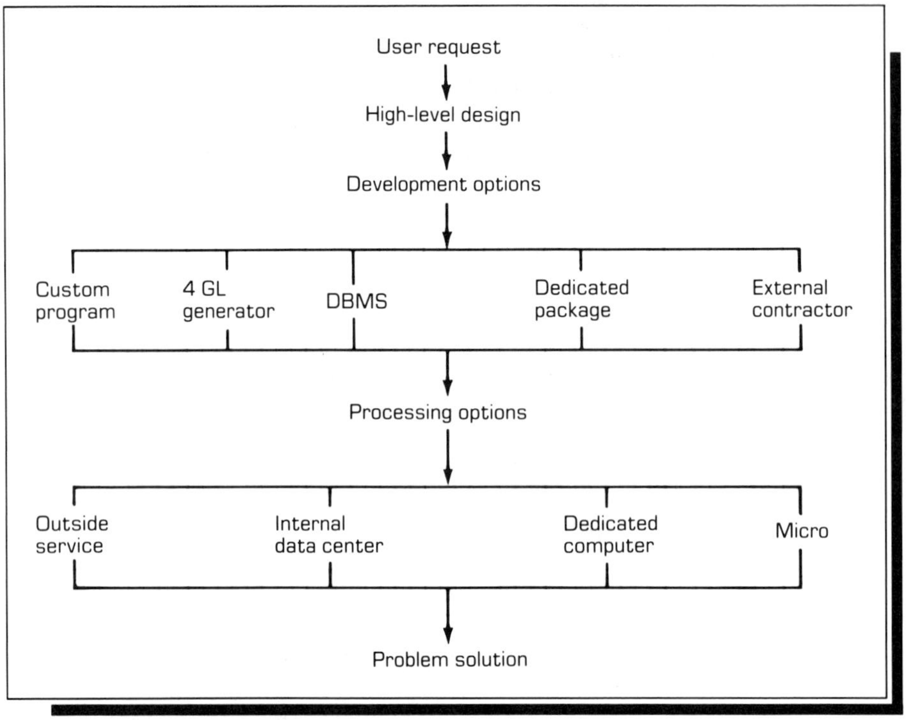

FIGURE 17-1 An application.

The acquisition of hardware, software, and services is closely related to other aspects of the management of information services, especially systems analysis and design. In particular, designers must consider the "make versus buy" option when evaluating a request for an information system. Given the shortage of systems analysis personnel and the time required to develop a custom system, combined with advances in software packages, a designer is obligated to search for and consider a packaged software solution for a requested system.

Figure 17-1 shows the development of an application. The process begins with a request from a user. ISD staff and the user work together to develop a high-level design. This design should describe the major objectives for the system and list input and output. It should define the contents of the database and major relations among the entities stored in the database.

One does not have to go to the level of detail needed to program the system, but there should be enough detail so that a reader can determine the important functions of the system by reading the high-level specifications. Why bother with this step if one is considering a package? Why not just look at the package?

One problem in buying software of any kind is comparing what the software vendor offers with what is needed. Without our own specifications, it is easy to be swayed by features in the package that are not needed. One can also overlook the absence of an important feature if there is no specification for comparison purposes. The specification becomes a type of benchmark; it is the blueprint against which one can evaluate different alternatives for developing an application.

Development Options

Figure 17-1 shows a series of development options that the design team must evaluate. The ISD staff acts as a consultant in this process; it provides the expertise needed to delineate and evaluate options.

One option is obviously a custom program or system. Historically, this option has been popular, especially for mainframe systems. However, the user may be willing to settle for fewer functions in order to have a system running sooner. The custom programming option will almost always be considered, as it becomes the basis for comparing the advantages of alternatives.

The development team can achieve a great deal of what the user wants, possibly at some cost in execution speed or response time, through the use of a 4GL or an applications generator. It is quite possible that for micros, this option should include the user's doing the actual development. Users may also develop applications in 4GLs for mainframe systems if they have the expertise, time, and interest.

A DBMS may offer the tools to build an application for a user. Especially on micros, these packages come close to being applications generators. They feature the ability to define menus as well as data relations, and to create a menu-driven application that looks a great deal like a custom-programmed system.

The dedicated package is an attractive alternative if one can be found. The user is likely to give up a few functions, and it may be necessary to modify the package to make it acceptable. A final option is to hire an external contractor or consultant to develop a system. Often when internal resources are unavailable, the outside consultant is the only alternative if a system is needed.

Acquisition Considerations

Assume that none of the tools for these options exists in house at the time. How does one go about acquiring them? In the case of customer programming, there should be little acquisition unless there is no language compiler. For most applications, one would choose the language that is already in use in the firm. For a specialized application like an expert system (ES), it would be necessary to evaluate the various languages and ES shells available in order to choose a particular product.

This evaluation should be done by looking at the demands for the application and then reviewing the capabilities of each product. A good comparison mechanism is a matrix in which the rows are features needed and the columns are different options—in this instance, different ES shells

TABLE 17-1 A Comparison Matrix

Feature	Vendor 1	Vendor 2	Vendor 3	. . . Vendor *n*
Performance				
Functions				
Time horizon				
⋮				
Cost				

and languages. See Table 17-1. If it is likely that the product acquired will be used for other applications, there will be features to consider beyond the ones for the current system.

The acquisition of a 4GL or a generator extends beyond the current application; one of these tools will definitely be used for other applications. Therefore, one will need to develop a number of general evaluation criteria in addition to those for the present application. Since this tool is likely to have a dramatic effect on the organization, the ISD should review a number of options and be sure its decision is a good one.

If the firm needs to acquire a DBMS, a full-scale study is probably necessary. For mainframes, a DBMS is a several hundred thousand dollar decision. Even for micros, when training and the need for multiple copies are considered, the cost of a DBMS is high.

For the external contractor, the specifications become the basic document for estimating the price and duration for the project. ISD staff members need to check vendor references and contact some past clients to determine the consultant's past performance.

Processing Options

Figure 17-1 shows some of the processing options available for the new system. An outside service is possible, though it is not the most frequently chosen option. When investigating outside services, one needs to talk to a random sample of customers to determine their satisfaction with service. What does the external service provide? How well does it run applications?

The internal data center is often the recommendation of the ISD staff. After all, the firm has made an investment in computers; if they are not fully utilized, the marginal cost of adding an application is quite small. Some applications will require a dedicated computer. An extremely large application will require its own computer(s), for example, a nationwide on-line system. Another application might require a mini or a micro to be dedicated to it because of the importance of the application or the amount of processing it requires. A factory might have a minicomputer dedicated to analyzing quality control data. Although it will not function at capacity, management wants the machine available with good response times whenever a quality control staff member needs it.

Acquisition Considerations

Later in the chapter, we shall discuss the acquisition of hardware in more detail. With the exception of the outside service option, each of the processing alternatives in Figure 17-1 may necessitate the acquisition of hardware. In addition to software considerations, then, the design team may have to become involved in the evaluation and selection of hardware.

The order of decision making in Figure 17-1 is important because the hardware decision may not be necessary. If the ISD chooses a dedicated package as the way to develop the system, they may find that it runs only on a particular computer. In fact, the package may require the entire computer, so that what one is buying is a problem solution rather than a package.

An Example

A garment manufacturing firm wanted to update its computer systems. The primary application was order entry, followed by accounting and sales reporting. The systems were old and ran in batch processing mode. The firm developed a high-level specification for a set of integrated applications including order entry, warehouse picking slip generation, shipping, accounts receivable, sales analysis, and finished goods inventory.

The design team sent the specifications to a number of computer vendors, expecting some of them to join with software houses for a complete proposal. The president of the firm also suggested sending the proposal to a software vendor whose advertisement he had seen in a garment industry magazine.

This software vendor had a series of applications designed specifically for garment manufacturers and sales firms. If the firm was small, it used a time-sharing computer run by the software vendor and paid for by the transactions. As the volume of transactions increased, it became more economical for the customer to buy a computer and the software, and to run the system internally.

The functions included in the software offered by this vendor encompassed almost everything desired by the garment firm; it also contained other modules, like work-in-process and raw materials inventory control, which had not even been included in the original specifications.

The design team reviewed the system extensively through demonstrations and visits to clients who were using the package. The designers also visited several clients of the computer hardware vendors who had responded to the request for a bid. They looked at several systems that were typical of what might result from cooperation between a software and a hardware vendor.

The vendor recommended by the president was judged to have a superior package. The design team, however, was concerned about the hardware on which it ran. This hardware was not popular for commercial processing, though it was used in a number of engineering applications. The hardware vendor did not have a good reputation for service, so it was necessary to contact users of the computer to gain their assessment of its reliability and service. The overall quality of the software was so high, however, that the designers decided to purchase the package and to accept the last-choice hardware. Fortunately, the hardware and package have performed well.

This example illustrates how the industry has changed. The design team at first expected to buy a new computer and to hire a staff to implement the system. There were doubts about whether the firm had enough skill to manage the development of such a major system, and in fact, it might have had to turn to an outside contractor to develop the application. The package, however, was in its third or fourth version and was written by individuals who knew the garment industry; the package was good and it already existed. Because it had been used extensively by other customers, the code was well debugged. The software, then, became the overriding criterion in making the choice, with hardware relegated to last place.

Hardware and Software Acquisition

Table 17-2 describes considerations in the acquisition of hardware and software.

Hardware

With hardware, there are two common approaches to acquisition: moving up with one's current vendor or issuing a request for proposal (RFP) to a group of vendors. Moving up with the vendor is frequently the course followed for mainframes or even minicomputers. For example, if the firm has a data center with a large number of UNISYS computers, the staff is

TABLE 17-2 Hardware and Software Acquisition

Acquire	Mainframe	Mini	Micro
Hardware CPU Storage Peripherals	RFP or move up with current vendor	RFP or move up with current vendor	Magazines, retail stores, internal personal computer store
Software			
Systems	Vendor	Vendor	Standard
Compilers	Vendor	Vendor or software firm	Vendor or software firm
4GL	Vendor or software firm	Software firm	Software firm
Generators	Software firm	Software firm	Software firm
DBMS	Software firm	Software firm	Software firm
Problem oriented	Software firm	Software firm	Software firm
Dedicated package	Software firm	Software firm	Software firm

TABLE 17-3 RFP for Hardware

1. Workload
    - Present and planned applications
        - Database requirements
        - On-line requirements
            - Terminals and types
        - Processing load
            - Total transactions by application
            - Peak transactions volumes
2. Network and communications requirements
3. Modularity and expansion
4. Operating system
5. Schedule
6. Evaluation
7. Vendor instructions

familiar with the UNISYS environment. There is a strong tendency to add new UNISYS computers or to upgrade existing ones, such as by adding a new processor and memory.

If one does not feel bound to a current vendor, it is necessary to undertake some research. There are a number of new computer vendors offering unique architectures; a firm has many options to consider in acquiring hardware. Table 17-3 outlines an RFP that might be sent to different vendors.

The first step is to describe the workload, both present and planned. The vendor is interested in sizing the equipment proposed; can the computer under consideration handle the workload and have some extra capacity for growth? To answer these questions, the vendor must have an idea of the demands placed on the equipment. Thinking back to our discussion of performance in the last chapter, the characteristics of processing that affect performance include the size of the database, the number of terminals, and transactions volumes, both total and peak load.

The vendor will need this information for current applications and those that are planned for the computer under consideration. In addition, telecommunications and networking are extremely important today; an RFP should discuss plans and lay out requirements for the kinds of network connections expected.

Systems designers are very interested in modularity and expansion. Can they simply add more memory and another processor if our workload expands? At what point will the firm outgrow this computer and have to replace it entirely? Some vendors offer systems that are quite modular; one can add capacity in small increments. DEC and UNISYS, for example, have an excellent reputation for supporting the same computer architecture across their lines of computers, so that it is easy to move to a larger machine if necessary. IBM, on the other hand, has several different architectures, ranging from its micros to the mid-range line of System 36 and System 38 and finally to its minis and mainframes of the 370 class. Moving from a System 38 to a 4300 is a nontrivial task compared with moving from one model of DEC's VAX to another.

Operating systems are not hardware, but they are such an integral component of hardware that they should be considered in an RFP. With DEC one is dealing with VMS across all of its VAX computers. With IBM, the System 38 has one operating system and the 370 machine language computers have at least three operating systems, depending on how one defines a distinct version of an operating system.

The RFP should contain a schedule for replying to the bids, for a decision to be made, and for the installation of the computer. It is also helpful to provide the vendor with information on what evaluation criteria will be used to judge the competing proposals. Finally, the RFP may include instructions to the vendor on the format of the response.

Evaluation

Once vendors have sent responses, the ISD staff must evaluate them. Evaluation should focus on the areas of most concern. In the preceding garment company example, evaluation of system performance was easy because it was possible to visit a manufacturing firm with similar volumes that was using the system. The computer proposed was larger than the one at the firm visited, so there were few concerns about hardware performance. Because of worries about hardware service and reliability, the design team had to obtain a list of other users of the equipment and check with them about these concerns.

The most difficult and expensive evaluation effort takes place if system performance is in doubt and it is necessary to test the system. In most instances, the vendor will try to match the customer's processing profile with that of another firm to demonstrate that the vendor's equipment can handle the load. If the application is unique or the computer is quite new (as is the case with some of the special machines now being constructed with large numbers of processors), a formal evaluation effort with benchmarks and synthetic jobs may be necessary.

If dominant criteria like the features of the operating system, communications capabilities, storage capacity, or modularity do not rule out vendors, leaving only one who meets the requirements, the ISD staff will have to go through a decision process to select the winner. A comparison chart such as the one suggested in Table 17-1 can be used for this purpose. The first version of the chart describes the offerings and capabilities of the final contenders on the firm's key evaluation criteria. If the selection is not obvious from this listing, the vendors can be scored subjectively on a scale of 1 to 7 for each feature. Weight the features on importance, multiply the weights by the scores, and sum to get a total for each vendor. Whatever the results, review the ratings and the overall picture of each vendor, and use the numbers as one part of the decision; the most important thing is to gain a consensus on what makes the most sense for the firm.

Micros

Table 17-2 suggests that one is not likely to issue an RFP for micros. For the purchase of individual micros, it is not worth the effort to put together a formal proposal. The sources of most information here are industry magazines, personal computer stores, and habit. The firm may have established a policy of supporting a certain number of brands, and the user is strongly encouraged to purchase one of them. Consultants in the ISD or a personal computer store in the company provide advice, given the user's plans for the system.

There may be a time when the firm wants to negotiate a volume purchase agreement or purchase a large number of micros. In this instance, it will have to prepare an RFP. Since software is important for micros as well, the user will indicate what functions must be performed by software that is to be included by the vendor. Typically with a micro, one wants at least a spreadsheet program, a word processor, and a DBMS.

Software

Table 17-2 also lists some sources for various types of software. Systems software, such as the operating system, most often comes from the vendor. Compilers for mainframes are also generally offered by the computer manufacturer. For minis and especially for micros, there are many sources of compiler-level languages.

Today's most popular 4GLs are offered by software houses rather than computer manufacturers for all types of machines, ranging from mainframes to micros. The same is true for applications generators; usually software vendors have developed these products.

The database management field is crowded; computer vendors and independent software firms all offer a variety of DBMS products. Problem-oriented languages may come from the vendor or, more likely, from independents. Finally, vendors offer some dedicated packages, while independent software houses offer a large number of products for different purposes.

Acquisition and Evaluation

Software acquisition follows guidelines similar to those outlined in the first section of this chapter on choosing software for a particular application. The firm needs to do a functional analysis of what features the software should possess. It is extremely important to see the software in actual use, or at least to see a thorough demonstration of the software.

For many vendors, there is no choice of operating systems software; in fact, as discussed previously, the user selects this software with the hardware. A vendor like DEC has one operating system for its computers while IBM has several operating systems, some within the same line of computers. A number of IBM customers are always considering whether to upgrade operating systems. Do not forget conversion costs in such an analysis. In fact, for firms that delay upgrades, it is usually the transition cost and effort rather than the additional rental cost of an advanced operating system that is responsible for putting off an upgrade.

With a compiler, one is interested in the language features supported. Does the compiler meet whatever standards exist for the language? Compilation speed is sometimes a consideration, as is the resulting execution speed of the compiled code. For mainframes and minis, the customer usually buys the compilers offered by the vendor. For micros, the user will have to conduct research on the different products offered for the computer.

The evaluation of software like generators and database management packages is complex. Generators come in all types; some generate a great deal of code, while others leave much to the programmer. In evaluating a generator, one major factor to consider is ease of use; how difficult will it be for the programmer to work with the product? The purpose of the generator is to improve productivity; if it is very difficult to use, gains in productivity may not occur.

Each DBMS is based on a model of data: hierarchical, network, or relational. Since the field seems to be moving toward relational databases, vendors are suddenly finding that their products are relational after all. The user needs to look at several aspects of a DBMS, including how entities and relationships are defined. What are the capabilities of the data definition language, and how easy is its syntax to follow?

The evaluator of a DBMS will also need to look at the presence and capabilities of a data dictionary. Most DBMS packages come with some kind of query language. Since the user is likely to work with this language, the evaluator must consider its power and ease of use. Some microcomputer DBMS packages also contain programming languages of their own (e.g., DBase and Paradox). A programmer or user can generate a complete application with menus, so that the ultimate user of the system does not have to understand the DBMS.

Problem-oriented languages will also require unique evaluations. For example, there are financial modeling languages; a user might want to compare one of them with an electronic spreadsheet on a micro. What is the nature of the user's problems? Which package best fits his or her needs? How easy is it to use? What are the cost comparisons?

We discussed dedicated packages earlier in the chapter. The most important consideration here is to designate a high-level system specification as the standard for comparison and evaluation. Do not be influenced by features in a package that will never be used; be particularly careful that users can perform their required tasks within the structure of the package.

Services

Why might a firm turn to an outside service? We have suggested that this might be necessary in developing a particular application because not enough in-house resources exist. A service may also be used because the firm is very good. For example, a number of companies, many with in-house computers, use ADP for payroll processing, since ADP has built a reputation for handling this rather unpleasant task well.

Firms also use outside services because it is cheaper to obtain informa-

TABLE 17-4 Alternatives for Services

Services	Processing	Data	Assistance
Vendors			×
Service bureaus	×	×	×
Information providers		×	
Accounting firms			×
Consultants			×

tion from them or because they cannot possibly obtain it themselves. The various stock quotation systems are successful for this reason. Finally, outside services are used because of the expertise that the outsider brings to a particular problem. See Table 17-4.

Computer vendors have always provided consulting services for clients, often as part of installing or maintaining a computer system. These vendors now see opportunities to expand their consulting and are moving to become integrators. In the past, vendors were quite careful about working with their own equipment only.

An integrator is a consultant who pulls together disparate types of equipment to create a system. Integration is required in factory automation, as things stand today, because almost no vendor is able to offer a complete system. To create the kind of factory a firm would like to have, the products of a number of different vendors will be required. The integrator ties all of these pieces of equipment together.

The Ford Motor Company chose IBM to be the integrator for its office automation systems. Currently, Ford uses a variety of systems, including those of IBM, Wang, and DEC. It is likely that IBM will try to tie all of these systems together so that, for example, there will be one electronic mail system across the firm. In addition to computer vendors, there are consulting companies that perform system integration work. Most accounting firms also have a management services staff that performs different types of consulting work.

The evaluation and selection of consulting services is a very subjective process. Most consulting is based on past reputation, so the potential client will have to check references carefully. Certainly the client should ask about similar past assignments and try to find out their results.

Data Communications

Table 17-5 shows some of the options available for communications services. We shall discuss the management of telecommunications in more detail in Chapter 20. Deregulation and the breakup of AT&T have created a much more complex communications environment.

One can always used the public switched network; however, the user is charged according to time and distance. An alternative to this charging scheme is WATS service, in which one basically pays a flat rate for a certain

TABLE 17-5 Communications Services

Data communications
Public switched
Dialed
WATS
Common carrier (value added)
Conventional
Packet-switched
Private leased
Low-speed
Voice
Broadband

volume of calls. WATS (800) numbers have become very popular for customer service in a number of firms.

In addition to the public network, there are common carriers who add value to the network. These carriers either construct their own network—for example, with microwave towers along a railroad right of way—or lease lines from the phone companies. The value-added carrier turns the owned and leased lines into a network and sells network services to customers. The network may support conventional communications for voice and data.

The firm may also choose a packet switched network in which data to be transmitted are split into packets of the same size for transmission. The packets have routing information and may follow different routes on the network to reach the same destination.

Finally, instead of choosing a public or common carrier, the firm can develop its own private network. It can lease lines for this purpose from AT&T or the phone companies, or construct a private communications system. Citibank in New York has developed a very comprehensive system, using a satellite, that makes it independent of any phone company for its communications. This approach is sometimes called *bypass* because the customer is bypassing some or all of the lines offered by the public phone companies.

How does the firm choose? We shall discuss this issue further in Chapter 20. Basically there is a tradeoff between cost and service. The Citibank system is rumored to be more costly than that of public phone companies, but the firm wanted better service and independence of phone companies.

Research

One way to prepare for acquisition and evaluation is to conduct research on an ongoing basis. Remember that the ISD staff is moving toward a consulting role; research is a major part of the consultant's job. We are not advocating research on the leading edges of computer science, but research that consists of information gathering. By keeping up on new products and developments, the ISD staff is in a better position to determine what options to consider when undertaking an acquisition project. In addition, the staff will be called upon for advice when a more minor purchase is being made.

Beyond information gathering, it is also a good idea for the researchers within ISD to do some experimentation. For example, a microcomputer store should purchase new software and evaluate it. Visicalc gave way to Lotus 1-2-3; Wordstar has been suffering from declining sales as two or three other word processors have become more popular. A microcomputer consultant is of little use to clients if he or she is unaware of what is happening in the field.

Experimentation also extends to the construction of prototypes. The firm might want to consider building a LAN in the microstore to learn more about the technology. A factory project might involve integrating equipment from three or four vendors and trying the new MAP protocol (discussed in the next chapter).

Leasing versus Buying

In the purchase of hardware, there is frequently the option of leasing, buying, or renting. (Micros are so inexpensive that they are rarely leased.) Rental rates are almost always higher than leasing. To determine the benefits of buying, the customer has to determine the life of the equipment and its residual value, which is quite risky with high-technology products.

There are two reasons for a company to lease instead of buying. The first is to transfer the risk of owning obsolete equipment to the leasing firm. The second is to achieve lower costs. How can a lease cost less than a purchase?

The leasing company may feel that it can place the computer with a second customer after the first customer's lease is up. The leasing firm can set a price that takes this possibility into account. Second, suppose that tax benefits will not help the company acquiring the computer; the leasing firm may be able to use them and reduce its lease price accordingly.

The Tax Reform Act of 1986 has changed the rules somewhat. This act repeals the Investment Tax Credit (ITC), which forced lessors to increase their rates. In the past, many companies passed on the 10 per cent ITC to the lessor in return for lower lease rates.

How does a lease protect against obsolete equipment? Vendors shorten the life cycle of today's computers by bringing out new models every few years. Most leases allow the customer to upgrade something like the CPU as long as the lease payments go up instead of down. The lessor counts on being able to market the replaced CPU somewhere else.

Cost Reduction

Sometimes it appears that companies go on a buying spree with respect to computer equipment and software. SmithKline Backman in Philadelphia is a good example of a firm that historically has not skimped on computers; it has 12 mainframes, 109 minis, and 2500 personal computers, plus various word processors.

Recently the CIO has been cutting back on equipment purchases. He rejected an IBM 3090 mainframe at $2 million and chose a used $1 million computer instead. In place of upgrading a Wang electronic mail system, the firm is getting by with the one that it already has. It is estimated that computer users increased their budgets over 18% annually from 1982 to 1984. SmithKline's increased 25% each year in the first half of the 1980s; now the company is living with a 6% annual increase.

When the current CIO came to SmithKline, the information processing function was disorganized and out of date. To modernize, the company spent large sums of money; now it is concentrating on obtaining the greatest return for that investment. The CIO is also encouraging the use of packages; instead of programming a new personnel system, SmithKline bought one from Cullinet for $125,000; the system was installed in 8 months, compared with estimates of a 3-year development period for a custom-programmed version.

Software at CMI

Bob Carlin, vice president of finance at CMI, was talking with Tom White, CIO, about software purchases.

"Tom, I just don't understand why we spend so much money on software. Just look at this request for $100,000 for a set of accounting programs. And this one here, where we just bought five copies of a new database system for micros at a cost of $500 each."

"Let me try to explain," Tom responded. "We spent about 2 months investigating the accounting packages. Our estimate to write the code ourselves was $250,000 and 2 years. With the package, we should have the system within a year. The other thing we found was that each division would be willing to consider using the package if it works out here in headquarters. That would really be nice because we would develop uniform charts of accounts across divisions."

"Yes, now I remember that that was one of the selling points last fall when you asked for approval and we agreed that it was best to go with the package. I just feel we spend a lot and want to be sure we get something for it."

"That's what we're trying to do. The users are pretty enthusiastic about the accounting package. On the databases for the micros, we're trying to anticipate demand."

"What do you mean?"

"Well, no one requested this specific package, but we have been reading glowing press reports about how easy to use it is and how it goes well with our spreadsheet package. We want to have our personal computer consultants learn and evaluate the package and be ready when some of our users come in and ask us for it."

"Does that mean we will have to replace everything done with our current database package?"

"I doubt that most users would want to do that; it is too much trouble to convert. We would just leave it up to users to decide. If they like the new package, they should use it for new applications. We will keep the old one around and continue to support it with consulting help. This is something I think we have to do to stay one step ahead of users and to help them."

"I see your point, but please keep the overall budget in mind. We have to do something besides buy computers and programs around here . . . "

Recommended Readings

Byte. (A popular magazine with a number of articles comparing microcomputer hardware and software.)

High Technology. (An excellent magazine that covers all aspects of technology in articles geared to the educated layperson.)

Lucas, H. C., Jr., *Information Systems Concepts for Management,* 3rd ed. New York: McGraw-Hill, 1986. (See the chapter on systems alternatives and acquisition.)

PC Magazine. (A magazine devoted to the industry standard micro; it includes comparison articles.)

Discussion Problems

17.1 Riteway Drugs has recently merged with Mainline Paper Products. The two companies have extensive computer applications, but they run on incompatible computers. Riteway has a number of on-line systems on its IBM mainframes (370 architecture). Mainline also has on-line systems, especially a state-of-the-art order entry system with terminals in customers' buying offices; this system runs on a large-scale Burroughs processor.

The chairman of Riteway-Mainline has asked for your advice. He has the following questions: Should we merge our two computer operations? What is involved in switching from one vendor's computer to another? Wouldn't we save money by having computers from just a single source? How would we determine capacity requirements for a merged operation? If we were to merge, which vendor should we choose?

17.2 A major money center bank decided in the 1970s to decentralize information processing completely. Departments and divisions were told to automate and to purchase whatever equipment they wanted. Later the bank decided to tie its systems together in a network. An outside contractor was hired, and the interface systems to join various computers to the network was rumored to have cost $50,000 each.

What steps could the bank have taken to provide freedom for the departments while maintaining some control over acquisition? Was it reasonable to expect the bank to consider this when it started decentralizing?

Questions

1. Why has so much emphasis shifted to software in the acquisition process?
2. What has happened to time-sharing services?
3. How does acquisition of software and hardware enter into systems design considerations?
4. Why might many firms consider a package over a custom-developed system?
5. How should one go about evaluating a package for acquisition?
6. What role does the hardware vendor play in the acquisition process?
7. How does the ISD evaluate a vendor's proposal for a system?
8. How does the evaluation of a microcomputer for purchase differ from that of a mainframe?
9. How much freedom does the user have in choosing an operating system?
10. Why is the evaluation of a DBMS difficult?
11. Why does a firm consider the use of outside services?
12. What are the choices available to the firm for telecommunications services?
13. What is responsible for rapid changes in the telecommunications market?
14. What role does research play in the acquisition of software and hardware?
15. What are the considerations in leasing a computer?
16. How can a firm stay current with technology and avoid constantly escalating expenditures for equipment and software?
17. What can the ISD do to help users who want advice on acquiring microcomputers?
18. How is equipment acquisition related to capacity planning?
19. How do computer vendors force the customer to update equipment and software?
20. What are the advantages for a customer of compatibility across a line of equipment?

PART IV

Managing Related Functions

18

Managing Factory Automation

In general, factory automation has proceeded with little input from the traditional ISD. Engineers have assumed primary responsibility for the design of factories and special equipment, while the processing of orders and scheduling has often been left to information services computers. Leading-edge manufacturing companies are integrating all systems that affect production in their factories.

In the future, there will be networks of computers; at the highest levels, computers will process forecasts, order information, accounting, and similar data, while at the lowest level, dedicated computers will control individual machines on the factory floor. All of these computers, however, will communicate with each other. Increasingly, managers of traditional ISDs are becoming more involved in factory automation; it is important for these managers to understand the issues in automating production.

The emphasis in manufacturing today is on efficiency and quality; how can the firm reduce costs and improve the quality of the products it manufactures? One approach is through automation, and automation involves extensive use of computers and computer-controlled machines.

Does automation reduce direct labor costs? In some cases it does, but the savings from automation should not be predicated on savings in direct labor. Direct labor costs in the United States range from 5 to 15% of a product's total cost, so there is not much leverage in reducing direct labor.

Automation has an impact beyond direct labor, however, and this impact helps reduce costs. Automation involves controlling the flow of information through the factory. Consider a manufacturer that makes electronic components. This manufacturer has a large factory with 32 work centers, where different kinds of tasks are performed in the production process. As workers finish products, they leave the tray containing the lot at the end of their work station. There is a traveler or shop work order attached to the tray.

A person who is classified as an indirect laborer picks up the tray, enters the lot number into a computer terminal, and indicates the number of the work center to which he or she is taking the tray. There are as many people moving goods around the factory as there are direct production workers. We must also add to this total of indirect workers individuals assigned to inspection and quality control.

How would one automate the factory? A number of steps can be taken, and the applicability of each will depend on the particular factory involved. One approach in the electronic manufacturing plant is to put a bar code on each tray of goods. The computer terminal would include a bar code reader, and the production worker would scan the tray out of a work center where work was complete and into a new work center.

Improvements in quality are highly dependent on the manufacturing process. To measure the yield of a process, it might be possible to weigh the lot automatically; the loss of weight at a work center should be proportional to the number of items scrapped. Some companies are able to use automatic equipment to inspect goods as well; Nissan has a robot inspector that can totally inspect the quality of paint on an auto body. The robot inspector finishes the job in 1 minute and can detect defects as small as a hundredth of an inch; a skilled human inspector requires 45 minutes to inspect the painted body.

Manufacturing Strategy

Is automation the final answer for the factory? A number of actions can be taken to improve the manufacturing environment; automation is but one part of a manufacturing strategy to improve productivity and quality.

Product Design

The electronics company previously described had allowed part numbers to proliferate. If a customer ordered a part that was already made, but wanted a red stripe on it instead of an orange one, the firm's engineers assigned a new part number. The route of the part through the factory was the same whether the stripe was red or orange; only the final step in production differed, that is, the color of the final paint stripe. The company estimated that about 300 parts covered 90% of what it manufactured; unfortunately there were some 60,000 part numbers!

Why is this proliferation of parts a problem? One step in automation was to install a Materials Requirements Planning System (MRP), which will be discussed later. This system contains a database of the routing through the factory for each part. (A routing is a list of work centers and the requirements for what has to be done to the part in the work center.) Imagine the difference between entering 800 routings and 60,000.

One important part of factory automation, then, is to think about the whole manufacturing process. Do not simply automate existing practices; look for ways to improve on what is being done. A number of stories of successful factory automation stress the need to redesign products so that they can be manufactured or assembled by automated equipment.

Human Resources

Often U.S. manufacturing plants are constrained by rigid job classifications and a system that encourages conflict between management and labor. For decades, labor and organizational theorists have been calling for a management system that fosters cooperation between labor and management. Today the threat of foreign competition is encouraging experiments in cooperation. A number of Japanese manufacturers are operating plants in the United States, and their success in managing human resources is being copied by U.S. firms.

Some of the approaches that have been successful include group assembly, in which a group of workers is responsible for a product. Success has also been reported where there are fewer status differences between labor and management; no special dining rooms or parking lots exist for executives. In a typical Japanese firm, the plant manager and the lowest-paid worker wear the same white uniform with their name stitched on the pocket.

A popular technique is the use of a quality circle. A group of employees are trained in this approach and spend time analyzing the quality of the products they manufacture. The suggestions from the quality circle are used to improve the manufacturing process.

Another Japanese strategy that has not been employed frequently in the United States is lifetime job security. There is less concern over making the work last and narrow job classifications if the worker knows that he or she has a job for life. Some U.S. firms follow this policy, but the practice is not widespread.

Manufacturing Systems

There is a wide variety of manufacturing in an industrialized country. At one extreme is continuous production, such as in an oil refinery. The process of refining oil has been highly automated for a number of years; relatively few production workers are needed because the process is a continuous one that is capable of being automated.

At the other extreme is batch production, such as found in a job shop. Here a number of different machines or machine centers exist. A product is routed through the job shop in a certain manufacturing sequence. Job shop scheduling is a classic operations research problem; there is a combinatorial number of ways to assign machines to products, and production planning in this environment is very complex.

Different kinds of assembly operations fall between the continuous processing of the oil refinery and the batch manufacturing of the job shop. The assembly line features workers who perform a set task or tasks on products as they move along a line. Automobile assembly is the most frequently cited example of the assembly line.

It would be nice to have the flexibility of the job shop and some of the efficiencies of the assembly line. Assembly lines function best with long runs of similar products; we do not want to stop the assembly line after making 10 or 15 units and make something else. The job shop has far less of a problem with small production quantities in small volumes.

Some of the automation techniques employed in factories try to combine the advantages of the job shop and the assembly line. The idea is to be able to make a small number of products and then shift rapidly to the manufacture of a small lot of a different product economically.

Materials Requirements Planning

For a number of years, experts in manufacturing in the United States have promoted an approach called materials requirements planning (MRP). We now are in the age of MRP II, in which there is a great deal of feedback in the planning process. MRP systems are built around the typical U.S. manufacturing model of a series of work centers, with products in different-sized batches flowing through a factory.

In order to isolate various work centers and create more independence, this typical factory features a number of buffer or work-in-process inventories. A buffer inventory is a form of organizational slack. It allows a work center to continue its production by drawing on the work-in-process inventory even if a work center that performs a prior operation on the product is not functioning.

The cost of the buffer inventory takes a number of forms. The first cost is the actual financing of the inventory; working capital is tied up in partially completed products. Buffer inventories also create an information processing problem; production control has to keep track of the work-in-process inventories and is likely to spend a great deal of time tracing orders.

We have seen plants where the production planning process is chaotic. In order to please customers, one customer's order is diverted partway through the manufacturing process and is assigned to a higher-priority customer. As deadlines are passed, production becomes more frantic and other orders are diverted. Rush jobs keep interfering with whatever planned production exists until one finds a factory that is operating at 50% of capacity and yet missing most of its completion dates.

MRP is designed to attack these problems in production scheduling. See

Figure 18-1. In an MRP system, the emphasis is on planning and on building goods when they are needed, not piling up in inventory. Sales forecasts, actual orders, and finished goods inventory are the inputs to production planning.

The planning process produces a master production schedule that indicates when various products are to be built. The master production schedule becomes the input to the MRP function; here products are exploded into their components, using a bill of materials program. For example, the bill of materials database contains the assemblies and subassemblies for a product. If the manufacturer plans to build 500 of product 1 and product 1 requires 3 of assembly A, it is necessary to produce or have available 1500 of assembly A.

MRP and the master production schedule are inputs for capacity planning. What can the factory make or outside producers supply over time? All of this information is fed back to production planning to generate a new, feasible master production schedule based on plant capacity. One idea behind this approach is to make goods as they are needed. We might think of the critical path module analogy; activities off the critical path do not need to be started right away, and the network shows the latest start date. Similarly, there is no need to begin building assembly A if it is not needed for 5 weeks and if it only takes 1 week to manufacture 1500 of them.

Figure 18-1 shows several feedback paths because it will take several iterations to develop a feasible production schedule. Also, as new orders or forecasts change, the production schedule will be revised. The most important part of the MRP philosophy is that production is planned instead of undertaken in reaction to a shortage.

To complete the management process, there are production control functions including the release of orders to the factory. Production control is responsible for tracking products as they are manufactured to the extent that it is important to know the location of orders.

Just-in-Time Manufacturing

A number of firms have reported impressive results with MRP systems, and it is an alternative that management should consider carefully. Another approach, which is not incompatible with MRP, has come from Japan. Just-in-time or JIT-manufacturing stresses minimal or nonexistent work-in-process inventories. All of the items needed for production arrive just in time for assembly. This approach requires close coordination among various parts of a factory and with suppliers. It is not uncommon to find hourly deliveries of products in a JIT system.

Another characteristic of JIT is *pull-through production.* In an MRP system, the emphasis is on *push-through production.* As workers complete their tasks, materials flow from their stage of manufacturing to the next, since the processing at the current work center has been completed.

Pull-through production is downstream production drawing working from a previous stage. Removal of a piece for final assembly initiates a "back to front" chain reaction. Figure 18-2 shows a diagram of the JIT process

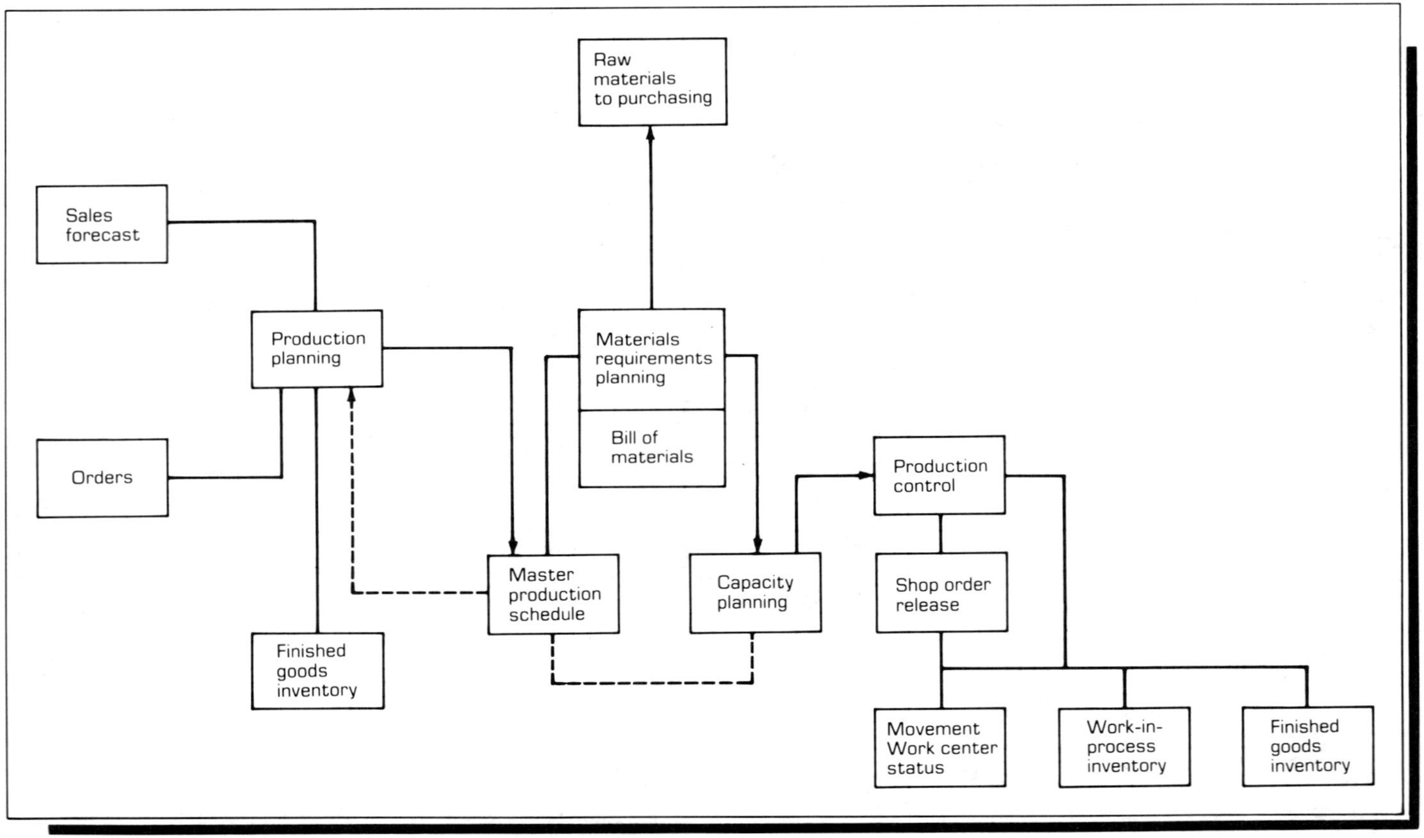

FIGURE 18-1 (above) Traditional materials requirements factory.

FIGURE 18-2 (below) JIT production. Under traditional manufacturing methods (top), parts are produced in large quantities at one time to reduce the cost of setting up equipment. Parts leaving feeder departments from the fabrication side of manufacturing pass through quality control before "queueing" up for assembly. Inventory in the queue contains a certain percentage of buffer stock as protection against product defects and other unforeseen problems. As work on a part ends at one station, the worker "pushes" the part through to the queue before the next assembly station, and so on to completion. JIT manufacturing (bottom), on the other hand, is based on the production of goods in small lots, with minimal or zero inventory. Testing and inspection are no longer relegated to a quality control department but become the responsibility of the individual line operator. Some physical signal, a *kanban*, must exist to tell an operator to ''pull'' a part or a lot into production or to deliver more parts. A finished part, or a small lot of parts, remains at an assembly station until the next worker is ready to ''pull'' it into production. (From Cortes-Comerer, 1986)

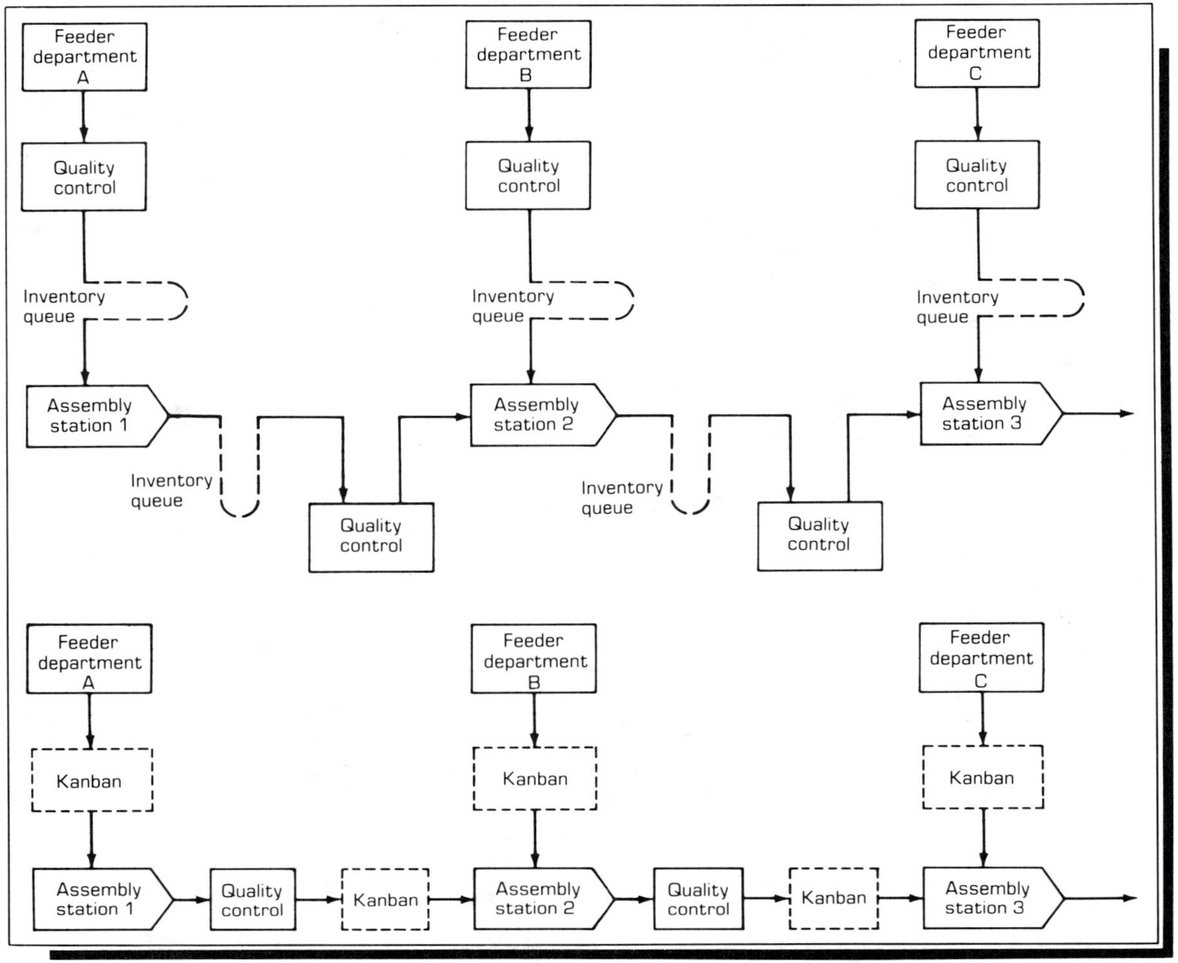

contrasted with more traditional manufacturing methods. Note the presence of inventory queues in the traditional factory. The JIT system features a *kanban* or signal to tell an upstream operator to pull a part, that is, to put a part or a lot into production or to deliver more parts. Finished lots or parts remain at their last assembly station until the next worker pulls them into production. In this system, workers also become responsible for quality control.

One major objective of JIT is to reduce inventory; it also provides flexibility, since it is easy to produce small batches instead of large job orders. To take full advantage of JIT, it is often necessary to reorganize the factory physically and organizationally. Figure 18-3 is an example from a Tektronix plant in Oregon that manufacturers hybrid integrated circuits.

The plant was originally laid out with equipment clustered by function, and each function was scattered among various plant locations. For example, the wire bonders were all grouped in one place and could handle up to 4000 parts. Parts typically passed through quality control several times.

To manufacture in smaller batches, Tektronix broke up the functional machine clusters into several U-shaped cells that in general contain one of each type of machine. Operators handle parts in queues of 10; each part is handled one step at a time. Workers learn to operate all equipment and can skip an operation while waiting for work to be completed at a station. This kind of physical and work organization provides job enlargement for the workers and allows them to focus on quality, since they are responsible for the entire product.

Robotics

One of the most visible symbols of factory automation is the robot. These devices are pictured frequently in the press, especially the dramatic welding robots for automobile bodies. It is estimated that there are about 20,000 robots operating in the United States. Japan claims some 200,000, but probably half of the Japanese machines simply pick something up and place it in another location; the machines are rarely reprogrammed.

There are a number of ways to use a robot, including painting, welding, inspection, machine loading, and assembly. Welding and painting applications are good uses of robots, as these tasks tend to be unpleasant and at times dangerous for human workers. Robots are also well suited to picking up material and moving it to a new location.

Assembly is an area of great future growth in robotics. In Japan, Seiko/Epson developed its own ultraprecise robots to automate watch production. The line can produce 100,000 watches per month in lots as small as 1000. Each robot follows a simple routine, like picking up a gear from one side of the workspace and placing it precisely on the watch. As a new model watch starts down the line, the robot has to prepare for another task, possibly changing its gripper for a screwdriver. The central computer monitors each robot and stops production if there is a problem.

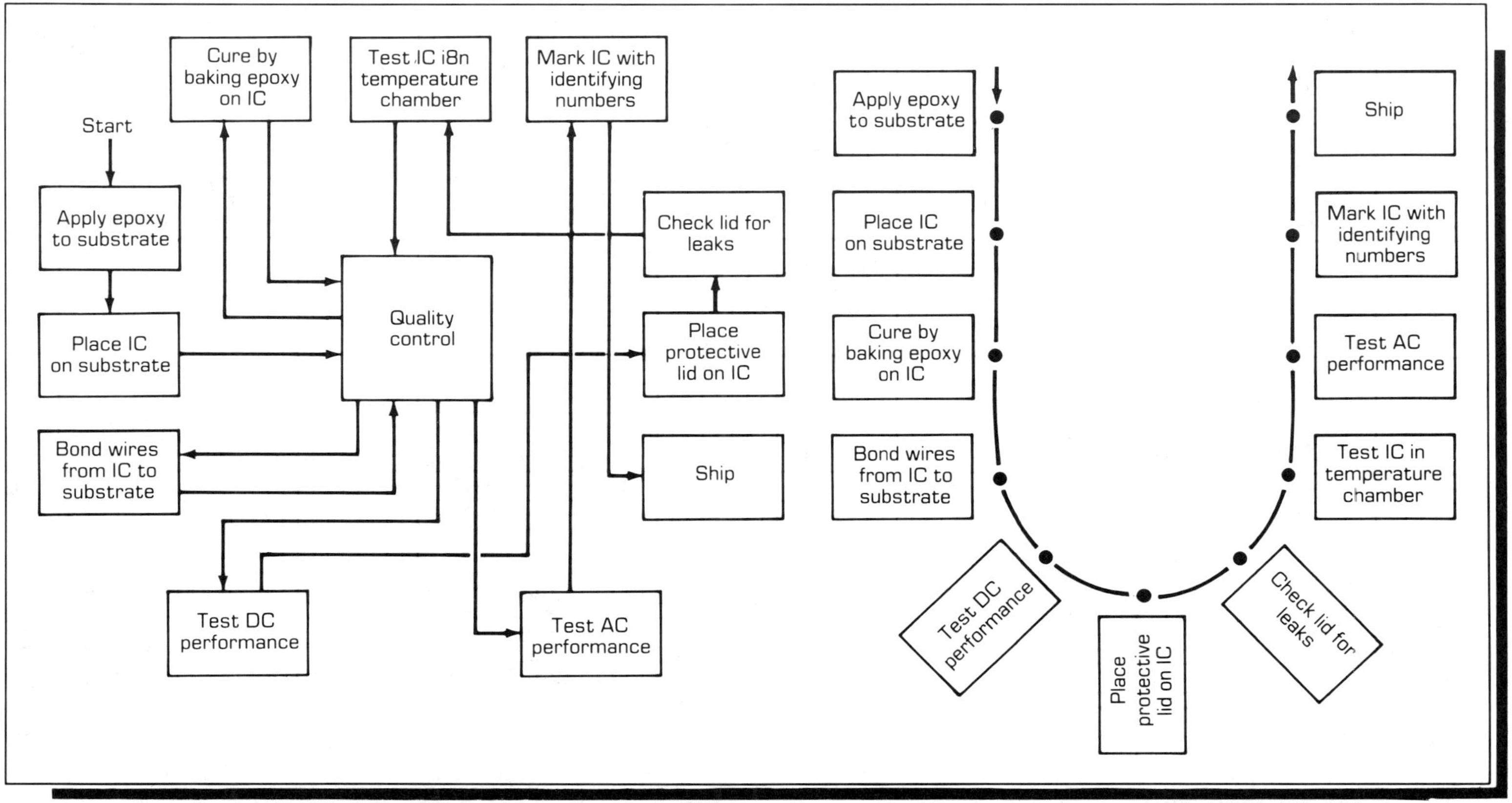

FIGURE 18-3 Factory reorganization. JIT makes use of the cell concept to arrange equipment progressively in U-shaped production lines that can produce one part or family of parts. At Tektronix in Beaverton, Oregon, equipment needed to manufacture a hybrid integrated circuit was formerly clustered by function, with each function scattered among various plant locations (left). A wire bonders, for example, would be grouped in one place and could handle as many as 4,000 parts. A part would pass through quality control several times on its way to another process. Manufacturing in small batches meant breaking up the clusters into several U-shaped cells that typically contain one of each type of machine (right). Operators handle parts in queues of 10, and each part is handled one step at a time. Workers learn to operate all the equipment, and can hop over an operation while waiting for work to be completed at a station. (From Cortes-Comerer, 1986).

Flexible Manufacturing Systems

As robots and computers are coupled with traditional manufacturing equipment like milling machines and multifunction machine tools, the firm is able to take advantage of flexible manufacturing techniques. The flexible manufacturing system (FMS) replaces stand-alone machine tools used in batch processing. The FMS is highly automated and is capable of producing a variety of metal parts in any order determined by the demand for products.

The FMS uses automation to eliminate manual setups; a central control computer directs each machine tool. The typical FMS might integrate eight machines and an automated materials handling system. The computer makes it possible to route products immediately without requiring work-in-process inventories. Because the system is so flexible, it is possible to make small lot sizes and to change products rapidly.

The Software Problem

One way to program robots is in a teaching mode. Many of the simple robots used for painting, for example, can be taught the necessary movements by human operators. The operator puts the robot in a learning mode and then manually moves the robot's paint sprayer to paint the item in front of the robot. When the robot is moved to the operating mode, it simply repeats the motions followed by the human trainer over and over again. As long as the item is properly positioned and the trainer did an adequate job of painting, the robot will function properly.

However, if the motions of the robot require more precision and/or tasks become more complicated, we encounter a software and programming problem. Some of the promise of FMS has yet to be achieved because of problems in the software controlling the systems. Similarly, it is not easy to program robots for all of the complex tasks involved in assembling different products. It has proven particularly difficult to program entire assembly lines like the one at Seiko, which is over 47 feet long.

Future Developments

Today's robots are sometimes classified as dumb, because they cannot process feedback on their performance. The next major advance in robotics will be systems that use feedback to modify their performance. As an example, a welding robot would be able to examine its weld and repair it if faulty.

Much of the feedback will be provided by machine vision systems. At Seiko, a robot with feedback from a television camera aligns a watch's small second hand with the tick marks on its face. The computer measures the distance between the needle-thin hand and the marks based on the image from the camera; the computer instructs the robot on which way to move the watch hand.

Similar kinds of vision and feedback systems will inaugurate the next generation of robots. Machines will be used in dangerous work and hostile environments and for boring tasks. Robots work on, no matter how fatiguing the task, and do not have the lapses in quality of human operators. They never go on strike or take holidays.

Sensors

Important underlying technologies for robotics include sensors and converters. A sensor allows the robot to sense something in the environment. In the preceding example, the robot used a TV camera to measure distances. Other examples of sensors include photocells, sound and motion detectors, sonar systems, and temperature sensors.

Typically, a robot requires changes from analog to digital signals and vice versa. See Figure 18-4. To measure the temperature, the robot needs a device that senses the temperature and feeds it to a transducer, which converts the analog temperature to a digital signal. The digital signal is coded to represent different temperatures; the computer in the robot recognizes the codes and can take action based on them.

The robot will also generate digital signals, which must be converted to analog voltages to control some of its motors. See Figure 18-5. Here the digital-to-analog conversion takes a digital signal and converts it to the voltage required to operate the motor.

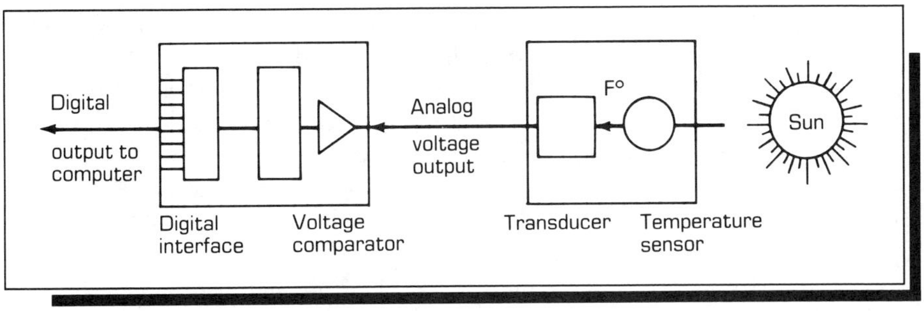

FIGURE 18-4 Analog-to-digital conversion.

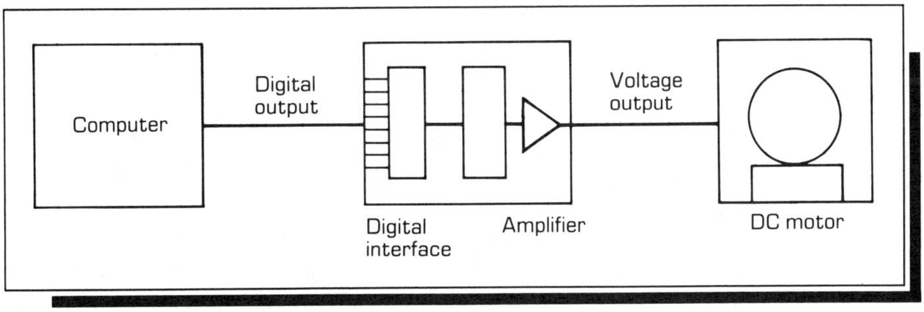

FIGURE 18-5 Digital-to-analog conversion.

The Role of the Robot

Robots are exciting and rather glamorous compared to a machine tool or other factory fixture. What is their role in automation? IBM has developed a highly automated typewriter assembly plant in Lexington, Kentucky. A robot lowers the typewriter assembly into a plastic housing and snaps the assembly into place. The robot has a hand that is sensitive to pressure and can feel whether the assembly pops out. If so, the robot can fix it right away rather than leaving the problem for a later stage of assembly.

Work in progress passes from one robot to another. The frame and paper feed structure go through a line of 56 relatively simple robots, each doing one job such as inserting a screw. IBM management feels that such specialization results in greater reliability than having a robot perform a variety of tasks.

Each robot repeats the same job over and over again. The conveyor network is the key to the entire operation; it makes sure that work in progress stops only at the right robot stations needed for a particular set of features. The robot makes the greatest contribution when it is integrated into a manufacturing system.

Integrating Factory Automation

A popular term today is *computer integrated manufacturing* (*CIM*). The goal of CIM is to reduce the mountain of paper that is associated with manufacturing a product. In addition, CIM should improve productivity, reduce indirect labor costs, and improve product quality. What is included in a CIM system? The first component is computer-aided design and engineering (CAD/CAE). These systems have been available for a number of years.

With CAD, an engineer at a workstation uses computer graphics to design a part. The design may be either original or a variation on an existing part; in the second case, the designer pulls a copy of the existing part from the database and modifies it. In either instance, the designer works with the graphics system, probably using a light pen or stylus and pad, to input the design. When finished, the designer prints the specifications for the part.

CAD can be integrated with computer-aided manufacturing (CAM). Suppose that the engineer's drawing actually generated the commands that are necessary to produce the part for a flexible manufacturing system. The work of the engineer, then, would be all that was necessary to go from design to production.

It has been estimated that a CIM factory might have a breakeven point as low as 25 to 30 per cent of capacity, whereas a conventional plant breaks even at 60 to 65 per cent of capacity. In addition, by running with fewer employees, a CIM plant should be able to avoid violent swings in employment. A more stable workforce should be better motivated and may also make it possible for management to consider a no-layoff policy.

There are now relatively few examples of CIM in the United States;

some of them are discussed later in the chapter. It is most typical to find islands of automation in a factory; management is now facing the task of tying the islands together and establishing control at the level of a manufacturing line rather than a machine cell. The highest level of automation will occur when a plant with multiple lines is under automatic control.

The size of automation efforts can be quite large; Chrysler has 3000 users in 18 different design centers sharing a huge computerized engineering database. The network has 550 workstations connected to 27 large computers. At the other extreme, a small manufacturing firm might buy a robot or two for specific tasks like painting or welding.

The Implementation Problem

All of the benefits suggested for more automated production will occur only if the automated systems work. Unfortunately, implementation has been a bit of a problem. One firm has spent over 3 years debugging its flexible manufacturing system! The Ford Motor Company's problems with a highly automated factory caused it to delay the introduction of its Taurus and Sable cars for 4 months. One GM plant has reached only 70 per cent of planned production levels and GM has had significant problems with another highly automated Buick factory.

In defense of these firms, many of their efforts are leading edge and involve significant R&D. However, these technological leaders have been embarrassed by the joint venture in Fremont, California, between Toyota and GM. The plant uses relatively old technology to assemble cars, but its productivity is reported to be higher than that of most of GM's new plants. Toyota is managing the plant; it emphasizes training and participative management, and features a relatively small group of middle managers. Decision making occurs as close to the assembly line as possible.

There are many ways to obtain greater factory productivity. Automation provides flexibility and an opportunity to rethink product design and the organization of work. A new management system may be needed to take full advantage of the technology.

Communications

Japanese companies reportedly design and build many of their own robots and automated assembly lines. In the United States the tendency has been for firms to integrate the products of a number of vendors. In fact, systems integration is one of the major bottlenecks in factory automation. Consider the task of developing a typewriter assembly line with 50 or 60 robots, some from different vendors, a materials handling system, machines to supply parts, and a central computer to control the line. What if all of these devices used a different protocol for communications?

GM, recognizing this problem in its factory automation efforts, has developed a standard communications protocol for factory operations called *manufacturing automation protocol* (*MAP*). GM has an estimated 40,000 programmable devices in its factories, and that number may grow by a factor of four or five in the next 5 years. Because of GM's size, it has tremendous leverage in the field, and a number of computer and automation vendors have agreed to design their equipment to communicate using this protocol.

MAP is a 10-megabit-per-second broadband, token bus communications standard in seven layers. Broadband transmission provides the capability for sending a large number of signals over the same network at the same time. To prevent messages from different devices from colliding, the network has a special bit pattern called a *token*, which is passed from station to station. When a station has the token, it can pass data to another station. Since the network will be used in real-time operations, the token scheme works best when the designer knows the maximum time any station will have to wait to transmit data. A broadband coaxial cable can link together many devices.

A number of vendors have agreed to develop devices to use the MAP protocol, including the large manufacturers of computer equipment. It remains to be seen if MAP will become an important standard for factory networks, as there are other standards that have been proposed as well. GM has taken the initiative in developing and demonstrating a working protocol. The GM truck factory in Pontiac, Michigan uses a MAP network to control an automated assembly line.

The Role of Information Services

Where does the traditional information services function fit in with factory automation? Figure 18-6 is an overview of an automated manufacturing company. A corporate computer processes traditional IS applications like order entry, accounts receivable, accounts payable, sales analysis, and possibly engineering. (There may be departmental computers or specialized workstations for some of these functions.)

The corporate computer communicates with the factory computer; in particular, the corporate computer sends order information to the factory. The factory computer handles production from scheduling through production control and monitoring. The firm may use MRP software or a JIT system. Quality control may run on this machine or on a special mini or micro with a package for statistical quality control analysis.

The factory computer communicates with various devices that are used in production. There may be minis or micros between the factory computer and the programmable controllers that give commands to the production machinery. Another possibility is that the controller manages a cell through a LAN; the cell contains devices like milling machines, robots, lathes, and so on.

Historically, information services has functioned at the corporate level and often at the level of the applications run on the factory computer. In some firms, production scheduling, MRP, and production control are actu-

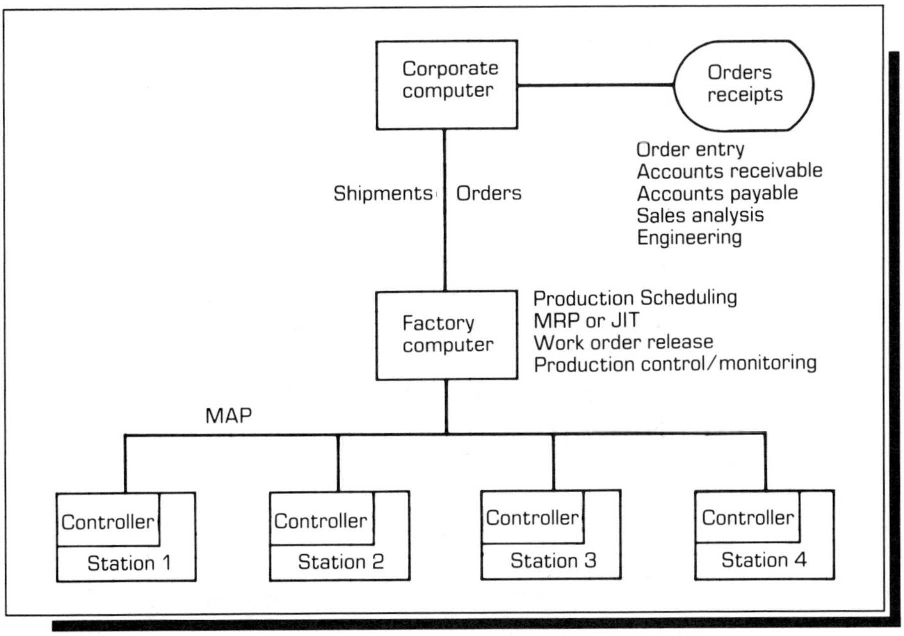

FIGURE 18-6 A possible factory automation architecture.

ally run on the corporate system. Does IS have a continuing role in this process? What about the efforts of automation in the factory?

In the next chapter, we shall argue that office automation is close enough to the traditional functions of IS to be included under the IS umbrella. However, factory automation requires a degree of specialization beyond what is available in the typical IS organization. The design of automated factories and their installation is the responsibility of the engineer, not the business systems analyst.

The traditional IS function will have to span the boundary between management and office systems and the factory. It is unlikely that the factory will want to run the order entry system or provide a sales analysis system. Conversely, corporate IS is not prepared to program robots and controllers for a machine cell. However, if the automated factory is to work, all of these various applications will have to communicate with each other.

Corporate information services has a number of responsibilities in factory automation. First, it has to be a member of a task force charged with implementing factory automation. Corporate IS has the key to interfacing traditional information systems with factory systems. IS in general also has experience in managing software projects; its project management skills can be useful to a team charged with developing factory automation.

In the case of factory automation, information services needs to participate in the development effort and to provide advice and consultation in the process. There is much technology available; the major problems are in design and integration, which are tasks constantly faced by information services staff members.

Some Examples

John Deere

At East Moline, Illinois, the sheet metal factory for the John Deere Harvester Works produces components for farm combines. The factory handles punching and welding of sheet metal. The company uses numerical controllers to send cutting and tooling instructions to over 30 machine tools on the shop floor. To avoid connecting each machine to a computer room, Deere Harvester decided to install a MAP-based factory floor network.

The firm can download numerical control (NC) programs to machine tools on the factory floor. Engineers can access and update programs and then send them to the shop floor automatically. Using a CAD system, the company can transfer programs across the LAN to the system for storage. Since the company is using an emerging standard, MAP, it should be possible to add equipment easily in the future.

Allen-Bradley

Allen-Bradley has developed a totally automated factory that has been cited as an example of what can be done with a relatively small facility. Allen-Bradley manufactures motor controls called *contactors* in the plant. The plant requires only a small number of workers, and the line can switch from one product to another without losing any time.

The process begins when an IBM mainframe receives and processes orders from Allen-Bradley's customers. The day the order is to be filled, the mainframe sends it to a VAX minicomputer in the plant. The VAX schedules production and starts the factory running every morning at 5 A.M.; it continues to run the plant all day.

The computer can locate and report on the status of every contactor by using laser-scanned bar codes on the contactors. There are 26 workstations in the production process. The computer helps workers spot problems in the line and has been able to hold stoppages to about 1 minute. The system is capable of generating 80 different manufacturing reports, though one has to wonder how that many reports can contribute to a reduction in paper!

Allen-Bradley figures that the system has cut the cost of a typical contactor by nearly 40 per cent. The major savings come from lower overhead due to less indirect labor and lower raw materials and work-in-process inventories and stockpiles of finished goods. The factory has 45,000 square feet and the system required a capital investment of $8 million; the total cost was $15 million, which is small compared to that of many other automation efforts.

General Electric

General Electric has constructed an automated dishwasher factory in Louisville, Kentucky. The automation effort required a complete redesign of the dishwasher so that it could be built with available automatic equipment and robots. The number of parts in the dishwasher was reduced from approximately 5600 to 850 in order to use more automated manufacturing techniques.

The remodeled plant required an investment of over $38 million. GE has found that the average number of dishwasher service calls has been reduced by 53 per cent since the new plant went into operation. The plant required 5 to 6 days to produce a dishwasher 2 years ago; it now requires only about 18 hours. Overall employee productivity has increased by more than 25 per cent and production capacity at the plant is up by 20 per cent.

The process of building a dishwasher, including parts production, unit assembly, and warehousing, is controlled and tracked by 34 Series Six programmable controllers developed by a GE division. Assembly operations are monitored from an overhead booth that contains three computer terminals connected to a DEC PDP 11/44 computer.

GE constructs the polypropylene tub and inner door using a proprietary process of injection molding. The tub mold weighs almost 22 tons; its injection machines are controlled by a Series Six programmable controller that monitors 32 different temperature points, 20 velocities, 5 gates, 7 pressure points, and a selection of counters.

While the tub is being constructed, metal structural and support parts are cut or stamped from steel coils. The plant makes 13 dishwasher models, each of which passes through a series of stations: 21 for tub assembly and 13 for the door.

The status of each unit is tracked through assembly by laser-scanned bar codes. An automatic camera recognition system developed by another GE division aligns the door hinges and tub structure during fabrication. Proper door latching requires tolerances of several thousandths of an inch.

Some portions of the process require human manual dexterity, such as the final parts assembly process. Each operator has about 15 seconds to perform an assembly step, but can continue for up to 45 seconds if a problem develops. If the worker cannot finish, he or she logs a signal to the controller and the unit continues down the line for later repair.

This example shows how GE has integrated a variety of technologies to produce a highly automated plant. The key to the automation effort was rethinking how a dishwasher should be designed and built. It is unlikely that the firm could have succeeded in automating the manufacture of the old dishwasher with its 5600 parts. As a by-product, the firm has lowered manufacturing costs and created a better product for its customers!

Recommended Readings

Business Week. (A general business magazines with occasional articles on manufacturing.)

Cortes-Comerer, "JIT Is Made to Order," *IEEE Spectrum* (September 1986), pp. 57–62. (A good explanation of JIT and traditional production techniques.)

High Technology. (A magazine devoted to the use of technology; contains frequent articles on factory automation.)

Liker, J. K., D. B. Roitmar, and E. Roskies, "Changing Everything All at Once—Work Life and Technological Change," *Sloan Management Review,* vol. 28, no. 4 (Summer 1987), pp. 49–61. (A good analysis of a partially successful attempt to automate production all at once.)

Orlicky, J., *Material Requirements Planning.* New York: McGraw-Hill, 1975. (A good introductory book on MRP.)

Wight, O., *MRP II: Unlocking America's Productivity Potential.* Williston, Vt.: Oliver Wight, 1981. (A book by one of the leading consultants on MRP.)

Discussion Problems

18.1 Alex Products decided to install an MRP system at its major plant. The plant has six different lines manufacturing electronic components for circuit boards. Since each of the lines is slightly different, Alex decided to implement a pilot system and then take one line at a time if the pilot worked.

The lines have a number of work stations, so that engineers had to input detailed routings for each product manufactured. This process took several months; during this time, the ISD worked with plant foremen to show them the new reports that they would receive.

The pilot seemed successful, and full-scale implementation proceeded. According to the manager of the ISD, however, each line seemed to take as much effort as the first one. In fact, the worst implementation experience occurred with the last line. How do you explain this lack of learning?

18.2 In the pharmaceuticals business, quality control is extremely important. Drug recalls or poor marks from government agencies are costly and embarrassing. Drug makers devote a great deal of time and money to quality control and inspection.

One such firm is very interested in automating as much of this process as possible. However, there are technical and management problems. Quality control needs the cooperation of manufacturing, which has the data needed to assess quality. On the other hand, quality control decides that a lot from production can be released for shipment and sale.

What approach can you suggest to solve the organizational problems in a joint project to automate some of the quality control functions?

Questions

1. Is factory automation designed primarily to save direct labor costs?
2. What costs might be reduced through automation?
3. What is the potential social cost of CIM?
4. What is MRP?
5. Why are routings important in an MRP system?
6. What is JIT inventory?
7. What conditions are required for JIT inventory to work?
8. Why do some CIM experts argue that one cannot automate only existing manufacturing procedures, and possibly not existing products as currently designed?

9. What motivated GM to develop the MAP protocol?
10. What is the advantage of having a standard like MAP?
11. Why would a firm want a network as opposed to point-to-point connections for equipment?
12. What are the advantages of group assembly?
13. What does a bill of materials processor do?
14. What are islands of automation?
15. What stands in the way of complete CIM in a factory?
16. What is the role of robotics in manufacturing?
17. What features will more advanced robots have?
18. Describe a flexible manufacturing system.
19. Why is software such a problem in factory automation?
20. What is a sensor? Why are sensors needed?
21. Why is there a need to convert analog signals to digital signals and vice versa?
22. What are the major challenges of managing factory automation?
23. What is the role of information services in factory automation?
24. What is unique about the Allen-Bradley factory?
25. What is most impressive about the GE dishwasher factory?

19

Managing Office Automation

Office automation is broadly defined as the application of technology to help individuals perform functions. What is an office? What are the typical tasks in an office? An office is a collection of individuals who process information rather than produce a product. An office consists of knowledge workers rather than factory workers.

It is probably clear that the assembly line is not an office and that the financial manager of the firm works in an office. Is the shipping department an office? It contains workers who are concerned with information such as how much a shipment weighs and where the shipment is to go. These workers record the fact that an order has been filled. Some researchers argue that a system to assist the shipping department is office automation, while a system to help on the production line is factory automation.

We shall adopt a broad definition of the office and state that office automation is a system that aids knowledge workers. A system controlling production or manufacturing machinery is a manufacturing system. The major distinction is between automating a production process and aiding an individual who must process information.

The Nature of Office Work

Office work is characterized by communications among the individuals in the office, documents, a supporting file system of documents and information, and a set of procedures executed by office workers. In addition to

TABLE 19-1 Some Components of Office Automation

Managerial and secretarial workstations
Word processing
Personal computer applications, e.g. (spreadsheets)
Electronic and voice mail
Filing systems
Presentation graphics
Computer conferencing

routine procedures, there are office activities that arise from requests made of office workers.

Thus, an individual in an office handles information such as reports, forms, letters, and memoranda. The worker may perform computations, verify information, and access different files. The office worker spends much time communicating, often over the telephone. Activity is stimulated by a request, such as a customer calling with a question, or by the passage of time, such as the preparation of a weekly report on sales. Other office activities include planning, work on special projects, and communications.

Office Technology

While there is much routine in an office, there are other activities that arise on an ad hoc basis. What kind of technology can support this variety of tasks? See Table 19-1. Some systems can be used on a routine basis; for example, a system to report sales could automate a manual tally sheet kept by order entry personnel. For nonroutine tasks, one can think about providing support for the generic functions that underlie the tasks. For example, word processing helps in the preparation of a wide variety of documents; the word processing system is a general-purpose tool for the office. Other such tools include electronic mail, conferencing systems, and forms processing systems.

Managerial Workstations

The managerial workstation is one device that can have a dramatic impact on the productivity of office workers. The workstation offers the following tools to aid the knowledge worker:

1. Word processing.
2. Electronic spreadsheets.
3. Filing systems.
4. Presentation graphics programs.
5. Electronic mail programs.
6. Network connections.

Word processing began with dedicated word processors, devices that could be used only in this task. As microcomputer programs became more sophisticated, word processing began to move from dedicated to general-purpose micros. Word processing is now being extended to desktop publishing systems so that near-typeset quality output will be possible at a modest cost.

Word processing improves both productivity and document quality. Productivity is higher because successive drafts of papers and reports do not need to be retyped. Once they have been entered, only changes and corrections have to be reentered. Because the document can be edited and polished on the system, the final output is free of correction fluid and erasures. Of course, word processing does encourage the author to go through a large number of drafts!

Electronic spreadsheets are some of the most popular microcomputer programs. Spreadsheet programs fit very well into the office environment. Many office tasks involve processing numbers such as budgets or analyses of the cost of a new project. The electronic spreadsheet program can be used for ad hoc decision support applications or for routine reports produced on a regular basis.

A filing system may be designed specifically for an office, or office workers can define their own files using a DBMS. These programs tend to be a bit more difficult for users than spreadsheets or word processors. However, advances in the quality of micro DBMSs for end users will make custom filing system more common.

Many office professionals are called upon to make presentations; a set of graphics programs can help save preparation time for presentations and should result in high-quality displays. Programs exist to create text and graphics on 35-mm slides or transparencies using a variety of output devices. Cameras taking direct signals from a CRT produce excellent 35-mm slides, and relatively inexpensive plotters produce high-quality transparencies.

The workstation needs a manager to make it easy for the user to access any of these programs. The manager is a type of "shell" that hides the operating system from the user. A number of these shells exist for MS DOS, the most popular microcomputer operating system. The next generation of operating system for personal computers should improve this interface by allowing the user to run several programs simultaneously in different windows on the CRT. For example, one could work on a document with the word processor, move to a window and prepare a spreadsheet, and then easily move the spreadsheet to the document. This kind of technology will greatly improve the capabilities and appeal of the managerial workstation.

Electronic Mail

One of the most important contributions of technology to the office is electronic mail. Office workers and professionals of all types spend a great deal of time communicating with each other. An electronic mail system is a new form of communications that falls between a telephone and a letter.

Electronic mail systems allow the user to send a message from a workstation (terminal) to another user. The sender addresses the message to a receiver and types the text; the sender then types a sequence of characters to indicate that the message is complete and should be sent.

The computer system routes the message to the recipient's electronic mailbox. When the recipient runs his or her mail program, the message is waiting to be read. The sender can send multiple copies of the message and can set up mailing lists so that by entering the name of a list, the entire group of people on the list will receive a copy of the message.

Mail systems offer users a great deal of flexibility for messages that are not urgent. Studies have shown that a large number of phone calls are not completed the first time they are dialed, either because the person called is not in or because the line is busy. If a message does not require discussion, putting it on the system has several advantages. First, the message is available whenever the recipient uses his or her computer. Second, the message is off line; the recipient can think about a reply without having to respond immediately, as in a phone conversation. Finally, the communication is asynchronous; the recipient is not interrupted by a phone call.

Electronic mail systems may serve one department, an entire organization, or a network of organizations. Our department in the university has used electronic mail for more than 5 years; we can communicate with other faculty members, graduate students, research assistants, students in classes, and secretaries. Since various individuals are in a number of different locations during the day, the mail system has proven invaluable in departmental communications. In fact, in more than one instance, an electronic message has reached someone before a telephone message.

In addition to communicating within the department, we are connected to two national and international networks. With a more complicated address, it is possible to send messages to a large number of faculty members and researchers on the Arpanet. This network ties together a large number of university computers and computers of certain government contractors. A similar network called Bitnet connects universities in the United States and Europe, along with a number of research laboratories.

A company wishing to establish an electronic mail system can use a common carrier and rent mailboxes for a small charge. Anyone on the system with a mailbox can send and receive messages; a number of companies have used this approach to pilot test electronic mail. Other firms have installed dedicated computers to support office automation and electronic mail. Digital Equipment (DEC) is a major vendor in this area and has installed over 12,000 of its All In One office automation systems, which feature electronic mail.

An Example

DEC itself is a major user of electronic mail. This multinational manufacturer of computers has over 60,000 active subscribers to its internal electronic mail system.

The user can file messages electronically, so that there is a record of messages related to a particular topic or sender. As with many systems, the user can write and edit a message, read and answer mail, forward mail, file mail, and create distribution lists so that one message can be sent to multiple recipients.

Some 62 per cent of the users at DEC work with the system; the rest use secretaries. A majority of system users feel that their personal productivity has increased by 5 to 15 per cent, but of course, this is only a subjective evaluation. At DEC an economic analysis suggested that electronic mail was less expensive than traditional communications mechanisms if the message required an additional phone call or copy of a message. For any copies or phone calls beyond the second, electronic mail is less expensive than an interoffice memo or telephone call.

Cost savings, however, are usually not the justification for an electronic mail system. Mail systems are attractive because they offer an additional form of communications and provide the organization with greater flexibility. The president of DEC indicated that it would be hard to manage the firm if it were impossible to communicate with the company's 60,000 stations around the world that are on the electronic mail system.

Voice Mail

In addition to electronic mail, voice mail systems are available. With these systems, a recorded voice message is left in the recipient's mailbox. One advantage of voice mail is that the only device needed to use the system is a telephone. Voice mail appeals to individuals who travel and do not have easy access to a terminal and to those who do not want to type messages.

The Ford Motor Company uses a voice mail system with over 2000 mailboxes for communications between sales representatives and sales managers; the system is expected to grow to 30,000 mailboxes in the future. A salesperson who is traveling uses an 800 toll-free number to call the system; in addition to leaving a message, the employee can check his or her mailbox. Voice mail offers an attractive approach to communications in situations where it is difficult to coordinate schedules to make phone connections.

Computer Conferencing

Computer conferencing is another type of communications. Common carriers and some firms have established teleconferencing facilities. Teleconferencing usually involves a meeting in which one group communicates with another at the same time. The least expensive teleconference uses a speaker phone. More elaborate versions involve meeting rooms with television transmission so that participants can see other members of the meeting at different locations.

Computer conferencing is quite different from teleconferencing because the communications are usually asynchronous. Individuals sign on to a central computer and join a conference. They review comments from other participants that were made the last time they were on the system, and then add their own contributions.

Computer conferencing can be appropriate for a team of individuals at different locations who are working on the same project. It is probably a good idea, however, to have individuals meet at least once in person before using the conferencing system. Periodic meetings may also be necessary to maintain social ties among the work group. Computer conferencing then becomes a mechanism for maintaining project progress between meetings of the project team.

DEC is offering a system called *VAX Notes,* which can be used for a computer conference. The system grew out of an informal communications network developed by DEC employees at research centers. With this system, the creator of a conference has the option of being its moderator. He or she establishes the agenda and topics to be covered and sets up a conference directory. The moderator may also set up a membership list. The system provides users with an electronic notebook containing information about the conferences in which the user is participating. Computer conferencing appeals to individuals who are already used to working with computers; the availability of packages like Notes should encourage others to try conferencing as well.

Managing Remote Work

Some firms are using communications technology to allow employees to work remotely, possibly at a satellite location or even at home. Company management is then faced with the problem of how to supervise these remote workers. Will remote workers become dissatisfied because of their lack of contact with colleagues? Will individuals working at home be distracted and produce lower-quality output?

Some labor unions and other groups have opposed work at home because they feel it is a way of exploiting laborers. For many individuals, the ability to work at home allows them to be employed—for example, mothers with children who lack adequate day care facilities. As communications and computer technology make it easier to provide remote work, the issues of managing it will demand more attention.

The Impact of Office Automation

Many organizations began their office automation in the administrative services area. The manager of the typing pool became the manager of office automation because this technology was first seen as primarily providing word processing services. Given the trends in the technology and a broad view of office automation, one expects that the CIO will ultimately be responsible for office automation and telecommunications.

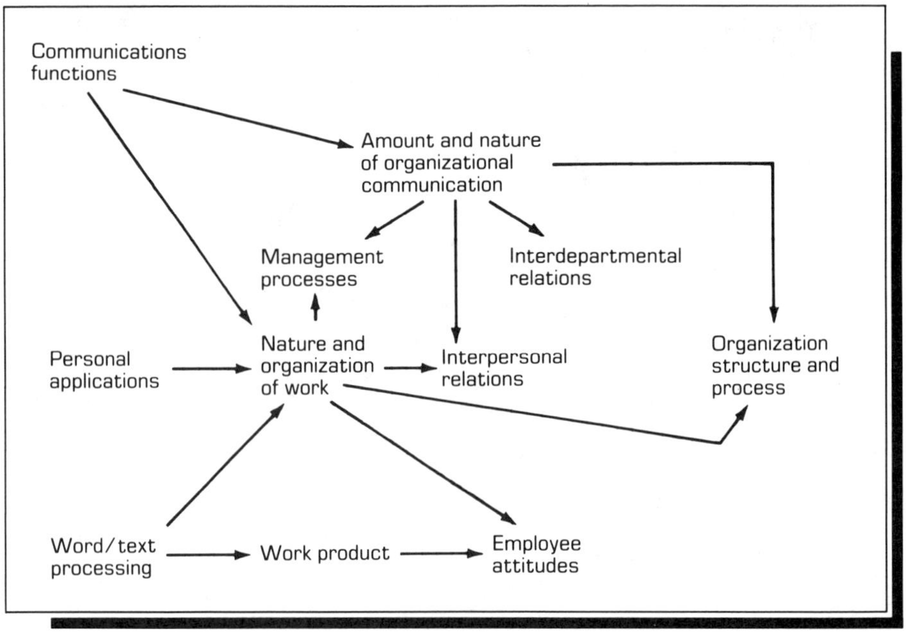

FIGURE 19-1 The impact of office automation. (From Olson and Lucas, 1982)

There have been relatively few studies of the impact of office automation on the organization. It is necessary to understand this impact in order to implement and manage the technology successfully. In this section, we present a predictive model of the impact of office automation on the organization as an aid to planning and managing this aspect of information processing in the firm (Olson and Lucas, 1982). See Figure 19-1.

The Nature of Work

1. Automated systems, especially word processing systems, can improve the quality of documents.

We have discussed the improvements in quality possible with word processing. Correspondence also benefits from the technology. For example, we expect reduced transformation through office automation. If office professionals begin to type more of their correspondence and reports instead of giving a secretary hand-written documents, there should be fewer transformation errors.

2. Automated offices permit increased specialization of skills to support administration.

One option for management is to reorganize the office for increased specialization. Clerical employees who become word processors may see this change as an advance and an increase in job scope. On the other hand, some critics of the technology feel that office automation will deskill workers and create a factory in the office.

Thus, management must consider the possible negative impact of specialization and plan jobs in such a way that the negative aspects of factory work do not become characteristics of the office. For example, assembly line workers report great dissatisfaction with their isolation. Office work should be structured so that individuals do not lose social contact with fellow workers.

3. Communications aspects of automated offices can alter the physical and temporal boundaries of work.

We have discussed the asynchronous nature of electronic mail. Since an electronic mail system is available whenever the computer system is operating, there are no time restrictions on message systems. For multinational firms, the technology makes it possible to communicate easily across time zones on a routine basis.

The characteristics of electronic mail can be used to create greater flexibility in the place and time of work. There is much interest in the idea of allowing some employees to work at home, using computer and communications technology to keep in touch with fellow workers. In fact, computer programmers are in the forefront of those involved in work-at-home projects.

Management can also consider using the technology to move entire work units to different locations, such as smaller satellite work centers closer to the place where employees live. While this arrangement provides additional flexibility, there are problems in managing and supervising workers at remote sites.

Impact on Individuals

4. Automated office systems can affect the identity and stress level of office workers, especially secretaries and clerical workers.

A few studies suggest that stress is a major problem with certain clerical jobs, especially those involving machine pacing of work, monotonous and repetitive tasks, and servicing of others. Management needs to consider the way jobs are defined in the automated office to reduce stress.

Managers are expected to experience little or no increase in role overload or stress from automated offices. There may be greater time pressure to respond to electronic memoranda than to those on paper, but since electronic messages replace phone calls, the recipient has time to frame a response without having to react immediately on the telephone.

5. Automated offices can affect the status and satisfaction of office workers.

An increased variety of tasks, increased skill levels, and direct feedback have been found to improve job satisfaction and status. Automation of some of the most routine and boring office jobs should help improve job satisfaction. As skill levels increase to use workstations and different programs, there will be new career paths in the office for clerical workers.

Management, however, must be careful not to design jobs and the organization so that decreased status and satisfaction are the result. Early experiments with word processing centers reduced the status and satisfaction of secretaries who lost contact with individual managers to become members of a typing pool.

6. Changes in the location of work can affect the professional's feeling of identification with organizational goals and the criteria for promotion.

If management provides professionals working on long-term projects with communications and computer equipment to work at home, will the professionals still identify with the firm? The use of the technology is this manner may encourage loyalty to the profession rather than to the organization providing the equipment.

7. Office automation can lead to improved efficiency of communication.

In the preceding DEC example, we discussed some of the increases in administrative efficiency claimed for the electronic mail system. We expect these advantages to accrue to most mail users, though the evaluation of these systems will probably remain subjective.

8. Office automation can lead to decreased face-to-face contact between a manager and a secretary, between colleagues, and between superiors and subordinates.

Mail systems can easily substitute for some forms of direct communication. What is the impact of this substitution? In the university, we felt it important to maintain regular faculty meetings and social functions to avoid depersonalization of the department.

9. Office automation can lead to an increase in the total volume of communication in the organization.

Due to the ease of using electronic mail, we expect there to be greater communication in the department. To the extent that management favors extensive communication, the mail system will have a positive impact on the firm.

10. Office automation can affect the total volume of communications between departments.

Departmental boundaries have been known to reduce communications activities. Electronic mail offers an easy way to transcend these boundaries without the negative features of the telephone. Management may want to use this aspect of electronic communications to restructure the organization. For example, one could place industrial engineers in the factory near the equipment for which they are responsible instead of in an office. The engineers are in one location for communications purposes; they could be distributed to the factory, with electronic mail facilitating communications with other engineering colleagues.

11. Office automation can affect managers' perceptions of the degree of rationality, flexibility, and scope of their work.

Some writers claim that management is emotional rather than rational; they see office automation as forcing rational systems on the manager, reducing the scope of movement and creativity. However, messaging systems still provide the opportunity for managers to control their communications. To the extent that these systems encourage communications across managerial levels, they will reduce the blockage or withholding of information that some managers adopt as a strategy.

12. Office automation can affect methods for monitoring and controlling work.

How does a manager monitor and control work that is done remotely? Will there be a temptation to pay clerical workers on a piece rate? Some union critics of work at home fear that even though the employee is tied to the firm by communications, this aspect of office automation marks a return to the type of contract labor that was banned a number of years ago. In addition, will managers feel comfortable supervising employees they cannot see?

13. Office automation systems can help increase the span of control of managers.

If a managerial workstation and electronic mail help the manager become more efficient, he or she should have more free time. The organization may be tempted to take advantage of this situation by increasing the number of subordinates reporting to the manager. This approach is quantifiable, whereas the other savings from office automation often are not. One major bank has justified its entire investment in office systems by the goal of increasing the span of control of middle management by one employee.

Interpersonal Relations

14. Office automation can reduce the quantity and quality of social interaction in the office.

We discussed this problem briefly when considering reduced face-to-face contact. Offices clearly help fill some social needs, and many people who work in offices are motivated by interaction with their peers. A satellite work center may be a better idea than remote work simply because it does allow more social needs to be met.

15. Office automation can affect the number of links within the organization and the volume of communications among the links.

We have described the characteristics of electronic mail that lead to more communications. Because messaging systems are easy to use, yet do not interrupt or disturb the recipient, they encourage more communications. This trend should result in communications between individuals who rarely communicated before the system was established. However, increased communications upward may cause overload for managers; receiving several hundred electronic messages a day can take the fun out of electronic mail.

Interdepartmental Relations

16. Office automation can affect the degree of interdepartmental conflict, interdependence, and definition of boundaries.

To the extent that mechanical obstacles account for departmental conflict, office automation should help to alleviate problems. Electronic mail can be used to communicate between and coordinate departments. The production department's night shift supervisor can send an electronic message to the shipping department's day shift explaining any problems in manufacturing.

Organization Structure

17. Office automation can facilitate changes in the definition of physical organizational boundaries.

Regardless of physical location, by using office technology, employees can contribute to the organization. One extreme position is that the organization could become a network of small work groups or even of individuals. At least the technology gives management the option of considering other physical structures for the organization. The CIO, faced with a shortage of programmers, may want to encourage remote work as a way of retaining or attracting employees.

18. Office automation can improve the ability of the organization to accommodate structural changes.

In the discussion of organizational structure in Chapter 2, we presented Galbraith's information processing approach to organizations. To the extent that office automation improves the ability of the organization to communicate and process information, it provides another tool for responding to a changing environment. Since messaging and other communications systems cut across organizational boundaries, reconfiguring the organization should be easier since communications paths can be kept intact.

Summary

Office automation has the potential to influence the organization in a number of ways. If management controls the process, it is possible to use this technology to improve communications, the quality of work, and the efficiency of managers. As with any technological change, management needs to plan for implementation and then manage the systems once they have been installed. In the next section we shall discuss some implementation steps for office automation.

Implementation

In the article referred to previously (Olson and Lucas, 1982), four characteristics of a high-potential prototype application for office automation were suggested:

1. A high volume of task-oriented communications.
2. Significant coordination requirements between (or within) departments.
3. Good working relationships among those involved.
4. Low levels of departmental conflict.

One must consider work design issues and pay attention to the composition of the work group and the social relations among employees. The impact model can be used to predict what might happen and to test various design decisions.

The implementer might want to make a simple list of the benefits and costs for the individuals involved. For each person, the positive and negative impacts of the system should be predicted. The implementer should try to redesign the system or the organization so that the negative factors are minimized before implementation.

Overall Strategy

Few implementation efforts have been reported for office automation. Our own experience suggests several important considerations. First, it is probably possible to implement word processing from the bottom up, but this is about the only office automation function for which one can start at the bottom.

We have found that having a senior manager use electronic mail for significant communications provides the greatest incentive for subordinates to use electronic mail themselves. Even if the high-level manager uses electronic mail through a secretary, the fact that the messages are coming from the manager is important in encouraging use.

The next step is to introduce managerial workstations. Past experience suggests that the implementer should locate several interested and highly visible managers in the organization for a demonstration. Then the workstations can be provided to anyone who requests one. Implementers should make the workstation easy to use and see that individuals have their own. Sharing is not consistent with the concept of an individual workstation.

For the most part, office systems are expected to be off the shelf. They deal with generic office functions like word processing, filing, spreadsheet analysis, and electronic mail. A number of products are available for these purposes. It is possible to subscribe to one of four or five publicly offered electronic mail systems. The firm can also purchase an in-house computer with electronic mail software that can be implemented relatively quickly.

Even if the office systems effort involves the design of a managerial workstation, we would recommend that off-the-shelf components be used. The major task of design should be delineating the functional requirements of office systems and then choosing and integrating packages. The high cost of custom development is not justified for most office systems.

An Implementation Procedure

Christie (1985) has suggested the following steps for implementing office systems, which will now be reviewed.

1. Be sure that there is a need for the system.

Try to avoid marketing a technological solution for which there is no problem. Assess the readiness of the organization and the users for the system.

2. Ensure commitment to the system.

Try to develop high-level commitment to the system; follow the top-down implementation strategy previously recommended. Senior management is an excellent model for others in the firm.

3. Provide support.

The introduction of a system is crucial, but do not forget to support it for ongoing operations. Users will not work with systems if implementers fail to support them. In addition, it is important to provide financial support; there must be sufficient terminals and micros. We have found that users do not like to disturb others; the appeal of this technology is that it belongs to the user rather than to others in the organization.

4. Involve key parties.

Form a project team to plan for the system. Include representatives of all the potential users. Part of the role of this team is to market the system in the organization.

5. Establish goals.

What are the different reasons for the system? What are the goals of the implementation effort?

6. Maximize awareness.

Try to ensure that others in the organization are aware of the system. The design team can hold review meetings, give demonstrations, and set up a pilot test using a common carrier mail system before committing the organization to an in-house system.

7. Analyze the problem.

Conduct a systems analysis and design for the office. What functions need assistance? What are the characteristics desired for the firm's word processor? Is a full workstation needed? What groups should be included in electronic mail?

8. Anticipate the penetration.

Plan for the rapid spread of information through the organization. Consider the impacts discussed in the previous section and plan for them.

9. Identify the impact on individuals.

Will pay, job security, and career opportunities change? These issues should be discussed with the design group and the system planned to take them into account.

10. Assess the time scale.

It will probably take longer than planned to develop and install the system. The usual technology problems will occur, as well as difficulties with individuals in the organization itself.

11. Be aware of laws and regulations.

Control over transborder data flows presents a real problem for multinational firms implementing large-scale office automation systems.

12. Plan for changes.

Refer to the previous section for concerns about the impact of the technology on individuals, the work group, and the firm as a whole.

13. Prepare for the changes.

Implementation may require physical changes to workplaces, as well as the installation of new computer equipment. The firm may want to review its entire telecommunications function as a part of this implementation process.

14. Select the appropriate equipment.

The equipment has to function properly for the application; it is the end users who will use the equipment, and their cooperation will determine the success of the effort. The technology must work; be sure that the level of sophistication is appropriate to the user and the problem. An overly sophisticated workstation may not be used.

15. Attend to the user interface.

Is the system user friendly? How easy is it to use the system? Can people be trained quickly to work with the system?

16. Attend to the needs of different user groups.

Part of the work of the design team is to anticipate problems that different user groups may have with the system. Certain identifiable departments or work groups may need special training or management attention for the system to succeed.

17. Implement the changes.

Follow the implementation plan to install the systems and begin operations. Most of these systems can be installed gradually; new departments can be added one at a time to an electronic mail system. Workstations can be provided to one professional at a time; staging the installation of the system should be fairly easy.

18. Monitor and evaluate the changes.

We have mentioned that it is difficult to evaluate the success of office systems on a quantitative basis. However, one should still try to gauge the impact of the implementation effort. It is also important to have feedback so that improvements can be made to the system.

19. Modify the systems.

If necessary, be prepared to make changes in the systems. A prototype and early testing should have revealed most problems with individual functions like electronic mail or word processing packages. However, the integration of these elements may create a problem. In addition, the workstation will probably need some refinement.

Managing Office Systems

Implementation is the most significant problem with office automation. How do implementers motivate and encourage users to adopt these systems? Once the systems have been installed, the same operational issues arise that occur with any computer-based system.

First, implementers need to be sure that the technology works. It is important to keep the electronic mail central computer working and available. Do not load the machine with so many other programs that it is hard to get a line or the mail program runs too slowly. The operations group must monitor the network to be sure that communications are possible. Finally, there needs to be support when something goes wrong with a terminal, modem, or user's workstation.

Second, implementers must provide support for users. There should be a telephone for help calls, and consultants should be available. Since these systems involve a large number of employees, normal turnover will create a need for constant training.

Third, office systems management requires an R&D effort; the firm must evaluate advances in the technology and adopt new technology where appropriate.

Finally, office automation and communications must be considered part of information processing in the firm in general. Plans for the technology should include these two components, particularly since there will be little distinction in the future between the use of a computer for office applications and its use for other purposes in the firm.

Recommended Readings

Christie, B., "Introducing Office Systems: Guidelines and Impacts." in Christie, B. (ed.), *Human Factors of Information Technology in the Office.* Chichester: Wiley, 1985. (A good collection of readings on office systems.)

Hiltz, S. R., and M. Turoff, "The Evolution of User Behavior in a Computerized Conferencing System," *Communications of the ACM,* vol. 24, no. 11 (November 1981), pp. 739–751. (A report on the use of a major computer conferencing facility.)

Olson, M., and H. C. Lucas, Jr., "The Impact of Office Automation on the Organization: Some Implications for Research and Practice," *Communications of the ACM,* vol. 25, no. 11 (November 1982), pp. 838–847. (The impact model discussed in this chapter.)

Discussion Problems

19.1 A major government financial institution was considering what to do with its two computer systems. Regular production work ran on an IBM computer with a 370 instruction set. For office automation, the firm had just purchased a VAX computer and the All in One package from DEC.

The vice president to whom information processing reported was concerned. "I am not sure how we are going to provide terminals. Will someone have to have two terminals on his desk, one for IBM and the other for the VAX? How do I decide what jobs to do on which computer? Right now, we want to have the VAX for office automation, but I know people will start building systems for themselves on that computer rather than the IBM mainframe."

Help the vice president prepare a policy statement on what applications will be developed on each computer. Is there a need to have two desktop terminals in order to use two different systems?

19.2 A major university decided to implement the office automation software that already existed on its minicomputer. The Information Systems faculty and several other groups in the school were heavy users of electronic mail. However, not all faculty members even had accounts on the computer system.

The dean's office felt that the system would be very useful for communicating with the faculty, particularly department chairmen. However, the deans themselves felt that they would probably not need to use the system. "The secretaries are the ones to use electronic mail," said one dean.

Three years after the idea of using electronic mail was first accepted, the system is still being used only by the IS faculty and a few others. How can the school move ahead with implementation?

Questions

1. What is an office?
2. How do office systems differ from other information systems?
3. Describe electronic mail.
4. What are the advantages of electronic mail?
5. How does electronic mail differ from voice mail?
6. How does computer conferencing differ from teleconferencing?
7. What are the advantages and disadvantages of computer conferencing compared with those of alternative communications methods?
8. Describe the software that might be included with an electronic workstation.
9. Why is electronic mail so appealing to a large multinational firm?
10. Why might one expect electronic communications to cut down on social interaction in the office?
11. How can office automation contribute to productivity and to the quality of output?
12. What are the problems of managing a remote work force?
13. How can office automation lead to overload and stress?
14. How does office automation provide the option to structure firms differently?
15. In what ways does office automation affect relations between departments?
16. How can office automation contribute to a manager's performance?

17. Is there a risk of turning professionals into clerical workers through office automation? If yes, how?
18. How is planning the implementation of office automation different from planning a traditional transactions processing system?
19. Should a firm consider designing its own office automation software?
20. How does one support users of office automation systems?

20

Managing Communications

Communications are of paramount importance to a modern organization. Historically, communications were face-to-face or written. The first advance in communications came with the telegraph, which allowed unheard-of speed in sending messages over long distances. The next major milestone was the telephone, which allowed voice communications from separate locations for the first time. Today we have the ability to send large amounts of data around the world in a matter of minutes.

There are three types of communications in the firm today:

1. Voice using a phone.
2. Data.
3. All other types.

Even though the first two categories have grown rapidly, the third category is quite large. It includes face-to-face meetings, written memoranda, mail, conferences, informal meetings, and so on. When researchers talk about voice communication, they are generally discussing voice via a phone, or telecommunications. Similarly, there is much information in the organization that is not transmitted; however, the technology of telecommunications plays a part when it is necessary to send data.

Historically voice and data communications have been considered separately. However, today's technology suggests that we should plan for all types of telecommunications services together; voice and data will utilize the same kind of network.

Fundamental Considerations

We are concerned primarily with the management of communications, not with the technology. However, a review of a few fundamentals will clarify some of the management issues.

Basics

Figure 20-1 shows a simple diagram of communications between computer devices. With today's communications technology, the first device needs an interface to convert its signals to signals that can be transmitted over the communications medium. An interface is needed by the second device to change the signals back into signals that this device can process.

Figure 20-2 is an example of this model of communications. Device 1 is a dumb terminal connected through a modem to a phone line. The phone, utilizing the public switched network, carries signals to a modem at a time-sharing computer. The modem modulates the signal for transmission, changing it from a string of bits to an analog signal for the phone network. The modem at the computer center converts the analog signal back to digital form for the computer.

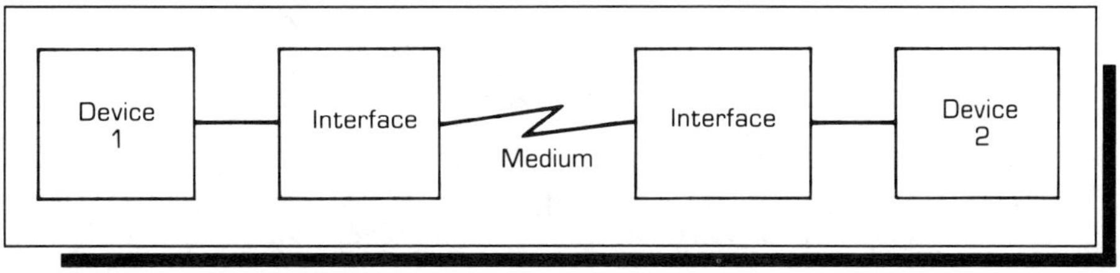

FIGURE 20-1 General communications. Communications between devices usually require some kind of interface between the device and the communication medium.

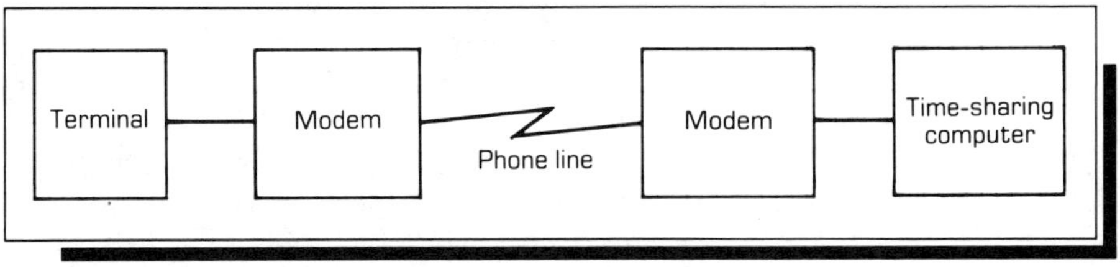

FIGURE 20-2 Example of communications. For a terminal connected to a time-sharing computer, we could use a device called a *modem* as the interface and a voice-grade phone line as the medium.

TABLE 20-1 Transmission Options

Type	
Serial	Block
One character at a time with start and stop bits	One block at a time
Asynchronous sender and receiver	Synchronized sender and receiver
Lines	
Simplex	One direction
Half duplex	Both directions, but one at a time
Full duplex	Both directions simultaneously on two lines

When configuring a communications network, the designer must be concerned with the type of transmission involved. Table 20-1 shows some of the options. In serial mode, characters are transmitted one at a time, with start and stop bits to delineate each character. Serial mode is associated with asynchronous transmission; no coordination is needed between the sending and receiving stations because each character is delineated. Serial, asynchronous transmission is used between the terminal and the time-sharing system.

In block mode, a block of data is sent all at once. For block mode to work, the sending and receiving ends have to be synchronized so that the receiving node can tell what is being sent. Because of this synchronization, transmission is faster in block mode than in serial mode.

Lines can send in one direction at a time, in which case the transmission is simplex. A half-duplex line sends data in both directions, but not at once. With full duplex, communications go in two directions at the same time on two different lines.

Figure 20-3 shows the modulation of digital signals by a modem for transmission over the phone line. The public phone network is analog, as there was no digital transmission when the telephone was invented. Given today's high volume of digital communications among computer devices, common carriers are installing a large number of digital links. Digital transmission is particularly well suited to fiber optics, which is one of the highest-capacity transmission methods available.

With digital transmission one does not have to use a modem for computer data; however, it is necessary to convert voice traffic to digital signals. This conversion is done by sampling the voice signal at very short intervals and characterizing the voice wave form digitally. The results are quite accurate because it is easy to detect transmission errors of a few bits as an outlier in a block of digital data.

Communicating devices use protocols to coordinate their actions. Sending and receiving stations adhere to the same conventions for establishing a link and sending data over it. The protocol is used to set up a session and establish a path from one transmission node to another, to correct and detect errors, to format messages, to control lines, and to sequence messages.

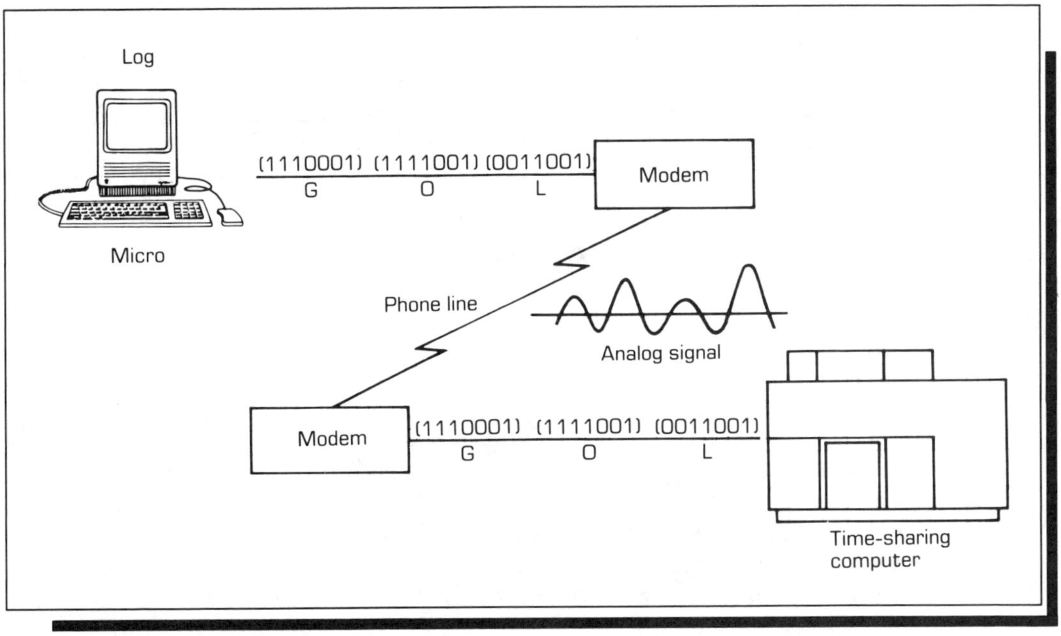

FIGURE 20-3 A modem changes digital signals from the microcomputer to analog signals for transmission over phone lines. Decoders at the time-sharing computer site change the phone signals back to digital code. When the time-sharing computer sends data to the microcomputer, the operation is reversed.

Networks

A network is a series of communications paths that link different nodes together. The nodes may be locations where data or voice traffic occur. The most familiar network is the public switched phone system. As we discussed in Chapter 17, there are a number of options available to a firm wishing to construct a network. The firm may use dial-up services that are routed over the public network. Another alternative is one of the value-added carriers, which has or leases its own lines and then sells communications services on the lines. Finally, the firm can develop its own private network by leasing lines, a strategy followed by some firms with worldwide or nationwide systems, such as the airlines.

In addition to these wide-area networks, there is great interest in LANs. These relatively low-speed networks allow a group of users to connect different devices for communications and sharing purposes. For example, workers might want to share a plotter; each user does not use a plotter often enough to justify having one at his or her micro. The network makes one available to everyone. Similarly, depending on the software vendor's requirements, it may be possible to put one copy of software on a shared disk and allow each person on the network to download a copy. This approach to management reduces diskette handling and makes it easier to control changes and new versions of software.

There is competition now among vendors of LANs and private branch exchanges (PBX). A PBX connects a large number of nodes together. New model PBXs are digital, and a number can transmit voice and data together. The most modern approach is to digitize speech at the telephone handset, which makes it possible to have all transmission in digital form.

Integrated Services Digital Networks

Communications carriers are racing to offer the integrated services digital network (ISDN). This digital network will extend nationwide, beyond the digital PBX that might be found in an office. The ISDN will work with the PBX to replace the several networks now used by many companies to handle phone traffic, data traffic, facsimile machines, and LANs.

From a consumer standpoint, these new services will offer display phones that show who is calling and will allow a caller to communicate in writing. The networks will allow households to have easy access to advanced services like home banking, videotext, and electronic mail, and even home security monitoring.

The goal of an ISDN is to offer users a universal communications facility. An ISDN has three major elements. The first is a digital, end-to-end communications channel under the control of the user. The second is a choice of narrow and wide bandwidth transmission services. The third element consists of standard interfaces and conversion facilities to permit widespread, transparent access by users.

Efforts are now underway to create the standards that will make ISDN possible. It is likely that ISDN will offer two kinds of service. Primary service will support large business users; total transmission capacity will be something like 1.5 million bits per second. Individual user service—for example, for individual terminal users—will provide 144,000 bit-per-second capacities.

The promise of ISDN technology is voice, data, and video communications, all using the same network. With ISDN, users would not have to worry about LANs and other networks; they could just plug in a personal computer or terminal the way one plugs an appliance into a wall socket. ISDN will also be used to integrate existing networks like LANs.

Naturally, for all of this equipment to work, there will have to be interface standards for the communications network. Devices to be connected to the ISDN will have to meet standards set up by the providers of communications circuits.

Electronic Data Interchange

The use of information technology as part of corporate strategy is an important objective for many firms today. Often this strategy involves linking one organization with another electronically. One popular arrangement is to place a terminal or microcomputer in a customer location that can access the firm's order entry system. Such an application draws the customer closer to the firm offering the service. To reduce costs, Detroit auto makers are connecting their computers directly to the computers of suppliers so that orders can be transmitted electronically. In fact, for concepts like JIT inventory to work, electronic communications may be required.

A broadly emerging standard, ANSI X.12, along with software to support the standard, is giving impetus to electronic data exchange. This standard provides transmission control, a transactions format, and content standards. Industries are developing subsets of the standard to fit their needs. For example, the apparel and textile industries are developing a subset that will automate not only billing and ordering but also transmission for fabric specifications.

The advantage of a standard can hardly be overstated. Rockwell International found that it had over 100 program modules to deal with companies and various divisions with which it exchanged data. A personal computer to interface company treasurers with bank on-line account balance query systems needs 80 to 100 different formats, one for each bank's system.

There will be growing pressure on ISDs to connect their firms with other organizations. The objectives for management are to reduce or eliminate paperwork and to strengthen the firm's link to customers and suppliers. The reduction in paperwork is accompanied by increases in the speed of communication, which reduces overhead. For example, a JIT inventory requires timely communications. The CIO will increasingly be developing managerial links with external organizations to accompany electronic ones.

Bypass

With increasing deregulation of the communications industry, organizations are thinking more about the issue of bypass. Bypass is to the practice of developing private communications alternatives to public carriers ranging from the local phone company to AT&T for long-distance service. Our university installed a microwave link between two campuses over a mile apart. The microwave was less expensive in the long run and provides more capacity than a leased line from the local phone company.

Ebasco Services, a New York engineering firm, uses a microwave terminal and a 2-foot antenna to send communications from its offices to an antenna operated by Satellite Business Systems, a long-distance carrier. In this way, Ebasco bypasses both the local New York phone system and AT&T's long-distance services. Other organizations are developing complete bypass systems; the University of Iowa is installing a $15 million fiber optic network to connect five locations.

Deregulation has led to many more options in designing a communications strategy for a firm. Because of constantly changing services and economics, management must continually revise and update its approach to communications.

Management Implications

From a management standpoint, computer networks are interesting for a variety of reasons. A network of computers is expected to be the predominant computing environment of the coming decade. We expect to see a variety of devices connected over different types of networks. See Figure 20-4. There will be mainframe computers connected to large databases, possibly accessed by a separate database computer.

LANs within the firm will be used to connect different devices together. For example, a group of micros might share a laser printer and a very large hard disk. In addition, there will be connections to other networks, such as those offered by the common carriers, to connect with other organizations.

Figure 20-5 shows how firms will try to connect their computers to reduce the amount of redundant keying required. A great deal has been achieved with transactions processing systems; the next advance will come with interorganizational systems.

Consider how much paperwork and duplication could be eliminated if a link existed between a vendor's and a customer's computers. An order for goods is entered by the customer directly into the supplier's computer; the order triggers shipping instructions as well as an electronic invoice. When the shipment arrives, the warehouse retrieves the purchase order and checks off the goods that are included. A clerk in the accounting department reviews the invoice and the purchase order to see that all items were delivered and that prices are correct. The clerk approves payment. If the customer does a lot of business with the supplier, the payment could be combined with other payments and sent at the end of the month in one check. Alternatively, the customer could be connected to the supplier's bank and send payment electronically.

Firms are now working on this type of data exchange. This approach will speed communications, reduce redundant effort, and reduce the cost of duplicate data entry by both parties.

Design of Communications Systems

Firms are grappling with the issue of what kind of communications architecture to develop for the future. The needs of the firm, the technology, and the communications industry all seem to be changing rapidly as the organization tries to plan.

Organizational Structure

One trend is clear: there is a strong impetus to centralize communications. Since the opposite trend is occurring with respect to computing and systems development, there is likely to be discomfort with the suggestion that com-

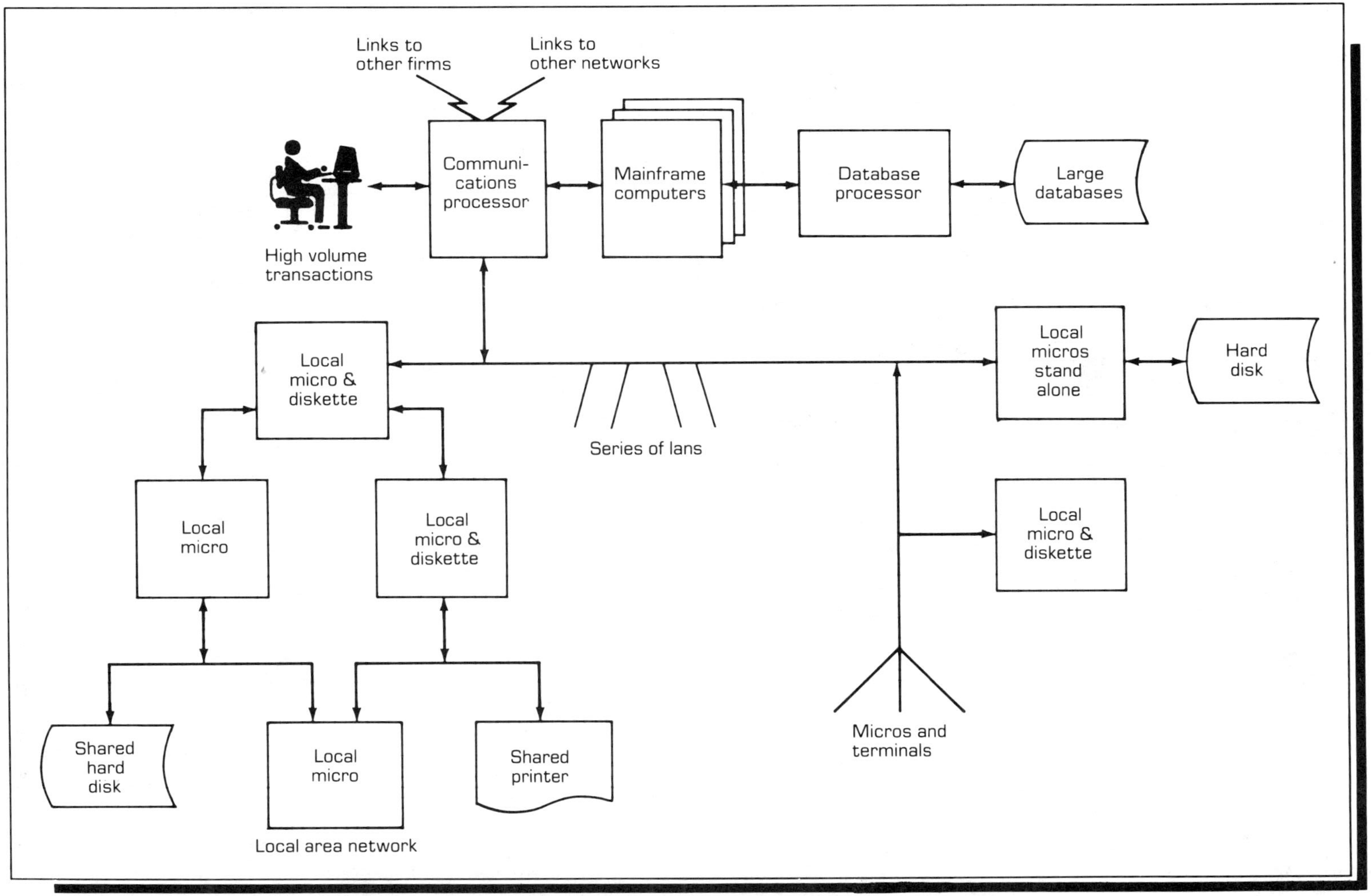

FIGURE 20-4 We predict that organizations will develop networks of mainframes, minicomputers, and microcomputers.

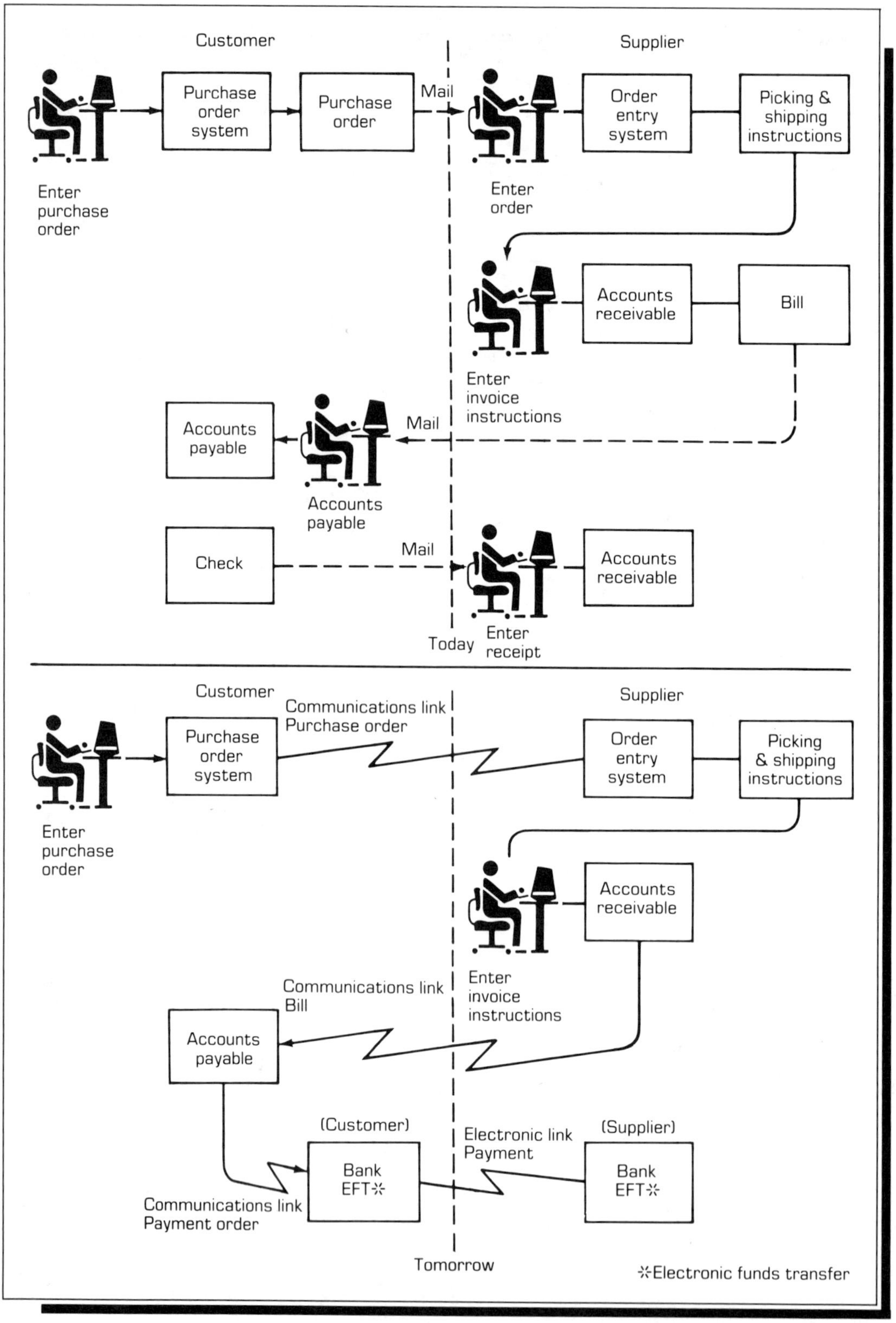

FIGURE 20-5 Above: today. Electronic connection between customer and supplies. Today's environment includes a lot of duplicate effort, entering and printing data. Below: tomorrow? In the near future, firms will establish direct computer-to-computer links to eliminate redundant operations.

munications is a central function. The argument must be made that communications serves to link information processing and voice transmission for the organization as a whole. Individual users should not be concerned with the network as long as it provides reliable service and allows them to send and receive the information they need to process. While there may be decentralized management for a number of functions, certain basic infrastructure activities are usually centralized, such as building maintenance, legal services, interface with public accountants, and so on. The communications network should be a part of the infrastructure because it is a common service and because coordinating it is extremely difficult if communications are decentralized.

Barriers to Networking

One of the major problems with networking is the lack of standards for computers and communications. These problems arise in two areas: the computer systems themselves and communications networks. There are digital networks, analog networks, and packet switched networks.

The International Standards Organization (OSI) has proposed a layered architecture as a standard. The standard consists of seven layers (see Table 20-2):

1. The bottom layer is the physical layer. It includes functions to activate, maintain, and deactivate the physical connection between two communications devices. It defines the characteristics of the physical circuit.
2. The data link layer covers synchronization and error control for data that are transmitted over the physical link.
3. The network layer routes communications through the network to their destination. It may disassemble and reassemble data units that travel over different routes.
4. The transport layer multiplexes independent message streams over a

TABLE 20-2 The OSI Layers

Layer	Function
Physical	Establish and maintain physical connections between devices
Data link	Synchronization and error control
Network	Route communications through the network
Transport	Multiplex independent message streams over a single connection
Session	Manage conversations between applications
Presentation	Manage data delivery, e.g., by converting character codes
Application	Manage resources during communication

single connection when desirable. This layer also segments data into the appropriate size for handling by the network layer.
5. The session layer manages and synchronizes conversations between applications. It resynchronizes data streams to be sure that a dialogue is not terminated before it should end.
6. The presentation layer ensures that data are delivered so that the receiving system can understand them. This layer might have to convert ASCII code to EBCDIC, depending on the devices communicating.
7. The application layer manipulates data. It handles resources for file transfers, virtual files, and terminal emulation.

The OSI model is often divided into two parts. The bottom three layers cover the components of the network needed to transmit a message. The top three layers reflect the characteristics of the end systems involved in the communications. These layers are not influenced by the medium actually used in transmission. The transport layer is the link between the top three and bottom three layers of the model. Some vendors are adopting the OSI standard, but it is not at all clear if and when the standard will allow the user to simply plug a device into a network.

Another problem in networking is incompatibility among computers. IBM has three computer architectures and several operating systems; it has marketed a communications network standard called SNA. IBM also markets LANs for its personal computers. Since the 370 computer architecture of IBM's mainframe and mini line uses EBCDIC code, someone with an ASCII terminal (the non-IBM standard code) cannot communicate with the 370 machine unless there is a special communications processor and program available in the 370 complex. Add to this confusion separate computer architectures of the mid-range system 36 and system 38 and the personal computer, and we are faced with a great deal of apparent incompatibility.

DEC has been capitalizing on its strengths of compatibility across its machine line and its network architecture. Using DECNET, a user can connect all of DEC's VAX line computers, including the Vaxmate, a personal computer that will execute PC-compatible programs. However, DECNET is not necessarily a standard to which other vendors can or will connect.

Each vendor has gained a parochial advantage by developing it own network. Unfortunately, this strategy was based on the false hope that companies would remain exclusively with a single vendor. In fact, management in most firms does not have sufficient control of computing to insist that only one vendor's equipment be used.

Until some of these compatibility and network standards issues are resolved, the designer of communications networks will have a difficult problem. The designer must evaluate the various options, visit other organizations, and project the communications environment in the next few years to determine what action is most appropriate now. It is probably a good idea to run a pilot test or two before committing the firm to one architecture. It is also vitally important to coordinate the communications plan with the overall plan for computer systems and new applications. It is quite possible that new applications will place requirements on a network that the design team will have to meet.

Design Approach

There are a number of steps to follow in the design of a communications network; the steps are similar to those followed in systems analysis and design of any type.

1. Define the problem. What is behind the request for a network? Since the network has the potential to affect all applications, present and future, in the firm, it is necessary to collect data from a wide variety of areas in the firm.

2. Develop the requirements and specifications for a network. At this stage, the designers need to determine what applications will make use of the net and to estimate message size and volume. It is also a good idea to think about performance requirements; if an on-line system is a part of the network, what response is expected at distant terminals? Will the delay inherent in satellite transmission preclude this type of transmission for the on-line application?

3. Configure the network. Prepare a plan documenting the requirements previously described. The plan should show major network links and traffic volumes. It should also list all of the applications and their characteristics. Finally, if the network will be used for voice traffic too, the document must show the estimated volume and duration of voice calls on the network.

4. Submit the document for bids. There are several options, as discussed earlier, such as AT&T, value-added services like MCI, Tymnet, and Telenet, and the configuration of a private network using any of a variety of carriers for transmission services and/or network equipment. For example, one can lease lines and purchase communications equipment from Telenet to set up a private packet switched network.

5. Evaluate the responses and alternatives. Cost, expandability, and performance will be the primary criteria in choosing an alternative. Given the complexity of the situation, the firm may want to use one of the consulting firms specializing in network design to help evaluate the responses; Manufacturer's Hanover, discussed later, followed this course in designing GEONET.

6. Choose an alternative and conduct a pilot test. It is important to determine if the technology will work as planned. A small network connecting dissimilar equipment is a good place to check out the capabilities of the devices chosen.

7. Install the network in stages. It may be possible to convert by geographic area or by application in order to control and manage change.

8. Evaluate the results. Before expanding the network, it is a good idea to determine how the net is performing and whether or not users are satisfied with it.

Managing Networks

Once installed, a network cannot be left alone. It is necessary to monitor the network and to check its performance. Also, as new applications are developed, the network may have to be expanded. If the network is private, the user will probably use monitors to check the lines and look for broken links or noise. Users will need a number to call when they suspect that a communications problem exists.

Examples

Brokerage Workstation Networks

Several retail-oriented stock brokerage firms, including Merrill Lynch and Shearson Lehman/E. F. Hutton, are developing networks of broker workstations. These firms provide a variety of financial services and feel they need to give brokers an automated advantage. Brokers often have to answer questions on the telephone with clients; the systems that are currently under design will place a tremendous amount of data and computational power in a workstation on the broker's desk. See Figure 20-6.

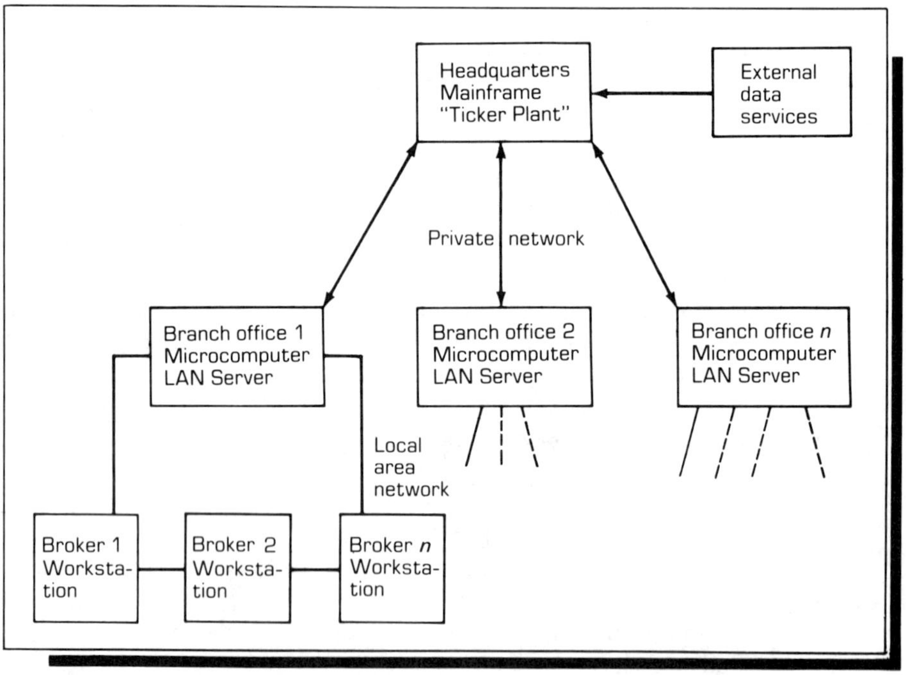

FIGURE 20-6 A brokerage system.

The systems involve three levels of hardware and software linked through private terrestrial and/or satellite communications networks. The systems will cost over $100 million. The applications feature large mainframe computers at headquarters. Microcomputers at regional branch offices are network servers, and there are thousands of microcomputer workstations for brokers and executives.

A "ticker plant" had headquarters will send a variety of data to a microcomputer LAN server in each branch office. The server makes these data available to workstations on each broker's desk. The broker can have the system automatically monitor different stocks for changes and can access a tremendous amount of data about financial markets and investments. The systems also provide office automation functions so that the broker can move data from the system into personalized letters for his or her clients. The workstations should provide these professionals with an information system which contributes directly to their productivity and to customer service.

Manufacturers Hanover Trust

Manufacturers Hanover Trust (MHT) is a major New York bank, the fourth largest in the United States. Two trends in business in the 1970s affected the bank. The first was increasing competition in the banking business due to deregulation, large swings in the economy, and a changing customer base. Banks now must earn income from services in addition to the traditional spread between funds invested and those loaned to customers. The second trend was tremendous growth in multinational businesses as large money center banks became more global in their business dealings.

During this time the bank operated four operations groups for computing, each associated with a different user community. Within these four organizational entities were a total of nine data centers operating different computers for their bank "customers." MHT was experiencing growth of 25% per year in communications costs as new on-line systems were installed.

In 1976 some 28 teleprocessing networks were supported by the various data centers for their on-line systems. Each of 200 retail branches had two different networks for unique applications or computers. The networks lasted an average of 18 to 24 months and were dumb; they provided no statistics on volume or activity.

Management at MHT felt that an integrated solution to their communications problems was needed. In 1978 the bank undertook a feasibility study to aid the design of a common network. Each business unit was asked to fill out a questionnaire on its planned growth of product offerings and enhancements: what volume of each type of communications service would it need? Analysts worked to discover existing information systems and to list specific details on traffic for each terminal and each type of message or transaction. The analysts also looked at the geographic distribution of traffic. Existing traffic was estimated at over 800,000 transactions per day, sufficient to justify an integrated corporate network if all traffic migrated to a new network.

The design team delineated five alternatives to be considered for a network for the bank:

1. Specialized networks (the status quo).
2. Public networks from common carriers.
3. Vendor networks.
4. Third-party design.
5. Internally designed and managed networks.

The design team met with their three major suppliers of computers: IBM, NCR, and DEC. It soon became clear that none of the vendors had a system that could accommodate all of the equipment in use at the bank.

The team retained a network consulting firm to evaluate the alternatives. The result of the analysis was a recommendation for a packet switched network following the X.25 international specification for packet switched protocols. The cost/benefit analysis showed that the network would not be cost justified based on the return on investment. The immediate advantage would be cost avoidance for new, specialized networks; in the long run, the network could be justified only by the belief that there would be added revenues and more customers from the services the bank could offer.

The bank proceeded with a pilot plan. It purchased Telenet communications processors and set up a private network of leased lines to provide a packet switched, internally managed network. The pilot interfaced an IBM computer in MHT with a Telenet communications processor, a retail NCR system using an NCR protocol, a corporate data center IBM system to the X.25 network, a time-sharing connection, and a terminal concentrator to the X.25 network.

After a successful pilot program in 1979, the bank undertook a full-scale implementation network now known as GEONET. This implementation proved more difficult than was forecast because electronic mail was coming to the bank. Telenet was chosen as the main supplier, and by the end of 1980 GEONET was running worldwide. By the end of 1981 the network linked midtown and downtown Manhattan, London, Hong Kong, Singapore, Bangkok, Kuala Lumpur, Djakarta, Tokyo, Seoul, and Caracas with a private X.25 net. The network provided access via public networks throughout the United States and 40 other countries on six continents. New services were added regularly and another $4 million was invested in expanding the network as communications operating costs continued to grow rapidly.

In 1982 and 1983 the network grew in coverage, but traffic volume was below planned targets by a significant margin. It was difficult to convert all of the high-volume, specialty networks to GEONET. Some users worried about response times for their high-volume operations like stock transfer.

Electronic mail expanded rapidly and had the highest volume of any user of the network; 5000 to 6000 employees used the mail system. Mail also stimulated the expansion of the network so that in 1984 it had equipment in 33 cities and 20 countries, along with 17 domestic locations. The plans called for expansion to over 30 additional locations. Areas not directly on the network had access to GEONET through public networks.

Bank officers are enthusiastic about the network; with large correspondent relations across the United States, the bank could not support this business without a network. The bank is also trying to connect electronically to all major corporate customers. Network availability provides great flexibility for changing markets; it is easy to add new applications and services because a separate network does not have to be configured for each new system.

Note, however, that the network requires continual expansion and management. The task force has spent a great deal of time helping to convert existing applications to GEONET, while at the same time expanding the network to provide new services. Network management requires that

1. Assistance be given to existing users of the network who are having problems.
2. Conversion support be offered to move existing applications to the new network.
3. The capacity and the need for new nodes be carefully evaluated and the network expanded as required.
4. Communications staff members keep abreast of standards, the capabilities of new equipment, and changes in tariffs and services offered by common carriers.

Harris Corporation

Harris is a producer of advanced communication and information processing systems; its management is familiar with the technology and had a desire to "showcase" its products in a private network. McCauley (1983) describes the development of a private network at Harris that features a variety of equipment along with satellite transmission.

The design effort for a network was stimulated by rising costs for communications, both voice and data. In 1979 corporate IS began a major program to improve the transmission of digitized voice and data communications over a private network. While data volumes were growing rapidly, the near-term justification for the network would be voice traffic. The analysis was done using PBX tapes of traffic at major locations.

The network consists of switch and access networks at headquarters in Melbourne, Florida, and three satellite ground stations at Melbourne, Dallas, and Westerly, Rhode Island. See Figure 20-7. The satellite network has a total of six wideband channels over three links, and each link has two carriers. The company rents space on the Western Union WESTAR III satellite, which provides 30 megahertz of bandwidth (corresponding to 60 megabits).

At each earth station, a Harris PBX functions as a tandem switch for voice routing. The switch selects the least expensive route for outgoing calls from among satellite links, Bell facilities, or WATS lines. Messages sent by

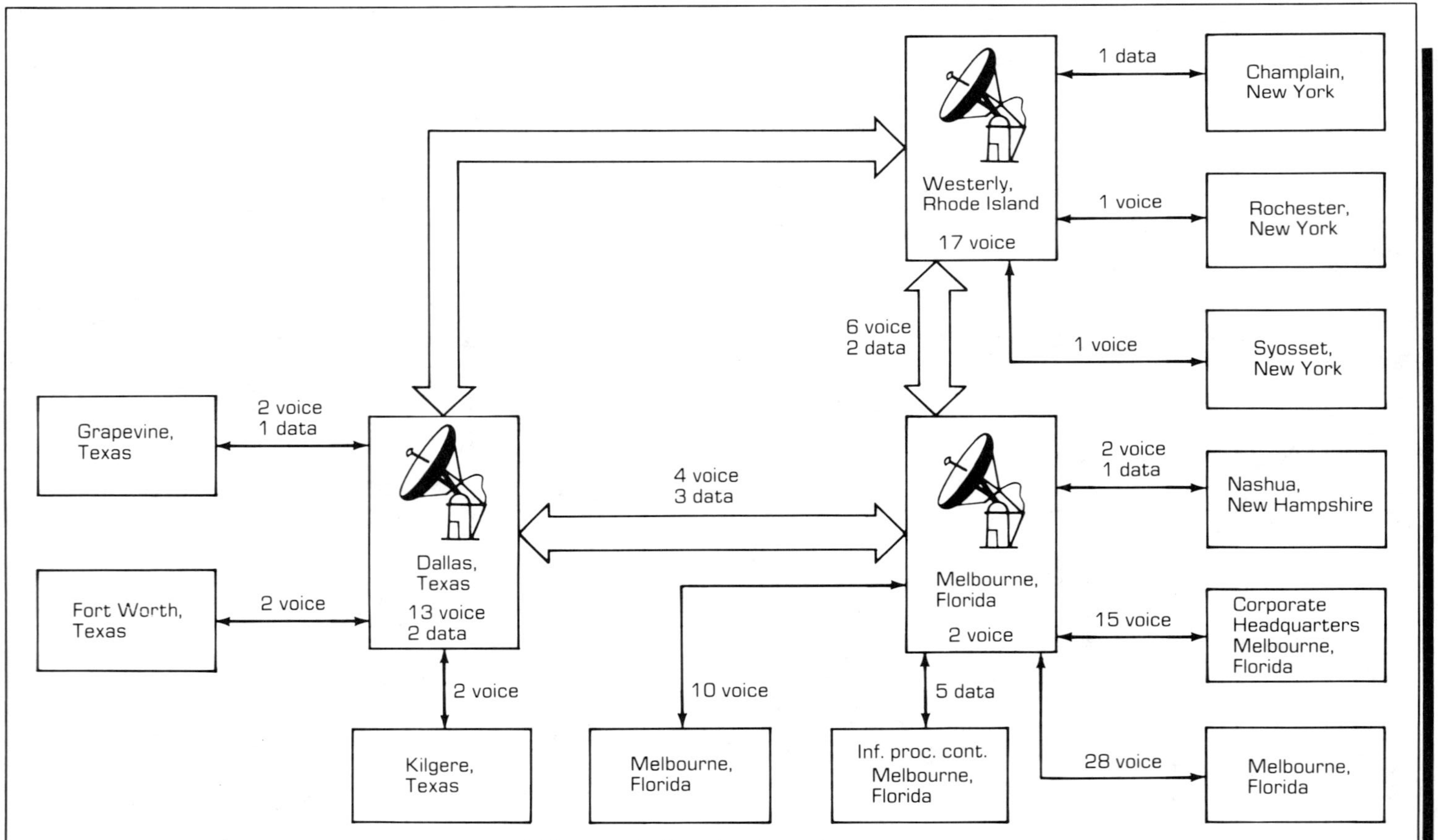

(a) Harris satellite network - first phase

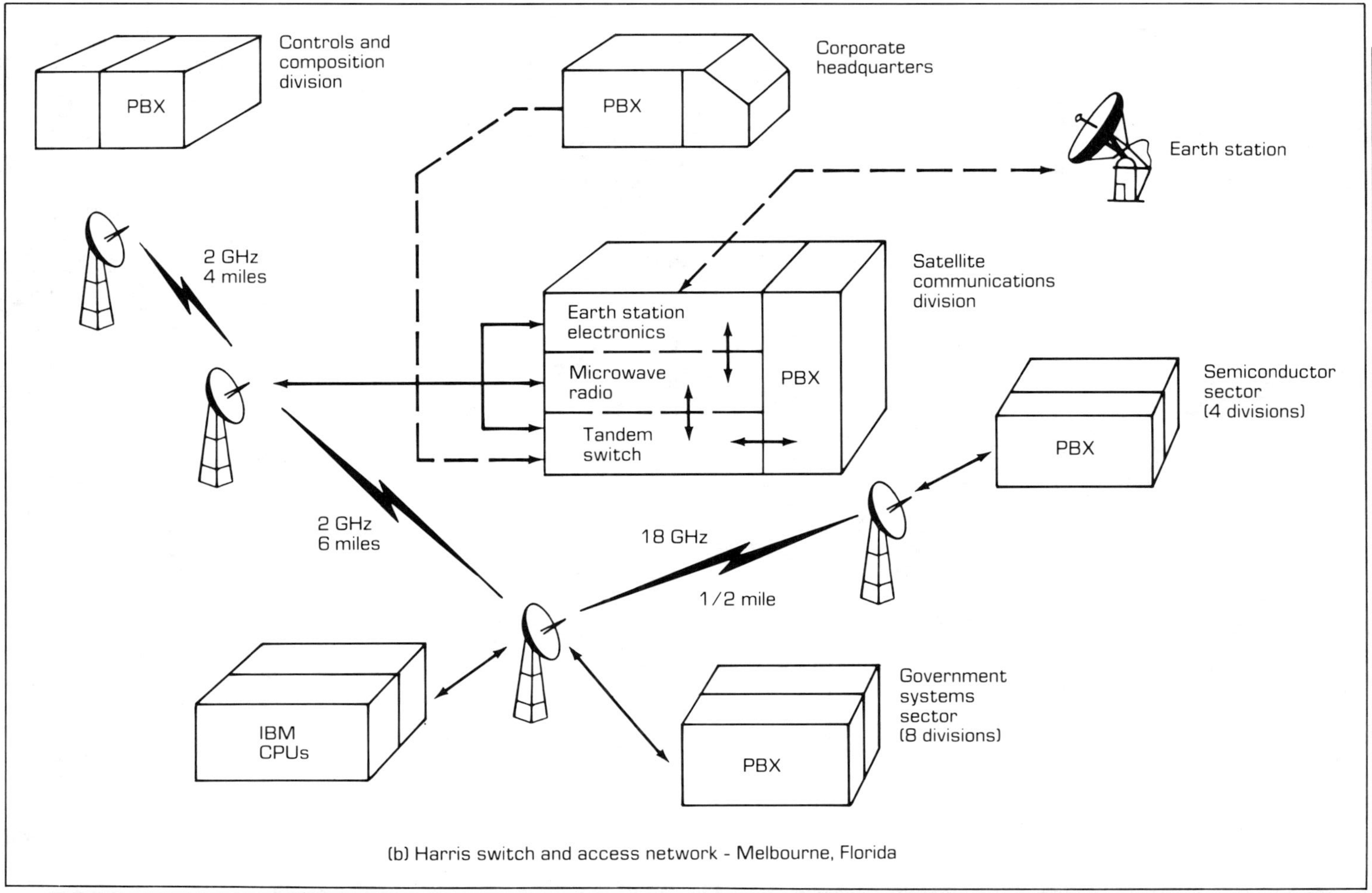

FIGURE 20-7 The Harris system. (From McCauley, 1983)

satellite are switched by another tandem switch at the receiving earth station to the local network.

Switched data and private-line data methods are used for data transmission. Switched data uses the voice switching facilities of the tandem switches and PBXs to establish connections; the communications facilities are satellites, microwaves, terrestrial tie lines, and FEX and WATS lines. The system uses modems and satellite-delay compensation units. Data circuits are point-to-point circuits, and no switching takes place. In Melbourne microwave connects the earth station with data communications equipment, so no modems are required for the digital system. The switched data service handles any synchronous protocol that functions in half-duplex mode and any asynchronous link protocol in common use.

Harris found that billing for private data is equal to or about 20 per cent less than common carrier charges. Voice billing on the network runs 10 per cent or less than alternative costs for the same service and no more than 65 per cent of Bell direct distance dialing rates.

Corporate IS found that the network effort forced management to pay increased attention to the cost and value of communications. The network program is credited with advancing IS programs by several years. In addition, the network effort accelerated the consolidation of IS, telecommunications, and office systems in the divisions by 2 to 3 years.

Harris believes that in the United States a satellite link is worth consideration by companies that have sales exceeding $500 million, two or more facilities located over 500 miles apart, and a volume of traffic between locations of 100,000 call minutes per month or the data equivalent.

McCauley (1983) feels that the greatest enthusiasm and approval for information services have come from the network project. It has advanced the larger concept of integrating telecommunications office systems and information processing. Shortly before the network was placed in operation, the senior IS position at Harris was elevated to company officer status.

Summary

Telecommunications for voice and data are rapidly converging; it is most logical for IS to take responsibility for communications. Data communications will soon overshadow voice traffic in most companies, particularly when factory automation and office automation are taken into account.

The IS area needs to include telecommunications in planning for information processing. Information services will need a communications staff and will have to apply its skills in systems analysis and design to the design of networks for the corporation. Successful implementation of a corporate network is a major and expensive undertaking. After implementation, IS must also manage the network; from the Manufacturers Hanover Trust example, we would expect that networks will continue to expand and add services.

Recommended Readings

"Manufacturers Hanover Corporation-Worldwide Network." Boston: Harvard Business School, 1984. (A case study of the bank's network and its development).

Lucas, H. C., Jr., *Introduction to Computers and Information Systems.* New York: Macmillan, 1986. (See especially the chapter on communications.)

McCauley, H. N., "Developing a Corporate Private Network," *MIS Quarterly*, vol. 7, no. 4 (December 1983), pp. 19–33. (A discussion of the Harris network described in this chapter.)

Discussion Problems

20.1 Consolidated Products wants to place terminals in customers' offices connected to its computer systems for order entry purposes. Consolidated is located in a small town in South Carolina. The ISD has been investigating the alternatives.

The first idea was to let customers dial into the computers on whatever long-distance carrier they normally use. However, the sales department thought that having to pay for the phone call might encourage some customers to send in paper orders; one purpose of the system was to replace paper orders.

Next, the ISD looked at two other possibilities: WATS lines and Telenet, a packet switching firm. The manager of IS is leaning toward Telenet, though it will be expensive at first because of the Telenet interface processor that must be installed to link to the network. "The advantage of Telenet," she said, "is that the network does some of the code conversion so that we don't have to worry about it."

What is your analysis of Consolidated's plan? What problems do you foresee in implementing the system?

20.2 A university wants to establish a LAN in its microcomputer laboratory. The LAN is to tie together a group of microcomputers and a laser printer. Eventually the school hopes to be able to license software in such a way that it could reside on a shared disk on the network; no longer would students have to check out diskettes containing the software.

The school is having a hard time deciding what kind of LAN to install. There are baseband and broadband LANs, and it is hard to know which one is best. If this works, the school may want to put one in on all faculty floors. One professor suggested a software LAN that is very slow but inexpensive. It connects the serial ports of the computers together and no circuit board is needed.

How should the university proceed to select a LAN?

Questions

1. What are the three types of communications used in firms today? How do they differ?
2. Why do we need conversion devices like modems?
3. Why is block mode transmission usually synchronous?
4. What is the advantage of digital transmission? The disadvantage?
5. What is a LAN?

6. Where is a LAN likely to be used?
7. What is ISDN?
8. What are the advantages of electronic data interchange?
9. Why are standards helpful for electronic data interchange?
10. What is bypass? Why is it possible now?
11. What are the arguments for centralizing communications management? For decentralizing it?
12. What are the issues with respect to computer compatibility and communications?
13. How does one approach the design of a communications network? Does this process differ from the design of an application?
14. What motivated Manufacturers Hanover Trust to develop GEONET?
15. Why did Harris develop a private communications network?
16. What is exciting about the Hutton system? How do communications play a part in this application?
17. Will PBX devices replace LANs in your opinion? Why or why not?
18. If the vision of a future computer system and network in this chapter is correct, what are the implications for the structuring of information processing in the firm?
19. What are the problems associated with developing a standard format for electronic document interchange?
20. Where do the savings originate with electronic document interchange?

PART V

Management Issues

21

Evaluation and Management Control

In Chapter 15 we discussed a framework for the control of information processing; part of that framework focused on management control. One of the major problems senior managers seem to have with information services is evaluating and then controlling this function in the firm.

Some of these problems probably arise because managers are not familiar with the technology and because the mission of information services is not clear. It is relatively easy to define the job of sales or production. The sales department usually has quotas and an expense budget. Their objective is to keep within the budget while meeting or exceeding sales quotas. What is a comparable goal for information services?

Unfortunately, management often fails to establish measurable goals for information processing. Since IS is a service function, senior management hears about service primarily when something goes wrong. To many users, information services is like a utility; one rarely writes letters of praise to the electric company when the lights are working. When the power fails, the electric company and sometimes the state utilities commission hear about it.

Evaluation

We can suggest some criteria for management to use in evaluating information services. See Table 21-1. These criteria are not as precise as the sales quotas previously mentioned; evaluating performance on the basis of the criteria is also difficult. However, if management is ever to feel comfortable with its control over information processing, it will have to make an effort to evaluate information services on the basis of meaningful criteria.

Given the lack of evaluation in many organizations, the CIO will have to sell the idea of being evaluated! The ISD will have to agree that the criteria selected by management are meaningful, and then will have to help measure its own performance against the criteria. In this section, we suggest some possible criteria for management evaluation of information services.

Meeting Business Objectives

We have stressed the importance of information processing in supporting the objectives of the business. There is much current emphasis on using the technology as a part of competitive strategy; the strategic use of IS is certainly one way to advance business objectives.

How does one measure this kind of contribution? It may be possible to perform a detailed evaluation of a specific system. The American Hospital Supply Corporation (now a part of Baxter-Travenol Laboratories) can monitor the sales entered by hospitals that have terminals connected directly to the American order entry system. These sales can be compared with sales during a comparable period before installation of the terminals, possibly adjusting for any general increase in sales for the whole firm.

A money center bank with a cash management microcomputer system compared business growth from customers with and without a workstation. Business increases were greater from customers with the workstation, but they were not significantly larger than overall business growth for the bank.

It is often difficult to show how a particular system adopted to gain a competitive advantage has made a financial contribution to the firm. One reason is that the system may be necessary simply to maintain one's present position. The first firm with a new innovation may achieve extra benefits, but firms that adopt the new technology later to keep up with the competition may simply protect their current position.

In the absence of a way to estimate the direct contribution made by

TABLE 21-1 IS Evaluation Considerations

Meeting business objectives (Table 21-2)
Progress on plan
User survey (Tables 21-3, 21-4)
Project performance
Budget performance
Operations
Response time
Availability
Report deadlines met
Maintenance experience
External review
Management involvement
Creative use of the technology

information systems, management can resort to more subjective measures. Table 21-2 contains a set of questions that senior management can complete to evaluate the effectiveness of information processing from its standpoint.

As part of this evaluation process, information services should prepare an inventory of applications. This inventory should probably be arranged in order of importance to the firm, with relatively minor applications placed in a single miscellaneous category. The inventory should contain the following information:

- Name of the application
- Business function supported
- Original investment
- Maintenance expenditures this year
- Objective measures of benefits
- Subjective evaluation of contribution
- Plans for the application

As an example, the cash management workstation supports the treasurer's office in firms doing business with the bank that offers the workstation. Objective measures of benefits would include the aforementioned analysis of the percentage growth in business from bank customers that use the workstation compared to those that do not. A subjective evaluation of the application would include comments from bank officers who are client contacts; these managers feel that the workstation ties the client more closely to the bank. It also provides a "window" on what the client is doing so that the bank officer can serve the client better. Future plans would include marketing efforts to sell the system and enhancements that are being considered.

An inventory of applications of this type makes management aware of the range of systems in the firm and provides the best information possible on their contribution. In addition to being one evaluation measure, such an inventory is a device for marketing information services to top management.

TABLE 21-2 Senior Management Evaluation of Information Processing

To what extent do you feel that:	Not at all						To a great extent
Information systems contribute to achievement of the firm's mission	1	2	3	4	5	6	7
Information services meets its objectives	1	2	3	4	5	6	7
Information services provides reliable service	1	2	3	4	5	6	7
Information services develops applications on time and within budget	1	2	3	4	5	6	7
Information services develops applications that give the firm a competitive advantage	1	2	3	4	5	6	7
Information services develops systems that satisfy users	1	2	3	4	5	6	7
We receive a good return for our investment in information systems	1	2	3	4	5	6	7
Information systems will be crucial to our success in the next 5 years	1	2	3	4	5	6	7

A Plan and a Vision

Chapter 6 is devoted to planning for information systems. One of the major roles for a plan is in the evaluation of information services. The plan should have a vision for the firm and for the role of information services. Subjectively, management can evaluate at the end of each year the extent to which progress has been made toward achieving the vision in the plan.

In addition, the plan should delineate the organizational structure of information processing in the firm. Senior management can talk with other managers to find out how well the structure is working and whether it needs to be modified. This kind of evaluation will have to be subjective, though questions similar to the ones in Table 21-2 can be used to collect more systematic data.

The plan also describes applications efforts, especially new applications. Management can determine if new applications under development are on schedule and if newly installed systems meet their design objectives. Progress on projects is one extremely good way to measure the effectiveness of IS management.

One way to evaluate specific information systems is to audit their costs and benefits; however, this approach is expensive for most complex systems. Instead of a full-scale audit, management might ask the design team to review the original justification for the system and to offer whatever evidence exists on its costs and benefits.

Another approach is to obtain a more subjective user evaluation of a system. Table 21-3 contains a series of questions asked in a research project we conducted to evaluate an information processing system used for decision support. The evaluator would develop questions related to the system under examination. Users of the system would complete the instrument. The

TABLE 21-3 Examples of Questions to Evaluate a System

1. Please indicate your level of satisfaction with:

	Completely dissatisfied						Completely satisfied
XYZ language	1	2	3	4	5	6	7
XYZ functions	1	2	3	4	5	6	7
XYZ response time	1	2	3	4	5	6	7
XYZ communications network	1	2	3	4	5	6	7
XYZ file documentation	1	2	3	4	5	6	7
XYZ language documentation	1	2	3	4	5	6	7
Database completeness	1	2	3	4	5	6	7
Database accuracy	1	2	3	4	5	6	7
Database currency	1	2	3	4	5	6	7
XYZ availability	1	2	3	4	5	6	7

2. What are the most significant features of XYZ for you?
3. What do you like best about XYZ?
4. What additional data would you like to see available through XYZ?
5. What improvements would you recommend for XYZ?
6. What are your major problems with XYZ?

evaluator would average together like questions to develop several measurement scales, which are reported back to management.

Unfortunately, it is difficult to calibrate the results for a single system. What does it mean to say that the average score for a system was 5.4 on user satisfaction, given a range of 1 to 7 for a response? To obtain the most from this kind of questionnaire, the evaluator has two choices. First, he or she can compare the responses of different groups of individuals. If managers who do not use the system have a satisfaction score of 6.4 and individuals who work on the system have a satisfaction score of 4.1, the numbers may indicate a problem with the way the system works, response time, user interface, or something similar.

A second way to use the instrument is to develop roughly comparable questionnaires for several systems. The results can be compared across systems to indicate applications where there may be problems. Over time, hopefully, management will see improvements in all systems as evaluated by their users.

General User Reactions

The instrument in Table 21-3 is aimed at a specific system. General user reactions can provide useful information for management when trying to evaluate information services. The questionnaire in Table 21-4 has been extensively tested in various organizations.

Examining the questions, we can see that individual items are rather general. The respondent is asked about his or her relationship with the IS staff, not about a specific application. This kind of global evaluation provides a total indication of user satisfaction with information processing services.

Of course, the evaluator must be careful to distinguish what information services are in the respondent's mind when completing the questionnaire. Is the user thinking primarily about his or her microcomputer? Is the staff a group of professional systems analysts working on a project, or is it a local departmental consultant on spreadsheets? If the organization uses an instrument like the one in Table 21-4, it should also include a section to determine with what systems and what staff member(s) the respondent works.

An instrument such as the one in Table 21-4 is an excellent way to begin a long-term evaluation of user reactions to information services. The instrument can be administered once a year and scores plotted over time. The objective would be to see if information services can increase its performance as evaluated by users of its systems and services.

Project Performance

One of the most important activities in the ISD is the development of new applications. Development projects generally have a budget, and we have

TABLE 21-4 Users' Evaluation of ISD

1. Relationship with the ISD staff			
	dissonant	:___:___:___:___:___:___:___:	Harmonious
	bad	:___:___:___:___:___:___:___:	good
2. Processing of requests for changes to existing systems			
	fast	:___:___:___:___:___:___:___:	slow
	untimely	:___:___:___:___:___:___:___:	timely
3. Degree of ISD training provided to users			
	complete	:___:___:___:___:___:___:___:	incomplete
	low	:___:___:___:___:___:___:___:	high
4. Users' understanding of systems			
	insufficient	:___:___:___:___:___:___:___:	sufficient
	complete	:___:___:___:___:___:___:___:	incomplete
5. Users' feelings of participation			
	positive	:___:___:___:___:___:___:___:	negative
	insufficient	:___:___:___:___:___:___:___:	sufficient
6. Attitude of the ISD staff			
	cooperative	:___:___:___:___:___:___:___:	belligerent
	negative	:___:___:___:___:___:___:___:	positive
7. Reliability of output information			
	high	:___:___:___:___:___:___:___:	low
	superior	:___:___:___:___:___:___:___:	inferior
8. Relevancy of output information (to intended function)			
	useful	:___:___:___:___:___:___:___:	useless
	relevant	:___:___:___:___:___:___:___:	irrelevant
9. Accuracy of output information			
	inaccurate	:___:___:___:___:___:___:___:	accurate
	low	:___:___:___:___:___:___:___:	high
10. Precision of output information			
	low	:___:___:___:___:___:___:___:	high
	definite	:___:___:___:___:___:___:___:	uncertain
11. Communication with the ISD staff			
	dissonant	:___:___:___:___:___:___:___:	harmonious
	destructive	:___:___:___:___:___:___:___:	productive
12. Time required for new systems development			
	unreasonable	:___:___:___:___:___:___:___:	reasonable
	acceptable	:___:___:___:___:___:___:___:	unacceptable
13. Completeness of the output information			
	sufficient	:___:___:___:___:___:___:___:	insufficient
	adequate	:___:___:___:___:___:___:___:	inadequate

Source: Baroudi, J., and W. Orlikowski, "A Short Form Measure of User Information Satisfaction: Research and Practice," *Journal of MIS*, Vol. 4 No. 4 (Spring 1988), pp. 44–59.

advocated that they be planned and managed. A key indicator for senior management is whether or not projects

1. Meet user needs and expectations.
2. Provide some return to the firm.
3. Are completed on time.
4. Are completed within budget.

The development of new systems is probably the most difficult task in the

ISD; it certainly has the most uncertainty of any project assigned to the IS staff. Success with projects is an extremely important aspect of evaluating information services.

Budget Performance

A relatively straightforward measure of performance is to compare ISD budgets with actual expenditures. Management should look closely at variances and learn the reasons for them. It is most likely that budget overruns will occur with new development projects rather than operations that are more stable.

Operations

In Chapter 15 we discussed several measures that are important to users of information systems. These indicators include response time, availability, and meeting deadlines. Response time is the time that elapses after a user enters information on a terminal or micro and the computer responds. As response times increase, users tend to become more dissatisfied.

It is a good idea for information services to establish response time targets, at least for the busiest shift, which is usually during the day. Targets might be something like an x-second response time on the average, with peak response times not exceeding y seconds. ISD operations should plot the target versus the number of hours in which it was not met.

Management will have to apply subjective standards to evaluate response time performance. For example, if only during 6 peak hours of the year did response time exceed the target, performance would be considered good. If response time was longer than the target for 200 peak hours during the year, performance would be considered poor.

Availability is a measure that should be reported in a manner similar to that of response time. One is interested in availability during the time when most people want to use the system. The base for availability should not be 24 hours a day for 7 days if the system is used only 8 hours a day, Monday through Friday.

In reviewing availability, one is interested in the number of outages and the duration of the problem. If operations reports only on the number of outages, it is not possible to gauge their disruption. Several outages of 5 minutes' duration are usually preferable to one that lasts for several days.

Operations should keep track of its performance in meeting deadlines as well. Deadlines usually apply to batch processing in which certain jobs must be run to completion by a certain hour of the day. For example, a manufacturing firm may need to have the movement of materials in the factory updated overnight so that new work orders can be distributed in the factory by 7 A.M. Deadlines also apply to certain types of reports that users need to complete their assigned tasks, such as the preparation of financial statements.

Operations should prepare a report of missed deadlines, showing the number of incidents and how late the deadline was. There should also be a grouping of deadlines according to importance; a work stoppage in the factory is far more serious than a 1-hour delay in an accounting report.

Operations Workload

Management should also request a report that describes the workload for operations. The report should be oriented toward the business, not the computer. For example, operations might report the following information for each month:

	Jan	Feb	Mar . . . Dec	Total Average
Orders shipped				
Units shipped				
Units produced				

According to Batiste (1986), these measures should be listed along with information processing performance; for example:

	Jan	Feb	Mar . . . Dec	Total Average
Transactions				
Database updates				
MRP runs				
Statements				
Payments				

One can also list MIS costs in a similar display by month. A one-page report similar to the one described here can help management understand the work that is done on the computer.

Maintenance

ISDs often regard maintenance as an annoyance; progress comes from new applications, not the revision of old ones. Unfortunately, users have a different view, especially if they will not be working with the new application. Users want existing systems problems solved and new enhancements added as soon as possible.

We have advocated the formation of a maintenance committee, with at least one supporting staff member from the ISD. This staff member should prepare a monthly report on the number of maintenance requests and the person-hours estimated to meet them. This report should show the status at the beginning of the month, the number of requests resolved, the number of person-hours worked, the number of new requests and estimated person-hours to meet them, and the present backlog at the end of the month.

This same report should be summarized for an annual review of maintenance. Management, users, and the management of information services must determine subjectively if the effort currently devoted to maintenance is satisfactory based on this report and on user reactions.

External Review

Even with all of the evaluation criteria just proposed, senior management may still feel uncomfortable with information services. In this case, the remaining option is to arrange for an external review of information processing. A consultant with experience in the field conducts a management audit of information services.

The consultant can help in evaluating information services based on the criteria previously discussed. He or she can also bring experience from other firms to bear. Management may feel that information processing is proceeding well where an outside consultant sees a very conservative portfolio of applications. These applications process transactions, but very little use is made of the information; computer systems contribute little beyond basic efficiencies in transactions processing.

The external consultant should try to evaluate two aspects of information services that are quite difficult for someone in the firm to consider.

1. What is the level of involvement of senior management, middle management, and users in the management of information services? An external observer may be able to convince management that its involvement in information processing is well below that of senior managers in other firms. On the other hand, management may feel more comfortable about its own role if the consultant judges it to be highly involved and effective in managing information services.

2. How creatively is the firm using the technology? It is easy to become insular in information processing; deadlines and pressures encourage hard work on immediate problems. There is little time for professionals to do reading in the field or attend conferences. An external consultant should be able to evaluate whether or not the firm is taking advantage of technology and to what extent it is on the leading edge. The consultant may also be able to advise the firm on whether to try to be on the leading edge or let others pioneer the technology.

Action and Control

Evaluation is only one part of management's task with respect to the control of information processing. It is also necessary to recognize problems and take action to solve them. What are some of the actions management can take to improve information processing in the firm? What can the CIO recommend to management for its role?

Planning

The most frequent problem with a plan is not having one. The CIO can encourage management and work with it to develop a plan, hopefully one that contains a clear vision of the future of the firm and the role of information processing in that future. Chapter 6 provides detailed recommendations for planning.

The second problem with a plan is more subtle: the failure to manage according to the plan. A plan is of little use if it is filed away after approval. It should be the road map for information services and for decision making. The plan can be remarkably helpful in making and justifying decisions. If a division wants to purchase a computer system dedicated to quality control for its major factory, the ISD and senior management can look at the plan to see if the request makes sense in terms of where the firm is headed. Suppose the computer in question will be the only one of that brand in the firm, or suppose it lacks communications facilities; the purchase would not fit the plan. The corporate plan might include a major systems development/acquisition project beginning in 8 months to look at quality control across the corporation. The division requesting the new system should participate in the project and hold its own plans in abeyance.

The third role for the plan was discussed earlier in this chapter; it is a benchmark against which senior management can evaluate the performance of information services. If the ISD is aware that the plan will be used for evaluation, it can manage its own activities to accomplish the objectives in the plan.

The recommendation, then, that one can give to senior management is to

1. Develop a plan.
2. Manage according to the plan.
3. Evaluate performance with respect to the plan.

User Reactions

We have found significant problems with user reactions and attitudes toward information processing. It is rare to find an organization in which users praise information services or express great satisfaction with their systems. Maybe lack of satisfaction and praise is simply the curse of a service function.

It is difficult to change attitudes and to recommend a single strategy to help resolve problems in this area. There are a number of steps that management might consider to gradually improve user reactions to information services.

1. If the problems are localized to one particular system, resources can be devoted to improving that system.
2. If the problems reflect a lack of help, consider setting up an informa-

tion center or help desk within information services. IS consultants in user areas are another possibility.

3. Be sure that new applications are developed with a design team; it is also helpful to have a user in charge of the team.
4. Insist on review meetings and see that senior management within ISD and the firm attends them for key development projects.
5. Consider the formation of a steering committee to help user management learn about the problems in the ISD and to facilitate high-level communications between ISD management and firm management.
6. Establish the improvement of user reactions to systems as an objective for the plan and for the IS staff.

Development Projects

Development projects that are late and over budget frequently cause problems for the organization. There are many possible reasons for this situation, ranging from lack of user participation to incompetence of the ISD systems professional. Management can take some of the following actions:

1. Be sure that users are participating meaningfully in the design process; they must influence key design decisions or make the decisions themselves.
2. Be sure that users understand the application; frequent review meetings and walkthroughs can help achieve this objective.
3. Be sure that the professional analysts are supported well; consider providing an analyst workstation to help automate the design process.
4. Be sure that structured design and top-down design approaches are followed by the professional analysts.
5. Be sure that alternatives to custom design, such as packages, are considered.
6. Determine if it is possible to use a generator or 4GL for at least part of the system.
7. Be sure that prototyping is used where it can help provide feedback for users on the system.

Operations

Problems in operations are often the easiest to solve. Computer professionals are used to planning capacity and expanding processing power. If response time is the problem, the system may have to be tuned or expanded. Often additional memory has a dramatic affect on response time for on-line systems. If added memory is not enough, more CPU power is likely to be necessary.

If the problem is availability, the firm may have to consider backup processors, uninterruptible power supplies, and exerting pressure on the maintenance vendor to improve the reliability of the computer.

Finally, problems with meeting schedules may be resolved by better scheduling, extra shifts, or even buying computer time somewhere else when a peak processing load exists. If these approaches do not work, additional computing equipment will be needed to provide adequate processing capacity.

Creativity/Vision

It is very hard to teach creativity or offer suggestions on how to develop a forward-looking vision for information processing in the firm. Management can employ outside consultants to provide this perspective. Another approach is to be sure that ISD staff members are active professionally; reading the literature and attending meetings are ways to keep abreast of the technology.

We have also suggested the creation of a position called the *technological strategist*, who is charged with the responsibility of bringing new technology to the firm. The objective here is not to encourage technology for its own sake; one does not want to buy technological solutions and then look for problems they can solve.

The technological strategist must be well versed in the business and be aware of senior management's vision of the future. He or she then helps map available and coming technology to the organization's plans and objectives. This individual is crucial in helping the firm use technology creatively and to its competitive advantage.

Management Involvement

Another chronic problem in business is management's lack of attention to information processing. Many managers do not consider technology to be strategic or even critical to the firm. As a result, it is very difficult to obtain support and involvement in designing systems or guiding IS.

If management does not recognize that this problem exists, how can it be solved? The CIO is probably in the best position to involve managers in IS activities. He or she must work diplomatically to encourage managers to evaluate, control, and manage information processing. Some of the mechanisms we have discussed in this book are designed for this purpose.

For example, the formation of a steering committee, a strong emphasis on planning, the use of systems review meetings, encouraging management to evaluate IS, and similar techniques should result in managers paying more attention to information processing.

Evaluation at CMI

Tom Roberts is addressing a quarterly meeting of ISD managers at CMI.

"Good morning. I would like to talk to you today about philosophy, my philosophy of how we can best serve CMI. A major part of that philosophy is to pull senior management into IS activities ranging from planning to systems design.

"I think that, in the past, managers felt quite uncomfortable with information processing and computing. They don't understand the technology; it is hidden away inside a computer. You can go into one of our factories and figure out what is going on. You can't see much inside a computer.

"The job of IS management is to show managers at CMI how they can play a role in information services. Our approach began with a plan; I know a lot of you thought it was wasted time earlier this year, but now we have a plan.

"We have been trying to pull out that plan and point to it whenever a major decision has to be made. It has helped, and I think that by next year we really will be managing to the plan. It won't just decorate your filing cabinets.

"What we want to do now, as a part of updating the plan for next year, is to prepare an annual report on information services at CMI. In essence, I want to evaluate our performance on a whole range of indicators. Your handout has a list of them, ranging from project completion to response time to user satisfaction.

"Nobody is going to be fired or lose a bonus as a result of the evaluation. What we will do is to see what's wrong and include actions in the plan to solve whatever problems come up. Basically, I am asking you to be honest and do some homework to get us numbers, questionnaires, and your own goals for the coming year. We've got to go through an evaluation to find out what needs to be improved.

Are there any questions?"

Recommended Readings

Batiste, J., "The Application Profile," *MIS Quarterly*, vol. 10, no. 3 (September 1986), pp. 207–213. (Presents a sample report on operations statistics related to business conditions and IS costs.)

Lucas, H. C., Jr., and J. Turner, "A Corporate Strategy for the Control of Information Processing" *Sloan Management Review* vol. 23, no. 73 (Spring 1982), pp. 25–36. (Discusses management action to improve the control of information services; suggests the need for the information strategist.)

Sprague, R., and B. McNurlin (eds.), *Information Systems Management in Practice*. Englewood Cliffs, N.J.: Prentice-Hall, 1986. (A book showing concern for end users and ideas on how to support them.)

Discussion Problems

21.1 The chairman of the ABZ Corporation was meeting with a consultant he had just retained to help solve some of ABZ's problems with information services.

He asked, "How much money should a firm of our size be spending on information processing?" The consultant said he would have to think about that for a while.

The chairman followed up with other question: "If we double our sales, how much should we then be spending on information systems?" How do you recommend that the consultant answer these questions? What data should he gather to provide an answer?

21.2 The President of Casual Clothes was angry; he had just reviewed his budgets for the coming year. The manager of information services and the controller were the victims of the president's anger. "We have sales of $50 million a year, and I have to spend over a $1 million a year on accounting and computers. What are we getting for all of that? You two go away and come back with an answer."

How should the controller and the manager of ISD go about convincing the president that the firm benefits from accounting and computing?

Questions

1. Why does management have trouble evaluating information processing?
2. How can one decide whether systems help meet business objectives?
3. How can the ISD show its contribution to the business?
4. What is the role of an IS plan in evaluation?
5. How can one measure user reactions to systems?
6. What role does the IS budget have in evaluating its performance?
7. What is the purpose of a report on operations?
8. What do most users want from computer operations?
9. How can one measure the quality of systems development efforts?
10. What is project performance? What are good indicators of successful performance?
11. What kind of maintenance information does management need?
12. What is the role of an external review of IS?
13. How does one judge how creatively a firm is using information technology?
14. What types of action can management take if it feels that information processing is not under control?
15. How does management encourage user participation in systems design?
16. What is the role of a technological strategist?
17. If management is not very interested in IS, how can the CIO help bring management's attention to this area?
18. Why should senior management obtain information from a variety of users about IS instead of just the ones who come to management?
19. What does it mean to "manage according to the plan?"
20. Using our earlier model of a control system, what suggestions in this chapter play the part of the standard, the actuator, the discriminator, and so on?

22

A Message for Management

In this chapter we provide recommendations on how senior and division/department managers can contribute to the management of information processing. Then we summarize some of the key points in the book for information services management.

Management in the Organization

There are five broad areas of concern on which firm management should focus in its information systems–related activities.

1. *Strategy and technology.* How can the firm use the technology to gain a strategic advantage? Are there ways to become the low-cost producer, choose a market niche, or differentiate the firm's product or services from those of others? Does the technology suggest a new product or new services to make the firm's product more attractive?

2. *Organizational structure.* What is the structure of information processing in the firm? What kind of structure does the firm want—centralized, decentralized, or distributed? Is the pattern of processing for equipment

important, or is the real issue what level of management has control over resources and systems development?

3. *Control and coordination.* Given an organizational structure for processing, how does management exert control to see that it is managed well? If the structure tends to be decentralized or distributed, how does management coordinate diverse individuals and groups to avoid making costly mistakes?

4. *Communications networks.* Most firms will develop communications networks, possibly including both voice and data. How does management prepare for this environment? What are the implications of a future network for the decisions made today on equipment acquisition?

5. *Systems development.* How should the firm develop applications? How many alternatives should be considered? What automation techniques are most suitable for the firm in systems development? What technology will improve productivity? What is management's role in design? What is the role of users?

Recommendations for Senior Managers

We offer the following recommendations to senior management to address these five areas of concern. Table 22-1 arrays these suggestions against the five concerns.

1. Look for strategic uses of technology; compare what the firm is doing with others in its industry. Look at the technology employed outside of the industry to see if it might be adapted to the business.

2. Define an organizational structure for information processing. Include the structure in a plan for IS.

3. Work with the ISD staff to develop an architecture of hardware, software, and communications. Include a scenario in the plan for the information processing environment toward which the firm is working.

TABLE 22-1 Senior Management Actions

Strategy and Technology	Organizational Structure	Control and Coordination	Communications and Networks	Systems Development
Seek strategic uses of information technology	Define organizational structure Determine coordination required	Define technical architecture Support end users Determine coordination required Establish coordination mechanisms Review budget	Plan for networks	Establish applications approval mechanism

Source: Lucas (1986).

4. Determine how computer support will be provided. What resources will be allocated to end users? How does the firm prevent frustration on the part of users who have problems working with the technology?

5. Determine the appropriate amount of coordination for information processing. Consider establishing approved lists for vendors of hardware and software. What actions of local managers have to be approved centrally? What is the firm trying to coordinate?

6. Establish a mechanism for the approval of a suggested application; look for common systems that can be used in more than one location. The firm might require that any application costing more than a certain amount be approved by the CIO within 2 weeks of submission for review.

7. Establish coordination mechanisms. All local information services staff members might be required to meet once a year. The CIO or central consultants might be expected to visit each company site twice a year for a review of plans and systems. Encourage local divisions to set up users' groups to review popular software.

8. Require that local budgets and plans for information processing be reviewed by the CIO in order to keep this individual aware of what is happening in the divisions. Encourage the CIO to play a coordinating and linking function for information services across the firm.

Recommendations for Divisional Managers

Table 22-2 contains a series of recommendations for divisional managers and shows how they are related to the five concerns of management presented earlier.

1. Look for opportunities for the strategic use of the technology in the division.

2. Determine an organizational structure for processing in the division. Just as the firm must have a structure, divisions will need to decide how to organize their information processing activities. Will there be data centers, or

TABLE 22-2 Actions of Divisional Manager

Strategy and Technology	Organizational Structure	Control and Coordination	Communications and Networks	Systems Development
Seek strategic uses of technology	Define organizational structure	Determine coordination required Encourage end-user computing	Plan networks	Encourage involvement in systems analysis Encourage use of new technologies Encourage end-user computing

Source: Lucas (1986).

will users each have their own computer with a possible network connecting them?

3. Follow the previous recommendations to establish policies for whatever degree of coordination and control seems appropriate at the local level.

4. Become involved in systems analysis and design. Insist on seeing alternatives on how each proposed application might be implemented. Attend review sessions and understand the policy implications of each system for the division.

5. Encourage the use of new technologies within information services. The 4GLs, applications generators, and prototyping can all contribute to systems development productivity.

6. Support end-user computing through experiments with workstations and 4GLs. Control microcomputers and end-user computing by supporting users rather than with rigid rules.

7. Develop a network plan that is consistent with corporate plans for networking. Keep the networking objective in mind when purchasing additional computer hardware and software.

Conclusions

Managers cannot expect to delegate responsibility for information processing to the IS staff and remain uninvolved. Information systems are too important a part of a modern organization's strategy and operations for senior or divisional management to remain aloof.

The CIO can do only so much alone; he or she requires management support and visible action in order to manage information processing successfully. The time requirements for management do not have to be excessive; information services is a part of the business that needs management attention, just as any other business function does.

To paraphrase the words of labor relations expert Douglas McGregor, by and large, management gets the kind of information processing it deserves.

Summary

The purpose of this book is to help the reader manage information processing in an organization. Figure 1-1 is a framework for this management task and provides a structure for the book as well. Management of information processing begins with the top management of the firm and the CIO.

Today organizations are concerned with the role of information processing in supporting the objectives of the firm. That role may involve operations of the firm, decision making, or the firm's basic competitive strategy.

We advocate that the firm develop a plan for information processing. The plan should describe the structure of processing in the firm, which leads to a pattern for processing ranging from centralized to distributed. Equipment, systems analysis, and control over decisions can all be structured in a centralized, decentralized or distributed manner.

The development of new applications is a key activity in information services. New applications affect the firm in a number of ways. At the level of the plan, management identifies the applications areas that are important in the coming 2 to 3 years. Especially strategic applications may be specified in more detail and assigned a high priority in the plan.

The plan becomes a guide for all levels of management in the firm regarding information processing activities and decisions. The CIO has to manage information systems personnel. The development of new applications begins the relationship between users and the ISD. We have suggested a strategy for applications development that begins with the delineation of a set of alternative ways to meet users' needs. In addition, our approach stresses heavy user influence on design, user understanding, and the use of modern design approaches.

Since many IS projects are over budget and late, project management is an important activity within the ISD. Because the demands for service are so great and IS staff is limited, there is growing emphasis on end-user support. Personal computer stores, information centers, and consultants all help extend the use of computers in the organization.

Managers are concerned with the control of the firm; information services is subject to top management control, budgetary concerns, and operational controls on systems. The operations area of the ISD must ensure that computer services are delivered to users, both for on-line and batch processing systems. Operations worries about capacity and the acquisition of new computing capabilities.

The CIO is becoming increasingly involved in related technologies like office automation, communications for both voice and data, and factory automation. Finally, a plan for information processing provides guidelines on the evaluation and management control of information services.

Different firms will approach the management of information processing in different ways. The purpose of the framework in Figure 1-1 is to provide the reader with an understanding of the issues that the organization must confront and the relationship among various aspects of information services management.

A Changing Environment

One of our themes has been the changing environment for information processing. We are in an era of user-dominated technology combined with new demands from senior management. The narrow view of information systems associated with the days of punched card data processing has given way to a broader, often strategic view of the technology.

Greater distribution of responsibility for information systems, including equipment, design, and control, creates more complexity in the organization. Distributed responsibility creates support and coordination problems for the information services staff. It also creates a sometimes unrealized demand for some type of central coordination.

These changes are being fueled by explosive user demands for new applications, whether multiuser systems for a department or individual applications for personal decision support on a micro. As users become more involved, influence in systems development moves to them.

All across the spectrum of information processing activities, information services is giving up control to user areas. While some IS professionals may fight this loss of power, in the long run it is probably a healthy development. Centralized professional computer and systems staff members have not been very successful operating in an environment in which they controlled the technology.

We predict that IS professionals will be far more successful, and probably much more satisfied, as consultants and advisors to managers and users in the organization. Corporate IS management will also fulfill more of a coordinating and less of a directing role. Information processing professionals will exert influence on members of the organization instead of control over technology.

Conclusion

The CIO is first and foremost a manager. This individual is a leader and spokesperson for information services in the firm. He or she should also be an advocate of technology, marketing the abilities and accomplishments of information services. The CIO links information services to other departments and managers.

The role of managers in information services constantly changes, but the task of management remains. Managers bring change to the organization and then control and coordinate its operations. For managers in IS, the key is to recognize fundamental changes and trends and separate them from fads. The product of information processing, new applications, creates major changes for both individuals and organizations.

Changes in the technology, in the way information processing contributes to the organization, and in the ability of non-IS professionals to use the technology all affect the management task of the CIO and other IS managers.

The success of many organizations in the coming decade will depend on how well they manage technology. Information systems professionals have a great deal to contribute to the organization. A tremendously powerful technology exists; our ability to manage it will determine its contribution to the organization and to society at large.

Recommended Readings

Lucas, H. C., Jr., "Managing the Revolution in Information Technology," *Sloan Management Review* (Fall 1986), pp. (An article with recommendations for management on coping with information processing.)

Questions

1. What are the areas of concern for senior managers with respect to information processing?
2. How does senior management play a role in the identification of strategic opportunities for the technology?
3. What is an architecture of hardware, software, and communications?
4. What is management's duty with respect to coordinating information processing?
5. How do the tasks of a divisional manager differ from those of a senior manager with respect to information processing?
6. On what decision is division management's IS responsibilities dependent?
7. How does division management link its plans to corporate plans for information processing?
8. Why do companies get the kind of processing they deserve?
9. Why is the development of applications such an important activity?
10. What is the role of an information systems plan?
11. How does the firm control information processing?
12. What is the role of the CIO in the firm?
13. Why is there so much change in the information processing field?
14. Why are users rapidly adopting micro- and minicomputers?
15. What do you think the most important management challenges are for the CIO in the next 3 years?

Index